D1428208

Front Cover Photograph:
Copyright 1978 Hans Wendt
All rights reserved
Reprinted by permission

Rear Cover Photograph:
Copyright 1974 Donnie L. Head
All rights reserved
Reprinted by permission

MAYDAY

iv

MAYDAY

Accident Reports and Voice Transcripts from Airline Crash Investigations

Marion F. Sturkey

Heritage Press International

MAYDAY: Accident Reports and Voice Transcripts from Airline Crash Investigations

First Edition

Library of Congress Control Number: 2005927457

ISBN 13: 978-0-9650814-3-6
ISBN 10: 0-9650814-3-5

Heritage Press International
204 Jefferson Street
P.O. Box 333
Plum Branch, SC 29845 USA

Manufactured in the United States of America

Acknowledgements

Grateful acknowledgement is extended to the U.S. National Transportation Safety Board and its predecessors, the Department of Commerce and the Civil Aeronautics Board, for making their Aircraft Accident Reports available to the public.

Grateful acknowledgement is extended to the U.S. National Aeronautics and Space Administration for its technical assistance in the creation of the Reports of the Presidential Commissions, which are available to the public.

Grateful acknowledgement is extended to the governments of France, the United Kingdom, Spain, the Kingdom of Thailand, the Kingdom of Bahrain, the Republic of Colombia, Canada, New Zealand, and to the International Civil Aviation Organization for making their Aircraft Accident Reports available to the public.

Grateful acknowledgement is extended to Hans Wendt, the renowned professional photographer, for authorizing the reprinting of his two unique post-collision photographs of PSA Flight 182 prior to ground impact.

Grateful acknowledgement is extended to Donnie L. Head, the renowned aviation photographer and historian, for authorizing the reprinting of 16 aviation photographs from his collection of approximately 44,000 such photographs.

Grateful acknowledgement is extended to the hundreds of unnamed aircraft accident investigators without whose skill and dedication this project would not have been possible.

Purpose of this Book

Aircraft Accident Reports are authorized by the United States and other countries identified herein. These voluminous reports are published for educational purposes.

This book contains summaries of Aircraft Accident Reports. Like the lengthy government reports upon which it is based, this book is published for *educational purposes* only. It is intended that the condensed content of this book will enable persons associated with the aviation industry to learn from past accidents.

The goal of airline accident investigation is to (1) determine the circumstances and causes of an accident in order to (2) prevent future accidents and loss of life. The aim is not to apportion blame or liability. In accord with those aviation safety principles, this book does not assign or imply fault or misconduct on the part of any government, any business entity, or any person living or dead. The purpose of this book is to *promote education*.

Experience is often a cruel teacher. Yet, by applying the lessons learned from past accidents we can enhance aviation safety in the future.

Table of Contents

-- Military and Aviation books by Marion Sturkey --

BONNIE-SUE: A Marine Corps Helicopter Squadron in Vietnam (first published in 1996) 509 pages, 21 photographs, 4 maps. A classic, the definitive work on helicopter warfare in Vietnam. Against the backdrop of the turbulent 1960s, *BONNIE-SUE* evolves into a saga of commitment, sacrifice, and brotherhood.

Warrior Culture of the U.S. Marines (first published in 2002) 212 pages, 3 illustrations. Axioms for warriors, Marine quotations, USMC battle history -- and much more -- for the world's warrior elite. Plus, plenty of upbeat and gung-ho satire exclusively for U.S. Marines. "Politically Incorrect" and proud of it!

Murphy's Laws of Combat (first published in 2003) 241 pages. A walk on the humorous side of military life. Military satire for the U.S. Armed Forces. Hundreds of tongue-in-cheek combat laws, axioms, and principles -- hilarious because of the inherent truth they contain. "Politically Impossible," but no profanity.

MAYDAY: Accident Reports and Voice Transcripts from Airline Crash Investigations (this book, first published in 2005) 461 pages, 23 photographs, 6 illustrations. For each accident the author walks the reader through the flight, the crisis, the "black box" transcript, the crash, the investigation, and Probable Cause. Learn from past accidents in order to further aviation safety in the future.

MID-AIR: Accident Reports and Voice Transcripts from Mid-Air Collision Investigations (coming soon) With the format used in *MAYDAY*, the author examines mid-air collisions involving commercial airliners, military planes, and general aviation aircraft.

MAYDAY

Accident Reports and
Voice Transcripts from
Airline Crash Investigations

For I dip't into the future, far as human eye could see,
Saw the Vision of the World, and all the wonders that would be;
Saw the heavens fill with commerce, argosies of magic sails,
Pilots of the purple twilight, dropping down with costly bales.

[Alfred Lord Tennyson, "Locksley Hall" in 1842]

Prologue: Setting The Stage

In the Beginning: The ancients dreamed of soaring with the birds. Several visionaries fabricated and donned bird-like wings and leaped from high towers or cliffs in attempts to fly. They all failed. For millennia the romantic concept of heavier-than-air flight remained in the realm of escapist fantasy.

Nonetheless, men continued to wistfully dream of flying. Greek mythology tells us that Daedalus and his son, Icarus, wanted to escape from a tyrannical king on the island of Crete. Fortunately, Daedalus was a professional craftsman and inventor, and flying offered the perfect solution to his dilemma:

Daedalus designed and constructed wings made of feathers and wax. He fastened these wings to his arms and to the arms of his son. He calculated that they could fly over the sea and find refuge on the mainland of Greece.

Yet, Daedalus knew that flying would be fraught with peril for anyone who refused to use prudent judgment. He cautioned Icarus not to fly too close to the surface of the sea, where the waves would drench his feathers. He also admonished Icarus not to fly too high, lest the sun melt the wax.

Alas! Once in flight, Icarus was overcome with the thrill of the experience. He ignored his father's advice. The enthralled young man began to soar higher, ever higher, swooping up toward heaven and the sun. The blazing sun soon melted the wax, and Icarus lost his wings. He plummeted down into the sea and perished.

Although Icarus was a fictional person, mankind can learn from his mythical folly. Aviation is not inherently dangerous, but it is unforgiving of human error and lapses in judgment.

History of Commercial Aviation: Over 2,000 years ago men began building and flying primitive kites. By the Fifth Century an English monk had discovered that moving air could support an *untethered* aerial craft in the manner that water supports a boat. He had the right idea. What he lacked was a means of propulsion more efficient than muscle power.

The development of the gasoline engine solved the propulsion dilemma. The famed Wright brothers were not the first to harness engine technology to propel their aerial craft. They were, however, the first to blend this efficient new power source with adequate stability and control features. In 1903 they designed and flew the first powered and controllable heavier-than-air machine.

Within a few years the rickety wood and fabric construction materials were replaced by sleek all-metal designs. Retractable landing gear reduced drag and increased speed. Flaps and slats enabled builders to fashion more streamlined wings, and new radial engines replaced the older in-line powerplants.

Soon the traveler who had once ridden a bus or train from New York to California found that he had a more attractive option. Instead of stops at scores of cities along the way, he could fly non-stop. Instead of enduring several days and nights on a bus or train, he could spend a few hours on a modern airliner. Commercial aviation was here to stay.

Powerful jet propulsion, proven in the fires of World War II, replaced piston engines and propellers. Big swept-wing jetliners with their pressurized cabins were soon equipped with state-of-the-art electronic navigation and communications aids. These new aerial transports ushered in exponential advances in speed, reliability, and economy. During the latter half of the Twentieth Century, commercial cargo and passenger flights linked every inhabited region on the Earth. Wilbur and Orville would have been proud.

Aircraft Accident Investigation: All modes of transportation are subject to mishaps: ships sink, trains derail, automobiles collide. Commercial aviation, while much more safe per mile than other modes of travel, is not immune to unique perils. Despite stringent safety standards modern airliners may catch on fire, fall prey to mechanical failure, encounter hazardous weather, or fail to land safely for a host of reasons.

Skilled teams of aviation analysts from government and industry investigate each airline accident. The object of these investigations is not to apportion blame or liability. Instead, the goal is to (1) identify the circumstances and causes of each accident in order to (2) prevent future accidents and loss of life. Readers should refer to "Purpose of this Book" on page viii.

Aircraft Accident Reports: When the big airship *Hindenburg* burned in 1937 the U.S. Department of Commerce report was a mere 56 pages long. In contrast, modern-day Aircraft Accident Reports are usually hundreds of pages in length and contain the results of detailed analyses, research, tests, and other investigative findings of fact. These technical reports are the primary source documents for each chapter in this book. After reading a chapter, a person desiring more detail should refer to the source document. Each such document is in the public domain and is identified in the Probable Cause section of each chapter.

An Aircraft Accident Report is the work product of a team of experts from government and the aviation industry. However, it is not always the "final word" on an airline accident. The initial report may be preliminary, and so-called final reports are often followed by updated or revised reports over a period of many years. Therefore, a report used as a source document in this book may not be the "final" report.

Recommendations: Each modern-day Aircraft Accident Report concludes with detailed recommendations for corrective action. These recommendations are intended to prevent similar accidents in the future. They cover a host of issues which may include flight crew training, air traffic control procedures, aircraft systems, airline management, etc. These proposals and the extent to which they are implemented are crucial to commercial aviation safety. Yet, they are ***another story*** and are ***not included in this book***.

Legal Standing: After an airline accident, swarms of attorneys descend upon survivors and the relatives of those who were killed. In theory, their aim is to see that "justice" is served. In reality, they have twin goals: (1) convince a jury that an airline, or an aircraft manufacturer, or a government, or *someone* was negligent and caused the accident, and (2) convince a jury to award actual and punitive damages -- money -- to them and their clients. They are not legally bound by the conclusions and findings contained in the Aircraft Accident Report.

Political and Judicial Influence: A nation may not endorse the content of another nation's Aircraft Accident Report. For example, EgyptAir Flight 990 crashed into the Atlantic Ocean on 31 October 1999, killing all 217 people aboard. The Aircraft Accident Brief prepared by the United States concluded that the Egyptian pilot, chanting "I rely on God," shut down both engines and dove the airliner into the sea. The evidence seemed compelling and beyond debate. Yet, the Egyptian Civil Aviation Authority disagreed and claimed that the report was "limited and incomplete."

Also, the judiciary may not agree with the findings detailed in an Aircraft Accident Report. For example, Air New Zealand Flight 901 crashed into Mt. Erebus, Antarctica, on 28 November 1979. The impact killed the 257 people on the aircraft. After a lengthy investigation the Ministry of Transport in New Zealand adopted an Aircraft Accident Report which indicated that the conduct of the pilots caused the accident. However, to the surprise of aviation industry analysts, a Royal Commission of Inquiry did not agree. The barristers -- without aviation expertise -- decreed that airline management, not the pilots, was the root cause of the tragedy.

Cockpit Voice Recorder Transcripts: For over a quarter-century, Aircraft Accident Reports have included a transcript of the Cockpit Voice Recorder (CVR) tape. However, readers are cautioned that transcription of CVR tapes is not a precise science. Instead, it is the best product possible from a collective technical effort. The resulting CVR transcripts, or parts thereof, can be misleading if taken out of context. In the words of the NTSB:

> [a] CVR transcript should be viewed as an accident investigation *tool [emphasis added]* to be used in conjunction with other evidence gathered during the investigation. Conclusions or interpretations should not be made using the transcripts as the sole source of information.

CVR transcripts included as a part of Aircraft Accident Reports often are extremely lengthy. Therefore, this book does not include the complete transcripts. The portion of transcripts quoted in this book generally begins just before the pilots encounter the dilemma that leads to the accident. Thereafter, non-pertinent cockpit noises and non-pertinent conversation are excluded in the interest of brevity. Persons wishing to review the complete transcript should refer to the source document.

Name of Manufacturer: Two manufacturing giants, Douglas and McDonnell, merged in 1967. They became McDonnell Douglas, which later merged with Boeing. Raytheon acquired Beechcraft. The European-built Fokker F-27 became the Fairchild F-27 when manufactured in the United States. Confusing!

For continuity this book uses the name of the manufacturer when an aircraft in question was built. Readers will not find *politically correct* references to a "McDonnell Douglas DC-3."

Format of this Book: Each subsequent chapter summarizes an Aircraft Accident Report and contains the following sub-headings:

Overview: . . . . . . Synopsis of the flight and the accident.
The Flight: . . . . . Description of the aircraft, crew, route, etc.
Trouble Ahead: . . Events which led to the accident.
The Accident: . . . The accident and its aftermath.
The Investigation: . Analysis and technical findings.
Probable Cause: . . Direct and contributing causes.

In addition to the sub-headings listed above, several chapters also conclude with a Postscript, a look at unique circumstances which followed the accident.

Errata: On a project of this complexity it is possible that errors may have crept in. The author will appreciate notification (*with credible documentation*) of any such errors so that they may be corrected in future printings or editions.

Those who cannot remember the past are condemned to repeat it.

[George Santayana, *The Life of Reason*, 1906]

The Zeppelin Airship *Hindenburg*

Luft Schiffbau Zeppelin Airship, registration LZ-129
6 May 1937, at the Naval Air Station, Lakehurst, New Jersey
97 aboard, 35 killed (plus 1 killed on the ground)

Overview: After a flight across the Atlantic Ocean the luxury airship *Hindenburg* reached the United States. The giant dirigible approached the mooring mast at Lakehurst, New Jersey. A muted detonation suddenly rocked the big airship, followed by a raging hydrogen-fueled inferno. Of the 97 people on board the craft, 35 perished in the flames.

The Flight: The 61 crewmembers, 36 wealthy passengers, and 2 dogs boarded the airship *Hindenburg* in Frankfort, Germany, for a flight to the United States. Arguably the finest airship in the world, *Hindenburg* had been designed to project the presumed technological superiority of the German Reich and its charismatic leader, Adolf Hitler. After flying over the Atlantic Ocean the giant dirigible approached its destination, the U.S. Naval Air Station (NAS) at Lakehurst, New Jersey, on the afternoon of 6 May 1937. The mooring would complete the first scheduled demonstration flight of the 1937 season:

> The flight . . . was authorized by a provisional air navigation permit from the [U.S.] Secretary of Commerce, and a revokable permit from the [U.S.] Secretary of the Navy to the American Zeppelin Transport, Inc.

Hindenburg, registration LZ-129, was one 118 rigid airships built by Luft Schiffbau Zeppelin of Friedrichshafen, Germany. Completed the previous year, she had been constructed around a framework of girders and tension wires. Sixteen compartments each held a bag of hydrogen "lifting gas." Each gas bag was formed by film placed between layers of fabric.

The builders had mounted Daimler Benz diesel engines, each producing 1,100 horsepower, in four external "engine cars." The engines powered huge 19-foot-diameter four-blade propellers that were armored with brass sheathing. Inside the cavernous ship, generators and two diesel powerplants provided electrical power for lighting, cooking, radio equipment, and steering.

The sheer size of the airship staggered the senses. The aerial giant measured 804 feet in length, almost a sixth of a mile. This immense *floating palace* would, its builders believed, usher in an era of luxury Zeppelin travel. Its internal gas bags held 7,036,000 cubic feet of volatile hydrogen. This "lighter-than-air" behemoth weighed 430,950 pounds, held 143,650 pounds of fuel, and could boast of the latest technology in luxury accommodations, radio communications, and safety equipment:

> During its nine months of operation in 1936 this airship had made more than 55 flights, flown 2,764 hours, cruised 191,583 miles, crossed the ocean 34 times, carried 2,798 passengers and more than 377,000 pounds of mail and freight . . . .

Trouble Ahead: As the big airship approached its destination on 6 May, thunderstorms began lashing NAS Lakehurst at 1540 Hours. Rain and lightning continued for 65 minutes. *Hindenburg* flew through heavy rain, but she steered clear of the thunderclouds above and waited for the weather to improve.

Lakehurst Tower kept a radio log from which the following verbiage has been abstracted. The exact words that were *spoken* are not known. The transcript, below, is a verbatim recitation of the words that were *written* in the radio log:

Tower: . . . . . . NAS Lakehurst Control Tower
Hindenburg: . . . The Airship *Hindenburg*

Tower: Conditions still unsettled, recommend delay landing until further word from station, advise [us of] your decision. (1642)

Hindenburg: We will wait 'till you report that landing conditions are better. (1652)

Tower: Conditions [are] now considered suitable for landing, ground crew is ready, thunderstorm over station, ceiling 2,000 feet, visibility 5 miles to westward, surface temperature 60 [degrees], surface wind west-southwest [at] 8 knots . . . . (1712)

<u>Tower</u>: Recommend landing now. (1722)

<u>Tower</u>: Overcast moderate, rain diminishing, lightning in west, ceiling 2,000 feet, improving visibility, surface wind [is] west-southwest [at] 4 knots, gusts under 10 knots, surface temperature 61 [degrees], pressure 29.70. (1800)

<u>Tower</u>: Conditions definitely improved, [we] recommend earliest possible landing. (1808)

Hindenburg acknowledged the last radio transmission from the Lakehurst Tower and then reeled in her two antennas. She sent no more radio messages to NAS Lakehurst. Her radio operator turned off the transmitters and the radio dynamotors.

As the ship approached the mooring mast in the rain she released 2,420 pounds of water ballast. Two minutes later at 1821 Hours she dropped her thick hemp "bow trail ropes." On the ground the 231 men in the landing party grasped both ropes and began to winch the aerial giant toward the mooring point.

The Accident: *Hindenburg* floated motionless 180 feet above the ground at 1825 Hours. The landing party supervisor noticed a sudden "fluttering" of the fabric outer cover on top of the airship in a "wave motion" above gas bag No. 5. Another witness, waiting atop the mooring mast, watched the flutter from his aerial vantage point, and so did others. The airship was leaking volatile hydrogen gas, and investigators would later report:

> We conclude that the first open flame, produced by the burning of the ship's hydrogen, appeared on the top of the ship . . . .

Within seconds a "ball of flame" appeared over the flutter. Most witnesses agreed that the fireball looked to be about 10 feet in diameter. A muffled detonation rocked *Hindenburg*, and within seconds fire engulfed the stern of the great ship.

A gigantic pillar of flames mushroomed hundreds of feet into the sky. The stern began to settle as fire spread forward all the way to the bow. The terrified men of the landing party scattered in all directions, running for their lives. From the blazing airship, many passengers and crewmembers leapt to their deaths.

A young reporter waited in the terminal where he was watching the mooring and narrating the spectacle for broadcast at a later date. His words described the approach of the aerial behemoth. Then, as fire suddenly broke out he exclaimed in horror:

> It's burst into flame! It burst into flame and it's falling! Get out of the way! Get out of the way! Oh, my God! What do I see? It's burning, bursting into flame, and it's falling on the mooring mast. This is terrible! This is one of the worst catastrophes in the world. [It is] crashing to the ground! Oh, the humanity! Oh, the passengers!

Within 32 seconds the once-proud *Hindenburg* lay mangled and burning on the ground. Hydrogen gas fueled the flames, which soon subsided. Of the 36 passengers, 13 died, and of the 61 crewmembers, 22 died. One member of the ground crew could not scamper away in time, and he also perished in the inferno. Scores of additional crewmembers, passengers, and men from the landing party suffered indescribably horrible burns.

The Investigation: Pursuant to the U.S. Air Commerce Act of 1926, the Bureau of Commerce began an investigation the next day. Analysts from the German Investigative Commission, U.S. Navy, U.S. Army, the office of the U.S. Director of Aeronautics, the U.S. Weather Bureau, and a host of experts from government and industry pitched in to help. Much of the potential evidence literally had gone up in smoke. Yet, two things were certain. For the fire to have occurred there must have been (1) a combustible mixture of hydrogen and oxygen and (2) enough heat to ignite the mixture.

The board considered both evidence and supposition. The ship's chief electrician survived, and he reported that no fuses or circuit breakers had "operated" prior to the fire. Electrical bonding was deemed adequate. Sabotage by an incendiary bullet, electric ray, or explosive device was high on the list of potential causes, but there was no evidence of such activity.

Hydrogen gas escaped, mixed with air, and ignited. That was beyond question, and gas leaks in airships are expected from time to time. Yet, why did the gas *ignite*? What heat source ignited the combustible hydrogen/air mixture?

The U.S. Bureau of Standards reported that the flammable limits of a hydrogen/air mixture range from about 5 percent hydrogen up to 62 percent hydrogen. The analysts noted:

The temperature at which chemical activity *[meaning, the combustion]* between hydrogen and oxygen [begins] is between 507 and 557 degrees Centigrade.

Could a short circuit in the electrical system have been the culprit? Had one of the engines "chunked" a propeller blade into the ship? Had a tension wire snapped, creating a spark? Ball lightning? A bomb? Could a carbon engine exhaust spark, with a temperature of about 530 degrees, have somehow penetrated the interior of the ship before being cooled by the outside air? Could high-frequency radio transmission from an external source be the elusive cause? Slowly the experts evaluated dozens of potential sources of ignition, then eliminated all of them except one. In the end, the obvious source of ignition could not be dismissed.

Probable Cause: The U.S. Secretary of Commerce published the lengthy *Airship Hindenburg Accident Investigation Report* on 21 July 1937. The investigative board had gradually zeroed in on the assassin of *Hindenburg,* a phenomenon known as "brush discharge." Commonly called St. Elmo's fire, brush discharge is a rapid release of static electricity into the air. This discharge produces a reddish or bluish glow that is visible only at night.

Experts reconstructed the loss of the airship. *Hindenburg* had flown through heavy rain from electrically charged thunderclouds while waiting for weather conditions to improve before mooring. The electrically charged rain caused a static electrical potential, relative to the ground, to build up on the craft:

The port bow trail ropes first made contact with the extremely wet ground 4 minutes before the fire. When they first left the ship they appeared to be quite dry.

Dry hemp ropes make poor electrical conductors. The static potential of the ship could not be harmlessly discharged to the ground through the dry ropes. However, as the landing party handled the ropes in the rain, the ropes gradually became *wet*.

As the moisture in the hemp ropes increased, their electrical conductivity increased. The electrical potential of the ship began to discharge to the ground through the wet ropes. This decreasing electrical potential, relative to the ground, caused *an increasing electrical potential between the ship and the air above it.*

Meanwhile the "flutter" began atop the ship -- leaking hydrogen gas was escaping. The gas mixed with air over the point of the leak and became flammable.

Simultaneously, the electrical potential between the ship and the air above it continued to increase. This eventually caused what normally would have been a harmless brush discharge of static electricity from the top of the ship into the air. Yet, because of the leak, the air over the ship contained a flammable hydrogen/air mixture. A U.S. National Weather Service analyst testified:

> This brush discharge would have continued for some time; it would have been invisible, being in daylight, [and] such a discharge would have ignited any adequately rich stream of leaking hydrogen that reached it, and from the point of ignition the flame would have shot back to the leak; there quickly [it] would have burnt a larger opening [in the fabric covering] and set going a conflagration of great violence.

The flammable mixture ignited. Flames raced to the point of the leak and created the "ball of fire" seen by many witnesses. Within seconds the fire burned through the fabric and into the heart of *Hindenburg.* A series of detonations followed, and fire rapidly spread throughout the airship. Within only 32 seconds the inferno reduced the pride of Nazi Germany to a burning mass of twisted metal on the ground. The board reached the following **Conclusion**:

> The cause of the accident was the ignition of a mixture of free hydrogen and air. Based upon the evidence, a leak at or in the vicinity of Cell 4 and [Cell] 5 caused a combustible mixture of hydrogen and air to form in the upper stern part of the ship in considerable quantity . . . .

The board further concluded it was "most probable" that a brush discharge ignited the flammable mixture escaping into the outside air through the fabric covering atop the airship.

TWA Flight 2
and
United Airlines Flight 718

<u>TWA Flight 2</u>:
Lockheed L-1049 Super Constellation, registration N6902C
30 June 1956, mid-air collision over the Grand Canyon, Arizona
70 aboard, 70 killed

<u>United Airlines Flight 718</u>:
Douglas DC-7, registration N6324C
30 June 1956, mid-air collision over the Grand Canyon, Arizona
58 aboard, 58 killed

Overview: A Lockheed L-1049 took off from Los Angeles and headed for Kansas City. Three minutes later a Douglas DC-7 took off from the same runway and headed in the same direction toward Chicago. On IFR flight plans in clear weather the two airliners collided at 21,000 feet over the Grand Canyon in Arizona. Both craft plummeted down and crashed in the canyon four miles below. All of the 128 people aboard the two airliners were killed.

The TWA Flight: Sixty-four trusting passengers walked out of the terminal at Los Angeles International Airport on 30 June 1956. They climbed up the mobile stairway and walked into the cabin of a Lockheed L-1049 Super Constellation, registration N6902C. Their airliner, Trans World Airlines (TWA) Flight 2, was bound for Kansas City, Missouri.

The four-engine aircraft took off from Runway 25, and Los Angeles Departure Control vectored the flight up through a low overcast. After the pilots reported "on top" at 2,400 feet they switched to the frequency of Los Angeles Center to confirm their en route ATC clearance. The captain had logged almost 15,000 hours of flight time. Backed up by his first officer and two flight engineers in the cockpit and two "hostesses" -- as TWA called them at the time -- in the cabin, the captain climbed toward his assigned cruising altitude of 19,000 feet.

The Super Constellation had been designed to the specifications of the eccentric entrepreneur, Howard Hughes. With its distinctive triple-tail and artfully curved fuselage, the "Super-Connie" reigned as the undisputed queen of the sky in the early 1950s. She could fly coast to coast in slightly over seven hours.

The United Flight: Three minutes after the TWA flight climbed skyward, United Airlines Flight 718 began rumbling down the same runway. The Douglas DC-7, registration N6324C, climbed up through the same overcast into the clear blue sky above. ATC cleared the pilots to climb in VFR conditions to 21,000 feet, the planned cruising altitude.

The DC-7 was painted in a proud red, white, and blue color scheme, and it had rolled out of the Douglas factory the previous year. The captain had 17,000 hours of flight time in his logbook. A first officer and flight engineer assisted him in the cockpit. Two young "stewardesses," as United called them, would cater to the needs of the passengers on the trip to Chicago, Illinois.

Trouble Ahead: In sunny skies, TWA Flight 2 droned eastward at 19,000 feet. Meanwhile, United Flight 718 headed in the same direction at 21,000 feet. Neither aircraft was equipped with a CVR, for this was the 1950s. However, radio messages between airliners, ATC facilities, and "aeronautical ground stations" were routinely recorded. The portion of the ATC transcript, below, begins after TWA Flight 2 requests an altitude change. The ground station relays this request to Los Angeles Center:

    Capt-United 718: . . . Captain, United Flight 718
    FO-United 718: . . . . First Officer, United Flight 718
    TWA-Ground: . . . . . TWA aeronautical ground station
    LA-Center: . . . . Los Angeles Center (ARTCC)
    SL-Center: . . . . Salt Lake Center (ARTCC)

TWA-Ground: TWA two is coming up on Daggett *[an electronic fix]*, requesting twenty-one-thousand feet. (0921)

[Los Angeles Center calls Salt Lake Center]

<u>LA-Center</u>: TWA two is requesting two-one-thousand, how does it look? I see he is [at] Daggett, direct [to] Trinidad, I see you have United seven-eighteen crossing his altitude, in his way at two-one-thousand.

<u>SL-Center</u>: Yes, their courses cross, and they are right together.

[Los Angeles Center calls the TWA ground station]

<u>LA-Center</u>: Advisory [for] TWA flight two, unable [to] approve two-one-thousand.

<u>TWA-Ground</u>: Just a minute, I think he wants a thousand on top, yes, a thousand on top until he can get [21,000 feet].

<u>LA-Center</u>: ATC clears TWA two, maintain at least one-thousand on top, advise TWA two his traffic is United seven-eighteen, direct Durango, estimating Needles at zero-nine-five-seven.

[the ground station radios the clearance to TWA Flight 2]

[At 0958, <u>United 718</u> reports passing over Needles at 21,000 feet, and estimates it will reach Painted Desert at 1031; the ground station forwards this report to Salt Lake Center]

[One minute later at 0959, <u>TWA 2</u> reports that it passed over Lake Mohave at 0955, "1,000 feet on top" at 21,000 feet, and estimates it will reach Painted Desert at 1031; the TWA ground station forwards this report to Salt Lake Center]

[both craft are at 21,000 feet; both have estimated that they will reach the <u>same place</u>, at the <u>same time</u>, at the <u>same altitude</u>]

[the two airliners collide at apx. 1030:30]

<u>FO-United 718</u>: Salt Lake [Center, this is] United seven-eighteen! Aaahhh! We're going in! *[screamed in a loud voice]* (1030:53)

<u>Capt-United 718</u>: Pull! Up! *[screamed in desperation]* (1030:53)

The Accident: At 1030:53 Hours the frantic radio transmissions from United Flight 718 were recorded by the aeronautical radio stations at Salt Lake City and at San Francisco. The ground station radiomen could not decipher the words, which had been screamed in a high-pitched voice.

Later the tape recording was subjected to spectrographic analysis, speech stretching, and a technique called "visible speech." These tests revealed that the first officer began screaming far above the normal male voice range. During pauses his microphone remained keyed, and analysts detected the shouted words of a second speaker. He was identified as the captain, and the pitch of his shouts was even higher. The analysts dryly noted that the two pilots were under "great emotional stress."

The two airliners had flown eastward over the Grand Canyon. The passengers lucky enough to have window seats had likely enjoyed the scenic view. Possibly, so had the pilots. Meanwhile, like two bugs racing toward the same morsel of food, the two aircraft slowly converged. Then they met:

> The initial impact occurred with the [United] DC-7 moving from right to left relative to the [TWA] L-1049. . . . The lower surface of the DC-7 left wing struck the upper aft fuselage of the Constellation with disintegrating force. . . . The collision ripped open the fuselage of the Constellation. . . . Most of the left outer wing [of the DC-7] separated during the collision.

Passengers were flung out into the sky as the Constellation cabin ripped open. The triple-tail empennage broke away. What was left of TWA Flight 2 dropped like the proverbial pallet of bricks into the canyon four miles below. Most of the wreckage tumbled down into a deep draw near Temple Butte.

The United DC-7, minus much of its left wing, began a steep spiral from which recovery was not possible. The mortally wounded airliner slammed into the face of a cliff a mile from the TWA Constellation. Much of the debris and some dismembered bodies showered down into a deep and inaccessible "chimney" below the impact site.

Neither aircraft had reported reaching the Painted Desert fix, so ATC issued a "missing aircraft" alert at 1151 Hours. Later that day searchers sighted smoke from the two crash sites deep down inside the Grand Canyon in Arizona. There had been a total of 128 people on the two aircraft. None of them survived.

Eager to peddle misfortune and scandal, the news media enjoyed a brief field day. ATC had known that the airliners were (1) flying at the *same altitude* (2) toward the *same place* in the sky, and (3) planned to get there at the *same time*. Insanity! Surely the heads of incompetent dolts at ATC would roll, the media crowed.

This rush to judgment proved to be premature. Those in the aviation community knew the truth. They knew that the presumed control exercised by ATC was more fantasy than fact.

The Investigation: A brief review is necessary. In the technical aftermath of World War II, modern aircraft instrumentation had made flight in IMC weather possible. Advances in electronics led to a national network of VOR stations for aerial navigation. In all types of weather, planes could fly on a network of "airways" in the sky. Nonetheless, a means of preventing aircraft from *colliding* on airways in the clouds was needed, and ATC was born:

ATC in the United States was in its infancy in 1956. Within en route "centers," civil servants in white shirts and bow ties became "controllers." Armed with microphones and headsets, they sat at desks facing rows of slanting metal trays. Each tray represented a given airway segment. The trays held handwritten "flight progress strips," each of which represented an aircraft that ATC had "cleared" on an IFR flight.

Each flight progress strip fit between bars on the tray, and each bar represented 1,000 feet of altitude. Therefore, in theory, if a controller could keep his flight progress strips separated, no aircraft could collide. Crude, but it worked.

En route radar coverage did not exist. Pilots radioed "position reports" to aeronautical ground stations. The ground stations used a telephone or teletype to relay the reports to the ATC "center." They relayed amended ATC clearances and pilot requests in the same manner.

This system worked well for aircraft (1) on an IFR flight plan, (2) in IFR weather conditions, (3) in controlled airspace. Under other conditions the United States' air traffic control system had severe limitations. These limitations became obvious after the Grand Canyon mid-air collision.

Investigators from the Civil Aeronautics Board (CAB) conducted a meticulous analysis of the accident. After leaving Los Angeles both flights initially flew on airways, and ATC had to separate them from each other and from all other IFR traffic.

Both flights later flew "off airways" in uncontrolled airspace. As they droned eastward both flights periodically radioed position reports to ATC. Consequently, ATC knew that both aircraft were eventually cruising at the (1) same altitude and estimating arrival at the (2) same electronic fix at the (3) same time. How could ATC have allowed the flights to progress in this manner, the public wondered? The answers lay in regulations well known only to ATC, civilian and military pilots, and the airlines:

First, in "uncontrolled airspace" off of airways, ATC was not required to provide, and in most instances *could not* provide, control services or advisories to aircraft on IFR flight plans. ATC procedures clearly stated:

[ATC] clearances authorize flight within control zones and control areas only; no responsibility for separation of aircraft outside these areas is accepted.

Second, although the TWA flight was at 21,000 feet, ATC had not cleared it to fly at that altitude. Instead, ATC had cleared the pilots to fly "1,000 feet on top," something totally different. The Flight Information Manual best explained the concept:

"1,000 feet on top" may be filed in an IFR flight plan, or assigned by ATC in an IFR clearance in lieu of a cruising altitude. [This] permits the flight to be conducted at any altitude . . . 1,000 feet or more above the cloud layer.

In other words, the TWA pilots could have been flying at any altitude 1,000 feet or more above the clouds. The captain had *elected* to fly at 21,000 feet.

Third, although both aircraft were at 21,000 feet, they were flying in clear sunny weather. Under such conditions, Civil Air Regulations required the pilots to maintain *visual* separation:

During the time an IFR flight is operating in VFR weather conditions, it is the direct responsibility of the pilot to avoid other aircraft.

Probable Cause: On 15 April 1957, roughly 10 months after the accident, the CAB adopted its Accident Investigation Report, File No. 1-0090. The board determined that both aircraft were flying in VMC weather in uncontrolled airspace. ATC was not required to enforce separation between them:

> [Air] traffic control services are not provided in uncontrolled airspace. *[and also]* Under visual flight rules . . . it is the pilot's responsibility to maintain separation from other aircraft.

The board found that ATC had issued proper clearances. After learning that both aircraft were flying in the same area at the same altitude, ATC was not required to issue an amended clearance or a traffic advisory. Notwithstanding their IFR flight plans, both aircraft were flying in *VFR conditions*. The old *see-and-be-seen* adage applied. The board concluded:

> The *Probable Cause* of this mid-air collision was that the pilots did not see each other in time to avoid a collision. It is not possible to determine why the pilots did not see each other.

Postscript: The Grand Canyon collision blared a wake-up call to the aviation industry. As an interim step, U.S. military radar sites began monitoring commercial airline flights. Congress created a new agency, which would evolve into the FAA. Within a few years new radar installations and electronic wizardry enabled controllers to separate IFR aircraft from takeoff until landing. Were the days of mid-air collisions long past?

Wishful thinking! Slightly over four years later, nine days before Christmas in 1960, two airliners plied the murky night sky over the city of New York. Armed with new high-tech equipment, ATC maintained *radio and radar contact* with both aircraft. Yet, they collided, killing everyone on board (see the chapter, "United Airlines Flight 826 and TWA Flight 266"). And, unfortunately, there would be more "mid-airs" still to come.

Braniff Airways Flight 542 (The Electra Story, Part 1)

Lockheed L-188 Electra, registration N9705C
29 September 1959, near Buffalo, Texas
34 aboard, 34 killed

This accident would lead to the most intriguing mystery in the annals of commercial aviation.

Overview: A Lockheed L-188 Electra cruised through the night sky at 15,000 feet. The left wing suddenly tore off of the aircraft, and complete structural disintegration followed. Wreckage rained down along a path almost three miles long near Buffalo, Texas. The 34 people on board were killed.

The Flight: When Lockheed engineers designed the four-engine turboprop L-188 Electra, they created a modern-day symphony of aluminum and technology. The craft met the demand for a swift medium-range airliner that would seat at least 100 passengers, and the prototype first flew in 1957. Engineers mated four powerful Allison jet engines to Aero Products propeller assemblies, making the Electra the fastest propeller driven airliner in the world. Within three years over 100 of these swift new aircraft were plying the skies over the United States.

An Electra, registration N9705C, took off from Houston, Texas, at 2244 Hours on 29 September 1959 as Braniff Airways Flight 542. The aircraft was almost brand new. It had rolled out of the California factory only 11 days earlier and had accumulated just 132 hours of flight time. On this "red eye" flight the Electra carried a light load of only 28 passengers and 6 crewmembers. The flight was bound for New York, but the schedule called for stops at Dallas, Texas, and Washington, DC. The two pilots, the flight engineer, and three "hostesses" had only recently completed their Electra transition training.

Trouble Ahead: Houston Departure Control soon turned the flight over to San Antonio Center, and at 2258 Hours the Electra reached its assigned altitude of 15,000 feet. For the 41 minute trip to Dallas the aircraft cruised at 275 knots. The year 1959 was in the pre-CVR era, but ATC transmissions were recorded. The brief transcript, below, has been *reconstructed* from technical sources. Consequently, some of the verbiage may not be verbatim:

FO: . . . . First Officer, Flight 542
FltEngr-Log: . . . . Flight Engineer's log, Flight 542
Radio-: . . . . (prefix) Radio transmission, Flight 542
Center: . . . . San Antonio Center (ARTCC)

FltEngr-Log: Altitude 15,000, airspeed 275 knots, [outside air temperature] 15 degrees, anti-icing off. (2300)

Radio-FO: San Antonio, Braniff flight five-forty-two is over the Leona VOR at fifteen-thousand [feet]. (2305)

Center: Roger, Braniff five-forty-two, now monitor Fort Worth on frequency one-two-zero-point-eight. (2305)

Radio-FO: [Braniff] five-forty-two, roger. (2305)

[at 2307 the First Officer radios the airline's base at Dallas and reports a deferred maintenance item, an inoperative sump pump]

FltEngr-Log: Transmission completed, 2307. (2307)

*[2 minutes later **the aircraft disintegrates** in flight at 2309]*

The Accident: The exchange of maintenance information with the airline's base in Dallas became the epitaph for the 34 people on Flight 542. Two minutes later at 2309 Hours the Electra ripped apart in the air. There was no radio distress message. The death of Flight 542 proved to be swift and terrible, and the CAB staff would later explain:

That the aircraft broke up violently is self-evident. That the break-up process was both quick and with little or no warning is clear. *[and also]* Structural failure of the aircraft occurred at approximately 2309 [Hours] while on course to the next fix, Trinidad Intersection.

First, a tooth-jarring vibration consumed the Electra airframe. The CAB would describe the break-up sequence:

> Separation of the left wing and the No. 1 gear box propeller QEC structure occurred at about the same time . . . . The horizontal stabilizer then broke up under impact of parts coming from the wing; wing planking from the right wing [broke off], the No. 4 powerplant tore loose, and the right wing outboard of the No. 4 engine separated. . . . The fuselage broke into two separate portions . . . .

Aerodynamic forces tore at the fuselage as it tumbled toward the ground, breaking it into several sections. The disintegration flung many passengers out into the dark Texas night. Some were still alive as they began the fall to the ground three miles below:

> Traumatic injuries to occupants, some of whom had fallen free of the aircraft, were severe and extensive with much mutilation.

The largest pieces of wreckage fell into a potato field several miles from Buffalo, Texas. People who fell to the earth inside the broken fuselage sections shared the fate of those who had been thrown out during the aerial break-up. No one survived.

The Investigation: A team of investigators from the CAB gathered at the site of the crash the following morning. They found the left wing and its engines over a mile from the potato field. Pieces of the right wing had been scattered helter-skelter across the Texas landscape. The distribution and nature of the wreckage pointed to a catastrophic in-flight structural failure:

> Damage to the airframe had been so great that no aircraft system, as such, survived . . . functional checks were impossible. *[and also]* The wreckage was strewn for a total distance of 13,900 feet from the first debris to the nose crater.

Night and day investigation soon established precisely *what* had happened: initial failure of the left wing, followed by the other structural failures. However, the *cause* of the break-up proved to be elusive. The wreckage revealed fire damage, but the fire had begun after the break-up.

Metal score marks indicated that the propeller assembly had been wobbling in the No. 1 nacelle. At the time, analysts believed that the wobbling was caused by the wing tearing away. In any event, standing alone, there was no known way a wobbling propeller could damage the massive Electra wing.

Metallurgists examined each piece of the crushed rubble. They found that the wing had been destroyed by powerful "cycles of reverse bending." This is called "flutter" in the aviation industry. Yet, flutter had *supposedly* posed no danger to an Electra wing. Plus, the flutter frequency of the wing and the nacelle were not the same, so harmonic coupling was deemed impossible:

> All of the flutter tests and analyses made by Lockheed during the original certification process and during the reevaluation showed the Electra wing to be flutter-free during and even above normal operating speeds and further disclosed that the wing has a high degree of damping.

Why had the wing ripped off in flight? What could have caused flutter in a supposedly flutter-free wing? Methodically the experts examined each possible cause, then eliminated it. In laboratory tests an Electra wing was deliberately weakened, twisted with hydraulic jacks, hammered, and subjected to loads far exceeding its design limits. Week after week the mighty wing withstood all the torture the engineers could throw at it. Technical analysts compiled thousands of pages of test data. The evidence indicated that the wing was too strong, too fail-safe, too immune to damage.

The CAB interviewed scores of local witnesses, many of them farmers. Separately and independently, most of the farmers said the same thing. Just before the crash all coon dogs within miles began howling. This was a clue, but the experts did not know what to make of it. Dogs can hear sounds far beyond the range of human hearing. What had the dogs heard? What had disturbed them? What significance, if any, did it have?

The entire aviation industry pitched in to help, but six months after the crash they all were stumped. A team of technical analysts from Boeing, Convair, NASA, the FAA, and representatives from all airlines flying the Electra met for five days to review the stymied investigation. They examined and then re-examined every conceivable vulnerability, every possible weakness. They made no progress. It seemed that there were no avenues left to explore, no more theories, no more data to analyze. Their "findings" consisted of reasons why *the wing could not have failed*. If the meeting had continued much longer they all could have been forgiven for going home thinking that the accident never had happened.

Probable Cause: The CAB had no *probable* cause. It also had no *possible* cause. All data indicated that it was not possible for the wing to have ripped off. Simply impossible!

The analysts had no way to know that an obscure principle of physics could tear the mighty Electra apart. Yet, they all were haunted by something they could not explain, something eerie, the reaction of the coon dogs. Aviation authority Robert J. Serling explained it best in his book, *Loud & Clear*:

> Lurking in every investigator's mind, like a nagging uneasy conscience, was the phrase uttered by one farmer and backed up by so many of his neighbors: "Every coon dog for miles around started howling."

By the middle of March 1960 the CAB was ready to place the Braniff crash in the "unsolved" category The analysts had been grasping at straws and coming up empty. The elusive cause of the crash of Flight 542 was beyond their reach. Then, **another** Electra shed its wings and plunged to earth.

> *Note: For the cause of both Electra crashes, see the following chapter, "Northwest Airlines Flight 710."*

Northwest Airlines Flight 710 (The Electra Story, Part 2)

Lockheed L-188 Electra, registration N121US
17 March 1960, near Channelton, Indiana
63 aboard, 63 killed

This accident is almost identical to a previous Electra crash. Six months earlier Braniff Airways Flight 542 (see the previous chapter) disintegrated in flight. All on board were killed. The ongoing investigation had failed to identify the cause, and that prior crash remained in the then-unsolved category.

Overview: In clear and sunny weather a Lockheed L-188 Electra cruised at 18,000 feet. A horrible vibration consumed the airframe, and both wings tore off of the fuselage. The debris tumbled to the ground near Channelton, Indiana. There were 63 people aboard the airliner, and all of them were killed.

The Flight: On the clear afternoon of 17 March 1960, Northwest Airlines Flight 710 took off from Chicago, Illinois, at 1438 Hours and headed toward Miami, Florida. The Lockheed L-188 Electra, registration N121US, cruised effortlessly at 18,000 feet and 260 knots. This aircraft had been delivered new in July of the previous year, and it was the first Electra in the Northwest Airlines fleet. It had amassed 1,786 flight hours and had sailed through a scheduled major inspection only eight days prior to this flight.

The captain, age 57, held an ATP certificate and had logged 27,523 flight hours during his career. The young first officer, age 27, held a Commercial Pilot certificate and had 2,974 hours in his logbook. Their flight engineer had over 5,000 hours of experience under his belt. In the cabin two female "stewardesses" and one male "flight attendant" took charge of the 57 passengers, including several children and one infant.

Trouble Ahead: Crew and passengers alike probably enjoyed the view as their flying machine sped over the Indiana farmland over three miles below. There was no hint of impending trouble.

Disaster would strike without any warning. The brief transcript, below, has been *reconstructed* from technical reports. Therefore, some of the verbiage may not be verbatim:

FO: . . . . . . First Officer, Flight 710
Radio-: . . . . (prefix) Radio transmission, Flight 710
Center: . . . . Indianapolis Center (ARTCC)

Radio-FO: Indy Center, Northwest seven-ten. (1445)

Center: Northwest seven-one-zero, Indianapolis Center. (1445)

Radio-FO: Northwest seven-ten is over Milford at eighteen-thousand [feet], estimating Scotland at one-five-one-two. (1445)

[Indianapolis Center acknowledges the position report]

Radio-FO: Center, Northwest seven-ten. (1513)

Center: Northwest seven-one-zero, Indianapolis Center. (1513)

Radio-FO: Center, Northwest seven-ten is over Scotland and maintaining eighteen-thousand [feet], estimating Bowling Green at one-five-three-five. (1513)

Center: Northwest seven-one-zero, roger, contact Memphis Center on frequency one-two-four-point-six at time, fifteen-thirty. (1513)

[the First Officer acknowledges the instructions]

*[12 minutes later **the Electra disintegrates** in flight at 1525]*

The Accident: First came a horrible vibration -- exactly like the precursor of doom that had destroyed the Braniff flight six months earlier. Then the right wing buckled:

The first parts to separate were pieces of the right wing upper surface . . . Separations of the left outboard powerplant and the left outer wing structure began almost simultaneously with the right wing separation . . . .

Startled by the sound of two loud explosions, many people looked skyward and witnessed the death of Flight 710:

> Suddenly two puffs of white smoke were seen. Seconds later these were followed by a large cloud of dark smoke. Two loud explosions were then heard, and [the wingless fuselage] was seen to emerge from the smoke cloud and fall nearly vertically, trailing smoke and flame.

With both wings torn off the aerodynamic drag on the fuselage was greatly reduced. At an incredible speed of about 600 knots it screamed down into a soybean patch near Channelton, Indiana. The impact hurled debris a quarter-mile away. The missing wings would be found over two miles from the fuselage crater.

Potential rescuers rushed to the crater at the main crash site, but they found that the fuselage had vanished. It was gone. There was no aluminum tangle of wreckage. There were no bodies. The rescuers looked down into a deep smoking cauldron that marked the grave of the 63 people aboard Flight 710.

At the terminal at Miami International Airport, people began to trickle in to wait for the arrival of friends on Flight 710, for it was scheduled to land at 1821 Hours. An hour before the scheduled landing a crying Northwest employee walked to the manual flight arrivals board. With a trembling hand, next to the lettering for Northwest Flight 710 he wrote one word: "CANCELLED."

The Investigation: The CAB promptly arrived at the crash site, but the fire in the bottom of the crater smoldered for five days. Finally a backhoe began excavating the site. Twelve feet below the surface the workers began finding what remained of the Electra fuselage. It had telescoped down into a fraction of its original size. The smoldering aluminum mass and the victims were all compacted together. They could not be separated. Individual bodies could not be identified. Strong men gagged and vomited as they recovered molten metal mingled with the mortal remains of the crew and passengers from Flight 710:

> Following the accident at Channelton, Indiana, Lockheed undertook a reevaluation program in which the entire Electra concept and design was audited.

Accident reconstruction experts soon found that the Northwest crash mirrored the Braniff tragedy. Therefore, the CAB quickly combined the two investigations into a single effort. In both instances the wings had failed and ripped off in flight. That was obvious. Lockheed and the CAB redoubled their efforts in the air and in the laboratory. They worked three shifts a day, seven days a week. To their surprise they stumbled upon two inconsistencies in the basic design of the aircraft:

Significant [dynamic] loads imposed on the wing . . . between the fuselage and the outboard nacelles . . . had not been included in the design loads. *[and also]* The dynamic response of the outboard nacelles in turbulence was different from that used in the original design.

In other words, in turbulence the outboard nacelles were taking more of a beating than engineers had predicted. Still, it was not enough to damage the mighty Electra wing. There had to be another factor, something elusive, something that was missing:

Since the Electra wing is basically flutter-resistant, in order to produce flutter there must be an external driving force.

Grasping at straws, analysts remembered reports of howling coon dogs at the time of the Braniff crash. If a propeller tip had gone supersonic it would create an unearthly wail, one that would induce the dogs to howl. Investigators made recordings of propellers at supersonic speed and played the tapes for the rural witnesses. Yes, they reported, that was the sound they had heard.

There are over 90 modes in which metal can vibrate or flutter. Gradually the lethal death mode came into focus, and it unmasked the assassin of the two Electras:

The reevaluation of the Electra disclosed that whirl mode [flutter in a nacelle] can induce flutter in a wing highly resistant to flutter. . . . It must be concluded, therefore, that the whirl mode [flutter in the nacelle] provided the driving force essential to destruction of the wing.

Whirl mode flutter was nothing new. In the aviation industry it had been understood for many years. Any spinning object is, in effect, a gyroscope, and any such device (a child's spinning top, electric fans, and aircraft propellers) can become unbalanced. In propeller-driven aircraft a blow, such as turbulence, will cause the whirling propeller to displace slightly. The gyroscopic tendency of the spinning propeller will push back against the displacing force and cause *whirl mode flutter.*

In the Electra airliner the frequency of whirl mode flutter in the nacelle was five cycles per second. This was normal and expected. It posed no danger. But, the experts discovered, if the flutter grew in magnitude its *frequency could decrease* to a mere three cycles per second. Tragically, this lower flutter frequency matched the harmonic frequency of the giant Electra wing:

> As whirl mode flutter progresses [in the nacelle] . . . its frequency can reduce from five to three cycles per second, where it will drive the wing in three cycles per second torsional and bending oscillations. These wing oscillations will *reinforce and perpetuate [emphasis added]* the whirl mode.

Once the fatal cycle began, it could not be stopped. Turbulence would cause slight whirl mode flutter in the propeller assembly. This flutter would increase within a weakened nacelle. As the strength of the flutter grew, its frequency would decrease to three cycles per second. Instead of absorbing (*damping*, in aviation parlance) the flutter as it was supposed to do, the wing would begin vibrating at the same frequency -- *harmonic coupling!*

> Propeller whirl mode [flutter] could persist undampened and couple with the wing, thus exciting it to failure.

The wing vibration would "excite" and accelerate the propeller flutter and feed the metallurgical malignancy. The engine mounts would snap and the wobbling engine and propeller unit, still in frequency with the wing -- harmonic coupling -- would fuel ever-wilder wing vibrations. The propeller tips would go supersonic (and any dog in the vicinity would howl). In a vicious sequence lasting only a few seconds the massive wing would shake itself to death and snap like a twig.

Probable Cause: For the Northwest crash the CAB adopted its Aircraft Accident Report, File No. 1-0003, on 24 April 1961. Four days later it adopted a similar report for the Braniff Airlines tragedy, File No. 1-0060.

The board found that both aircraft had been in level cruising flight at normal cruise speeds. Damage to an outboard nacelle had gone undetected. Clear air turbulence caused whirl mode flutter in the weakened nacelle. The flutter grew, decreased in frequency, and spread to the wing. The wing began to vibrate at the same frequency. This out-of-control harmonic coupling grew stronger and stronger, and it tore the wings off the airliner.

The problem was not the strength of the wing. It was more than strong enough. Yet, it did not have the necessary "stiffness" to damp the sinister whirl mode flutter from the nacelle. The CAB found that the *Probable Cause* of the two accidents was:

separation of the [wings] in flight due to [whirl mode] flutter induced by oscillation of the outboard nacelles.

The board also found two *contributing* factors:

[First was] a reduced stiffness of the [wing] structure.

[Second was] the entry of the aircraft into an area of severe clear air turbulence [which initiated the fatal flutter sequence].

United Airlines Flight 826
and
TWA Flight 266

<u>United Airlines Flight 826</u>
Douglas DC-8, registration N8013U
16 December 1960, mid-air collision over New York
84 aboard, 84 killed (plus 8 killed on the ground)

<u>TWA Flight 266</u>
Lockheed L-1049 Super Constellation, registration N6907C
16 December 1960, mid-air collision over New York
44 aboard, 44 killed

Overview: A new Douglas DC-8 and a Lockheed L-1049 Super Constellation descended for landing at separate airports in New York. ATC had radar contact with both aircraft; ATC controlled both flights. Nonetheless, the two airliners collided in the murky sky and fell to earth. The 128 people on board, plus eight more on the ground, died in the collision and fiery crashes.

The United Flight: United Airlines Flight 826 took off from O'Hare Airport in Chicago and headed east toward Idlewild Airport (also called New York International Airport, and later renamed JFK International Airport) in New York. The new Douglas DC-8, registration N8013U, carried a light load of only 77 passengers and a crew of seven. The four-jet passenger airliner had been delivered to the airline in December of the previous year and had logged 2,434 hours in the air.

At a takeoff weight of 214,790 pounds the DC-8 had clawed its way skyward at 0911 Hours. The IFR flight plan specified flight level 270, a speed of 478 knots, and a time en route of 1 hour and 29 minutes. At 1022:41 Hours the controller at New York Center confirmed: "radar contact."

The TWA Flight: Eleven minutes before the United flight left Chicago, Trans World Airlines (TWA) Flight 266 took off from Columbus, Ohio. The TWA airliner headed for LaGuardia Airport, a different air terminal in New York. The sleek Lockheed L-1049 Super Constellation, registration N9607C, carried a slim passenger load of 39 in addition to its crew of five. For this flight the Constellation weighed 101,144 pounds with its passengers and its 2,600 gallons of fuel. The airliner had been plying the world's airways since 1952 and had amassed 21,555 hours in the air.

The pilots planned on a flight time of 1 hour and 32 minutes. Toward the end of the trip they approached the eastern seaboard at 19,000 feet and followed the instructions of New York Center. At 1019 Hours as the Constellation descended through 11,000 feet the controller voiced the comforting words: "radar contact."

Trouble Ahead: The United DC-8 was equipped with a FDR, but neither airliner had a new-technology CVR. Nonetheless, ATC recorded all radio transmissions. ATC could track the *position* of each aircraft on radar. Yet, the state of transponder technology in the year 1960 did not provide an *altitude* display for the controller. He relied on pilot radio reports in order to afford altitude separation for aircraft under his control.

The portion of the ATC transcript, below, contains radio traffic between the controllers and the two flights. At no time were the United DC-8 pilots and the TWA Constellation pilots in radio contact with the same controller:

> United 826: . . . . . United Flight 826
> TWA 266: . . . . . . TWA Flight 266
> Center: . . . . New York Center (ARTCC)
> LG-AppControl: . . LaGuardia Approach Control
> IW-AppControl: . . Idlewild Approach Control

Center: United eight-two-six, [your] clearance limit is Preston Intersection . . . maintain flight level two-five-zero. (1015)

[the United pilots acknowledge the clearance limit at 1015]

[TWA 266 reports passing the Allentown VOR at 11,000 feet; Center confirms radar contact at 1019]

Center: United eight-two-six, Center, radar contact. (1022:41)

[Center reports the Idlewild Airport weather to United 826; the United pilots then begin a descent at 1024:37]

Center: United eight-twenty-six, cleared to proceed on Victor thirty until intercepting Victor one-twenty-three and that way to Preston. It'll be a little bit quicker. (1025:09)

[the United pilots acknowledge the clearance at 1025:20]

[Center clears TWA 266 to descend to 9,000 feet and contact LaGuardia Approach Control]

LG-AppControl: TWA two-sixty-six, maintain nine-thousand, report the zero-one-zero [radial of] Robbinsville [VOR], ILS Runway four, landing Runway four . . . . (1026:22)

[Center clears United 826 to descend to 11,000 feet at 1026:49]

[TWA 266 reports passing the 010 radial of the Robbinsville VOR; LaGuardia Approach Control clears the pilots to descend to 8,000 feet at 1028]

Center: United eight-twenty-six, I show you crossing the centerline of Victor thirty at this time. (1028:41)

[the United pilots acknowledge that they are on Victor 30, and they ask Center how far they are from Victor 123]

Center: United eight-twenty-six . . . I show you fifteen, make it sixteen, miles [from] Victor one-twenty-three. (1028:56)

[at 1029:49 LaGuardia Approach Control clears TWA 266 to descend to 6,000 feet for radar vectors to the ILS course for Runway 4; the pilots acknowledge the instructions]

Center: United eight-two-six, descend to and maintain five-thousand feet . . . looks like you'll be able to make Preston at five-thousand [feet]. (1030:07)

[at 1032:09 LaGuardia Approach Control instructs TWA 266 to turn right to a heading of 130 degrees to intercept the ILS]

Center: United eight-two-six, if holding is necessary at Preston, [use a] southwest one minute pattern, right turns, the only delay will be in descent. (1032:16)

United 826: Roger, no delay, we're out of seven-[thousand feet].

[LaGuardia Approach Control clears TWA 266 to descend to 5,000 feet; the pilots acknowledge the clearance at 1032:22]

LG-AppControl: TWA two-sixty-six, traffic *[meaning, another aircraft]* at two-thirty, six miles, northeast bound. (1032:47)

[the TWA pilots acknowledge the "traffic advisory" at 1032:51]

[United 826 reports descending through 6,000 feet at 1033:01]

[in response to a query from LaGuardia Approach Control, TWA 266 reports descending through 5,500 feet at 1033:08]

[both flights are now cleared to the same altitude, 5,000 feet]

Center: United eight-twenty-six, roger, and you [have] received the holding instructions at Preston; radar service is terminated, contact Idlewild Approach Control . . . . (1033:20)

[the United pilots reply "good day" and switch to Idlewild Approach Control]

LG-AppControl: TWA two-sixty-six, turn left now, heading one-three-zero. (1033:21)

TWA 266: Roger, heading one-three-zero. (1033:23)

LG-AppControl: TWA two-sixty-six, roger, that appears to be jet traffic *[meaning, it is moving fast]* off to your right now, three o'clock at one mile, northeast bound. (1033:26)

United 826: Idlewild Approach control, United eight-twenty-six, approaching Preston at five thousand. (1033:28)

*[4 seconds later **the airliners collide** at 1033:32]*

The Accident: The two aircraft collided at an altitude of 5,175 feet in the clouds over Staten Island. The No. 4 engine on the big DC-8 sliced through the top of the TWA Constellation like a giant meat cleaver. The mid-air impact tore the Constellation apart, and no one aboard had a chance to survive:

The Constellation broke into three main sections following the collision . . . . Numerous pieces of aircraft structure were strewn over a wide area in the vicinity of Miller Field.

The rear of the Constellation cabin and the empennage tumbled earthward. The forward part of the cabin and the left wing followed. The two main sections of the severed fuselage fell down onto Miller Field, and smaller pieces of debris rained down into the surrounding neighborhood. An intense fire consumed all remnants of the Constellation fuselage. There had been 44 people on board, and the collision and fiery crash killed all of them.

Meanwhile, on the DC-8 the impact had torn off the outer right wing and the No. 4 engine. The high-speed collision also ripped away many of the enhanced lift devices on the left wing. These detached pieces from the DC-8 showered down onto Miller Army Air Field a mile below:

Both main landing gear doors, the outboard section of the right wing, and the No. 4 engine impacted in the Miller Field area.

Despite the damage the pilots retained partial control over the DC-8. They made a valiant attempt to save their airliner, but its wounds eventually proved to be too great. The craft staggered eight miles to the northeast, sinking lower and lower:

The DC-8 continued on a northeasterly heading and crashed into the heavily populated area of Brooklyn.

The airliner rammed through tall buildings and exploded at the intersection of Sterling Place and Seventh Avenue. Flaming wreckage cartwheeled in all directions. The left wing burned in the street, and mangled remains from the fuselage burned atop a nearby building. The fuel-filled right wing and the No. 3 engine tore through the Pillar of Fire Church, sending a *pillar of fire* hundreds of feet into the snowy sky. Ironically, the revisionist Methodist sect had drawn its name from a miracle related in *Exodus 13:21*. The ancient Israelites had relied upon a "pillar of fire" to lead them out of slavery in Egypt:

[A] 15-foot section [of the left wing] cut through and came to rest in a building at 126 Sterling Place, leaving two feet of the wing protruding through the roof.

The crushed rear of the United DC-8 cabin tumbled down the street after the impact, throwing an 11 year old boy out into a snowbank. Two policemen found him there, horribly burned and in shock. Yet, he sat up and cried through blackened lips to the officers: "My name is Stephen. Mommy? Daddy?"

The young boy hailed from Wilmette, Illinois. He was on his Christmas vacation and had been going to meet his grandparents, who were waiting for him at Idlewild. Instead, an ambulance rushed him to the hospital.

Against the backdrop of the two fiery crashes in the city and the tremendous loss of life, the desperate efforts to save young Stephen became a non-stop "media event." Alerted by television and radio, compassionate New Yorkers flocked to the hospital to donate blood, or to donate skin for grafting to cover the boy's terrible burns. Yet, although the entire nation rooted for the youngster, his life slipped away the following day.

Stephen's death completed the casualty toll; he was the 136th fatality. All of the people aboard the two airliners, plus eight more on the ground, perished in the collision and crashes. However, it could have been much worse. The DC-8 fell only 250 feet from Public School No. 41. Hundreds of young children had rushed to the windows to watch the orange flames boiling skyward.

The Investigation: The FDR on the DC-8 fixed the time of the collision at 1033:32 Hours. Two ATC controllers, each of them responsible for separate areas of airspace, separately had cleared the two flights to descend to the same altitude, 5,000 feet. LaGuardia Approach Control was providing vectors to guide TWA Flight 266, the Constellation, toward the ILS course for Runway 4:

> At no time prior to the one-mile advisory was any information furnished to Flight 266 which would have alerted it to a conflict.

ATC handled the United DC-8 differently. The United pilots made position reports to ATC, but they were responsible for their own navigation. They did not receive ATC radar vectors. Twelve seconds before the collision, New York Center had handed the United flight off to Idlewild Approach Control. Still, long before the handoff Center had issued a clearance limit. That aerial "fix" in the sky, Preston Intersection, was a point beyond which the

United pilots were not authorized to fly:

> Preston Intersection is defined as the intersection of the 346 degree radial of the Colts Neck [VOR] and the 050 degree radial of the Robbinsville [VOR].

Normally the United pilots would have tuned one of their VOR receivers to the Colts Neck VOR and the other receiver to the Robbinsville VOR. The cockpit instruments would have displayed the radials from both VOR stations, easily allowing the pilots to identify the intersection. However, investigators discovered that the United pilots had radioed their maintenance base to report a problem -- one of their two VOR systems was inoperative:

> ATC was not advised of the fact that United [Flight] 826 was operating with a single [VOR] receiver.

With only one operative VOR it was still *possible* to identify a VOR intersection, but it was more difficult. The pilots would have to switch their single operative receiver back and forth from one VOR frequency to the other, constantly checking and cross-checking the radials. This would consume a lot of time, and it would not be as accurate as a simultaneous cockpit display.

Investigators learned that difficulties had continued to mount for the United pilots. At 1025:09 Hours, ATC issued them a revised clearance for a new route. This shortened the distance to Preston Intersection. Significantly, it reduced the time available for the pilots to repeatedly re-tune their only operative VOR receiver to establish the location of the intersection. Investigators opined:

> The crew committed a primary error by apparently failing to record and note the time and distance required to comply with their new clearance.

Both flights had been cleared to 5,000 feet, so identification of Preston Intersection was crucial. If the United pilots did not stop (that is, enter the mandated *holding pattern*) at the intersection, they would (1) leave the airspace reserved for them and (2) head toward airspace reserved for the TWA flight.

Probable Cause: The CAB adopted its Aircraft Accident Report, File No. 1-0083, on 12 June 1962 roughly 18 months after the accident. The board found that the United DC-8 did not enter a holding pattern at Preston Intersection, as ATC had instructed:

> When radar service was being terminated at 1033:20 [Hours], Flight 826 had already proceeded eight or nine miles beyond Preston [Intersection].

The board found that the ATC clearances and handling of the two flights had been proper. The LaGuardia controller who vectored the TWA Constellation had seen the radar return from the United DC-8. He watched the two "blips" converge on his radar display. Yet, the controller had no way to know the *altitude* of the errant flight. Accordingly, ATC radioed routine "advisories" to the TWA Constellation. At the time of the last such advisory at 1033:26 Hours the collision was a mere six seconds away. The board noted the following ***Probable Cause*** of the accident:

> [United] Flight 826 *[the DC-8]* proceeded beyond its clearance limit and the confines of the airspace allocated to the flight by Air Traffic Control.

The CAB found two factors that ***contributed*** to the accident:

> [First was] the high rate of speed of the United DC-8 as it approached Preston Intersection.

> [Second was] the change of clearance which reduced the en route distance along Victor 123 by approximately 11 miles.

Pan Am Flight 214

Boeing 707, registration N709PA
8 December 1963, near Elkton, Maryland
81 aboard, 81 killed

Overview: On a stormy December night a Boeing 707 flew in a holding pattern while waiting to land. Lightning struck the aircraft. A fuel tank exploded, the left wing broke off, and the airliner crashed in flames. There were 81 people aboard the airliner, and the explosion and crash killed them all.

The Flight: Pan American World Airways (Pan Am) Flight 214 took off from San Juan, Puerto Rico, and headed north. During a brief stop in Baltimore, Maryland, the captain got a briefing on the rough weather along the route to Philadelphia, Pennsylvania, his final destination. The briefing included details about thunderstorm activity in the Philadelphia area. At 2024 Hours the flight took off for the expected short 20 to 25 minute trip.

The captain, age 45, and the first officer, age 48, both held ATP certificates, and they had logged a total of 31,012 hours of flight time. Backing them up were their experienced second officer, their flight engineer, plus four flight attendants in the cabin. Their aircraft, a sleek Boeing 707, registration N709PA, happened to be the first production model of that type from the Boeing factory. Consequently, it was the very first American jet airliner to go into scheduled airline service, and by the time of this final flight it had accumulated 14,609 hours in the air.

Trouble Ahead: A rare winter thunderstorm, including lots of visible lightning, lashed the Philadelphia area. The controller soon radioed the Pan Am pilots:

> Philadelphia weather [is] now seven-hundred scattered, measured eight-hundred broken, one-thousand overcast, six miles with rainshowers, altimeter two-nine-four-five, the surface wind is

two-hundred-and-eighty degrees at twenty with gusts to thirty. I've got five aircraft [that] have elected to hold until . . . extreme winds have passed, . . . would you like to hold until the squall line passes Philadelphia, over?

The pilots elected to wait. They entered a holding pattern at 5,000 feet on the 270 degree radial of the New Castle VOR. Along with other airliners they "stacked up" in the holding pattern while waiting for the weather to improve. National Airlines Flight 16 was holding in the "stack" 1,000 feet above Pan Am Flight 214. Through periodic breaks in the thunderstorm clouds the pilots of the National airliner could see the lights on the Pan Am flight circling below them.

There would be no CVR tape. The portion of the *reconstructed* ATC transcript, below, has been created by reference to multiple source documents, most notably the CAB report, so some of the verbiage may not be verbatim. The transcript begins as the pilots tell Philadelphia Approach Control that they are ready for their approach clearance:

> Pan Am 214: . . Pan Am Flight 214 (call-sign, "Clipper")
> National 16: . . . National Flight 16
> AppControl: . . . Philadelphia Approach Control

Pan Am 214: Philadelphia Approach, Pan Am two-fourteen, we're ready to go. (2050:45)

AppControl: Clipper two-fourteen, stay in the [holding] pattern, I'll pull you away as soon as I can.

Pan Am 214: Roger, no hurry, just wanted you to know that . . . we'll accept [an approach] clearance.

> *[8 minutes pass; then National Flight 16, a DC-8, asks about its priority for landing]*

AppControl: National sixteen, you're third in line for landing.

National 16: OK.

AppControl: How's the turbulence in your area, National sixteen?

> *[lightning strikes Pan Am Flight 214, a **fuel tank explodes**, a wing breaks off, and the airliner falls earthward in flames; in*

futility one of the pilots screams into his microphone]

<u>Pan Am 214</u>: Mayday! Mayday! Mayday! Clipper two-fourteen out of control! Here we go! (2058:56)

<u>AppControl</u>: Clipper two-fourteen, did you call Philadelphia?

[there is no response from Flight 214]

[the First Officer on National Flight 16 watches as Pan Am Flight 214 falls earthward in flames]

<u>National 16</u>: Clipper two-fourteen's going down in flames!

[lightning now strikes National Flight 16; obviously shaken, the First Officer keys his microphone]

<u>National 16</u>: Philadelphia, we'd like to [leave here and go] to the New York area -- either Newark or Idlewild.

[the controller reports conflicting traffic to the northeast, but the National pilot <u>strongly</u> replies]

<u>National 16</u>: We do not want to stay here!

<u>AppControl</u>: Roger, [I] understand, National sixteen, ah . . . turn right . . . take a one-eight-zero heading . . . this could put you into a possible smoother area.

<u>National 16</u>: It's smooth enough. We're getting lightning.

[the controller tries in vain to contact Pan Am Flight 214]

<u>AppControl</u>: Clipper two-fourteen, Philadelphia Approach.

<u>AppControl</u>: Clipper two-fourteen, this is Approach Control.

<u>AppControl</u>: Clipper two-one-four, are you still on this frequency?

[there is no response]

<u>The Accident</u>: The Boeing 707 broke apart in the air. The fuselage fell into a cornfield near Elkton, Maryland, at 2059 Hours. Nearly 600 pieces of wreckage were strewn along a path over four miles long. There had been 73 passengers and 8 crewmembers on board, and none survived:

The complete left wing . . . was found approximately 1.8 miles east-northeast of the main impact crater.

Over 130 witnesses observed various aspects of the break-up of the airliner. Of these witnesses, 99 saw the flaming aircraft in the sky, and 72 saw a "ball of fire" concurrent with, or immediately following, lightning striking the airliner.

The Investigation: Specialists from the CAB reconstructed the flight. From analyzing the wreckage it was evident that the aircraft was on fire long before it struck the ground. The ailerons and spoilers on both wings evidenced extreme fire damage, and:

there was molten aluminum alloy splattered on the forward upper surface of the leading edge of the horizontal stabilizer.

Multiple lightning strike marks covered the left wingtip. In many places the metal surface of the wing and the rivet heads had melted. The largest of the lightning strike locations was an inch-and-a-half diameter hole in the wing surrounded by fused metal. Numerous smaller "lustrous craters" dotted the wing surface. It was obvious that an initial explosion had occurred in the left wing reserve tank, followed by explosions in other fuel tanks:

The center tank bottom skin was separated [and] stiffeners and access doors were bowed outwards.

Why had the fuel tanks exploded? Never before had lightning brought down a commercial airliner in the United States. True, lightning had *struck* airliners on many occasions, but there had been no catastrophic fuel tank explosions. In fact, just moments after lightning struck the Pan Am airliner, lightning also struck National Flight 16:

The crew of [National Flight 16] observed a lightning strike on their aircraft while in the holding pattern. Later examination of the aircraft revealed evidence of lightning damage to the left wing tip and empennage.

Analysts delved into the mystery. They knew that lightning begins when the resistance of air to the passage of electricity breaks down. A luminous (thence the word, *lightning*) "stepped leader" advances from a cloud toward the ground. The experts explain:

> The intensified electric field causes an upward moving streamer
> to . . . advance toward the stepped leader. . . . An avalanche of
> electron flow follows, discharging the cloud to the ground.

The electrical potential of lightning varies from 10,000,000 to 100,000,000 volts, and the current can exceed 100,000 amperes. The heat may reach 15,000 degrees Centigrade. This extraordinary heat supersonically expands the air and creates the echoing sonic boom commonly called thunder. Meteorological experts explain how lightning can strike an aircraft in flight:

> If the stepped leader of a [lightning] stroke approaches a flying
> aircraft, the intense electric field induces streamers from the
> extremities of the aircraft out toward the approaching stroke.
> The stepped leader contacts one of these streamers, completing
> the ionized channel to the aircraft and raising the potential of the
> aircraft to the order of 100 megavolts. . . . These streamers can
> have sufficient energy to ignite fuel vapors.

Engineers knew that, under the proper circumstances, lightning could ignite a fuel/air mixture within a fuel tank. However, fuel itself is not flammable. To ignite and burn (explode) the fuel first must be mixed with air. Even then it may not be flammable. Below a lower limit the mixture will be too lean to ignite, and above an upper limit it will be too rich.

Even if a fuel/air mixture inside a tank is within the flammable range, a lightning strike on the aircraft will not normally do any damage. To ignite and explode the mixture, electrical arcing must occur *inside* the tank:

> Lightning discharges can be hazardous to aircraft fuel systems
> by possibly igniting the fuel vapor within the tanks. Direct
> strokes may penetrate the wall of the tank and cause internal
> sparking.

Analysis of the fuel tanks from Flight 214 revealed no evidence of internal sparking or arcing. Inside the fuel tanks, investigators discovered no pitting or scoring. There was no technical way they could link the explosion to lightning. Yet, many highly credible witnesses had seen a lightning discharge of "exceptionally great magnitude" totally envelop Flight 214. Then the aircraft tumbled earthward on fire, out of control.

Probable Cause: The CAB adopted its Aircraft Accident Report, File No. 1-0015, on 25 February 1965. The CAB admitted a partial defeat. Members of the board agreed that lightning was somehow the culprit, but the exact mechanics of ignition remained an unsolved mystery.

Reconstruction of the accident confirmed that vapor in the left reserve tank had been within the flammable range. Yet, no one knew precisely how an electrical arcing force had penetrated inside the tank. Was there a fuel leak? A loose rivet or seal? Had fuel vapor escaped from a tank? If flammable vapor outside a tank had ignited, how could the resulting fire ignite vapor *within* the tanks? Although unable to pinpoint the exact cause, the board concluded:

> There is no logical explanation for the ignition of the flammable vapor [in the fuel tanks] other than some effect stemming directly from the lightning strike.

The board found the ***Probable Cause*** of the accident to be:

> lightning-induced ignition of the fuel/air mixture in the No. 1 reserve fuel tank with resultant explosive disintegration of the left outer wing and loss of control.

Pacific Airlines Flight 773

Fairchild F-27, registration N2770R
7 May 1964, near San Ramon, California
44 aboard, 44 killed

Overview: A turboprop Fairchild F-27 routinely cruised toward San Francisco, California. A mentally deranged passenger shot both pilots, and the airliner dove into the ground. The homicidal shooting and the subsequent crash killed all 44 people on board.

The Flight: Pacific Airlines Flight 773 took off from Reno, Nevada, before daylight on 7 May 1964. It swooped down for an intermediate stop at Stockton, California. There, 41 passengers and 3 crewmembers got ready for the next leg of their trip, a short flight to San Francisco.

Pacific had purchased the Fairchild F-27, registration N2770R, new from the manufacturer in 1959. The turboprop commuter airliner sported two Rolls-Royce engines, each equipped with Rotol four-blade propellers. By the date of this final flight the reliable F-27 had accumulated 10,252 hours in the air.

Flight 773 took off from Stockton and headed for San Francisco at 0638 Hours. The captain, age 52, held an ATP certificate and had logged 20,434 hours of flight time. His first officer, age 31, held a Commercial Pilot certificate and had 6,640 hours of aerial experience in his logbook. Behind them in the cabin the lone flight attendant, age 30, stayed busy tending to her 41 passengers.

Oakland Center soon established radar contact with the flight. At 0645:10 Hours the Center controller began vectoring the pilots toward the final approach course for the airport at San Francisco. Oakland Center handed the flight off to Oakland Approach Control at 0646:49 Hours.

Trouble Ahead: One of the passengers was a disillusioned and troubled man who wanted to die. He had made plans to end his life before the airliner landed at San Francisco. Unfortunately the manner in which he planned to commit suicide would be a death sentence for everyone aboard Flight 773.

The F-27 was not equipped with a CVR, and was not required to be so equipped. However, it did have an FDR. Also, ATC recorded radio transmissions to and from the flight. The portion of the ATC transcript, below, begins as the pilots near the approach course for the airport at San Francisco:

FO-Pacific 773: . . . First Officer, Pacific Airlines Flight 773
AppControl: . . . . . . Oakland Approach Control
United 593: . . . . . . United Airlines Flight 593

[at 0647:53 Hours, Oakland Approach Control gives the pilots the local altimeter setting; the controller then tells the pilots that their radio transmission was somewhat garbled]

FO-Pacific 773: Roger, how do you read now? (0648:09)

AppControl: It's still the same . . . sounds like overmodulation.

*[the controller hears an **unintelligible high-pitched scream** which later would be deciphered as shown below]*

FO-Pacific 773: Skipper's shot! We've been shot! [I was] tryin' ta help! (0648:15)

AppControl: Say again?

[there is no response]

[the controller loses radar contact with Flight 773; he makes repeated futile efforts to contact the flight by radio]

[3 minutes later United Flight 593 contacts the controller]

United 593: There's a black cloud of smoke coming up through the undercast at . . . three-thirty, four o'clock position right now, looks like [an] oil or gasoline fire. (0651:20)

The Accident: Shortly after the high-pitched radio message at 0648:15 Hours the controller noticed that the radar return from Flight 773 was weakening. The return dimmed and slowly faded from the Approach Control radar display. Flight 773 and all aboard were beyond mortal aid:

Witnesses . . . described extreme and abrupt changes in [the] attitude of Flight 773, coupled with erratic powerplant sounds and a large ball of fire following the final impact.

The F-27 dove down into a hillside near San Ramon, California. From the primary impact location, pieces of wreckage were thrown over 1,000 feet from the crash site. An intense fire raged in and around the impact crater. There were 44 people aboard, and there were no survivors.

The Investigation: Investigators from the CAB faced a daunting challenge as they sifted through the rubble. They determined that all flight control surfaces had been attached to the aircraft at the time of impact. The landing gear and the flaps had been retracted, and there was no evidence to indicate that the aircraft was on fire prior to hitting the ground. Analysts determined that both engines were capable of producing power prior to impact. There was no indication of a malfunction of any aircraft system:

The cockpit area was so completely destroyed by the impact that only four small pieces of the instrument panel were retrieved.

The FDR revealed that Flight 773 had been cruising at 213 knots at an altitude of 5,000 feet. The first FDR anomaly took place immediately before the ATC tape recorded the screaming voice. The aircraft then turned and descended 3,200 feet in just over 20 seconds, an incredible 9,000 foot per minute rate of descent. The F-27 recovered from the dive, pulled up, and climbed 1,100 feet. Then it nosed over and dove into the ground.

The CAB carried the Oakland Approach Control radio recording to Bell Telephone Laboratories. It was subjected to spectrogram analysis. Comparison with prior recordings revealed that the final desperate radio message from Flight 773 was voiced by the first officer. Using cutting-edge technology the "Bell Labs" technical staff deciphered his words: "Skipper's shot! We've been shot! [I was] tryin' ta help!"

Because of that "been shot" message the CAB asked the Federal Bureau of Investigation (FBI) for assistance. The FBI began a criminal investigation, and its agents sifted through the debris. They recovered a piece of tubing from the captain's seat, and it contained a unique indentation. The FBI analyzed the tubing, and the resulting report proved to be an eye-opener:

> Microscopic examination of this tubing at the [FBI] laboratory disclosed silvery metallic smears in an indention in the tubing. Spectrographic analysis of these smears revealed the presence of lead and antimony. The FBI [concludes] that the indentation in the tubing was made by a bullet.

In the wreckage the FBI agents found the remains of a pistol, a Smith & Wesson, Model 27, .357 magnum revolver. Laboratory tests revealed that remnants of human tissue still adhered to the pistol, and clothing fibers were embedded in the tissue. The pistol contained six *empty* cartridges. The FBI investigation established that the pistol had been bought by a passenger who will hereafter be identified as "John Doe":

> The gun, with ammunition and a cleaning kit, had been purchased by passenger John Doe on the evening of May 6, 1964. Mr. Doe had advised both friends and relatives that he would die on either Wednesday, the 6th of May, or Thursday, the 7th of May.

John Doe was a passenger on the fatal flight. In addition to documentation of the purchase, FBI forensic tests positively linked him to the pistol.

John Doe, the federal agents learned, was a troubled man who had been in emotional distress in recent weeks. He was deeply in debt. Over half his salary was committed for loan repayments, and he had marital problems as well. Each day during the week prior to the crash, John Doe had talked to various relatives about his "impending death." He wept profusely on 5 May.

On the night of 6 May, the night before the crash, Doe showed the pistol to numerous friends. He specifically told one of them that he planned to shoot himself:

> On that same evening he had purchased two [life] insurance policies in the total amount of $105,000.

In Reno late on the evening of 6 May, Doe spent several hours gambling in various casinos. One casino employee asked him if he was having a "good night" at the tables, and Doe replied: "It won't make any difference after tomorrow."

After the flight from Reno early the next morning, one fortunate passenger deplaned at Stockton. He later told investigators that he remembered John Doe. The passenger recalled that Doe had been hand-carrying a small package. He was in a front row seat, right behind the passageway leading to the F-27 cockpit.

Probable Cause: On 28 October 1964, slightly over six months after Flight 773 plunged to earth, the CAB adopted the Aviation Accident Report, File No. 1-0007. The board concluded:

The total evidence clearly indicates that the captain and first officer of Flight 773 were shot by a passenger. As a result, the uncontrolled aircraft began the descent which ended in impact with the hill.

The *Probable Cause* statement consisted of only one sentence:

The board determines [that] the Probable Cause of this accident was the shooting of the captain and first officer by a passenger in flight.

Mohawk Airlines Flight 40

BAC-111, registration N1116J
23 June 1967, near Blossburg, Pennsylvania
34 aboard, 34 killed

Overview: A BAC-111 took off from Elmira, New York. Within minutes after takeoff the airliner suffered a catastrophic loss of pitch control. It climbed, then dove, then climbed again. Finally it nosed over and dove into the ground. The impact killed all 34 people on board.

The Flight: Mohawk Airlines Flight 40 took off from Runway 24 at Chemung County Airport at Elmira, New York, at 1439 Hours on 23 June 1967. The pilots contacted New York Center three minutes later and climbed toward an intermediate altitude of 6,000 feet. There the British Aircraft Corporation (BAC)-111 jetliner, registration N1116J, leveled off pending a further clearance.

The captain, age 43, held an ATP certificate. He had relatively little time in the BAC-111, but his logbook reflected a respectable 13,875 flight hours. The younger first officer, age 33, held a Commercial Pilot certificate and had accumulated 4,814 hours in his logbook. Only 30 passengers were seated in the spacious cabin of the BAC airliner; it could have held three times that many. These trusting passengers fell under the care of two young flight attendants, both of whom were only 21 years of age.

Trouble Ahead: At 1444 Hours the controller cleared Flight 40 to climb to 16,000 feet. ATC did not receive a response. Despite several attempts to reestablish radio contact, there were no further transmissions from the flight. Three minutes later the controller noted an inexplicable phenomenon. The Flight 40 radar return seemed to slow down for one sweep of the antenna, then move laterally at the end of the next sweep.

The portion of the CVR transcript, below, begins as ATC clears the flight to 16,000 feet. The first officer is flying the airliner:

Capt: . . . . . Captain, Flight 40
FO: . . . . . . First Officer, Flight 40
Att-Radio-: . (prefix) Attempted radio transmission, Flight 40
Center: . . . . New York Center (ARTCC)

Center: Ah, Mohawk forty, climb now and maintain one-six-thousand [feet]. (1444:11)

*[the aircraft begins a rapid **uncommanded climb**; it will reach 7,500 feet in 32 seconds]*

Capt: Aaahhh! (1444:12)

Capt: We're not going to have that! (1444:17)

Att-Radio-Capt: [New York Center,] ah, [this is Mohawk] forty, climb to and maintain si -- say again -- what? (1444:24)

[the pilots do not know it, but their radio contact with New York Center has been permanently cut off]

FO: Ah, feel -- it's not doing that, actually -- it's hard to tell just what it is. (1444:33)

Capt: Aaahhh, let's see -- pull back on your speed. (1444:41)

[the pilots can not control the "pitch" of the aircraft]

FO: Wait a minute . . . there's something screwy here.

Capt: I know it.

Att-Radio-Capt: [Center,] ah, Mohawk forty is having a little control problem here, we'll -- aaahhh -- we'll advise you, ah, we may have to -- aaahhh -- declare an emergency. (1444:49)

FO: Yeah, that's gonna be [unintelligible].

*[the aircraft abruptly **levels off** at 7,500 feet for 20 seconds; the Captain takes over the controls]*

Capt: I got it. I got it. (1445:04)

Capt: Tell [Center] we're unable to maintain six-thousand, [we are] goin' back to Elmira.

FO: We're making a [turn] back to Elmira?

Capt: [Yes,] to Elmira at six-thousand.

Att-Radio-FO: Ah, New York [Center], Mohawk, ah, New York, Mohawk forty, [we would] like to return to Elmira -- aaahhh -- aaahhh -- [at] six-thousand [feet]. (1445:14)

*[the aircraft begins a **steep descent** of 3,700 feet]*

Capt: We lost all control. We don't have anything! (1445:16)

FO: We're in manual *[non-hydraulic mode]* now. (1445:26)

Capt: Yeah, but I can't do anything. (1445:27)

Capt: You turned it off? -- Put it back in the second [hydraulic] system. (1445:32)

Capt: Let's go up for a minute . . . easy now, easy. (1445:42)

FO: Looks like somethin's 'a matter. (1445:54)

Capt: Pull back! Pull back! Keep workin', we're makin' it.

Capt: Pull back -- straight now. (1446:06)

*[the aircraft suddenly shifts from a descent to a **rapid ascent**, it will climb 1,300 feet in 26 seconds]*

Capt: Climb now -- that's it -- easy now -- now, cut the -- cut the gun, we're in now. (1446:11)

FO: Ooohhh-weee! I don't like that! (1446:23)

Capt: OK -- aaahhh -- we better turn back toward Elmira -- now wait a minute, wait -- aaahhh -- let's go straight ahead. (1446:31)

*[the aircraft begins to nose over for **another descent**]*

Capt: What have we done to that [expletive] tail surface, 'ya have any idea? (1446:37)

FO: I don't know -- ah -- I just can't figure it out -- ah -- we've lost both systems. (1446:44)

*[the aircraft **dives earthward**]*

Capt: I can't keep this [expletive] from [unintelligible] -- all right, I'm gonna use both hands now. (1446:47)

<u>FO</u>: OK!

<u>Capt</u>: Both hands!

<u>Capt</u>: Pull 'er back! Pull! Power! Both hands! Back! Both hands! (1446:54)

<u>Capt</u>: Pull back! (1447:10)

<u>Capt</u>: I've gone out of control! (1447:11)

[end of the CVR tape at 1447:17]

The Accident: Numerous witnesses on the ground watched the final dive of the BAC-111. Most of them reported that smoke trailed back from the tail of the aircraft. One witness described a white discharge of vapor behind the airliner. Two other witnesses saw a large section of the tail fall off the aircraft. Smaller pieces then fell off too, and the craft dove out of view:

> The aircraft impacted in a heavily wooded area near the crest of a hill. . . . The fuselage, [parts from] both wings, and both engines were located within the main impact area.

The BAC-111 dove into a small hill a mile east of Blossburg, Pennsylvania. Although the impact angle was steep, the crash threw pieces of wreckage along a path over a quarter-mile long. During the final dive the outboard portion of the right wing had broken off, along with various parts of the empennage. The largest piece of the vertical fin was found 510 feet back along the flight track. The rudder was discovered 430 feet behind the vertical fin.

The alarmed ATC controller had watched as the radar signature of Flight 40 dimmed, then vanished. He vectored a small Piper Aztec to the area where he last "painted" the airliner. The Aztec pilot soon radioed back the bad news. He found the funeral pyre of what once had been Flight 40.

The Investigation: NTSB investigators found the rudder and vertical fin assembly far away from the main wreckage. There was evidence of severe fire damage *prior* to impact with the ground. The entire length of the vertical fin displayed sooting, molten metal splatters, and damage from intense heat. Analysis revealed that the forward spar in the fin had failed due to extreme high temperature that caused the metal to lose strength and rip away in flight.

Electrical wiring in the tail had been burned away, including the wiring for the VHF antenna. This accounted for the severance of air-to-ground radio contact after 1444:11 Hours. Investigators then made a startling discovery. They found the reason why the pilots had lost pitch control:

> The elevator control rods, located on the rear side of the aft spar in the lower section of the vertical fin, were destroyed by fire.

Why? Witnesses had reported an in-flight fire and a structural break-up in the air. Yet, there was no evidence of a pre-impact fire forward of the empennage. What heat source could have started a fire in the rear of the aircraft? What flammable material could have fueled the combustion there?

> A review of the [maintenance] log sheets of N1116J revealed that there were numerous discrepancies concerning its pneumatic system, including the APU.

During the three months before the crash there had been 55 maintenance "squawks" concerning defects or problems with the system. Searching through the wreckage, investigators discovered a defective APU non-return valve. Both of the valve flaps were severely deformed, and this had caused the valve to malfunction:

> The purpose of the non-return valve is to prevent main engine bleed air from flowing back into the APU.

However, with the valve flaps deformed, hot air had flowed (1) through the defective valve, then (2) through an *open* air delivery valve, then (3) through the APU, and (4) into the airframe plenum chamber. This super-heated air eventually ignited the acoustic blankets lining the walls of the chamber. Temperatures were calculated to be in the range of 648 to 882 degrees Centigrade. The NTSB investigators determined:

> The primary combustible fueling the fire was hydraulic fluid, which was fed to the fire under pressure when the flexible hoses in the hydraulics bay failed due to excessive heat.

Heat from burning acoustic blankets weakened the high-pressure hydraulic hoses. They eventually ruptured. Flammable hydraulic fluid, under pressure, spurted out and ignited. From then on it was just a matter of time. Flight 40 and all on board were doomed.

A "chimney effect" sucked flames up into the vertical fin. Fire destroyed the elevator control rods, the electric trim tab wires, and both hydraulics systems. This caused a total loss of pitch control, resulting in the uncommanded climbs and descents. The pilots had no control over the elevator.

Fire ultimately weakened the vertical fin, rudder, and horizontal stabilizer, causing them to rip off when the aircraft accelerated in its final dive. Loss of the tail assembly caused negative G forces on the wings, causing part of the right wing to break off from the aircraft prior to ground impact.

Probable Cause: The NTSB adopted its Aircraft Accident Report, File No. 1-0004, on 18 April 1968, ten months after the loss of Mohawk Flight 40. The board found that the *Probable Cause* of the accident was:

> the loss of integrity of the empennage pitch control systems due to a destructive in-flight fire which originated in the airframe plenum chamber and, fueled by hydraulic fluid, progressed up into the vertical fin. The fire resulted from engine bleed air flowing back through a malfunctioning non-return valve and an open air delivery valve, through the auxiliary power unit in a reverse direction, and exiting into the plenum chamber at temperatures sufficiently high to cause the acoustic linings to ignite.

The board noted that the pilots did not know what caused the loss of pitch control. They were unaware of the existence of the fire. There were no smoke or temperature sensing devices in the tail that could send a fire warning to the cockpit. Even if the pilots had known of the fire, there was nothing they could have done about it. The tail of the aircraft is inaccessible in flight, and there are no fire extinguishing systems there. Once it began, there was no manual or automated way to extinguish the fire in flight.

ALM Flight 980

Douglas DC-9, registration N935F
2 May 1970, ditched in the Atlantic Ocean near St. Croix
63 aboard, 23 killed

Overview: A Douglas DC-9 took off from New York and arced out over the Atlantic Ocean. After in-flight weather delays and two destination changes, the pilots made three unsuccessful attempts to land. The airliner ran out of fuel and ditched in the ocean near St. Croix. Of the 63 people aboard, 23 were killed either (1) by the impact during ditching, (2) by failure to get out of the sinking airliner, or (3) by drowning prior to rescue.

The Flight: Fifty-seven travelers began gathering at the JFK International Airport terminal in New York around mid-morning on 2 May 1970. Antilliaanse Luchtvaart Maatschappij (ALM) Flight 980 was waiting to whisk them south to the last "New World" remnant of the old Dutch colonial empire. Their destination was the tiny sub-tropical island of St. Maarten (also called St. Martin) in the Netherlands Antilles.

The Douglas DC-9 chosen for this flight, registration N935F, was almost new. It had been built and delivered to Overseas National Airways (ONA) the previous year and had accumulated only 2,505 hours of flight time. Pursuant to a lease agreement, ONA provided the aircraft and the flight crew, and ALM provided the cabin attendants.

The young captain, age 37, had logged roughly 12,000 flight hours, including 1,700 hours in the DC-9. His even younger first officer, age 25, had documented 3,500 hours of flight time in his logbook. Both pilots held ATP certificates. Their navigator had accumulated a wealth of line experience. In the compact passenger cabin, ALM had provided three attendants: a purser, a steward, and a young stewardess.

At a takeoff weight of 103,322 pounds, Flight 980 lifted off from Runway 13R at 1114 Hours and headed south over the

Atlantic. Once reaching flight level 290 the airliner cruised toward St. Maarten at Mach 0.78. If all went as planned the aircraft would land at about 1440 Hours with a minimum of 7,000 pounds of fuel remaining. However, a little over an hour into the flight the pilots encountered thunderstorms along their flight path. They slowed to turbulence penetration speed, deviated around the worst storms, and descended in an attempt to avoid the rough weather.

Trouble Ahead: San Juan Center cleared the flight to descend further to 10,000 feet as the pilots approached the West Indies. Shortly thereafter the controller radioed bad news:

> San Juan Air Route Traffic Control Center advised that the St. Maarten weather was below landing minimums.

The captain had no choice. He asked for and received a revised ATC clearance to divert to San Juan, Puerto Rico. However, while the flight was heading toward San Juan, ATC reported that the weather at St. Maarten had improved.

Armed with this updated information, the captain decided to head toward St. Maarten once again. He got a new clearance and changed course back toward the Dutch island. Concerned, he noted that he had only 5,800 pounds of fuel remaining. Flight 980 arrived over the radio beacon, the only navaid available, on St. Maarten. Clouds and rain shrouded the airport below:

> The tower controller advised that the weather was 800 feet scattered, estimated ceiling 1,000 feet broken, 5,000 feet overcast, visibility 2 to 3 miles.

At 1515 Hours the captain began an ADF approach. On final, gear and flaps down, the airliner broke out of the cloud base, and through the rain the first officer spotted the airport. Unfortunately the aircraft was not properly lined up with the runway and was not able to land.

The captain circled left at low altitude and tried to make a contact approach. Keeping the airport in sight proved difficult in the rain. Consequently, this second landing attempt also failed because of poor runway alignment. Once again, gear and flaps down, the flight circled around for a third try. This time the captain was able to line up with the runway, but he found that he was too high and too fast to land.

Retracting his gear and flaps, the captain abandoned attempts to land on St. Maarten. At 1531 Hours the pilots radioed San Juan Center and got clearance to divert to St. Thomas at 4,000 feet. During the climb the alarmed pilots and navigator watched as their fuel gauges slowly bobbled downward. When the fuel totalizer settled down it indicated only 850 pounds of fuel remaining.

The DC-9, including its CVR and FDR, would end up at the bottom of the sea in water over a mile deep, so no verbatim CVR transcript is available. Yet, ATC documented radio traffic. The transcript, below, includes those radio messages plus *reconstructed* intra-cockpit conversation based upon testimony before the NTSB. *Reconstructed* verbiage is prefaced by a double asterisk (**). The portion of the transcript, below, begins as the crew discusses their low fuel supply after abandoning attempts to land at St. Maarten:

Capt:　. . . . . Captain, Flight 980
FO:　. . . . . . First Officer, Flight 980
Nav:　. . . . . . Navigator, Flight 980
Radio-:　. . . . (prefix) Radio transmission, Flight 980
Center:　. . . . San Juan Center (ARTCC)

Capt: **It *[meaning, the fuel gauge]* can't be right! Our en route checks showed no problems.

Nav: **It *[meaning, the fuel gauge]* was bobbing around from thirteen-[hundred-and]-fifty to two-thousand pounds.

Capt: **There is no way we could have only eight-hundred-fifty pounds left, no way we could have less than two-thousand.

Center: **ALM nine-eighty, this is San Juan Center, traffic at twelve o'clock, ten miles. (1532)

Radio-FO: **ALM nine-eighty, roger. (1532)

Center: **ALM nine-eighty, San Juan Center, what altitude are you requesting? (1533)

Radio-Capt: Anything you've got [that is] higher, I'm a little short on fuel and I gotta get up. (1533)

[Center clears the pilots to climb to 12,000 feet at 1533]

Capt: **Our fuel? -- What do you think?

Nav: **It's hard to figure . . . why don't we head for St. Croix, it's closer than St. Thomas.

[the First Officer requests a revised clearance to St. Croix, which is 11 miles nearer than St. Thomas]

Center: **ALM nine-eighty is cleared direct to St. Croix, maintain flight level one-two-zero.

Capt: **Those fuel gauges, I've got to believe them. We ought to keep the water in sight, don't want to flame out in the clouds.

[the Captain requests a descent; Center approves it]

Radio-Capt: [Center,] OK, there's a possibility I may have to ditch this aircraft, I am now descending to the water. (1539)

[the Captain tells the Purser and Navigator to prepare the cabin and the passengers for ditching]

[Center reports that rescue efforts will begin immediately]

[the Captain descends to a height 20 feet above the waves]

[the engines flame out; the DC-9 settles toward the sea]

Radio-FO: [This is ALM] nine-eighty -- aaahhh -- we're ditching!

[Flight 980 drops off San Juan Center radar at 1548:40]

The Accident: Before the engines failed the captain descended below the clouds and leveled off a mere 20 feet above the waves. When his low fuel pressure lights flickered he lowered full flaps. Within seconds the engines flamed out. Only 30 miles short of St. Croix and safety (only five minutes' flying time) the captain and his DC-9, now merely a *glider*, struck the water at 90 knots.

Seat belts restrained most passengers, but some seat belts failed, and some passengers were standing up. The sudden impact with the water flung them violently forward through the cabin. Many suffered incapacitating injuries.

The aircraft remained intact and floated for about 10 minutes. The main passenger door in the front of the cabin had jammed in the closed position. The steward kicked open the galley door, and passengers began leaping out into the water. Others clambered out through the over-wing emergency exits. There were five big 25-man inflatable life rafts aboard the DC-9, but in the wild scramble to exit the aircraft none were taken outside. One of the huge rafts accidentally inflated inside the galley, temporarily pinning the first officer to the galley bulkhead.

Dozens of orange life preservers soon dotted the surface of the ocean around the slowly sinking DC-9. Many of those in the water had serious injuries, and the navigator and first officer played a key role in their survival:

> The navigator found an emergency escape slide floating in the water and, with the help of a female passenger, inflated it. The first officer, who had no life vest, climbed on top of the slide and assumed command of the main group of survivors who gathered around the slide.

Those who were not severely injured saved the day. They used their neckties, belts, and clothing to tie themselves to those less fortunate. Then there was nothing to do but wait, console those who were battered and bleeding, and pray that they would be found. Two search airplanes droned high overhead and dropped life rafts, but they fell too far away:

> Recovery of the [40] survivors by helicopter began [about] 1 1/2 hours after the ditching.

Over an hour after the ditching the first rescue craft rotored into view. Two U.S. Coast Guard helicopters plucked 11 survivors from the ocean. A U.S. Navy helicopter rescued 26 more people who were still alive. The last three persons found alive, including the first officer, were hoisted up into a U.S. Marine Corps CH-46 helicopter a half-hour later. Three lucky survivors required no medical treatment, but the 37 others sustained broken bones, internal injuries, lacerations, and various types of impact trauma.

The remaining 23 people aboard the jet airliner, including two children and the stewardess, all died. They either (1) were killed or incapacitated by the impact with the water, (2) were unable to get out of the sinking aircraft, (3) drowned or succumbed to their injuries in the ocean prior to rescue, or (4) drifted away and were lost at sea forever.

The Investigation: The CVR and FDR had sunk to the bottom of the Atlantic, but the flight crew reported that most of the aircraft systems had performed as expected. The sole exception, they said, was the fuel quantity indicating system. They told the NTSB that the gauges "bobbled" on climbout from St. Maarten and then settled down to show only 850 pounds of fuel remaining.

The NTSB reconstructed the crew's fuel management during the flight. Prior to leaving New York the aircraft had been loaded with 28,900 pounds of jet fuel. That would have been enough for the proposed flight, plus a reserve of 1 hour and 8 minutes. The DC-9 should have arrived at St. Maarten with over 7,000 pounds of fuel left in its tanks. The problem was that the flight had not gone according to plan:

> First, thunderstorms resulted in a lower airspeed, lower altitude, and deviation around the cells early in the flight.

> Second, the pilots later used engine power in excess of planned long range cruise settings.

> Third, after a descent north of the Virgin Islands, the remaining third of the flight was flown at low altitude.

Each of these three factors caused a higher than normal rate of fuel consumption, and it rapidly got worse. The flight diverted toward San Juan after learning of bad weather at St. Maarten. If the pilots had continued to San Juan and landed, all would have been well. But, far out over the ocean, they elected to change course -- again -- and head back toward St. Maarten:

> At that time, the aircraft [already] had been airborne for 3 hours and 37 minutes, 11 minutes longer than the [entire] originally planned flight time of 3 hours and 26 minutes.

Bad news continued to snowball. The new route to St. Maarten took longer than expected. Investigators calculated that the DC-9 held only about 4,300 pounds of remaining fuel when it arrived over the radio beacon at the Juliana Airport on St. Maarten. Total fuel exhaustion was only about 33 minutes away. Yet, the pilots made three time consuming approaches in an attempt to land. They used up the precious fuel that could have taken them and their passengers safely back to St. Thomas.

After the three unsuccessful approaches at St. Maarten the pilots were almost out of fuel. Yet, they initially tried to fly 109 miles over the sea to St. Thomas. Then they changed course toward closer St. Croix. They attempted to conserve fuel by using a low power and low airspeed climb, a tactic less fuel efficient than a full power climb would have been.

According to a fuel consumption study, by this time the flight could not have reached either St. Thomas or St. Croix. The pilots barely had enough fuel to try -- one final time -- to land at St. Maarten. Otherwise the DC-9 was destined to run out of fuel somewhere over the ocean, which it did.

Probable Cause: Almost a year after the accident the NTSB adopted its report, NTSB-AAR-71-8, on 31 March 1971. The board found that the flight crew "should have been well aware" that, after the delays and destination changes, they would arrive at St. Maarten extremely low on fuel:

> The captain should have realized that he was at or near minimum fuel for successful diversion to his alternate [airport].

Based upon the evidence, including the fuel consumption study, the board determined that the fuel quantity indicating system did not malfunction. The board reasoned that the reported erratic action of the gauges on climbout from St. Maarten could have resulted from (1) turbulence, (2) the low fuel state, or (3) the nose-up attitude during the climb. The board found the ***Probable Cause*** of this accident to be:

> fuel exhaustion, which resulted from continued unsuccessful attempts to land at St. Maarten until insufficient fuel remained to reach an alternate airport.

The board found a ***contributing*** cause of the accident to be "the reduced visibility [at St. Maarten] because of rainshowers." This condition was not known to the crew in advance.

Air Canada Flight 621

Douglas DC-8, registration CF-TIW
5 July 1970, near Toronto, Canada
109 aboard, 109 killed

Overview: As a DC-8 glided down to land at Toronto, Canada, one of the pilots accidentally deployed the spoilers 60 feet above the ground. The aircraft rapidly dropped down onto the runway. The impact ripped off one engine, but the airliner staggered back into the air. A series of in-flight explosions caused another engine to tear away, and then a wing broke off. All 109 people on board died in the crash and resulting fire.

The Flight: Air Canada Flight 621 left Montreal, Canada, at 0717 Hours early on Sunday morning, 5 July 1970. The flight was bound for Los Angeles, California, with an intermediate stop in Toronto, Canada. Aboard the airliner were 100 passengers and 9 crewmembers. None of them had any inkling that they would be dead in 52 minutes.

The DC-8, registration CF-TIW, was almost brand new. After its manufacture in the United States it had been delivered to Air Canada on 30 April 1970, about two months before this fateful flight. The Canadian Ministry of Transport issued a Certificate of Airworthiness for the sleek new four-engine airliner. On this flight the light passenger and fuel load brought the takeoff weight to only 220,993 pounds, far below the maximum of 350,000 pounds.

The captain, age 50, had begun his flying career in the Royal Canadian Air Force during World War II and had logged 20,000 flight hours. His first officer, age 40, also was a former military pilot, and he had 9,322 hours in his logbook. A flight engineer and six flight attendants rounded out the DC-8 crew. Flight 621 droned routinely toward Toronto. The aircraft performed flawlessly in all respects, and the weather was calm and clear as they approached the airport for landing. Eight miles from Runway 32 the pilots turned the airliner onto the final approach course.

Trouble Ahead: Both pilots were aware that, prior to landing, Air Canada policy required arming the spoilers while the aircraft was still 1,000 feet or more above the ground. Nonetheless, both the captain and first officer had been using a different procedure. On this flight the captain asked the first officer to delay arming the spoilers until they were "on the flare."

The portion of the CVR and ATC transcript, below, begins as the pilots discuss the spoilers. The captain is flying the airliner:

Capt: . . . . Captain, Flight 621
FO: . . . . First Officer, Flight 621
FltEngr: . . . . Flight Engineer, Flight 621
Radio-:   . . . . (prefix) Radio transmission, Flight 621
Tower: . . . . Toronto Airport Control Tower
DepControl: . . . . . . Toronto Departure Control
AirCanada 254:   . . . Air Canada Flight 254

FO: . . . spoilers on the flare? (0802:41)

Capt: OK, brakes, three green, four pressures . . . all right, give [the spoilers] to me on the flare. (0802:45)

[1 minute and 57 seconds pass, routine cockpit conversation]

FO: Spoilers to go, and the boards [are] clear. (0804:42)

Tower: [Air Canada] six-two-one, Toronto Tower, cleared to land, Runway three-two. (0805:52)

[the First Officer acknowledges the clearance at 0805:55]

FO: Here we have a green -- the VASI appears to be a little bit high, yet you're low on the glide path. (0806:10)

Capt: Yeah -- oh, this thing takes you a way down the runway . . . it's a noise abatement glide path. (0806:17)

FO: Yeah -- takes the whole airfield that way. (0806:28)

[the aircraft is 60 feet above the runway, ready to land]

Capt: OK, [arm the spoilers]. (0806:33)

*[the spoilers **deploy**; the aircraft loses lift and sinks rapidly]*

Capt: No! No! No! (0806:34)

FO: Sorry! Oh, sorry, Pete! (0806:35)

[sound of the engines spooling up at 0806:36]

*[sound of **extremely hard impact** with the runway at 0806:37; the No. 4 engine rips off of the right wing; fuel gushes out]*

FO: Sorry, Pete! (0806:39)

[the pilots do not know how badly the aircraft is damaged; they plan to climb and circle around for another landing attempt]

Capt: We've lost [some of] our power. (0806:44)

Tower: Air Canada six-twenty-one, I [see] you on the overshoot, *[meaning, the aborted landing]*, and you can contact Departure [Control] on one-nineteen-nine, or do you wish to come in for an immediate [landing] on Runway five right? (0806:52)

Radio-Capt: We'll go around. I think we're all right. (0806:58)

Tower: OK, contact Departure [Control].

Capt: Get the gear up please, Don. (0807:10)

[sound of landing gear retracting at 0807:12]

FO: What about the flaps? (0807:13)

Capt: Flaps twenty-five. (0807:14)

FltEngr: Number four generator's [inoperative]. (0807:22)

[the No. 4 generator is not operative because the No. 4 engine has torn off of the aircraft, but the pilots do not know that]

Capt: OK, get the crossfeed off first -- good. (0807:24)

Radio-FO: Toronto Departure Control, Air Canada six-twenty-one is overshooting on -- aaahhh -- Runway thirty-two. (0807:46)

DepControl: Air Canada six-twenty-one, confirm [that you are] on the overshoot. (0807:57)

Radio-FO: Affirmative. (0807:59)

DepControl: OK, sir, your intentions, please? (0808:00)

Radio-FO: Roger, we would like to circle back for another attempt on [Runway] thirty-two. (0808:04)

DepControl: Sir, the runway is closed, debris on the runway, your vector will be for a back course for two-three left . . . turn right heading zero-seven-zero, [maintain] three-thousand feet. (0808:08)

Capt: We've lost number four engine. (0808:24)

FO: Have we? (0808:24)

[fuel gushing from the damaged right wing suddenly ignites]

Tower: Six-twenty-one on the overshoot, [your] wing's on fire!

AirCanada 254: His number four engine is on fire . . . that [DC]-eight is losing all sorts of fuel out of the back end there.

Capt: OK, [shut down the] number four [engine]. (0808:42)

FO: Number four engine? Number four, right? (0808:49)

Capt: Number three is jammed too . . . there it is, the whole thing is jammed. (0808:58)

[sound of a "crackling" explosion at 0809:08]

FO: What was that? What happened there, Pete? (0809:09)

Capt: That's number -- that's [engine] number four -- somethin's happened -- [unintelligible]. (0809:13)

FO: Oh, look! We've got a -- a -- . (0809:14)

[sound of a loud explosion at 0809:15]

FO: Pete! Sorry! (0809:19)

[sound of a louder explosion at 0809:20]

Capt: All right --. (0809:22)

DepControl: [Air Canada] six-two-one, [what is] the status of your aircraft, please? (0809:22)

[sound of metal tearing at 0809:23]

Radio-Capt: We've got an explosion. (0809:24)

FO: Oh, look! We've got flames! Oh! Gosh! (0809:26)

Capt, FO, or FltEngr: We've lost a wing! (0809:31)

[the DC-8 impacts the ground; end of the CVR tape at 0809:35]

DepControl: [Tower], do you see him? (0809:44)

Tower: He's gone, Jerry. (0809:46)

[uncertain, Departure Control queries Air Canada Flight 254]

DepControl: Air Canada two-five-four, do you see the traffic at one o'clock, about four-and-a-half miles?

AirCanada 254: [Departure Control, Air Canada] six-twenty-one has -- aaahhh -- crashed. He went down in flames.

The Accident: Only 60 feet above the runway the captain had asked the first officer to "arm" the spoilers. In response the first officer inadvertently pulled the spoiler lever back to the "extend" position. The spoilers immediately deployed, robbing the wings of crucial lift, and the aircraft sank rapidly. The captain rammed the throttles forward and pulled back on his control column, but it was too late. The DC-8 *slammed* down onto the asphalt:

> When the aircraft struck the runway [the] Number 4 engine and pylon separated from the aircraft and fell on the runway.

Pieces of metal plating from the bottom of the wing sheared off, and fuel from a ruptured tank rushed out and trailed back behind the aircraft. The first officer quickly retracted the spoilers. With the throttles firewalled the airliner accelerated -- on three engines -- and clawed its way skyward. The pilots climbed to 3,100 feet and circled back toward the airport to try another landing.

Fuel gushing out of the right wing ignited. Within 30 seconds the fire caused an explosion near the location where the No. 4 engine had broken away from the wing. Debris rained earthward:

> Six seconds later a second explosion occurred in the vicinity of Number 3 engine, and the engine with its pylon ripped free of the wing and fell to the ground in flames.

Five seconds later a third explosion racked the damaged right wing. The outboard section folded upward and broke away, throwing the DC-8 into a death spiral. Trailing smoke and orange flames, the aircraft dove into the ground. The fiery impact at 220 knots killed the 109 people aboard.

The Investigation: Canadian investigators from the Aircraft Accident Investigation Division of the Ministry of Transport delved into the crash. They quickly excluded weather and mechanical problems as possible causes; the accident sequence was clear:

> The spoilers were deployed when the aircraft was about 60 feet above the runway. As a result, the aircraft sank rapidly.

> When the spoilers deployed the wings lost crucial lift. At a rate of 24 feet per second the aircraft fell toward the runway. The impact damage caused the subsequent explosions and crash.

On the DC-8 airliner, spoilers may be armed in flight by raising the spoiler activating lever to the "arm" position. This allows the spoilers to deploy automatically after the main landing gear touches down on the runway. However, the first officer on Flight 621 did not merely lift the lever. He also pulled it back rearward to the "extend" position. This caused the spoilers to deploy instantly. The board explained the obvious hazard:

> Multiple motions [of the activating lever] with a single raising, pulling, pulling and raising, readily lend themselves to confusion and mistakes and . . . the consequences of extending the ground spoilers in flight near the ground are catastrophic.

Investigators found that the first officer had been accustomed to waiting until the DC-8 was safely on the runway. He then would lift the activating lever and pull it rearward to deploy the spoilers. Investigators reasoned that, through force of habit, he prematurely took the same action "on the flare" when the captain asked him to arm the spoilers.

Probable Cause: The Ministry of Transport submitted detailed findings to a Board of Inquiry. Months later the lengthy Report of the Board of Inquiry formatted the findings in a manner unlike that suggested by the ICAO. Instead of a Probable Cause, the Canadian report separately lists *Conclusions* and *Circumstances*.

The board concluded that the captain and first officer knew the prescribed procedure for arming and deploying the spoilers and did not follow that procedure. Also, the first officer erred in pulling the spoiler activating lever to the "extend" position instead of the "arm" position. Nonetheless, board did not *crucify* the deceased captain and first officer as many laymen had predicted. Instead, the board's more significant findings are listed below:

[First], there was a design defect in [the DC-8] in that it was possible, by a single movement of the activating lever, to cause the ground spoilers of this aircraft to be deployed while it was in flight with its undercarriage down . . . .

[Second was] the failure of the manufacturer of [the DC-8] to provide a gate . . . to guard against such inappropriate manual operation of the ground spoiler lever in flight.

[Third were the] equivocation, inaccuracies, and misinformation in the manufacturer's aircraft flight manual . . . and in the Air Canada aircraft operating manual [about spoiler deployment]. In none of these manuals was there any warning that the ground spoilers of a DC-8 aircraft could be deployed while such an aircraft was in flight with its [landing gear] down and . . . in two of these manuals . . . it is erroneously stated that the lever is prevented from going to the extend [position] while in flight by a mechanical system.

[Fourth], Air Canada ground school instructors . . . did not know that the ground spoiler activating lever could be pulled back manually to cause the ground spoilers to be deployed [in the manner that doomed Flight 621].

[Fifth], Air Canada and the Ministry of Transport failed to detect this hazard to safe operation of the DC-8 aircraft.

[Sixth], the failure of the Ministry of Transport to detect the deficiencies and misinformation in the manufacturer's aircraft flight manual [relating to spoiler deployment].

Southern Airways Flight 932

Douglas DC-9, registration N97S
14 November 1970, near Huntington, West Virginia
75 aboard, 75 killed

Overview: After a football game the Marshall University team boarded a charter flight. The trip back to their college promised to be routine. Unfortunately, on final approach at night in rain and fog their Douglas DC-9 flew into tall trees over a mile from the runway. The fiery crash near Huntington, West Virginia, killed all 75 people on board.

The Flight: The gridiron *Pirates* of East Carolina University and the *Thundering Herd* from Marshall University squared off on Saturday afternoon, 14 November 1970. East Carolina won 17-14 in a defensive struggle between the two small colleges.

After the game the 37 football players from Marshall University, 8 coaches, and 25 loyal fans and supporters boarded chartered Southern Airways Flight 932. They took off from Kinston, North Carolina, at 1838 Hours as darkness settled in, and they headed toward their academic home at Huntington, West Virginia. The anticipated 52 minute trip progressed smoothly at flight level 260. Soon the Douglas DC-9 airliner, registration N97S, began a descent toward Huntington's air terminal, the Tri-City Airport.

In addition to the 70 passengers there were 5 crewmembers aboard Flight 932. The captain, age 47, held an ATP certificate and had flown for Southern Airways for 21 years. He had logged 18,557 hours in the air. His young first officer, age 28, held a Commercial Pilot certificate and had 5,872 hours of experience in his logbook. Two young "stewardesses" staffed the cabin, and a Southern Airways charter coordinator tagged along as the liaison between the airline and Marshall University.

As the DC-9 descended toward the airport, Indianapolis Center handed the flight off to Huntington Approach Control. The new controller cleared Flight 932 for a *non-precision* localizer approach to Runway 11 and reported weather conditions at the airport:

> . . . the Huntington weather, three-hundred scattered, measured ceiling five-hundred, variable broken, one-thousand-one-hundred overcast, visibility five [miles], light rain, fog, smoke, ceiling ragged, variable, four-to-six-hundred.

Because this was a charter flight, special instrument approach minima applied. The MDA would be 1,240 feet as usual, but the required forward visibility would be increased to one mile.

Trouble Ahead: The localizer at Huntington would give the pilots directional guidance only. The ILS at the Tri-City Airport did not include an electronic glideslope. Responsibility for maintaining the proper altitude fell solely upon the pilots. In the dark, visibility was hampered by fog, rain, and smoke. If the pilots could not see the runway lights from the 1,240 foot MDA they would have to terminate the landing attempt and execute a missed approach.

The charter coordinator sat in the jumpseat in the cockpit. The portion of the CVR transcript, below, begins as the flight approaches the electronic outer marker. The captain is flying the twin-jet DC-9 airliner:

> Capt: . . . . Captain, Flight 932
> FO: . . . . First Officer, Flight 932
> ChCoord: . . . . . Charter Coordinator, Flight 932
> Radio-: . . . . . . (prefix) Radio transmission, Flight 932
> AppControl: . . . Huntington Approach Control

ChCoord: Hope we don't have it *[meaning, the bad visibility and turbulence]* this way all the way in, it's rough. (1926:43)

FO: There she *[meaning, the outer marker]* is. (1927:58)

Radio-FO: [Approach Control,] Southern nine-thirty-two, we're over the outer marker now, proceeding outbound.

AppControl: Nine-thirty-two, roger, report the marker inbound.

Capt: Slats and [flaps] five. (1928:11)

Capt: From the lights on the ground, it looks like fog . . . [have] you checked the missed approach [procedure]? (1928:35)

FO: All right, [for a missed approach] you pull up to twenty-seven-hundred feet by the east course of the ILS to Shoals Fan Marker, then report Shoals, then straight out . . . .

FO: I believe half those lights [on the ground] should be off to our left. Kinda hard to say, though. (1930:03)

Capt: We're in a rainshower, all right. (1930:43)

FO: Yeah, I know it.

Capt: We sure are, the temp' is dropping. (1930:49)

FO: Yeah -- aaahhh -- that rain is mixed in with fog.

   [sound of windshield wipers begins]

FO: OK, you got the no smoking [sign on], ignition, radar standby, auto shutoff armed, waiting on the gear, got the spoilers?

Capt: [Spoilers] armed.

   [sound of "click" from arming the spoilers]

Capt: That thing captured! How did it capture? You [are] getting a glideslope capture, and you ain't got a glideslope. (1931:26)

FO: It might capture on the -- aaahhh -- on ILS, Frank, regardless of the glideslope. I don't have no capture, though.

Capt: OK, give me twenty-five [degrees of flaps]. (1931:49)

FO: Got twenty-five flaps, all is squared [away].

Capt: We ought to be over the outer marker at twenty-two-hundred feet. . . . [Are] you going to call out minimums?

FO: Yeah, I sure will, I'll sing 'em out to you -- as you get on down it, aaahhh, this rough air, ought to give us a little break.

Capt: Well, if it's like [the controller] said, if it's not blowing any harder than he says it is, why --.

FO: Down draft.

Capt: Must be a little rainshower. (1933:17)

FO: [We are] back in the soup *[meaning, in the clouds]*. (1933:19)

Capt: Jerry, I'm going to be flying about one-[hundred]-thirty.

FO: I'm going to check the time for you, [the runway will] be about two minutes from the, ah, outer marker.

[sound of the outer marker at 1933:43; it ends at 1933:47]

Radio-FO: Southern nine-thirty-two, the marker inbound.

AppControl: Southern nine-thirty-two is cleared to land, you can advise [us] on the lights, the wind is now three-four-zero degrees [at] seven [knots].

[sound of flap selector at 1933:59]

Radio-FO: OK, the lights [will] be good about step three, I guess.

AppControl: That's where they are, with the rabbit *[meaning, the sequence flashers]*, advise when you want them cut.

Radio-FO: Very good.

FO: [You are] on the [airspeed] bug. (1934:09)

FO: OK, I got the time for you. -- [We are] a thousand feet above the ground, [sink] rate and airspeed good -- speed a little fast, looks good -- got bug and twelve [knots].

Capt: See [the runway lights]? (1934:55)

FO: No, not yet -- it's beginning to lighten up a little bit on the ground here at -- ah -- seven-hundred feet. (1935:01)

FO: Bug [airspeed] and five. (1935:03)

FO: We're two-hundred [feet] above [the MDA]. (1935:06)

ChCoord: Bet it'll be a missed approach. (1935:10)

FO: Four-hundred [feet above the airport elevation]. (1935:18)

Capt: Is that the approach [MDA]? (1935:19)

FO: Yeah.

[the Captain begins a missed approach; he starts rotation and pushes the throttles forward at 1935:20]

FO: Hundred-and-twenty-six [knots]. (1935:21)

[the aircraft begins a shallow climb at 1935:23]

*[the First Officer looks at the radio altimeter and **shouts**]*

FO: Hundred [feet]! (1935:25)

[1 second later, sound of impact with treetops at 1935:26]

[the aircraft climbs, rolls inverted, then dives earthward]

[final impact; end of the CVR tape at 1935:32]

The Accident: The captain began a missed approach at 1935:21 Hours, and the DC-9 started a shallow climb. Seconds later the aircraft flew through the tops of tall trees on a hilltop 5,543 feet west of the runway threshold. The wings and fuselage sawed a swath 279 feet long through the treetops. On the right wing this initial impact ripped off several sections of the leading edge, a trailing edge flap, a movable vane, and a flap track.

Severely wounded, the DC-9 desperately clawed for altitude and safety. However, the damage to the wing proved to be fatal. The airliner climbed, slowly rolled inverted, and then dove down onto a hillside a quarter-mile from the point of impact with the trees. A gigantic orange fireball exploded up into the night sky:

> At 1936 [Hours] tower personnel observed a red glow west of the airport. When no response to radio calls was received, the tower controller initiated the emergency procedures.

Firefighting crews made their way to the crash site, but there was nothing they could do. In the words of the NTSB, most of the aircraft was "melted or reduced to a powder-like substance." One witness reported "charred pieces of bodies all over the place."

Alerted by telephone, the Cabell-Huntington Hospital sealed all entrances and geared up to treat the injured. Their effort was for naught. All 75 people aboard the DC-9 had perished in the worst sports-related disaster in the history of the United States.

The Investigation: Investigators from the NTSB pieced together what had happened. Simply stated, the DC-9 had flown too low, clipped the trees, and crashed roughly a mile short of the runway. The investigative staff noted:

The aircraft descended through the MDA approximately 2 miles from the end of the runway. . . . The major thrust of the investigation was focused on uncovering the reason or reasons which might explain this descent.

Despite the captain's remarks about "capturing" a nonexistent glideslope, the autopilot proved not to be a factor. The captain had used it for directional guidance only.

The CVR tape recording revealed that the pilots periodically saw several lights through breaks in the clouds. However, the tape indicated that they never acquired visual contact with the runway lights. As they tracked inbound the pilots' remarks confirmed that they were (1) properly concerned with their altitude and were (2) monitoring it closely. In view of the restricted visibility at night in the rain and fog, they knew their altitude was crucial. They planned for a possible missed approach, and the first officer made the required altitude call-outs.

The statements made by the pilots on final approach clearly indicated that they did not know the aircraft was descending below the MDA. In fact, the captain began a missed approach at what he *thought* was the MDA. What could have gone wrong? Were the altimeter and VSI displaying accurate information for the pilots? Probably not, for investigators soon discovered:

> It is possible that a static system error caused the barometric altimeter to read higher than the actual altitude of the aircraft, and produced a decrease in the indicated rate of descent on the vertical speed indicator. . . . The existence of [such] an error is consistent with certain indications on the flight data recorder.

Investigators found an alarming clue. The FDR and CVR tapes suggested the existence of a large barometric altimeter error. When the first officer's altitude call-outs were compared to the altitudes documented on the FDR, they did not match. The aircraft was flying roughly 200 feet below the altitude verbally reported by the first officer. At what the pilots *thought* was the 1,240 foot MDA, the aircraft had descended to about 100 feet above the treetops:

> Evidence supportive of an altimeter error can be derived from the cockpit voice recorder. During the final stages of the descent the first officer made four altitude call-outs. All of

these call-outs . . . were [about] 200 feet higher than the actual altitude of the aircraft as reflected by the flight data recorder.

The descent continued. The FDR and CVR tapes showed that the captain began rotation for the missed approach two seconds after the "four-hundred" call-out, and rotation took another 1.7 seconds. During those crucial 3.7 seconds before starting to climb the aircraft descended an additional 90 feet. That further descent, combined with the probable 200 foot altimeter error, pounded the last nail into the coffin for Flight 932.

Probable Cause: Seventeen months after the loss of Flight 932 the NTSB adopted its report, NTSB-AAR-72-11, on 14 April 1972. The report revealed that the technical experts knew *what* caused the crash, but exactly *why* remained somewhat fuzzy.

The airport lighting system and the localizer had functioned properly. There was no pre-impact mechanical problem with the DC-9. The captain began a missed approach at what he *believed* was the MDA. However, he was about 300 feet too low, and the aircraft flew into the trees. The board ruled that the *Probable Cause* of this accident was:

> the descent below Minimum Descent Altitude during a non-precision approach under adverse *[meaning, poor visibility]* operating conditions without visual contact with the runway environment.

The board noted that, to a certainty, it was "unable to determine the reason for this descent" The board members concluded that a likely explanation was "an altimetry system error."

Postscript: The fiery crash had wiped out the entire Marshall University football team and coaching staff. At the Division I-AA college nothing was left of the football program. Nothing. Many alumni and friends of the university urged that the football program be scrapped.

Instead of giving up and quitting, Marshall University started from scratch. In the autumn of 1971 new coaches fielded a team of freshmen, walk-ons, wannabes, and many who had no business trying to play college football. That first year was a disaster. Yet, the gridiron amateurs of the *Thundering Herd* somehow pulled off a miracle upset of Xavier on the last play of one home game. *The Herald-Dispatch* would report:

> It was one of the few highlights of a [football] program that endured years of futility.

However, as the years passed the team rose like a phoenix from the ashes of the fiery 1970 tragedy to become a national football powerhouse. In 1992 and 1996, Marshall University won Division I-AA national championships. In 1997 the school moved up into Division I-A. During the 1990s the men of Marshall University won more football games than any other college team in the United States. In 1999 the team reached the pinnacle of gridiron success. Marshall played 13 games and won them all. Undefeated! To date, since the move to Division I-A, the elite *Thundering Herd* has won five Mid-American Conference championships and has earned seven bowl berths.

In November 2000, two hours before the Marshall football team locked horns with Miami of Ohio, thousands of fans and alumni gathered outside Marshall Stadium. The band played the Marshall University alma mater. Then the crowd witnessed the unveiling of *We Are Marshall Memorial Bronze*. Below the huge sculpture the memorial displays the names of 75 people -- the athletes, coaches, supporters, and the flight crew -- who were lost on Southern Airways Flight 932. An inscription reads:

> They shall live on in the hearts of their friends and families forever, and this memorial records their loss to the university and to the community.

Allegheny Airlines Flight 485

Convair CV-580, registration N5832
7 June 1971, at New Haven, Connecticut
31 aboard, 28 killed

Overview: A Convair CV-580 headed for the coastal airport at New Haven, Connecticut. With no forward visibility in thick fog, the captain descended far below the MDA. He skimmed over Long Island Sound only 25 feet above the water. Flying blind, the Convair clipped the tops of beach cottages on the shoreline. Of the 31 persons aboard, 28 died in the crash and fire.

The Flight: Early on the morning of 7 June 1971, Allegheny Airlines Flight 485 took off from Washington, DC. After three missed approaches in thick fog the airliner slipped down and landed at New London, Connecticut. Twenty lucky passengers deplaned. Fourteen unlucky people boarded, bringing the total passenger count to 28. The flight took off again at 0933 Hours and headed for nearby New Haven, Connecticut.

The aircraft had been manufactured in 1956 as a piston-powered Convair CV-440 and delivered to Braniff Airways. Eleven years later Pacific Airmotive Corporation converted it into a modern turboprop transport. Powered by twin Allison turbine engines, the updated airliner was promoted as an "Allison Prop-Jet" by the marketing whizzes. The new Convair CV-580, registration N5832, reentered service with Allegheny Airlines in 1967.

The captain, age 39, held an ATP certificate and had logged 12,107 hours of flight time. His slightly younger first officer, age 34, held a Commercial Pilot certificate and had logged 4,150 hours. Their flight attendant, age 27, had been employed by Allegheny Airlines since 1964.

Trouble Ahead: As Flight 485 neared New Haven the pilots saw that the airport was shrouded by a blanket of fog that extended out over Long Island Sound. The airport had no ILS, so the captain decided to try a VOR straight-in approach to Runway 2. This approach would allow a descent to the 380 foot MDA out over the sound. The pilots would track inbound over the water, zip over the coastline, and land on the runway 14 feet above sea level.

The portion of the CVR transcript, below, begins as Westchester Approach Control clears Flight 485 for the VOR approach to the airport. The captain is flying the aircraft:

> <u>Capt</u>: . . . . Captain, Flight 485
> <u>FO</u>: . . . . First Officer, Flight 485
> <u>Radio-</u>: . . . . (prefix) Radio transmission, Flight 485
> <u>Tower</u>: . . . . New Haven Airport Control Tower
> <u>AppControl</u>: . . . . Westchester Approach Control

<u>AppControl</u>: OK, and you can intercept the final approach course on that heading, you'll be right at Pond Point [Intersection], you're cleared for a VOR approach. (0947:01)

<u>Radio-FO</u>: OK, thank you, sir, [we are] cleared for the approach, Allegheny four-eighty-five. (0947:06)

<u>AppControl</u>: Roger, you're welcome.

<u>Capt</u>: What was that wind, do you remember off-hand?

<u>FO</u>: A hundred-and-eighty [degrees] at five [knots].

<u>AppControl</u>: OK, and Allegheny four-eighty-five, contact New Haven Tower, one-two-four-point-eight now, you're [at] Pond Point inbound [to the airport]. (0947:25)

<u>Radio-FO</u>: 'K, [one]-twenty-four-eight, thank you a lot. (0947:30)

<u>AppControl</u>: You're welcome, sir.

<u>Capt</u>: Before you talk to [the tower], will you give me fifteen [degrees of flaps] and gear down, please? (0947:34)

[sound of landing gear extension at 0947:39]

<u>FO</u>: There ya go. (0947:40)

<u>Radio-FO</u>: New Haven Tower, Allegheny four-eighty-five is, ah, passin' the point comin' inbound. (0947:47)

<u>Tower</u>: Roger, four-eighty-five, runway your choice, sir, the wind

[is] one-nine-zero degrees at five [knots], altimeter two-niner-niner-six, Runway two or [Runway] twenty. (0947:53)

Capt: Well, tell him -- aaahhh -- well, that's all right, we'll take [Runway] two for the approach runway. (0948:01)

Radio-FO: OK, the way it looks we'll take [Runway] two, it will be all right. (0948:04)

Tower: Roger, cleared to land, Runway two. (0948:07)

[the pilots acknowledge with 2 microphone clicks at 0948:09]

Capt: Out of a thousand [feet]. (0948:11)

FO: Twenty-four [degrees of flaps]? (0948:11)

[the pilots complete their landing checklist]

Capt: Give me forty [degrees of flaps]. (0948:22)

FO: I'm telling you -- out of five-hundred [feet]. (0948:29)

FO: Looks about a hundred feet atop --. (0948:34)

Capt: They sure do. (0948:35)

Capt or FO: Not very good, is it? (0948:37)

FO: Top minimums -- I don't have it *[meaning, I don't have the runway in sight]*. (0948:42)

FO: Decision height. (0948:44)

[the Captain does not stop his descent]

FO: You got a hundred-and-five [knots], sinkin' five-[hundred feet per minute]. (0948:52)

Capt: All right -- keep a real sharp eye out here. (0948:56)

*[already below the MDA, the Captain **continues to descend** into the blinding fog at a rate of 500 feet per minute]*

FO: OK.

FO: Oh, this [unintelligible] is low! You can't see down through this stuff! (0949:10)

Capt: I can see the water. (0949:20)

Capt: [Unintelligible] I got [visibility] straight down. (0949:22)

*[the aircraft has descended to **an altitude of only 25 feet**]*

FO: I can see the water! We're right over the water! (0949:23)

FO: Man, we ain't twenty feet off the water! (0949:26)

FO: Hold it! (0949:29)

[1 second later, sound of the first impact at 0949:30]

[sound of more impacts; end of the CVR tape at 0949:31]

The Accident: Gear and flaps down, the aircraft skimmed over Long Island Sound toward the airport. Ahead was a solid opaque sea of white. Zipping blindly along through the dense fog, the aircraft reached the invisible shoreline:

> The aircraft struck the upper portion of three beach cottages at a height of approximately 29 feet msl and came to rest at a point 270 feet from [the point of] initial impact.

The Convair plowed through the tops of the houses, tore down electrical power lines, slammed down onto the ground, and skidded to a stop. The impacts crushed the cockpit, but the rest of the fuselage remained more or less intact. Fuel poured out of ruptured wing tanks and ignited. Several explosions rocked the downed aircraft, followed by a fire that consumed the fuselage. The fire also destroyed several homes and caused major damage to other structures and the electrical power lines.

Two badly burned passengers escaped through an emergency exit over the wing and crawled to safety in a water-filled ditch. The impact had thrown the first officer through the side of the crushed cockpit. Rescuers later found him lying 20 feet from the blazing wreckage. Critically injured and burned, he would survive after amputation of both legs.

The remaining 28 persons aboard all died. The majority of the bodies were found huddled around the rear service door, which they apparently could not open. With one exception the occupants did not succumb to traumatic injuries. Instead, trapped in the burning cabin, they died from "chemical asphyxiation and thermal injury, or a combination of both."

The Investigation: Investigators began looking for the cause of the crash. They knew, obviously, that the airliner had been flying far too low, but they did not know why. They turned to the FDR for answers, and what they found shocked them:

> The cause of this accident [lay] in the area of flight operation: specifically, the judgment and decision-making capability of the captain and his interaction with the first officer.

Before the crash at New Haven the airliner had landed at New London in thick fog. The MDA for the New London approach was 610 feet. Yet, the FDR revealed that the captain had descended to a height of 175 feet on each of the first two approaches. On the third approach he dropped down to only 125 feet. Somehow he landed after the fourth approach.

Armed with that information, investigators began reconstructing the crash at New Haven. The FDR and CVR confirmed that the captain began a straight-in approach toward Runway 2. Beginning at 1,600 feet, this approach allows an over-water descent to the MDA of 380 feet *if* -- and only *if* -- the forward visibility is at least one mile. However, the visibility was nowhere near a mile. It was only 100 to 200 feet at the airport, and a mere 50 to 60 feet at the site of the accident along the shoreline. The fog extended up to an altitude of about 400 feet. Only 16 seconds before the impact the first officer had exclaimed:

> Oh, this [unintelligible] is low! You can't see down through this stuff!

The FDR disclosed that during the final minute of flight the Convair descended at a steady rate of about 500 feet per minute. Investigators turned to the CVR tape. With regard to the *nuances* of the first officer's statements, they found it "obvious that he attempted in several ways to alert the captain to the growing danger created by the continued descent." Yet, the captain flew lower and lower until the aircraft was only 25 feet above the water.

Based on the CVR tape, both pilots saw the water just beneath the aircraft. The first officer, who survived, testified that he saw "the buildings" suddenly appear dead ahead in the fog. The captain apparently saw the cottages at the same time. One second before impact the FDR showed an abrupt vertical acceleration increase to 2.4 G's. The captain had tried to pull up, but it was too late.

Probable Cause: Almost one year after the crash the NTSB adopted Aircraft Accident Report NTSB-AAR-72-20 on 1 June 1972. The board knew that on each of the three missed approaches at New London the captain had intentionally descended far below the MDA of 610 feet. The board reported:

> In retrospect, the three missed approaches at [New London], each one of which was associated with a deliberate descent below the specified minimum descent altitude, must be considered in the overall analysis [of the crash at New Haven].

During the ill-fated approach at New Haven the board noted that the first officer properly made the required airspeed, altitude, and sink rate call-outs. Although the captain acknowledged reaching the MDA of 380 feet, he continued the descent. There was no acquisition of forward visibility until the pilots saw the beach cottages looming out of the mist right in front of them. The board was unable to determine why the experienced and proficient captain descended so far below the MDA. The board found that the *Probable Cause* of this accident was:

> the captain's intentional descent below the prescribed minimum descent altitude under adverse weather conditions without adequate forward visibility or the crew's sighting of the runway environment. The captain disregarded advisories from his first officer that the minimum descent altitude had been reached.

The board noted that it was "difficult to reconcile the actions" the captain exhibited during the flight. The board was "unable to determine what motivated the captain to disregard prescribed operating procedures and altitude restrictions."

Delta Airlines Flight 9570

Douglas DC-9, registration N3305L
30 May 1972, near Fort Worth, Texas
4 aboard, 4 killed

Overview: A heavy airliner completed a touch-and-go near Fort Worth, Texas. Then a much smaller Douglas DC-9 on a training flight approached for landing. The DC-9 pilots flew into a wingtip vortex created by the heavy airliner. The swirling winds flipped the DC-9 inverted, and it crashed. The impact and fire killed the three pilots and an FAA inspector on board.

The Flight: Delta Airlines scheduled Flight 9570, a training flight, on 30 May 1972. Two of its pilots were captain-trainees. Under the watchful eye of a designated check-pilot, the trainees were candidates for a type rating in the DC-9. The training flight took off from Love Field in Dallas, Texas, and headed for nearby Greater Southwest International Airport near Fort Worth.

The young check-pilot, age 35, had been flying with Delta for five years. He was the pilot in command on this flight, during which he would evaluate the two trainees. One of them, age 32, held an ATP certificate and had logged 7,800 flight hours. The other, age 35, held a Commercial Pilot certificate and had logged 6,220 hours. An FAA Air Carrier Operations Inspector rode in the cockpit to monitor the evaluation program.

Powered by twin Pratt & Whitney turbofan engines, the Douglas DC-9, registration N3305L, arrived at the airport near Fort Worth. The trainees each completed an ILS approach. With one of them seated back in the cabin, the other shot a VOR approach and circled to land on Runway 13.

Trouble Ahead: Operating under VFR procedures, the trainee extended his downwind leg. He planned to land behind American Airlines Flight 1114, a heavy DC-10 on short final approach.

The portion of the CVR transcript, below, begins as the DC-9 parallels the runway downwind. From his seat on the right, the Delta check-pilot asks the trainee to make a full-stop landing:

CkPilot: . . . . . .   Check-Pilot, Flight 9570
CaptTrainee: . .   One of the Captain-Trainees, Flight 9570
Radio-: . . . . . .   (prefix) Radio transmission, Flight 9570
Tower: . . . . . .   Greater Southwest Airport Control Tower

Tower: [Delta] ninety-five-seventy, plan your, ah, landing [after] the DC-ten over the outer marker now on [Runway] one-three, he'll be [making] a touch-and-go. (0720:41)

Radio-CaptTrainee: Roger.

[the Captain-Trainee requests a full-stop landing on Runway 13]

Tower: OK, that'll be fine, use [Runway] one-three for full stop, caution, turbulence.

CaptTrainee or CkPilot: Passing abeam one-three now. (0721:34)

CkPilot: There's fifteen seconds now -- let -- get abeam of him now. (0721:42)

[the Captain-Trainee extends his downwind leg to increase the time and distance behind the DC-10]

CaptTrainee: All right, there's twenty seconds *[meaning, 20 seconds beyond a position abeam the end of the runway]*, gimme thirty degrees [of flaps]. (0721:55)

CaptTrainee or CkPilot: Turning base, full stop. (0722:06)

CaptTrainee: Fifty degrees [of flaps], before landing checklist [is complete]. (0722:18)

[the Captain-Trainee rolls out on final approach at 0722:56]

[sound of the middle marker at 0723:19]

[the DC-9 slowly angles into a wingtip vortex from the DC-10]

CkPilot: A little turbulence here. (0723:23)

*[the DC-9 flies into the center of the **powerful vortex**, which snares the airliner and causes a "snap-roll" to the right]*

CkPilot: Let's go around! (0723:30)

CaptTrainee or CkPilot: Takeoff power! (0723:30)

[sound of the stick-shaker at 0723:30]

CaptTrainee or CkPilot: I've got it! (0723:31)

CaptTrainee or CkPilot: Ooohhh! (0723:33)

[sound of impact; end of the CVR tape at 0723:34]

The Accident: The flight and the landing approach had been normal in all respects until the DC-9 crossed over the runway threshold. Sixty feet above the runway the airliner rolled left, then right, then left again. Then the craft snap-rolled 90 degrees to the right, and the right wing dug into the runway. The wounded airliner continued to roll right. Inverted, it slammed down onto the runway and began a half-mile long slide:

Fire propagated from the ruptured wing fuel tanks to the airplane's fuselage subsequent to initial impact.

Fuel spewed from ruptured tanks in the wings and fed a boiling inferno. Firefighting crews at the airport saw the crash. Even before the airport crash alarm sounded they sped toward the rising column of black smoke and orange flames. Aided by crews from the city of Fort Worth, they eventually doused the flames, but they were unable to save the four men aboard.

The two Delta pilots in the cockpit and the FAA inspector had been killed by "massive impact trauma." The pilot riding back in the cabin survived the crash. Trapped in the burning upside-down plane, he died from "smoke and carbon monoxide inhalation." The medical examiner determined that he would have survived if there had been no fire.

The Investigation: Investigators found that there were no malfunctions of the aircraft or its systems. They turned to the data from the FDR and the voice recording from the CVR and soon discovered the reason for the crash.

Analysis showed that the DC-9 had crossed over the threshold of the runway only 53 to 54 seconds behind the much larger and much heavier DC-10. At takeoff the heavy transport had weighed 330,000 pounds, well over four times the weight of the smaller DC-9. Trailing back from the wingtips of the heavy DC-10 were two invisible, swirling, horizontal tornadoes. In aviation lingo they are known as *wingtip vortices* or *wake vortices*, and they are usually called "wake turbulence" by ATC.

Reconstruction of the accident showed that these powerful vortices had ***extreme circular air velocities*** on the order of 150 to 220 feet per second. Because of existing meteorological conditions the vortex from the left wing of the DC-10 was centered along the centerline of Runway 13 as the DC-9 approached to land.

The DC-9 flew above and to the left of the invisible vortex as it approached the runway. But as the twin-jet crossed the runway threshold it angled into the clockwise vortex from the left:

> The DC-9 descended into the influence of the left [wing] vortex generated by the DC-10, approaching the vortex from the left at a convergence angle of 7 degrees.

The initial upward pressure on the right wing caused a roll to the left. The FDR showed that the pilot applied right aileron and overcorrected to the right, then overcorrected back to the left. Then the DC-9 angled into the lethal core of the vortex.

The swirling airflow caught the aircraft in an aerodynamic vice from which there would be no escape. The vortex whipped the right wing down and the left wing up. Full left aileron had no effect. The aircraft rolled inverted and crashed.

This accident marked only the second known instance wherein a wingtip vortex had led to the crash of a modern airliner. The pilots had been caught low and slow, deep within the influence of the vortex airflow field. Computer analysis revealed:

> The left [wing] vortex of the DC-10 would have remained in the runway threshold zone for more than two minutes in the absence of external disturbing forces, which normally cause breakup or dissipation [of a wingtip vortex].

Ironically, a left crosswind component had caused the vortex from the left wing of the DC-10 to drift over the runway centerline. Normally it would have swirled off to the left of the runway and dissipated. Also, the normal no-wind or headwind condition would have moved the vortex farther downwind from the approach end of the runway. Unfortunately, in this instance there was a tailwind component. This tailwind, combined with the left crosswind, moved the vortex directly over the runway. The NTSB noted:

> Occurrence of these meteorological conditions, combined with intersecting approach paths, is rare.

On the fatal approach the Delta pilots had been flying under VFR procedures, and they sequenced their aircraft only 53 to 54 seconds behind the DC-10. At approach airspeed this equated to slightly more than two miles of longitudinal separation. If the flight been receiving radar vectors in either a VFR or an IFR environment, ATC would have afforded the pilots *six* miles of longitudinal separation.

Probable Cause: Ten months after the loss of Flight 9570 the NTSB adopted its Aircraft Accident Report, NTSB-AAR-73-3, on 13 March 1973. The board found the *Probable Cause* to be:

> an encounter with a trailing vortex generated by a preceding heavy jet, which resulted in an involuntary loss of control of the airplane during final approach.

Until the crash of Flight 9570 there had been a widespread belief that wake vortices were a danger only to small single-engine types of aircraft. The board noted that ATC had cautioned the Delta pilots about "turbulence." Yet, the board stressed that the pilots did not have enough information to evaluate the possible location of a wake vortex, or its danger to them:

> The core of the vortex was stationary along the runway centerline at a height of approximately 60 feet above ground level, and was not visible to the crew of the DC-9.

The board acknowledged that there were "no prescribed recovery procedures" for avoiding a wake vortex upset. The board found the reaction of the pilots to be "normal under the circumstances." In addition, the board pointed out that the DC-9 had already made two landings behind the DC-10 and had experienced no problems.

Texas International Airlines Flight 655

Convair CV-600, registration N94230
27 September 1973, on Black Fork Mountain, Arkansas
11 aboard, 11 killed

Overview: The pilots of a Convair CV-600 tried to circumvent a line of thunderstorms. In the *clouds*, in the *rain*, at *night*, they attempted to navigate *visually*. Zipping along far below the MEA, 100 miles off course, they blindly flew into Black Fork Mountain, Arkansas. The fiery crash instantly killed the 11 people on board.

The Flight: Texas International Airlines Flight 655 swooped down and landed at El Dorado, Arkansas, at 1953 Hours on the stormy night of 27 September 1973. The baggage handlers and the ground crew readied the turboprop airliner for the next segment of the trip, a flight to Texarkana, Arkansas.

Meanwhile, the pilots were concerned about weather conditions. Radar had painted a solid line of thunderstorms lying across their proposed route, and lightning was already visible to the southwest. In part, a National Weather Service forecast cautioned:

> . . . ceilings 500 overcast, [visibility] 1 mile in showers and thunderstorms . . . moving northward at 15 knots. Moderate to severe turbulence at all levels in or near thunderstorms.

The airliner was a Convair CV-600, registration N94230. It had rolled off the General Dynamics assembly line 25 years earlier as a medium range piston-powered airliner. After it completed many years of line service with American Airlines, Texas International bought the craft and converted it to turbine power in 1967. During its airline service the reliable twin-engine transport had amassed 51,208 flight hours.

The captain, age 41, had been flying with Texas International for 14 years. He held an ATP certificate, and his logbook reflected

11,800 hours of flight time, over half of which was in the CV-600 airliner. His younger first officer, age 37, held a Commercial Pilot certificate and had logged 7,106 hours. Only one flight attendant staffed the cabin. The young woman, age 23, had been employed by Texas International for 11 months.

To circumvent the storms to the west the pilots elected not to activate their computer-stored IFR flight plan. Instead, they called the local flight service station and explained that they planned to navigate *visually* to Texarkana without any type of flight plan.

Trouble Ahead: The pilots took off from Runway 22 at 2015 Hours. Rain pelted the airliner as the pilots headed north in the dark, trying in vain to maintain eye contact with lights on the ground below. The first officer was flying the airliner. The captain scanned the radar display and tried to direct the first officer around the storms that lay across their route of flight.

The portion of the CVR transcript, below, begins as the flight heads north. Neither pilot makes any radio transmissions:

Capt: . . .   Captain, Flight 655
FO: . . . .   First Officer, Flight 655

FO: [On our radar display] it looks like twenty-four miles to the end [of the line of storm cells], I don't mind, do you?

Capt: I don't care, just as long as we don't go through it.

FO: The visibility is dropping. (2025:45)

Capt: Yeah . . . raining all over the place.

Capt: You [see] something down there? (2027:17)

FO: What's all this, lights, in those fields? What the [expletive] are they, chicken farms? (2027:31)

Capt: Yeah. -- That's what they are.

FO: They're planning on growing a few eggs, ain't they?

[sound of whistling; 6 minutes pass; the flight continues north and skirts the eastern edge of the line of thunderstorms]

FO: I can't get this [expletive] stupid radar [unintelligible]. You got any idea where we're at?

Capt: Yeah, [a heading of] two-sixteen'll take us right to the VOR, two-oh-nine, I got. (2033:43)

Capt: I'm not concerned with that, I could care less. . . . I guess you're right, that [storm] is just extending on and on and on as we go along, 'cause it hasn't moved . . . .

Capt: What's [the] Hot Springs [frequency]? What's Hot Springs VOR? Is it ten-zero, is that right? (2034:47)

FO: Yeah, yeah, uuuhhh, that's right. We don't want to get too far up the [expletives], it gets hilly.

Capt: Why don't you [descend to] two-thousand [feet]. If we get up there anywhere near Hot Springs, we get in the [expletive] mountains. (2035:41)

FO: Uh, you reckon there's a ridge line along here somewhere?

Capt: Fred, you can quit worrying about the mountains 'cause [our altitude] will clear everything over there. (2036:27)

FO: That's why I wanted to [climb] to twenty-five-hundred feet. That's the Hot Springs highway right here, I think.

Capt: You're 'bout right.

FO: Texarkan -- naaaww, it ain't either. Texarkana's back here.

Capt: Texarkana's back over here, somewhere.

FO: Yeah, this ain't no Hot Springs highway.

Capt: I don't know, Fred, we keep gettin' another [storm cell] poppin' up every time -- every time.

FO: If we keep this up *[that is, flying north]* indefinitely, we'll be in Tulsa. (2038:11)

[sound of laughter; 2 minutes and 30 seconds pass]

FO: That's probably Hot Springs. (2040:41)

Capt: Yep, could be. Yeah, that might be either it or . . . .

FO: Well, I'm getting out of the clouds here, Mac, but I'm getting right into it --.

Capt: Oh, looks like you're all right.

FO: Do you see any stars above us? We're going in and outta some scud. . . . I sure wish I knew where the [expletive] we were.

FO: [Our radar is] paintin' ridges and everything else, boss, and I'm not familiar with the terrain. (2042:04)

Capt: Yeah, I'd stay down [low]. You're right in some, right in the base of the clouds . . . we're gonna be able to turn in a minute.

FO: We're in [the edge of the storm], we're in solid now.

Capt: Are we? Start your turn, standard rate . . . level out . . . we should be out of it in 'bout two miles.

[4 minutes pass; routine cockpit conversation]

FO: There's thirty left -- naaaw, thirty-five, [expletive]. (2046:57)

Capt: Keep on truckin' -- just keep on a-truckin'.

FO: Well, we must be somewhere in Oklahoma.

Capt: Doin' all the good in the world.

FO: Have any idea what the frequency of the Paris VOR is?

Capt: Nope, don't really give a [expletive]. Put, uh, about two-sixty-five, heading two-sixty-five. (2047:52)

FO: Two-sixty-five? I would say we [expletive] up. (2047:56)

[sound of laughter]

Capt: Fred, descend to two-thousand [feet]. (2049:00)

FO: Two-thousand [feet], coming down. -- Here we are [at two-thousand feet], we're not out of [the clouds].

Capt: Let's truck on.

Capt: 'Bout five [degrees] to the right, shift over a little bit if you can . . . that's all right.

Capt: That's all right, you're doin' all the good in the world. I thought we'd get, I thought [the storm] was moving that way on me, only, we just kinda turned a little bit while you was looking at the map . . . first time I ever made a mistake in my life.

FO: I'll be [expletive]. Man, I wish I knew where we were so we'd have some idea of the general [expletive] terrain around this [expletive] place.

Capt: I know what it is -- the highest point out here is about twelve-hundred feet . . . and then we're not even where that [highest terrain] is, I don't believe. (2050:38)

FO: I'll tell you what, as long as we travel northwest instead of west -- and I still can't get Paris [VOR] --.

Capt: Go ahead and look at [the map].

[sound of protracted whistling]

FO: Two-hundred-and-fifty [degrees], we're about to pass over Page [VORTAC], you know where that is? (2051:56)

Capt: About a hundred-and-eighty degrees to Texarkana. (2052:07)

FO: About a hundred-and-fifty-two [degrees]. (2052:15)

FO: Minimum en route altitude here is forty-four-hun --. (2052:17)

*[**sound of impact**; end of the CVR tape at 2052:19]*

The Accident: In level flight at an altitude of 2,025 feet the airliner slammed into a rock cliff 600 feet below the top of Black Fork Mountain near Mena, Arkansas. The head-on impact at 188 knots subjected the Convair and those inside to over 600 G's. In the words of the NTSB, "the aircraft disintegrated."

The airline declared Flight 655 to be "missing" at 2225 Hours. Soon civil and military authorities began an air and ground search along the *assumed* direct route of flight. Coordinated by the 43rd Aerospace Rescue and Recovery Squadron and the Civil Air Patrol, 224 aircraft flew 478 sorties and 1,235 hours in an effort to find the missing airliner. The exhaustive search turned up no trace of the CV-600. Pitching in to help, the Arkansas Army National Guard sent military search teams. Tragically, one of their search helicopters crashed and killed the entire crew.

Three days later a controller at Fort Worth Center volunteered a telltale clue. He recalled seeing an unidentified VFR target on his scope after 2000 Hours on 27 September. The target had been far, far to the north of the route supposedly taken by Flight 655. Nonetheless, weary search teams combed the remote area, and they spotted the wreckage at 1730 Hours on 30 September:

> The [Convair pilots had] deviated about 100 miles north of the direct route to their destination.

A military helicopter hovered over the mountainside and lowered potential rescuers down on a hoist. None of the 11 people on the doomed flight had survived the impact. The medical examiner ruled that everyone on board had succumbed because of "multiple, extreme, and traumatic injuries."

The Investigation: NTSB analysts reconstructed the flight and the weather conditions it encountered. Before landing at El Dorado the pilots had radioed the local flight service station to obtain the latest weather information. They told the FAA employee that their onboard radar was "painting a solid line [of storms] about 50 miles west of El Dorado." A cold front had extended across the direct route from El Dorado to Texarkana. Weather radar in Little Rock, Arkansas, detected heavy rain around the storm cells.

The FDR showed that the flight headed north, far away from the direct preplanned route to Texarkana. The pilots initially climbed to only 1,500 feet. In the final stages of the flight their altitude varied from 2,200 feet to 2,025 feet. The first officer was worried about terrain clearance, and he had remarked at 2042 Hours:

> I sure wish I knew where the [expletive] we were. . . . [Our radar is] paintin' ridges and everything else . . . .

Seven VORTAC's and five radio beacons were available along the route from El Dorado to the crash site. Also, Fort Worth Center would have provided radar services upon request. However, the pilots did not contact any ATC facility. Also, they did not notify their dispatcher that they had not activated their IFR flight plan or that they had deviated from the direct route.

The pilots tried to find a way around the line of storm cells. They made only sporadic electronic navigation efforts. The CVR revealed that the captain had only a *general idea* of his position.

Over and over the first officer voiced concern about the mountains, somewhere nearby. Repeatedly he told the captain that he did not know their position, as exemplified by his statement:

> Man, I wish I knew where we were so we'd have some idea of the general [expletive] terrain around this [expletive] place.

In the final minutes of flight the aircraft was over the Ouachita Mountain Range. Ironically, at the precise moment of impact the first officer was telling the captain about the MEA. It was over 2,000 feet higher than the altitude at which they were flying.

Investigators uncovered one last irony. In the minutes prior to impact the pilots did not aurally monitor the Page VORTAC. The transmitter was located atop a hill. Its automated broadcast stated: "Page VOR, caution, elevation two-thousand-seven-hundred feet." This hill towered 600 feet above the altitude at which the pilots were flying. In the dark, they were heading straight toward it.

Probable Cause: Seven months after the loss of Flight 655 the NTSB adopted its report, NTSB-AAR-74-4, on 11 April 1974. The board found that there was no failure or malfunction of the aircraft or its systems. The board pointed out that the captain did not file any type of flight plan. Further, the board opined that Texas International did not adequately control the actions of the pilots and did not monitor the progress of the flight.

The board stressed that the pilots did not utilize all available navaids and available ATC services. The board made it clear that the flight descended to an altitude far below the MEA. Flying blind in the rain and clouds at night, the captain and first officer had no visual cues or warning prior to impact with the mountain. The board found that the *Probable Cause* of this accident was:

> the captain's attempt to operate the flight under visual flight rules in night instrument meteorological conditions without using all the navigation aids available to him, and his deviation from the preplanned route without adequate position information.

Pan Am Flight 806

Boeing 707, registration N454PA
30 January 1974, at Pago Pago, American Samoa
101 aboard, 97 killed

Overview: A Boeing 707 tried to land in the rain at night at Pago Pago International Airport in American Samoa. On short final approach on the ILS the aircraft sank below the glideslope. In "black hole" conditions the pilots flew into the jungle a half-mile short of the runway. No one sustained critical injuries during the crash, but a post-crash fire killed 97 of the 101 people on board.

The Flight: Pan American World Airways (Pan Am) Flight 806 took off from Auckland, New Zealand, early on the night of 30 January 1974. With 91 passengers and a crew of 10, the plane was bound for Los Angeles, California, with en route stops in American Samoa and Hawaii.

The Boeing 707, registration N454PA, had been delivered new to Pan Am in 1967. On this flight it carried 117,000 pounds of jet fuel to power its four engines. The captain and the first officer held ATP certificates, and the other two flight deck crewmembers held Commercial Pilot certificates. Six flight attendants carried out their traditional hostess duties in the passenger cabin.

High over the Pacific Ocean, 160 miles from the airport, the pilots contacted Pago Pago Approach Control at 2311 Hours. The ATC controller cleared the flight to fly direct to the Pago Pago VORTAC, and the pilots began a long en route descent. Over the ocean at night, the pilots headed for small Pago Pago International Airport on the tiny tropical island of Tutuila in American Samoa. There was no control tower at the airport, for arriving aircraft were few and far between. Approach Control, located in a building a half-mile from the runway, provided all necessary ATC services.

Trouble Ahead: At 2324 Hours the controller cleared Flight 806 for an ILS/DME approach to Runway 5. Ten minutes later the pilots reported that they had intercepted the final approach course. There was rain at the airport, but the approach should have been simple. The pilots could track straight inbound on the ILS.

The portion of the CVR transcript, below, begins as the pilots intercept the localizer. The captain is flying the airliner:

> <u>Capt</u>: . . . . Captain, Flight 806
> <u>FO</u>: . . . . First Officer, Flight 806
> <u>Radio-</u>: . . . . . . (prefix) Radio transmission, Flight 806
> <u>AppControl</u>: . . . Pago Pago Approach Control

<u>AppControl</u>: [Clipper] eight-oh-six, right, understand [you are] inbound on the localizer, report about three [miles] out, no other reported traffic, winds zero-one-zero degrees at one-five, gusting to two-zero [knots]. (2335:10)

<u>Capt</u>: OK, mileage check.

<u>FO</u>: OK, ya' got eight miles [from the VORTAC at the airport].

<u>FO</u>: OK, I have the runway [lights] in sight.

<u>FO</u>: Two-thousand [feet] on the radio altimeter.

<u>Capt</u>: Seven miles DME.

[the aircraft is about 400 feet below the ILS glideslope; sound of increase in engine power]

<u>FO</u>: Seven miles, and the altimeters check.

[the aircraft is still about 350 feet below the glideslope; sound of further increase in engine power]

<u>Capt</u>: A bit bouncy out here.

<u>AppControl</u>: Clipper eight-oh-six, it appears that we've had a power failure at the airport. (2338:50)

[there is no power failure; heavy rain between the controller and the runway has merely blocked his view of the runway lights]

<u>Radio-FO</u>: [This is Clipper] eight-zero-six, we're still getting the VOR, the ILS, and the [runway] lights are showing.

[the aircraft rises and intercepts the glideslope]

AppControl: [Can you] see the runway lights? (2339:05)

Radio-FO: That's charlie *[meaning, affirmative]*.

AppControl: We have a bad rain shower here, I can't see them from my position [a half-mile from the runway].

Radio-FO: We're five [miles] DME [from the airport] now, and they still look bright. (2339:29)

AppControl: OK, no other reported traffic, the wind is zero-three-zero at twenty [knots], gusting to twenty-five, [after landing] advise [me] when [you are] clear of the runway.

Radio-FO: Pan Am eight-zero-six, wilco *[meaning, will comply]*.

Capt: Keep your eye on [the runway], I'll stay on the gauges.

Capt: Keep your eye on [the runway].

[sound of the windshield wiper motor begins]

*[the aircraft flies into windshear (a **headwind** and an **updraft**); the airspeed increases, the aircraft rises above the glideslope, and the Captain reduces engine thrust]*

Capt: [Give me] flaps fifty.

FO: You're by Logotala [Hill, two miles from the airport].

Capt: Let me know when you've got the runway [in sight].

FO: Now -- you have the runway?

FO: You're a little high. (2340:22)

*[the aircraft flies into more windshear (a **tailwind** and a **downdraft**); the airspeed quickly drops; with low engine thrust the aircraft **sinks rapidly**]*

FO: One-hundred-fifty knots.

[the aircraft sinks below the glideslope at 2340:31]

[sound of 280 foot radio altimeter warning at 2340:33]

FO: You're at minimums. (2340:33)

FO: Field in sight. (2340:35)

FO: Turn to your right.

FO: Hundred-and-forty knots.

[already far below the glideslope, 3/4 mile from the runway the
rate of descent increases *to 1,500 feet per minute]*

[sound of impact at 2340:42]

The Accident: The aircraft sank below the glideslope. Rate of
descent steadily increased. At 140 knots the pilots blindly flew
into the jungle 3,865 feet short of the runway. The Boeing 707
plowed through thick vegetation for 775 feet, shedding its landing
gear, outer wing panels, ailerons, flaps, and all four engines. The
fuselage skidded to a stop near the one-lane dirt service road that
led to the middle marker transmitter:

> The aircraft came to rest about 3,090 feet from the approach end
> of Runway 5 at Pago Pago International Airport.

Dense jungle vegetation cushioned the crash. Survivors would
report that impact forces were mild, not much worse than a normal
landing. The passenger cabin remained intact, and no one aboard
had been critically injured. Unfortunately, fuel gushed from the
ruptured wing tanks and ignited, and raging fires broke out on the
right side of the fuselage.

One passenger opened an emergency exit on the right side of the
aircraft, and searing flames roared into the cabin. Other passengers
opened two over-wing exits on the left side, and six people
managed to scramble out. Everyone else rushed to the front and
rear of the aircraft, apparently expecting to find an open exit.
Instead they found only choking smoke and flames, and they all
perished huddled on the floor. Toxicological examinations on their
remains would reveal that they died because of "smoke inhalation
and massive first-, second-, and third-degree burns."

A small fire truck and two firemen were stationed at the airport,
and their headquarters sounded the alarm at 2343 Hours. The
NTSB would later take note of the difficulty faced by the firemen:

> Response was delayed because of confusion as to whether a
> house or an aircraft was involved [and] by heavy rain and two
> chained gates across the road [leading] to the accident site.

Firemen had to make their way up the narrow and winding dirt access road and break through two locked gates to reach the middle marker site. By the time they arrived 14 minutes after the crash, an inferno had melted most of the fuselage. Those trapped inside were beyond earthly aid.

One passenger who got out of the aircraft died in the hospital nine days later. The third officer, the only crewmember to escape, also died within days. Of the 101 people on board Flight 806, only four passengers ultimately survived.

The Investigation: The CVR established that the first officer had the airport lights in sight when the aircraft was eight miles from the runway. He commented several times that he could see the runway or the airport lights.

NTSB investigators checked the FDR, and it revealed that the flight had encountered windshear. Fifty-one seconds before impact the aircraft had been on the glideslope, but then it flew into strong horizontal and vertical changes in wind direction. A sudden headwind, caused by outflowing winds from the rainstorm at the airport, caused a sharp increase in airspeed. Combined with a powerful updraft of up to 4,000 feet per minute, this caused the aircraft to rise high above the glideslope. The captain reduced engine thrust to compensate.

However, as the flight passed over Logotala Hill two miles from touchdown, the wind suddenly changed again. The airliner flew (1) out of the headwind and updraft, and (2) into a tailwind and downdraft. Airspeed dropped from 160 knots to 140 knots:

> About 16 seconds before impact the aircraft started a rapid descent of about 1,500 fpm.

With reduced engine thrust combined with reduced airspeed, the aircraft sank below the glideslope. At that time the captain was transitioning to a visual approach. Peering through the heavy rain, trying to keep the runway lights in sight, neither he nor the first officer detected the high rate of descent. Investigators noted:

> The heavy rainshower . . . probably caused visual cues to diminish to the extent that the increased sink rate would have been extremely difficult, if not impossible, to recognize.

Only seconds from touchdown, through the heavy rain the pilots were trying to maintain visual contact with the runway lights. The first officer called out the decreasing airspeed. Unfortunately he did not make crucial glideslope or rate of descent call-outs. The investigators *theorized* that he was concentrating on visual contact with the runway, trying to detect the VASI.

There were no lights in the jungle below, so the pilots could not visually determine their height above ground. Just 15 seconds before impact their rate of descent increased to an *unthinkable* 1,500 feet per minute. Concentrating on the runway lights half obscured by rain, the pilots did not detect the danger. They did not increase the angle-of-attack or the engine thrust, and the airliner flew down into the jungle.

Probable Cause: Ten months later the NTSB adopted the initial Aircraft Accident Report, NTSB-AAR-74-15, on 8 November 1974. Yet, because of knowledge gained from subsequent accidents and because of an appeal the NTSB later reopened the investigation. A new report, NTSB-AAR-77-7, was adopted on 6 October 1977 almost four years after the crash.

The board found that windshear encountered by the flight was caused by a heavy rainstorm moving down the runway toward the approach end. The rain was progressively obscuring the high intensity runway lights. Thus, ironically, the closer the pilots came to the runway, the harder it was for them to see the lights. Analysis indicated that the VASI was totally obscured.

Tragically the obstruction to visibility peaked at the crucial time when the captain was transitioning to a visual approach. The board found the *Probable Cause* of this accident to be:

> the flightcrew's late recognition [of], and failure to correct in a timely manner, an excessive descent rate which developed as a result of the aircraft's penetration through destabilizing wind changes. These winds consisted of horizontal and vertical components produced by a heavy rainstorm . . . . The captain's recognition was hampered by restricted visibility, the illusory effects of a "black-hole" approach, inadequate monitoring of flight instruments, and the failure of the crew to call out [the] descent rate during the last 15 seconds of flight.

TWA Flight 514

Boeing 727, registration N54328
1 December 1974, near Berryville, Virginia
92 aboard, 92 killed

Overview: A Boeing 727 headed for Dulles International Airport near Washington, DC. Tragically, the pilots and controller did not understand each other's intentions, and the pilots descended below the MEA. In murky skies the airliner slammed headlong into a rock cliff on Mount Weather, Virginia, 25 miles from the airport. The fiery crash killed the 92 people on board.

The Flight: Early on the cold, stormy, and rainy morning of 1 December 1974 the passengers began filing aboard Trans World Airlines (TWA) Flight 514 at Columbus, Ohio. Eleven minutes behind schedule at 1024 Hours, the flight took off for a planned trip to Washington National Airport, just across the Potomac River from downtown Washington, DC.

The Boeing 727, registration N54328, had been delivered new to TWA four years earlier and had accumulated 11,997 hours of flying time. The two pilots were TWA veterans, and they were backed up by an experienced flight engineer. Four flight attendants in the cabin took charge of their light load of 85 passengers. Two of these young women had been flying the line for 17 months. The remaining two were new employees who had completed their TWA training 24 days before this final flight. Both of these new flight attendants were only 22 years of age.

Trouble Ahead: Eight minutes after takeoff, Center informed the pilots that all landings at Washington National Airport had been stopped because of high crosswinds. The pilots elected to divert to Dulles International Airport about 20 miles west of the nation's capital. Center instructed them to intercept the 300 degree radial of the Armel VOR, descend to 8,000 feet, and expect a straight-in approach to Runway 12.

The Armel VOR was located at Dulles Airport. Intercepting the 300 degree radial would allow the flight to track inbound on a heading of 120 degrees. That track matched the final approach course and runway heading, a simple "straight-in" approach. ILS approaches were used for other runways at Dulles International, but only a VOR/DME approach was available for Runway 12.

Center soon handed off the pilots to Dulles Approach Control. The portion of the CVR and ATC transcript, below, begins as the controller clears the flight for an approach while the airliner is still 44 miles from the airport. The first officer is flying the aircraft:

Capt: . . . . Captain, Flight 514
FO: . . . . First Officer, Flight 514
FltEngr: . . . . . Flight Engineer, Flight 514
UnidCrew: . . . . Unidentified crewmember, Flight 514
AppControl: . . . Dulles Approach Control

AppControl: TWA five-one-four, you're cleared for a VOR/DME approach to Runway one-two. (1104:05)

[the Captain acknowledges the clearance]

Capt: Eighteen-hundred [feet] is the bottom *[meaning, minimum altitude to the final approach fix]*.

FO: [I will] start down.

[the Captain reviews the approach chart and explains the airport elevation, MDA, and final approach fix at 1105:06]

FO: I hate the altitude jumping around [due to turbulence].

Capt: We have a discrepancy in our VOR's, a little but not much. Fly yours, not mine. (1106:15)

FO: [This turbulence] gives you a headache after a while, watching [the instruments] jumping around like that. (1106:42)

FO: You can feel the wind down here now. (1107:27)

[the Captain refers to the "dumb sheet," the approach chart; it shows that the minimum altitude at their location is 3,400 feet]

Capt: You know, according to this dumb sheet it says thirty-four-hundred [feet] to Round Hill is our minimum altitude.

[the Flight Engineer asks for the source of that information]

Capt: Well, here -- Round Hill is eleven-and-a-half DME.

FO: Well, but --?

Capt: When [ATC] clears you, that means you can go to your --.

UnidCrew: Initial approach?

UnidCrew: Yeah.

Capt: Initial approach altitude.

FltEngr: We're outta' twenty-eight-[hundred feet and descending] for eighteen-[hundred feet].

UnidCrew: Right. One-[thousand feet] to go.

FltEngr: Dark in here. (1108:14)

FO: And bumpy too.

[sound of an automated altitude alert at 1108:25]

Capt: I had [visual] ground contact a minute ago.

FO: Yeah, I did too.

FO: [Unintelligible] power on this [expletive]. (1108:29)

Capt: Yeah, you got a high sink rate.

FO: Yeah.

UnidCrew: We're going uphill *[meaning, toward rising terrain]*.

FltEngr: We're right there, we're on course.

UnidCrew: Yeah. Yeah.

Capt: You ought to see [the] ground outside in just a minute. Hang in there, boy.

FltEngr: We're getting seasick [from the turbulence].

FO: Boy, it was -- wanted to go right through there, man.

UnidCrew: Yeah.

FO: Must have had a [expletive] of a downdraft.

[sound of the 500 foot radio altimeter alert as the aircraft flies over the steep up-slope of Mount Weather at 1109:14]

<u>FO</u>: Boy!

<u>Capt</u>: Get some power on! (1109:20)

[sound of the 100 foot radio altimeter alert at 1109:21]

[sound of impact; end of the CVR tape at 1109:22]

<u>AppControl</u>: TWA five-one-four, say your altitude. (1109:54)

[there is no response]

The Accident: The airliner descended in thick clouds and rain and tracked inbound toward the VOR at 225 knots. At an altitude of 1,670 feet (130 feet below where they *intended* to be) the aircraft cut a swath 500 feet long through the tops of tall trees. It then disintegrated when it impacted a solid rock outcropping on the western slope of Mount Weather near Berryville, Virginia, 25 miles northwest of the airport.

Fed by about 19,300 pounds of remaining fuel in the tanks, an intense ground fire consumed much of the wreckage. Local fire departments and potential rescuers found their way to the remote site later that day, but there was nothing they could do. All 92 people aboard the aircraft had died because of "traumatic injuries" sustained during the crash.

The Investigation: Investigators from the NTSB soon found that this was an operational accident. There were no malfunctions of the aircraft or its systems. Simply stated, the pilots had descended far below the MEA and had flown their aircraft into a mountain. Yet, the *reasons* for such a descent were not so simple.

Accident reconstruction experts analyzed the chain of events prior to the crash. They found that ATC had vectored the flight to intercept the 300 degree radial of the Armel VOR at a point 80 miles from the airport. From there the pilots tracked inbound toward the navaid. This portion of the flight was *not* a part of the published VOR/DME approach.

Without an altitude restriction, Approach Control cleared Flight 514 for the approach when the aircraft was 44 miles from the airport. Investigators faced two crucial questions:

First, why did the pilots descend to 1,800 feet in an area where mountains were higher than that altitude?

Second, why did the Dulles Approach Control clearance not include an altitude restriction?

The CVR revealed that the pilots were unsure of the altitude to which they should descend. Telling his first officer and flight engineer about the "dumb sheet," the approach chart, the captain remarked that the MEA prior to reaching Round Hill Intersection was 3,400 feet. Yet, after a cockpit discussion the captain decided he could descend to 1,800 feet. That was the minimum altitude between Round Hill Intersection and the final approach fix, and he was "cleared for the approach." Investigators would report:

The captain believed that when he approached the airport in a radar environment for a non-precision approach he would not be "cleared for the approach" without an altitude restriction unless he could make an unrestricted descent to the final approach fix altitude.

Lending credence to the captain's belief was a near-tragedy that occurred six weeks earlier at the same location. ATC had given another flight "cleared for the approach" instructions west of Round Hill. Like the doomed TWA flight, this prior flight also descended to 1,800 feet. Fortunately the visibility was better. The pilots saw the mountains, climbed, and narrowly escaped disaster.

The controller had a different understanding. He did not handle the flight as a "radar arrival." Consequently, he did not provide an altitude restriction that would have kept the flight safely over the mountains west of Round Hill. He expected the pilots to fly the approach as depicted on the approach chart and adhere to its altitude restrictions. Chiming in, the FAA *claimed* that the chart identified the high terrain west of Round Hill:

It does appear to the Board that there was a deficiency in the [approach] chart.

Investigators examined the approach chart. They noted that the profile view did *not* depict either (1) Round Hill Intersection or the

(2) MEA and high terrain to the west. However, the MEA of 3,400 feet *was* shown on the plan view of the chart.

Probable Cause: The NTSB took almost a year to finalize its Aircraft Accident Report. It adopted NTSB-AAR-75-16 on 26 November 1975 and found that the accident resulted from a tragic "misunderstanding." ATC expected the pilots to fly the approach depicted on the chart. Conversely, the pilots believed that they had been cleared to descend immediately.

The board emphasized that this "general lack of understanding" caused the accident. The board members noted: "Neither the pilot nor the controller understood what the other was thinking." The board found the *Probable Cause* of the accident to be:

the crew's decision to descend to 1,800 feet before the aircraft had reached [Round Hill Intersection] where that minimum altitude applied. [This decision resulted from] inadequacies and lack of clarity in the air traffic control procedures which led to misunderstanding on the part of the pilots and of the controllers regarding each other's responsibilities.

The board pointed out that the pilots should not have descended until they passed Round Hill Intersection. On the other hand, the board found the ATC clearance to be inadequate and "not precise or definitive." The board listed three *contributing* factors that led to the tragedy:

[First], the failure of the FAA to take timely action to resolve the confusion and misinterpretation of air traffic terminology, although [the FAA] had been aware of the problem for several years. [TWA and the U.S. Air Force had put the FAA on notice that "cleared for the approach" could be misinterpreted.]

[Second, ATC issued the] approach clearance while the flight was [(1)] 44 miles from the airport [(2)] on an unpublished route [(3)] without clearly defined minimum altitudes.

[Third was the] inadequate depiction of altitude restrictions on the profile view of the approach chart for the VOR/DME approach to Runway 12 at Dulles International Airport.

Pan Am Flight 1736
and
KLM Flight 4805

Pan Am Flight 1736
Boeing 747, registration N736PA
27 March 1977, runway collision at Tenerife, Canary Islands
396 aboard, 335 killed

KLM Flight 4805
Boeing 747, registration PH-BUF
27 March 1977, runway collision at Tenerife, Canary Islands
248 aboard, 248 killed

Overview: In the Canary Islands in blinding fog a Boeing 747 began its takeoff run without a takeoff clearance. At 140 knots it collided with another Boeing 747 that was taxiing on the runway. Of the 644 people aboard the two jumbo-jets, 583 perished in the collision and intense fires that followed.

The Pan Am Flight: Pan American World Airways (Pan Am) Flight 1736 left New York on 27 March 1977 and headed for Las Palmas Airport in the Canary Islands. In antiquity this chain of islands had been known as the "Fortunate Isles" because of warm and fair weather that lasted for most of the year. Spain's famed volcanic archipelago, stretching for 250 miles off the northwest coast of Africa, had proven to be a popular vacation spot in recent times. Throughout Europe for several decades, airlines and cruise ships had zeroed in on this tourist Mecca.

Most of the passengers looked forward to several days or weeks of leisure in the balmy Atlantic paradise. As their airliner cruised high over ocean the trip seemed routine. Four Pratt & Whitney turbines powered the Boeing 747, registration N736PA, which had accumulated 25,725 hours in the air. The captain and first officer both held ATP certificates, and each had logged over 21,000 hours of flight time. Their flight engineer had logged 15,210 hours in the air. Back in the cabin the six flight attendants had their hands full with 387 passengers, over 60 per flight attendant.

The KLM Flight: Another jumbo-jet, KLM Dutch Royal Airlines (KLM) Flight 4805, left Schiphol Airport in Amsterdam early on the same morning with 248 people aboard. This special KLM flight also was headed for the airport at Las Palmas, and it had been chartered by Holland International Travel Group. The Boeing 747, registration PH-BUF, had been in service for six years and had amassed a total of 21,195 hours of flight time.

During the flight the passengers learned that their captain was featured in the current KLM in-flight magazine. He was KLM's chief flying instructor, a senior pilot of great prestige. He had been flying for 30 years, and now he specialized in training veteran pilots for his employer's Boeing 747 airliners. Back behind the flight deck crew, 11 flight attendants staffed the cabin.

Trouble Ahead: While both airliners were crossing the Atlantic a small bomb exploded in a florist shop in the terminal at Las Palmas. A terrorist group claimed responsibility, and Spanish authorities closed the airport to search for a possible second bomb. ATC diverted inbound flights to one of the archipelago's other airports on the island of Tenerife.

KLM Flight 4805 and Pan Am Flight 1736 landed at Tenerife Airport at 1338 Hours and 1415 Hours, respectively. They found the airport packed with other diverted flights. However, the airport at Las Palmas soon reopened, and aircraft waiting at Tenerife began asking for clearance to taxi to the single runway for takeoff. Las Palmas was only 25 minutes away. The passengers were eager to get there and check-in at their plush hotels or board the waiting luxury cruise ships, but a problem arose:

Weather conditions [at] the airport were getting rapidly worse.

Thick fog began descending on Tenerife. Three smaller airliners managed to taxi out to the runway and take off. Next the KLM flight began to taxi toward Runway 30. To get the airliner to the proper takeoff position, ATC told the pilots to taxi onto the runway and taxi down to the approach end.

The Pan Am flight was ready to go too. ATC instructed the Pan Am pilots to taxi onto the runway and taxi toward the approach end -- just like the KLM pilots were doing. ATC planned to have the Pan Am airliner soon turn off onto a vacant taxiway. That would clear the runway for the KLM airliner to take off. Because of the thick fog neither the KLM pilots nor the Pan Am pilots could see each other, and the tower controller could not see either aircraft. He relied on radio reports from the pilots in order to determine their position on the airport.

The portion of the CVR and ATC transcript, below, contains the verbiage from both the Pan Am and the KLM cockpits and the tower. The transcript begins as the KLM flight is taxiing down the runway. Far behind, out of sight in the fog, the Pan Am aircraft is taxiing in the same direction down the same runway. The captain is at the controls in each aircraft. In compliance with international practice the Pan Am radio call-sign is "Clipper":

PanAm-Capt: . . . . . Captain, Pan Am Flight 1736
PanAm-FO: . . . . . . First Officer, Pan Am Flight 1736
KLM-Capt: . . . . . . Captain, KLM Flight 4805
KLM-FO: . . . . First Officer, KLM Flight 4805
KLM-FltEngr: . . . . Flight Engineer, KLM Flight 4805
Radio-: . . . . (prefix) Aircraft radio transmissions
Tower: . . . . Tenerife Airport Control Tower

Radio-KLM-FO: [Tower,] you want us to turn left at Charlie one, Taxiway Charlie one? (1659:28)

Tower: Negative, negative, taxi straight ahead -- aaahhh -- up to the end of the runway and make back-track. (1659:32)

Radio-KLM-FO: OK, sir. (1659:39)

[2 minutes later the controller radios the Pan Am pilots]

Tower: Clipper one-seven-three-six, Tenerife. (1702:01)

Radio-PanAm-FO: [Tower,] ah, we were instructed to contact you and also to taxi down the runway, is that correct? (1702:03)

Tower: Affirmative, taxi onto the runway and -- aaahhh -- leave the runway [at the] third [taxiway] to your left. (1702:08)

Radio-PanAm-FO: Third [taxiway] to the left, OK. (1702:16)

Tower: KLM four-eight-zero-five, how many taxiways -- aaahhh -- did you pass? (1702:49)

Radio-KLM-FO: I think we passed Charlie four [taxiway] now.

Tower: OK -- at the end of the runway make [a] one-eighty [degree turn] and report, ah, for ATC clearance. (1702:55)

Radio-PanAm-FO: Would you confirm that you want Clipper one-seven-three-six to turn left at the third intersection? (1703:35)

Tower: Third one, sir -- one, two, three -- third one. (1703:38)

PanAm-Capt: Good, that's what we need, the third one. (1703:39)

Tower: Clipper one-seven-three-six, report leaving the runway.

Radio-PanAm-FO: [Roger], Clipper one-seven-three-six. (1703:56)

[the KLM flight reaches the approach end of the runway, turns around, and requests its ATC clearance]

Radio-KLM-FO: [Tower], KLM four-eight-zero-five is now ready for takeoff, and we are waiting for our ATC clearance. (1705:50)

Tower: KLM four-eight-zero-five, you are cleared to the Papa Beacon, climb to and maintain flight level nine-zero, right turn after takeoff, proceed [on] heading zero-four-zero until intercepting the three-two-five radial from Las Palmas [VOR]. (1705:53)

*[the KLM flight has its en route clearance but **does not have takeoff clearance**; yet, the Captain releases his brakes]*

KLM-FO: Wait a minute, we don't have an ATC clearance!

[the KLM Captain ignores his First Officer's warning]

KLM-Capt: Let's go, check thrust. (1706:12)

[sound of the KLM engines spooling up at 1706:14]

[the KLM First Officer does not challenge his Captain further; he "reads back" the en route clearance during the takeoff run]

Radio-KLM-FO: Ah, roger, sir, we're cleared to the Papa Beacon, flight level nine-zero, right turn out [to heading] zero-four-zero until intercepting the three-two-five [radial of the Las Palmas VOR], and *we are now at takeoff [emphasis added]*. (1706:17)

[ATC does not know the KLM plane is on its takeoff run]

Tower: OK, stand by for takeoff, I will call you. (1706:21)

PanAm-Capt: No, uuuhhh --. (1706:22)

[the Pan Am pilots radio that they are still on the runway]

Radio-PanAm-FO: And, we're still taxiing down the runway, [this is] the Clipper one-seven-three-six. (1706:22)

Tower: Papa Alpha *[phonetic for "Pan Am"]* one-seven-three-six, report [when] clear [of the runway]. (1706:25)

Radio-PanAm-FO: OK, we'll report when we're clear. (1706:29)

Tower: Thank you.

*[the concerned Pan Am Captain is **not sure** of the KLM pilots' intent, so he heads for the nearest taxiway to clear the runway]*

PanAm-Capt: Let's get the [expletive] out of here! (1706:30)

[meanwhile, the KLM Flight Engineer queries his Captain]

KLM-FltEngr: Is he not clear [of the runway] then? (1706:32)

KLM-Capt: What do you say? (1706:34)

KLM-FltEngr: Is he not clear, that Pan American? (1706:34)

KLM-Capt: Oh, yes! *[spoken emphatically]* (1706:35)

[the Pan Am Captain sees the landing lights of the KLM aircraft materialize out of the fog, headed straight toward him]

PanAm-Capt: There he is! Look at him coming! [Expletive], that [expletive] is coming! Get off [of the runway]! Get off [of the runway]! Get off! (1706:40)

[the KLM pilots do not yet see the Pan Am aircraft dead ahead]

KLM-FO: V-one. (1706:43)

[the KLM Captain suddenly sees the Pan Am airliner on the runway ahead of him]

<u>KLM-Capt</u>: [Unintelligible exclamation]! (1706:47)

[the KLM aircraft lifts off and <u>almost</u> clears the top of the Pan Am aircraft below on the runway]

[sound of the impact at 1706:50]

The Accident: Accelerating down the runway at 140 knots, the KLM captain saw a ghostly apparition materialize dead ahead in the fog. In a moment he recognized the outline of the Pan Am aircraft. In desperation he hauled back on his control column and tried to take off. He *almost* made it.

The KLM aircraft lifted off and began to climb. Its fuselage skimmed over the top of the Pan Am aircraft, but then its main landing gear and engines tore through the Pan Am fuselage. The KLM airliner slammed back down onto the runway 450 feet beyond the point of the collision. It skidded for over 1,000 feet and exploded into flames. The fire consumed the KLM airliner and killed all 248 people on board:

> An immediate and raging fire must have prevented emergency [evacuation] because all of the aircraft's doors remained shut.

While still taxiing on the runway the Pan Am pilots had spotted the KLM plane rushing out of the fog toward them. They jammed their throttles forward, trying to evade the monster hurtling down the runway toward them. Too late:

> In the Pan Am aircraft the first class lounge disappeared as a result of the impact [by the KLM airliner], as well as nearly the whole top of the fuselage.

In the Pan Am cabin many passengers were killed instantly by the impact. Others fell prey to flames and choking smoke. A fortunate few managed to leap out of the mangled remains of the Boeing 747. There were 396 people on the Pan Am airliner, and the collision and fire killed 335 of them.

Because of thick fog the burning aircraft were not visible from the control tower. The controller heard a series of explosions. An aircraft on the parking apron soon radioed that it saw a red glow in the mist. Alerted, the fire brigade slowly drove around the airport and eventually stumbled upon the two flaming wrecks.

Despite the best efforts of the firemen the fires burned until 0330 Hours the following morning.

The Investigation: Spanish, Dutch, and American investigators began searching for answers. They recovered the CVR and FDR from both aircraft and found the tapes to be in good condition. This was indeed fortunate, for the keys to the puzzle lay in the content of the tapes.

When the KLM first officer had "read back" the en route ATC clearance, he added the phrase: "we are now at takeoff." What did that phrase mean? What was "at takeoff"? When investigators first heard those words on the tape, they had no idea that they had been spoken while the KLM flight was roaring down the runway. The investigators noted:

> The tower, which was not expecting the aircraft to take off, as it had not given [takeoff] clearance, interpreted the sentence as: "We are now at takeoff *position [emphasis added]*."

Neither the tower nor the Pan Am pilots had been *certain* what the phrase meant. Both responded out of caution. The controller replied: "OK, stand by for takeoff, I will call you." The Pan Am crew chimed in to remind the KLM pilots and the tower that they were still taxiing down the runway.

Investigators learned there was confusion in the KLM cockpit as well. The KLM first officer had warned: "We don't have an ATC clearance [to take off]!" The captain ignored the statement. The flight engineer realized that the Pan Am aircraft might be on the runway ahead, hidden by the fog. Twice he asked the captain if the Pan Am flight had cleared the runway ahead, but the captain brushed aside both questions and continued the takeoff run.

From the CVR tapes, investigators found that the alarmed Pan Am pilots had been heading toward a taxiway to clear the runway. Then, through the fog the Pan Am captain spotted the landing lights on the onrushing KLM airliner 9.5 seconds before impact. He firewalled his throttles, but there was not enough time to get out of the way.

Aboard the KLM airliner the first officer had intoned "V-one" seven seconds before the collision. The KLM captain *apparently* saw the Pan Am airliner about one second later. He prematurely pulled back on his control column to try to take off. His craft mushed into the air, but his engines and main landing gear failed to clear the top of the Pan Am aircraft.

Probable Cause: The Spanish government published its lengthy "Colision Aeronaves" report over a year later on 7 December 1978. The board found that, *without takeoff clearance*, the KLM captain began his takeoff run. In thick fog the KLM aircraft collided with the Pan Am aircraft, which was still on the runway. The board found the ***Fundamental Cause*** of the accident to be four-fold, in that the KLM captain:

[First], took off without clearance.

[Second], did not obey the "stand by for takeoff" [instructions from the tower].

[Third], did not interrupt [his] takeoff on learning that the Pan Am [aircraft] was still on the runway.

[Fourth], in reply to [his] flight engineer's query as to whether the Pan Am [aircraft] had left the runway, replied emphatically in the affirmative.

The report listed several factors which ***contributed*** to the accident:

[First, the KLM captain was in a hurry.] . . . if he did not take off within a relatively short space of time he might have to [postpone] the flight [because of "duty time" restrictions].

[Second], layers of low-lying [fog restricted] visibility.

[Third], two radio transmissions took place at the same time. The "stand by for takeoff, I will call you" [transmission] from the tower coincided with Pan Am's "we are still taxiing down the runway" [transmission]. [The KLM pilots may not have clearly heard either message, both of which were crucial.]

[Fourth], when the KLM [first officer stated], "we are now at takeoff," the controller, who had not been asked for a takeoff clearance, and who consequently had not granted it, did not understand that [the KLM aircraft] was taking off.

Southern Airways Flight 242

Douglas DC-9, registration N1335U
4 April 1977, at New Hope, Georgia
85 aboard, 64 killed (plus 8 killed on the ground)

Overview: When a Douglas DC-9 tried to penetrate a severe thunderstorm, massive amounts of heavy hail and rain caused both engines to fail. The pilots tried to land on a narrow rural roadway. The airliner sideswiped trees, utility poles, fences, and skidded into the community of New Hope, Georgia. There were 85 people on board, and 64 of them died in the crash and fire. The accident also killed eight people on the ground in New Hope.

The Flight: At 1554 Hours on the stormy afternoon of 4 April 1977, Southern Airways Flight 242 took off from Huntsville, Alabama. The airliner headed for Hartsfield International Airport in nearby Atlanta, Georgia, only 25 minutes away. Two Pratt & Whitney turbines powered the reliable twin-jet Douglas DC-9, registration N1335U, owned by McDonnell Douglas Leasing Corporation and leased to Southern Airways.

The DC-9 carried 81 passengers, and two pilots and two flight attendants comprised the crew. The experienced captain, age 54, had been flying for Southern Airways for 17 years, and he had been promoted to captain on the DC-9 two months before this final flight. He held an ATP certificate and had logged 19,380 flight hours. His young first officer, age 34, held a Commercial Pilot certificate and had 3,878 hours in his logbook. When not flying with Southern Airways he was a military pilot in the U.S. Navy Reserve. The two experienced flight attendants, ages 22 and 26, had flown a total of 6,312 hours with Southern Airways:

A squall line extended northeastward from near Meridian, Mississippi, through northern Alabama and northeastern Georgia.

The pilots knew that they would fly into rough weather. A cold front was sweeping across their path. Looking at his onboard radar weather display three minutes after takeoff, the captain opined: "Well, the radar is full of it *[meaning, full of thunderstorms]*, take your pick." With the first officer flying the aircraft the captain and Huntsville Departure Control tried to figure out the least turbulent route through the storms.

Trouble Ahead: Flying through rain and light turbulence at 17,000 feet, the pilots contacted Atlanta Center. A few moments later, looking at the storms on his radar display, the captain told his first officer: "Looks heavy, nothing's going through that."

Suddenly violent turbulence and downdrafts forced the flight to drop 3,000 feet. Huge chunks of hail shattered -- but did not crush in -- the windshield. The portion of the CVR transcript, below, begins as the first officer fights to regain control and climb:

<u>Capt</u>:	Captain, Flight 242
<u>FO</u>:	First Officer, Flight 242
<u>FltAtt(F)</u>:	Flight Attendant in Front cabin, Flight 242
<u>FltAtt(R)</u>:	Flight Attendant in Rear cabin, Flight 242
<u>Radio-</u>:	(prefix) Radio transmission, Flight 242
<u>ICS-</u>:	(prefix) ICS transmission, Flight 242
<u>PA-</u>:	(prefix) Public Address system, Flight 242
<u>Center</u>:	Atlanta Center (ARTCC)
<u>AppControl</u>: . . .	Atlanta Approach Control

<u>FO</u>: [I] got it, [I] got it back, Bill! [I] got it back! (1608:37)

*[extreme turbulence, sound of **heavy rain and large hail**]*

<u>PA-FltAtt(R)</u>: . . . in the unlikely event that there is a need for an emergency landing, we do ask that you please grab your ankles, I will scream from the rear of the aircraft . . . [if] you hear us holler, please grab your ankles! (1608:38)

<u>Radio-Capt</u>: [Center, this is Southern] two-forty-two, uh, we just got our windshield busted and -- uh -- we'll try to get it back up to fifteen-[thousand feet], we're [at] fourteen. (1609:15)

<u>Center</u>: Southern two-forty-two, you say you're at fourteen now?

<u>Radio-Capt</u>: Yes -- uuuhhh -- couldn't help it. (1609:27)

[the No. 1 engine begins to fail at 1609:34]

FO: Left engine won't spool! (1609:36)

Radio-Capt: [Center], our left engine just cut out. (1609:37)

Center: Southern two-forty-two, roger, and, uh, [I have] lost your transponder [signal], squawk five-six-two-three. (1609:43)

Radio-Capt: Five-six-two-three, we're squawking. (1609:49)

FO: Autopilot's off, I've got it, I'll hand-fly it. (1609:59)

Center: Southern two-forty-two, you can descend and maintain one-three-thousand now, that'll get you down lower. (1610:00)

[the No. 2 engine begins to fail at 1610:02]

FO: My -- the other engine's [failing] too, [expletive]! (1610:04)

Radio-Capt: Stand by, we lost both engines. (1610:10)

FO: All right, Bill, get us a vector to a clear area. (1610:14)

Radio-Capt: Get us a vector to a clear [airport], Atlanta. (1610:16)

Center: Southern two-forty-two, contact Approach Control [on] one-two-six-point-nine, and they'll try to get you straight into Dobbins [Air Force Base, north of Atlanta]. (1610:30)

FO: Give me -- I'm familiar with Dobbins -- tell them to give me a vector to Dobbins if they're clear. (1610:36)

[the First Officer tries to re-start the engines]

FO: Ignition override -- it's gotta work. (1610:50)

[electrical power to the CVR is interrupted for 1 minute and 4 seconds, then restored at 1613:00]

Radio-Capt: Uh, Atlanta, [do] you read Southern two-forty-two?

AppControl: Southern two-forty-two, Atlanta Approach Control, go ahead. (1613:08)

Radio-Capt: We've lost both engines, how about a vector to the nearest [airport], we're at seven-thousand feet. (1613:11)

AppControl: Southern two-forty-two, roger, turn right heading one-zero-zero, will be vectors to Dobbins for a straight-in approach,

Runway one-one, altimeter two-niner-five-two, your position is fifteen, correction, twenty miles west of Dobbins. (1613:18)

PA-FltAtt(R): Ladies and gentlemen, please check that your seatbelts are securely [fastened] across your pelvis area.

FO: What's the Dobbins weather, Bill? How far is it?

[for 1 minute and 13 seconds more the pilots follow Approach Control's radar vectors toward Dobbins Air Force Base, where they hope to glide down and make an emergency landing]

Radio-Capt: [Approach Control], we're out of -- uh -- fifty-eight-hundred [feet, and our airspeed is] two-hundred knots. (1614:40)

FO: What's our [bug] speed? Let's see, what's our weight, Bill? Get me a bug speed. (1614:44)

AppControl: Southern two-forty-two, do you have one engine running now? (1614:45)

Radio-Capt: Negative, no engines. (1614:48)

Capt: Just don't stall this thing out. (1615:04)

[the pilots continue to glide toward Dobbins Air Force Base]

AppControl: Southern two-forty-two, Dobbins weather is two-thousand [feet] scattered, estimated ceiling three-thousand [feet] broken, seven-thousand overcast, visibility seven miles. (1615:46)

Radio-Capt: OK, we're down to forty-six-hundred [feet] now.

AppControl: Roger, and you're approximately, uh, seventeen miles west of Dobbins at this time. (1616:00)

Radio-Capt: I don't know if we can make that or not. (1616:05)

[on the ICS the Flight Attendants discuss what they should do]

ICS-FltAtt(F): Sandy? *[Sandy replies]* [The pilots] would not talk to me, when I looked in [the cockpit] the whole front windshield is cracked . . . so what do we do? (1616:28)

ICS-FltAtt(R): Have [the pilots] said anything?

ICS-FltAtt(F): Ah, [the pilot] screamed at me when I opened the [cockpit] door [and said] just sit down, so I didn't ask him a thing, I don't know the results or anything, I'm sure we decompressed.

ICS-FltAtt(R): Aaahhh, yes, [and] we've lost an engine.

ICS-FltAtt(F): I thought so.

ICS-FltAtt(R): OK, Katty, have you briefed all your passengers in the [first class cabin]?

ICS-FltAtt(F): Yes, I told them, I checked the cockpit . . . .

ICS-FltAtt(R): Take off your shoes . . . I took off my socks so I'd have more ground pull with my toes . . . .

ICS-FltAtt(F): That's a good idea, too . . . thank you, bye-bye.

> *[the pilots realize they can not reach Dobbins Air Force Base; they get vectors toward a closer airport at Cartersville, but they do not have enough altitude to reach it]*

Capt: I'm picking out a clear [farm] field. (1617:08)

FO: Bill, you've got to find me a highway. (1617:12)

Capt: Let's get the next clear open field. (1617:17)

Capt: [I] see a highway! Over [there]! (1617:35)

FO: Right there! Is that [road] straight?

Capt: No. (1617:39)

Capt: We'll have to take it. (1617:44)

> *[sound of the landing gear extending at 1617:58]*

Radio-Capt: [Approach Control], we're putting it on the highway, we're down to nothing. (1618:02)

FO: Flaps! (1618:07)

Capt: They're at fifty [degrees].

FO: Oh, [expletive], Bill, I hope we can do it!

Capt: There's a car ahead!

FO: I got it! I'm going to land right over that [car]. (1618:14)

<u>FO</u>: I've got it, Bill! I've got it now! I got it! (1618:25)

<u>Capt</u>: OK, don't stall it. (1618:30)

<u>FO</u>: I gotta bug! We're gonna do it right here! (1618:31)

[the rear Flight Attendant sees trees zip past, and she yells]

<u>PA-FltAtt(R)</u>: Bend down and grab your ankles! (1618:33)

<u>FO</u>: I got it! (1618:34)

[sound of impacts begins at 1618:36 and continues until the end of the CVR tape 7 seconds later at 1618:43]

The Accident: The first officer did an exemplary job, considering the circumstances. He lined the DC-9 up on a narrow two-lane road, Georgia State Spur 92. With the gear down, flaps at fifty degrees, slats extended, he flared to land.

The left wing smashed through two small trees, but the sturdy airliner maintained the flare. As it settled toward the road below, both wings knifed through utility poles and large trees. Still, the left main landing gear touched down on the left side of the road 570 feet beyond the point of first impact with the trees. Could they grind to a safe stop?

The left and right wings continued to strike trees and utility poles on both sides of the highway.

Then, at almost 100 knots the left wing plowed into a roadside embankment. Breaking into five main pieces, the fuselage skidded another 1,260 feet and tumbled into the rural community of New Hope, Georgia. NTSB investigators would later note:

A combination grocery store-gasoline station was destroyed by fire. A truck and five automobiles were destroyed, and an automobile and a house were substantially damaged. [Further], numerous trees, shrubs, lawns, utility poles, powerlines, mail boxes, highway signs, and fences were damaged.

The flaming remains of the DC-9 smashed through gasoline pumps at a store in New Hope, setting ruptured gasoline lines, the store, and several vehicles on fire. Fortunately there was a rural volunteer fire department in New Hope. Firemen drove two fire trucks to the accident scene. One truck and one crew fought the inferno at the gas station, while the other truck and crew hosed down the burning wreckage of the DC-9.

Of the 85 people on the aircraft, 64 were killed by the crash and the fire. Postmortem examinations showed that the captain and first officer died because of "extensive trauma." Thirty-one of the passengers died due to "extensive traumatic injuries," most of which involved "crushing of the upper torso and head." The other fatalities resulted from a combination of trauma and "burning and smoke inhalation." The crash and the fires that followed also killed eight people in the New Hope community.

Both flight attendants survived. The front flight attendant would recall that a "fireball" erupted after the first few impacts. She remembered "passengers on fire" before the aircraft stopped sliding. Five horribly burned survivors who had been seated behind the wings recalled that "smoke, fire, debris, and bodies" hampered their escape from the tangled wreckage.

The Investigation: Why had the pilots flown into the line of violent thunderstorms? Why had the engines failed?

Investigators examined the weather conditions encountered by Flight 242. During a short 10 minute period while the airliner was climbing out from Huntsville, 1.2 inches of rain fell at the airport in Rome, Georgia. That equated to an *incredible rate* of over seven inches per hour, and it fell into the path of Flight 242:

> The [NWS reported] cells of *extreme [emphasis added]* intensity containing thunderstorms with *extreme [emphasis added]* rain-showers. The cells [were] . . . northeast of the Rome VOR.

Southern Airways dispatchers had learned of tornado watches and severe thunderstorm watches. Five minutes after Flight 242 took off a tornado was spotted on its flight path near Rome. Another tornado would sweep through the suburbs of Rome at 1600 Hours, six minutes after the flight took off and headed for that very spot. According to a National Weather Service report:

> The [storm] system that moved across northeast Alabama and northwestern Georgia on the afternoon of April 4 was one of the most severe systems in the United States in the past three years.

It also was one of the fastest-moving storms on record. About 20 tornadoes and 30 severe thunderstorms were in the system.

Examination of the two DC-9 engines revealed many bent and broken blades. The missing blades and blade fragments had been ingested into the high-pressure compressors. This caused extreme damage and rendered the engines inoperative.

Probable Cause: The NTSB staff adopted NTSB-AAR-78-3 on 26 January 1978. The board found that Flight 242 penetrated a severe thunderstorm while in cruising flight at 17,000 feet. The engines ingested extraordinarily large volumes of rain and hail, lost rotational speed, and the compressors began to stall.

Before takeoff from Huntsville the pilots had gotten a routine weather briefing. They knew of the squall line, but they had been given scant information on the severity of the thunderstorms on their flight path near Rome. Southern Airways dispatch employees did not alert the pilots to the *extreme* nature of the weather hazards or the tornadoes. The captain's decision to penetrate the storm was based solely upon his onboard radar display. The board found the *Probable Cause* of the accident to be:

> the total and unique loss of thrust from both engines while the aircraft was penetrating an area of severe thunderstorms. The loss of thrust was caused by the ingestion of massive amounts of water and hail which, in combination with thrust lever movement, induced severe stalling in and major damage to the engine compressors.

The board found several ***contributing*** factors which included:

> [First], the failure of the company's dispatching system to provide the [DC-9] flightcrew with up-to-date severe weather information . . . .

> [Second], the captain's reliance on airborne weather radar for penetration of thunderstorm areas.

> [Third], limitations in the [FAA] air traffic control system which precluded the timely dissemination of real-time hazardous weather information to the flightcrew.

PSA Flight 182
and a
General Aviation Aircraft

PSA Flight 182
Boeing 727, registration N533PS
25 September 1978, mid-air collision over San Diego, California
135 aboard, 135 killed (plus 7 killed on the ground)

General Aviation Aircraft
Cessna 172, registration N7711G
25 September 1978, mid-air collision over San Diego, California
2 aboard, 2 killed

Overview: A big Boeing 727 was cleared to land at San Diego, California. Instructed to maintain *visual separation*, the airline pilots did not see a small Cessna 172. The two aircraft collided and fell to the earth. All 135 people on the Boeing airliner, the 2 Cessna pilot-occupants, and 7 people on the ground died in the collision, crashes, and fire.

The PSA Flight: Pacific Southwest Airlines (PSA) Flight 182 departed Los Angeles, California, at 0834 Hours on 25 September 1978 for the short trip down to San Diego. The passengers and crew assumed that this would be a quick flight. Unfortunately it would end about three minutes sooner than planned.

The Boeing 727, registration N533PS, had amassed a total of 24,088 flying hours. The captain, age 42, held an ATP certificate and had 14,382 hours of experience in his logbook. His first officer, equally rated, had over 10,000 hours in the air, around 5,800 of which were in the Boeing 727. Backing them up in the cockpit was their experienced flight engineer. An off-duty PSA captain was riding in the cockpit, but he was not part of the crew. Four flight attendants were responsible for the 128 passengers.

Flight 182 contacted San Diego Approach Control at 0853 Hours and descended toward the southern California metropolitan area. The weather was clear and sunny, and the pilots soon reported the airport in sight. Approach Control cleared the airliner for a *visual approach* to Runway 27 at Lindbergh Field in San Diego.

The General Aviation Flight: A small Cessna 172 owned by Gibbs Flite Center had taken off from Montgomery Field, six miles northeast of Lindbergh Field. Aboard the four-seat Cessna were a flight instructor and his experienced "student." They flew to nearby Lindbergh Field where they practiced ILS approaches.

The instructor, age 32, was an employee of Gibbs Flite Center, and he held a Commercial Pilot and Flight Instructor certificate. His "student" also was a Commercial Pilot, and on this flight he was practicing instrument flying procedures. The two Cessna pilots completed their second ILS approach at Lindbergh Field and began a climbout to the northeast.

At 0859:01 Hours, Lindbergh Tower instructed the Cessna pilots to contact Approach Control, and one minute later ATC reported "radar contact." Approach Control instructed the Cessna pilots to *maintain VFR conditions* at or below 3,500 feet and fly a specified heading. The pilots acknowledged the ATC instructions.

The Cessna pilots had not filed an IFR or a VFR flight plan and none was required, for the weather was clear with a reported visibility of 10 miles. Nonetheless, the pilots had the benefit of Stage II terminal radar services in the busy sky over San Diego. Thus far they had complied with all instructions from Lindbergh Tower and San Diego Approach Control.

Trouble Ahead: As the small Cessna climbs out from the airport, Flight 182 is descending to land. The first officer is flying the airliner. The portion of the CVR transcript, below, begins after Flight 182 contacts Approach Control. The airspace over San Diego is crowded, and ATC is in radio contact with several aircraft, not just the Cessna and Flight 182. In the interest of brevity, radio contacts with other aircraft are omitted:

Capt: . . . .   Captain, Flight 182
FO: . . . .   First Officer, Flight 182
FltEngr: . . . . .   Flight Engineer, Flight 182

UnidCrew: . . . .   Unidentified crewmember, Flight 182
OffDutyCrew: .   Off-duty Captain in the cockpit, Flight 182
Radio-: . . . . . .   (prefix) Radio transmission, Flight 182
Tower: . . . . . .   Lindbergh Field Control Tower
AppControl: . . .   San Diego Approach Control

Radio-FO: Approach [Control], PSA one-eighty-two's out of nine-five, descending to seven-thousand, the airport's in sight. (0857:01)

AppControl: PSA one-eighty-two's cleared [for] *visual approach [emphasis added]*, Runway two-seven. (0857:06)

Radio-FO: Thank you, cleared [for a] *visual approach [emphasis added]*, [Runway] two-seven. (0857:09)

[over 2 minutes later Flight 182 receives the first ATC advisory]

AppControl: PSA one-eighty-two, traffic [at] twelve o'clock, one mile, northbound. (0859:30)

Radio-Capt: We're looking [for the traffic]. (0859:35)

[Flight 182 receives the second ATC advisory]

AppControl: PSA one-eighty-two, additional traffic's -- ah -- twelve o'clock, three miles, just north of the field, northeastbound, a Cessna one-seventy-two climbing VFR out of one-thousand-four-hundred [feet]. (0859:39)

Radio-FO: OK, we've got that other [traffic at] twelve. (0859:50)

AppControl: Cessna seven-seven-one-one-golf, [this is] San Diego Departure, radar contact, *maintain VFR conditions [emphasis added]* at or below three-thousand-five-hundred [feet], fly heading zero-seven-zero, vector [to the] final approach course. (0859:57)

[Flight 182 receives the third ATC advisory]

AppControl: PSA one-eighty-two, traffic's at twelve o'clock, three miles, [climbing] out of one-thousand-seven-hundred. (0900:15)

FO: Got 'em [in sight]. (0900:21)

Radio-Capt: Traffic in sight. (0900:22)

AppControl: [PSA one-eighty-two], *maintain visual separation [emphasis added]*, contact Lindbergh Tower [on] one-three-three-point-three, have a nice day now. (0900:23)

FO: Flaps two. (0900:25)

Radio-Capt: OK. (0900:28)

Radio-Capt: Lindbergh, PSA one-eighty-two, downwind. (0900:34)

[Flight 182 receives the <u>fourth ATC advisory</u>]

Tower: PSA one-eighty-two, Lindbergh Tower -- ah -- traffic [at] twelve o'clock, one mile, a Cessna. (0900:38)

[the pilots look for the Cessna but do not see it; they discuss where it might be]

Capt: Is that the one we were looking at? (0900:42)

FO: Yeah, but I don't see him now. (0900:43)

Radio-Capt: OK, we had it there a minute ago. (0900:44)

Tower: [PSA] one-eighty-two, roger. (0900:47)

Radio-Capt: I think he passed off to our right. (0900:50)

Tower: Yeah. (0900:51)

Capt: He was right over here a minute ago. (0900:52)

FO: Yeah. (0900:53)

Tower: How far are you going to take your downwind, one-eighty-two? Company traffic is waiting for departure. (0900:53)

Radio-Capt: Ah, probably about three to four miles. (0900:57)

Tower: PSA one-eighty-two, [you are] cleared to land. (0901:07)

Radio-Capt: One-eighty-two's cleared to land. (0901:08)

FO: Are we clear of that Cessna? (0901:11)

FltEngr: Supposed to be. (0901:13)

Capt: I guess. (0901:14)

OffDutyCrew: I hope. (0901:20)

Capt: Oh, yeah, before we turned downwind I saw him [at] about one o'clock, [he is] probably behind us now. (0901:21)

FO: Gear down. (0901:31)

[sound of landing gear extension at 0901:34]

FO: There's [an aircraft] underneath [us] -- I was looking at that inbound [aircraft] there. (0901:38)

[the pilots suddenly see the Cessna directly in front of them]

Capt: Whoop! (0901:45)

FO: Aaaggghhh! (0901:46)

*[sound of the **collision** at 0901:47]*

OffDutyCrew: Oh, [expletive]! (0901:47)

Capt: Easy, baby! Easy, baby! What have we got? (0901:49)

FO: It's bad. (0901:52)

Capt: Huh? (0901:52)

FO: We're hit, man! We are hit! (0901:53)

*[the airliner, right wing low, begins to **spiral earthward**]*

Radio-Capt: Tower, we're going down, this is PSA! (0901:55)

Tower: OK, we'll call the [crash] equipment for you. (0901:57)

UnidCrew: Whhhooo! (0901:58)

[sound of stall warning at 0901:58]

Radio-Capt: This is it, baby! (0901:59)

UnidCrew: Bob! (0901:59)

Capt: Brace yourself! (0902:03)

UnidCrew: Ma, I love yah! (0902:04)

[end of the CVR tape at 0902:04]

[3 seconds later, impact with the ground at 0902:07]

The Accident: Both aircraft were flying in the same direction, with the big Boeing 727 rapidly overtaking the small Cessna 172. From behind, the airliner caught up with the hapless Cessna and slammed into it 2,600 feet above the ground.

Enhancement of two in-flight post-collision photographs would show massive damage to the airliner's right wing and its control surfaces. Several leading edge devices were totally ripped away. A large part of the wing leading edge, back to the front spar, had been bashed in. A raging fire trailing back from ruptured fuel cells in the wing made it impossible to photographically analyze damage to the trailing edge devices.

After impact the Boeing 727 began a shallow right descending turn. The fire increased in intensity as the doomed airliner arced down toward the ground. Electrical power to the CVR was lost at 0902:04 Hours. Three seconds later, nose far down, banked 50 degrees to the right, Flight 182 dove into a residential area of San Diego three miles north of the airport. No one on board had a chance. Seismological instruments recorded the massive ground impact, and all 135 people aboard died instantly. The crash and the intense fire that followed killed seven people on the ground and destroyed or damaged 22 homes:

> The Cessna 172 was damaged extensively by the collision and fell to the ground in pieces.

Unlike the airliner, the small Cessna 172 did not *arc* down to the ground. Instead, the small aircraft "broke up immediately and exploded." Both pilots were killed instantly.

The Investigation: ATC had maintained radar and radio contact with both aircraft, and both were receiving active Stage II terminal radar services. How could this accident have happened?

The key lay in the ATC terminology, *maintain VFR conditions* and *visual approach*. In the clear sky over San Diego those terms placed the burden to "see and avoid" other aircraft on the pilots. After issuing "visual" clearances, conflicting traffic warnings from ATC became mere *advisories* to aid the pilots:

> After Flight 182 was cleared for the visual approach . . . federal regulations required the crew to "see and avoid" other aircraft.

In reconstructing this mid-air collision, NTSB investigators documented three traffic *advisories* from Approach Control and another from Lindbergh Tower. The controllers had pointed out potentially conflicting traffic to the pilots of Flight 182. However, between 0858 Hours and 0905 Hours, Lindbergh Tower was in radio contact with six airborne aircraft. Consequently, investigators could not be certain *which* aircraft the PSA pilots saw when they replied, "traffic in sight."

Analysis suggested, however, that the PSA pilots were looking at a *different aircraft* when they said the traffic was in sight. The ATC controllers had no way to know this. In any event the PSA pilots did not have, or keep, the Cessna in sight and did not convey this information to the controller.

ATC issued its last advisory to Flight 182 at 0900:38 Hours, 69 seconds before the collision. ATC reported that the Cessna was one mile ahead and flying essentially the same heading:

> [A cockpit] visibility study showed that when the [last two] advisories were issued, the Cessna would have been almost centered on both [PSA] pilot's windshields.

An *overtaking* aircraft is responsible for avoiding a slower aircraft under visual separation procedures. Yet, verbiage in the Boeing cockpit showed that the pilots thought the Cessna had passed behind or beneath them. Instead, it was dead ahead.

The automated "conflict alert" sounded in Approach Control at 0901:28 Hours, a mere 19 seconds before the collision:

> indicating to the controller that the predicted flight paths of Flight 182 and the Cessna would enter the computer's prescribed warning parameters.

The controller radioed an advisory to the Cessna pilots:

> Traffic in your vicinity, a PSA jet, [he] has you in sight, he's descending for [landing at] Lindbergh.

ATC did not radio a similar advisory to Flight 182, for its pilots had reported (erroneously) that they had the Cessna in sight. The final crucial seconds ticked away, and the two aircraft collided.

Probable Cause: Seven months after the accident the NTSB adopted the Aircraft Accident Report, NTSB-AAR-79-5, on 20 April 1979. The board made it clear that the pilots of both aircraft had been responsible for maintaining *visual* clearance from other aircraft in flight. They also were required to comply with ATC instructions in the controlled airspace around Lindbergh Field.

The board found that the Cessna pilots failed to maintain the heading assigned to them by Lindbergh Tower. However, the much faster airliner was overtaking the Cessna. It was unlikely that the Cessna pilots could have seen the huge airliner bearing down on them from behind.

The board *theorized* that when ATC told the airline pilots that the Cessna was straight ahead, one mile away, the airline pilots did not see it. They likely saw a different aircraft and *assumed* that it was the Cessna reported by ATC. However, the controller took no action, for the airline pilots *said* they had the Cessna in sight. The NTSB found the ***Probable Cause*** of this accident to be:

> the failure of the flight-crew of Flight 182 to comply with the provisions of a maintain-visual-separation clearance, including the requirement to inform the controller when they no longer had the other aircraft in sight.

The NTSB members found that a ***contributing*** cause was the ATC procedure in use. This procedure authorized controllers to "use visual separation procedures to separate two aircraft on potentially conflicting tracks" in the controlled airspace around Lindbergh Field. ATC had the *capability* to "provide either lateral or vertical radar separation to either aircraft" but did not do so.

United Airlines Flight 173

Douglas DC-8, registration N8082U
28 December 1978, at Portland, Oregon
189 aboard, 10 killed

Overview: A Douglas DC-8 approached Portland, Oregon, for landing. In VFR conditions with the airport in sight, the pilots circled while checking a potential problem with the landing gear. Preoccupied, they ran out of fuel and crashed. There were 189 people on board and -- miraculously -- 179 survived.

The Flight: Three days after Christmas in 1978, United Airlines Flight 173 left Denver, Colorado, and headed for Portland, Oregon. The Douglas DC-8, registration N8082U, was a "stretched" version of the original design, and it could carry over 250 passengers. The airliner had been manufactured in 1968 and delivered to United Airlines on 22 May of that year. Four Pratt & Whitney turbines provided the thrust necessary to whisk passengers from coast to coast or from continent to continent.

For the 2 hour and 26 minute trip to Portland in clear VFR weather the pilots would have an hour of fuel in reserve. Checking fuel status in flight would be easy. For the fuel tanks on the DC-8 there are eight fuel quantity gauges in the cockpit. Plus, there is a "totalizer" that registers the total amount of fuel in all the tanks. In addition there are gauges that continually monitor the rate of fuel flow to each of the four engines:

> The total amount of fuel required for the flight to Portland was 31,900 lbs. There [were] 46,700 lbs of fuel on board when the aircraft departed the gate at Denver.

The experienced captain, age 52, had been employed by United Airlines for 27 years. He held an ATP certificate and had over 27,000 flight hours in his logbook. The first officer, age 45, had logged 8,209 hours and held a Commercial Pilot certificate. The flight engineer had amassed 3,895 hours of experience. Five seasoned flight attendants were responsible for the care of the 181 passengers, including six infants.

Trouble Ahead: The airliner neared its destination right on schedule, just as darkness was setting in. With the airport in sight, the first officer called for landing gear extension. Surprise! When the captain lowered the gear the aircraft suddenly yawed to the right. Everyone aboard felt a hard *jolt* and heard a loud *thump*.

Instead of landing the captain decided to fly south of the airport and troubleshoot the abnormal jolt and noise. In the cockpit the right main landing gear "down-and-locked" light did not illuminate. The gear *looked like* it was down and locked. Was it? The captain wanted to take all practical precautions. He was in no hurry, for the nearby airport lights were in sight, and he had plenty of fuel.

At 1712 Hours the captain began holding at 5,000 feet. The holding pattern kept the aircraft within sight of the airport lights. The crew radioed the United maintenance base and reviewed the problem. Also, just as a precaution the captain instructed the flight attendants to prepare the cabin and passengers for an emergency evacuation. In the remote event that the landing gear collapsed when the DC-8 landed, he wanted to be prepared:

> The aircraft continued to circle under the direction of Portland Approach [Control] . . . southeast of the airport.

Meanwhile, as the minutes ticked away the engines continued to gulp down precious fuel at a normal rate. The crew periodically discussed the amount of fuel remaining. Somehow, though, the *reality* of the situation did not sink in. They could see the airport lights. They could land at any time. The only possible problem seemed to be the landing gear.

At 1750 Hours the captain decided to wait until the flight attendants completed their preparations in the cabin. He would land in about 15 minutes, he said. The flight engineer, who had been watching the dwindling fuel supply, replied:

> Fifteen minutes is gonna really run us low on fuel here.

No one else shared the flight engineer's concern. The portion of the CVR transcript, below, begins as the crewmembers leisurely discuss the landing gear anomaly and the on-going preparations in the cabin. The first officer is flying the airliner:

Capt: . . . . Captain, Flight 173
FO: . . . . First Officer, Flight 173
FltEngr: . . . . . Flight Engineer, Flight 173
FltAtt: . . . . Flight Attendant, Flight 173
Radio-: . . . . . . (prefix) Radio transmission, Flight 173
AppControl: . . . Portland Approach Control

FltEngr: [Our maintenance manager says that] you guys have done everything you can, and I [told him that] we're reluctant to recycle the gear for fear something is bent or broken and we won't be able to get it [back] down. (1751:16)

Capt: Ah, call the ramp, give 'em our passenger count, including [infants], tell 'em we'll land with about four-thousand pounds of fuel and tell them to [notify] the fire department. I want United mechanics to check the airplane after we stop. (1751:35)

FltEngr: Yes sir. (1752:02)

[routine cockpit conversation for 1 minute and 28 seconds]

FltEngr: [Our maintenance manager] wants to know if we'll be landing about five [minutes] after [1800 Hours]. (1753:30)

Capt: Yes.

[routine cockpit conversation for 3 minutes and 23 seconds]

FO: How much fuel you got now? (1756:53)

FltEngr: Four, four -- thousand -- in each -- four-thousand pounds.

Capt: You might, you might just take a walk back through the cabin and kinda see how things are going, OK? (1757:21)

Capt: I don't want to hurry [the Flight Attendants], but I'd like to [land] in another, oh, ten minutes or so. (1757:30)

[the Flight Engineer leaves the cockpit and goes into the cabin]

*[with only 4,000 pounds of fuel remaining, **fuel exhaustion** will occur in 18 minutes; yet, the Captain and First Officer routinely discuss the landing gear and the cabin preparations]*

[after 4 minutes the Flight Engineer returns to the cockpit]

Capt: OK, how are the people [in the cabin]?

FltEngr: Well, they're pretty calm and cool, ah, some of 'em are obviously nervous, ah, but for the most part they're taking it in stride -- they -- I stopped and reassured [some of them]. (1801:39)

Capt: OK, well, about two minutes before landing -- that will be about four miles out -- just pick up the mike, the PA, and say, ["] Assume the brace position.["] (1802:08)

FltEngr: We got about three-[thousand pounds left] on the fuel, and that's it. (1802:22)

[with only 3,000 pounds of fuel remaining, **fuel exhaustion** *will occur in 13 minutes]*

[the aircraft is headed toward the airport, which is only 6 miles away; however, the Captain turns away and flies toward a point 18 miles from the airport]

[almost 4 minutes pass; a Flight Attendant enters the cockpit]

Capt: How are you doing? (1806:19)

FltAtt: Well, I think we're ready . . . they've assigned helpers and showed people how to open exits . . . they've got able-bodied men by the [emergency exits]. (1806:21)

Capt: OK, we're going to go in [and land] now, we should be landing in about five minutes.

FltEngr: I think you just lost number four [engine], Buddy, you --.

FO: Better get some cross-feeds open there or something.

FltEngr: OK.

FO: We're goin' to lose an engine, Buddy. (1806:46)

Capt: Why? Why? (1806:49)

FO: Fuel! Open the cross-feeds, man! (1806:52)

Capt: Open the cross-feeds there or something!

FltEngr: [The fuel gauges are] showing fumes. (1806:55)

Capt: [They are] showing a thousand [pounds] or better.

FO: I don't think [the fuel is] in there. (1807:00)

FO: [The engine has] flamed out. (1807:06)

Radio-Capt: United one-seven-three would like clearance for an approach into [Runway] two-eight left, now. (1807:12)

AppControl: United one-seventy-three heavy, OK, roll out heading zero-one-zero -- [will] be a vector to, visual [approach], Runway two-eight left, and -- aaahhh -- you can report when you have the airport in sight suitable for a visual approach. (1807:17)

FltEngr: We're going to lose [engine] number three in a minute too. It's showing zero [fuel remaining]. (1807:27)

Capt: You got a thousand pounds! You got to!

FltEngr: [There was] five-thousand [pounds of fuel] in there, Buddy, but we [used] it.

[over 1 minute passes]

Capt: You gotta keep 'em running, Frostie. (1808:42)

FltEngr: Yes sir.

FO: [Let's] get this [aircraft] on the ground! (1808:45)

Radio-Capt: United one-seven-three has got the field in sight and we'd like an ASR to, uh, [Runway] two-eight left. (1808:50)

AppControl: OK, United one-seventy-three heavy, maintain five-thousand [feet]. (1808:58)

Radio-Capt: Maintain five-[thousand feet]. (1809:03)

FltEngr: We're down to one-[thousand] on the totalizer. (1809:16)

FltEngr: Number two is empty. (1809:17)

[1 minute and 30 seconds pass]

Radio-Capt: How far [do] you show us from the field? (1810:47)

AppControl: Aaahhh, I'd call it eighteen flying miles. (1810:51)

FltEngr: Boy, that fuel sure went to Hell all of a sudden, I told you we had four-[thousand pounds]. (1810:59)

Capt: There's, ah, kind of an interstate highway type thing along that bank on the river -- in case we're short. (1811:14)

Capt: That's Troutdale [a small airport] over there -- about six of one, half-dozen of the other. (1812:04)

Radio-Capt: What's our distance now? (1812:42)

AppControl: Twelve flying miles. (1812:45)

Capt: [The airport is] about three minutes -- four. (1812:52)

FltEngr: We've lost two engines, guys! We just lost two engines, [number] one and [number] two. (1813:25)

FO: You got all the pumps on and everything? (1813:28)

FltEngr: Yep.

AppControl: United one-seventy-three heavy, contact Portland Tower, one-one-eight-point-seven, you're about eight or niner flying miles from the airport. (1813:29)

Capt: They're all going [meaning, the engines are flaming out]! We can't make Troutdale! (1813:38)

FO: We can't make anything! (1813:43)

Capt: OK, declare a mayday. (1813:46)

Radio-FO: Portland Tower, United one-seventy-three heavy. Mayday! We're -- the engines are flaming out. We're going down. We're not going to be able to make the airport. (1813:50)

[end of the CVR tape at 1813:58]

The Accident: The DC-8 had turned into an expensive glider. Electrical power to the CVR was lost when the engines flamed out, causing all the generators to fail. About 44 seconds later, with the flaps and gear down, the wings cut through two tall trees. Another 541 feet along its flight track the airliner mushed into a wooded area that cushioned the crash. Trees ripped off both of the wings and the landing gear. However, the fuel tanks were empty, so there was no fire. The airliner plowed through an unoccupied house as it skidded to a stop five miles from the airport.

The Port of Portland Fire Department (airport), the Portland Fire Department (city), and the Multnomah Rural Fire District rushed a total of 39 fire and rescue vehicles to the crash site. Because there was no fire the firefighters took charge of extrication, search and rescue, and triage functions. There were homes and apartments in the vicinity, but only two unoccupied houses were destroyed:

> The 10 persons who were killed in the crash died from impact trauma. Some passengers sustained serious injuries during the evacuation.

Many injuries were incurred as people crawled out of the jagged wreckage in the dark. Twenty-two people were hospitalized with "serious injuries ranging from multiple fractures of extremities to fractures of cervical vertebrae." Yet, there had been 189 people on board Flight 173, and only 10 of them were killed.

The Investigation: NTSB investigators soon found that the landing gear had been down and locked. Corrosion had weakened a joint in the right main landing gear retract cylinder. When a piston rod end broke free, it allowed the gear to *fall* from the retracted position to the down-and-locked position. The sudden stop when the gear slammed into position caused the heavy jolt and noise. It also damaged the gear position indicating system, which prevented the down-and-locked light from illuminating in the cockpit. Also, because the right gear was down before the left gear, aerodynamic drag caused the strong yaw to the right.

Investigators turned to the fuel system. They checked the fuel flow indicators, fuel quantity gauges, and totalizer. Each gauge that they tested provided accurate fuel measurement. There was no indication of erroneous fuel metering and no indication of abnormal fuel flow to the four engines. Investigators pointed out:

> The fuel quantity indicating system accurately indicated fuel quantity to the crew. *[and also]* All of the aircraft's engines flamed out because of *fuel exhaustion [emphasis added]*.

Flight 173 had reached Portland within two minutes of the estimated arrival time. The rate of fuel consumption was normal, and the tanks held enough fuel for another hour of flight. The captain began holding at 1712 Hours, and investigators noted:

> Throughout the landing delay, Flight 173 remained at 5,000 feet
> with landing gear down and flaps set at 15 degrees. Under these
> conditions the Safety Board estimated that the flight would have
> been burning fuel at the rate of about 13,209 lbs per hour -- 220
> lbs per minute.

The aircraft simply flew around the Portland area for 1 hour and
2 minutes until the fuel supply was exhausted. The fuel gauges
were visible to the pilots and flight engineer. The crew knew how
much fuel was left in the tanks, and they knew the consumption
rate. The fuel exhaustion time was totally predictable. Yet,
preoccupied with the landing gear, the crew somehow failed to
equate (1) the decreasing fuel remaining with (2) the *time*
remaining until total fuel exhaustion. When the engines began
flaming out and the crew realized the impending peril, they were
too far from the airport. Time had run out.

Probable Cause: Less than six months after Flight 173 crashed
the NTSB adopted NTSB-AAR-79-7, the Aircraft Accident Report,
on 7 June 1979. Other than the failure of the right landing gear
retract mechanism, the board found no evidence of any failure of
the aircraft's structure, engines, flight controls, or systems. No
problem was found in the fuel measuring system, and there initially
had been plenty of fuel in the DC-8 tanks. The board found that
the *Probable Cause* of this accident was:

> the failure of the captain to monitor properly the aircraft's fuel
> state and to properly respond to the low fuel state and the
> crewmembers' advisories regarding fuel state. This resulted in
> fuel exhaustion in all engines. His inattention resulted from
> preoccupation with a landing gear malfunction and preparations
> for a possible landing emergency.

The board found that a *contributing* cause was the:

> failure of the other two flight crewmembers either to fully
> comprehend the criticality of the fuel state, or to successfully
> communicate their concern to the captain.

American Airlines Flight 191

Douglas DC-10, registration N110AA
25 May 1979, at Chicago, Illinois
271 aboard, 271 killed (plus 2 killed on the ground)

Overview: A Douglas DC-10 accelerated down the runway at Chicago, Illinois. As the aircraft took off the No. 1 engine and pylon ripped off of the left wing. The DC-10 climbed to a height of 375 feet. Then it slowly rolled inverted, dove into the ground, and exploded. The crash and fire killed all 271 people on board.

The Flight: From the gate at O'Hare International Airport at Chicago, Illinois, 258 passengers and 13 crewmembers boarded American Airlines Flight 191 for a trip to Los Angeles, California. None of them could have had any possible inkling that their flight would be cut short. It would last only 35 seconds.

The pilots began to taxi toward Runway 32R at 1459 Hours. They selected 10 degrees of flaps and extended the slats. For their gross weight of 379,000 pounds they calculated the takeoff speeds: V-1, 139 knots; V-r, 145 knots; and V-2, 153 knots.

The DC-10, registration N110AA, had been delivered from the factory on 25 February 1972 and had accumulated 19,871 flight hours. Three huge General Electric CF6-6D engines, each rated at 40,000 pounds of thrust, powered the airliner. The captain, age 53, held an ATP certificate and had logged 22,500 flying hours. His first officer, age 49, held a Commercial Pilot certificate and had 9,275 hours of flying experience. Their flight engineer had logged over 15,000 hours in various types of transport category aircraft. Ten flight attendants staffed the cabin to care for the 258 unwary and trusting passengers.

Trouble Ahead: Flight 191 taxied into position on the runway. There was no indication of any problem or impending hazard. At 1502 Hours the tower controller issued the takeoff clearance. The first officer began a rolling takeoff and stabilized the thrust from his three engines when the airspeed reached 80 knots.

The portion of the brief CVR and ATC transcript, below, begins as the captain acknowledges the takeoff clearance:

<u>Capt</u>: . . . . . .   Captain, Flight 191
<u>Radio-</u>: . . . . .   (prefix) Radio transmission, Flight 191
<u>Tower</u>: . . . . .   Chicago Airport Control Tower
<u>IntraTower</u>: . . .   IntraTower remarks and conversation

<u>Radio-Capt</u>: American one-ninety-one [is] under way. (1502:46)

<u>Capt</u>: V-one *[139 knots, the "go" or "no-go" decision speed].*

<u>Capt</u>: V-r *[145 knots, the rotation speed].* (1503:30)

*[all thrust from the **No. 1 engine is lost** at 1503:31]*

<u>Capt</u>: [Expletive]! (1503:32)

[the DC-10 lifts off from the runway at 1503:33]

[the CVR stops recording at 1503:33]

[the controller in the tower has seen the engine and pylon tear off of the left wing]

<u>IntraTower</u>: Look at this! Look at this! He lost an engine. [The emergency] equipment, we need [the emergency] equipment. He blew an engine. Oh, [expletive]!

<u>IntraTower</u>: Right by that [unintelligible].

[the DC-10 climbs straight ahead and accelerates to 172 knots; then the airspeed begins to decrease]

<u>Tower</u>: American one-ninety-one heavy, [do] you want to come back [and land], and on what runway?

[there is no response from Flight 191]

<u>IntraTower</u>: He's not talking to me.

<u>IntraTower</u>: Yeah, and he's gonna lose that wing.

<u>IntraTower</u>: There he goes! There he goes!

[the aircraft impacts the ground at 1504:08]

The Accident: The takeoff roll seemed normal until one second prior to rotation. At that time the No. 1 engine, slung on a pylon under the left wing, suddenly tore off of the aircraft. The entire engine and pylon assembly ripped away, rotated up and over the wing, and then fell onto the runway below.

From their cockpit instrumentation and the sudden left yaw the pilots knew they had lost the *thrust* from their No. 1 engine. The engines are not visible from the cockpit, so the pilots had no way to know that the engine and pylon assembly had ***ripped off*** of the aircraft. They followed the engine failure emergency procedure. Already past the V-1 (*"go"* or *"no-go"*) decision speed, they lifted off 6,000 feet down the runway.

Powered by two remaining engines (the No. 2 engine embedded in the vertical stabilizer and the No. 3 engine slung under the right wing) the DC-10 climbed straight ahead and accelerated. The pilots seemed to have complete control of the aircraft. However:

> During the climb the aircraft began to decelerate from 172 KIAS at an average rate of about 1 knot per second. At 20 seconds after liftoff at 325 feet agl and 159 knots the flight began a roll to the left . . . .

The wings rolled past the vertical position, and the roll continued until the aircraft was inverted. The DC-10 dove down into an open field and exploded upon impact. All 271 people on board died in the crash and the fuel-fed inferno that followed:

> The aircraft exploded . . . and was scattered into an open field and a trailer park. The disintegration of the aircraft structure was so extensive that little useful data was obtained . . . .

Flying flaming debris killed two people on the ground, and two others suffered severe burns. Burning wreckage from the crash sailed in all directions and destroyed several cars, a home, and an old aircraft hanger.

The Investigation: Checks of records and in-person interviews soon uncovered the cause of the pylon failure. Eight weeks before the accident, American Airlines mechanics at Tulsa, Oklahoma, had removed the engine and pylon assembly for scheduled maintenance. NTSB investigators discovered that the pylon failure:

resulted from a complete failure of the forward flange of the aft bulkhead after its residual strength had been critically reduced by a ***maintenance-induced crack*** *[emphasis added]*.

A maintenance-induced crack! Improper forklift handling of the big pylon and engine assembly, which weighs 13,477 pounds, had caused a crack in the supporting structure. This crack escaped detection at the time, and normal flight operations gradually enlarged it to 13 inches in length. Under the routine stress of takeoff thrust the pylon finally tore off of the aircraft.

The FDR revealed that Flight 191 had accelerated to 172 knots within nine seconds after lifting off from the runway. It began a shallow 1,150 foot per minute climb and reached a height of 375 feet above the ground. With an engine and pylon gone, one would *assume* that the aircraft was still flyable. The power from the two remaining engines should have been adequate. Unfortunately the hidden damage had severely crippled the airliner:

[When] the pylon separated from the aircraft [it] severed four hydraulic lines . . . which were routed through the wing leading edge . . . these hydraulic lines [operated] the leading edge slat control valve . . . and the actuating cylinders which extend and retract the outboard leading edge slats.

With hydraulic pressure lost and no check valve to retain the hydraulic fluid, dynamic air pressure caused the left outboard slats to retract. In the words of the investigators, "the uncommanded movement of these leading edge slats had a profound effect on aerodynamic performance." On the outboard portion of the left wing the *stall speed increased* to 159 knots.

The pilots began slowing down to reach the specified engine-out speed of 153 knots. As the airspeed dropped through 159 knots -- the *new stall speed* of the outboard left wing -- the outboard left wing stalled and began to drop. The DC-10 began a roll to the left despite the application of right rudder and right aileron. Eight seconds later the aircraft rolled past a 90 degree left bank. The nose dropped, and three seconds later the aircraft dove into the ground. The time from liftoff to impact had been only 35 seconds:

At impact the left wing's outboard slats were retracted while [all other] slats were extended to the takeoff position.

Loss of the No. 1 a.c. bus had caused the slat position indicating system to fail. The pilots did not know that the left outboard slats had retracted. The stick-shaker motor had lost its power supply too, and it failed to function. Analysis confirmed that the DC-10 would have remained flyable and fully controllable at any airspeed above 159 knots.

Probable Cause: The NTSB adopted Aircraft Accident Report NTSB-AAR-79-17 on 21 December 1979, seven months after the loss of Flight 191. The board found that *the pilots did everything right* based upon information available to them. Having passed the V-1 airspeed their decision not to abort the takeoff was logical.

The board noted that once airborne, due to the loss of the slat position indicating system and the stall warning system, the pilots had an "inadequate opportunity to recognize and prevent" the stall. They followed their prescribed emergency procedures for engine failure. Had they known the nature of the hidden damage to their craft they could have prevented the stall:

> The aircraft could have been flown successfully at speeds above 159 KIAS, or . . . the nose could have been lowered and the aircraft [could have been] accelerated out of the stall regime.

The board found glaring inadequacies in the original design and certification of the DC-10. The board pointed out that, although it had been considered an improbability, a pylon *could* break off of the aircraft. Such a pylon failure, the resulting structural and systems damage, and the asymmetric slat retraction were "not considered" when the airliner was certified. Also, the board found that the stall warning system "lacked sufficient redundancy." The board found the *Probable Cause* of the accident to be the:

> asymmetrical stall and the ensuing roll of the aircraft because of the uncommanded retraction of the left wing outboard leading edge slats and the loss of stall warning and slat disagreement indication systems [due to] *maintenance-induced damage [emphasis added]* leading to the separation of the No. 1 engine and pylon assembly at a critical point during takeoff. The separation resulted from damage by *improper maintenance procedures [emphasis added]* . . . .

The board found a large number of factors which **contributed** to the accident. Five of these factors are listed below:

[First was the] vulnerability of the **design** *[emphasis added]* of the pylon attach points to maintenance damage.

[Second was the] vulnerability of the **design** *[emphasis added]* of the leading edge slat system to the damage which [caused the asymmetric slat retraction and the asymmetric stall].

[Third were] deficiencies in the FAA surveillance and reporting systems which failed to detect and prevent the use of improper maintenance procedures.

[Fourth, the board found that] Douglas and the FAA failed to determine and disseminate the particulars regarding previous maintenance damage incidents.

[Fifth was] the intolerance of prescribed operational procedures to this unique emergency.

Postscript: In terms of loss of life this crash would remain the worst aviation disaster in the United States for 22 years. It would be surpassed by a quadruple terrorist hijacking on 11 September 2001 (see the chapter, "The '9/11' Terrorist Attacks").

Clandestine Marijuana Flight

Douglas C-54 Skymaster, registration N8060C
19 November 1979, near McCormick, South Carolina
2 aboard, 2 killed

Exclusive of a brief <u>Postscript</u>, this project excludes the conduct and results of investigations by local, state, and federal Law Enforcement agencies, some of which had been monitoring the whereabouts and prospective usage of the aircraft in question prior to this final flight. Exclusive of the <u>Postscript</u>, this project is limited in scope to the aeronautical aspects of the flight and the NTSB investigation which followed.

Overview: In predawn darkness a Douglas C-54 Skymaster flew toward a clandestine sod landing strip in rural McCormick County, South Carolina. The big C-54 crashed and burned over three miles short of its destination. The two pilots, the only persons aboard, died in the crash. Law Enforcement agents confiscated the illicit cargo -- over seven tons of marijuana.

The Flight: Before dawn on 19 November 1979 a Douglas C-54 Skymaster, registration N8060C, droned low over the southeastern United States. No flight plan had been filed, and there were no passengers. Over 15,000 pounds of marijuana, packed into burlap bags, had been loaded into the cavernous cargo bay.

The C-54 was the ideal aircraft for this type of flight. This four-engine "freighter" was the military version of the pre-turbine era DC-4 commercial airliner. In view of the circumstances a look at the history of the venerable C-54 Skymaster is warranted:

Based upon a United Airlines' request for a four-engine long range airliner, Douglas developed the DC-4 as the war clouds gathered prior to World War II. After the Japanese attacked United States military installations at Pearl Harbor, Hawaii, in December 1941 the U.S. government took over the production line to further the war effort. The Douglas C-54 Skymaster, the military version of the commercial DC-4, first rolled off the assembly line two months later on 14 February 1942. During the war Douglas rolled out 1,162 of these reliable workhorses.

Powered by four R-2000 Pratt & Whitney radial engines, the Skymaster went to war hauling both troops and military cargo. Its large fuel capacity gave it intercontinental range. During World War II the C-54s made over 79,000 ocean crossings, most of them in the Pacific Theater, losing only three aircraft in the process. Later the C-54 garnered its greatest fame during the so-called Cold War when it became the backbone of the Berlin Airlift in 1948 and 1949. With a maximum takeoff weight of 73,000 pounds, the C-54 served in the U.S. Air Force and the U.S. Navy (designated as the R-5D) until the late 1960s.

Commercial versions of the Skymaster hauled passengers for airlines in the United States well into the jet age. The airlines finally began retiring the DC-4s and converted C-54s in favor of faster jet-powered airliners. The reliable transports quickly found new homes with foreign airlines. They hauled passengers and served as "freighters" and "tankers" throughout the world well into the 1990s.

When the marijuana-laden C-54 reached western South Carolina in the predawn darkness, the pilots were the only two people on board. Both were airline pilots; both held ATP certificates and current first-class FAA medical certificates. The captain, age 56, was a resident of Sherman Oaks, California, and had earned type ratings in many Douglas transports, including the more recent DC-8 and DC-9 jetliners. His logbook reflected an impressive 23,500 flight hours. The first officer, age 43, lived in Homestead, Florida, and was type rated in the DC-8. In addition to over 5,000 hours with commercial airlines, he had logged over 3,000 flight hours in various military aircraft.

Trouble Ahead: The pilots used VOR triangulation to navigate toward a clandestine airstrip. Once there, improvised runway lighting would enable them to bring the C-54 down onto the sod runway. Then their waiting off-loading crew could take over.

Fate threw a wild card into the plans. In late November before 0600 Hours it was still dark, as anticipated for this type of "cargo" operation. However, upon arrival the two pilots could not see the make-shift runway lights. An impenetrable layer of opaque ground fog blanketed the terrain. The pilots knew that they were over the *vicinity* of the airstrip, but they could not see it.

In the dark the pilots circled and waited, hoping that the fog would dissipate before daylight. It did not. Then came the final twist of fate -- fire broke out aboard the aircraft. Smoke filled the cargo area and cockpit, and flames worked their mischief on the fuselage. The pilots had to land (1) before getting overcome by smoke, or (2) before fire destroyed the structural integrity of their craft. The NTSB would later take note of the in-flight peril:

> Witnesses reported the loud sound of engines and the aircraft burning in flight. The weather was foggy and it was dark.

Where could they land? Where? The closest suitable location was Greenwood County Airport. It had a 4,993 foot long asphalt runway plus a VORTAC and a NDB for instrument approaches. Yet, considering the nature of their cargo the pilots did not dare to try to land there. Also, that airport was 19 miles to the northeast, and the pilots had to get their burning C-54 on the ground without delay. They had only one viable option.

The Accident: Unable to see the sod airstrip lights through the thick fog, the pilots nonetheless tried a *desperate* visual approach. Gear down, they headed toward a primitive runway they could not yet see. In the dark they skimmed over the tops of trees that stuck up through the fog blanket. Then their luck ran out. The burning C-54 clipped an electrical power line along state road S-33-38, flew low over a small farm field, and blindly plowed into tall trees at the end of the field. The NTSB reported:

> The aircraft crashed in a remote, heavily wooded area, while approaching a sod landing strip . . . in low visibility conditions.

Trees crushed the front of the cockpit and ripped off parts of the wings, engines, propellers, and nacelles. The fuselage ground to a stop within only 150 feet in a wooded area nine miles north of the town of McCormick, South Carolina. Fire consumed part of the cockpit and cabin of the doomed C-54. Alerted by local residents, firefighters flocked to the scene and hosed down the burning wreckage. The NTSB would later note:

> Law Enforcement agents reported that the cargo on board, bales of marijuana not consumed by fire, weighed 15,000 pounds.

The two pilots were beyond mortal aid. They died in their seats. Their bodies had been crushed by the tree impacts and by the cargo from the cabin. Upon tree impact the marijuana bales, collectively weighing over seven tons, had hurtled forward through the cargo area and into the cockpit. Tissue samples from the pilots' remains would later be carried to the Division of Clinical Chemistry at the Medical University of South Carolina. All tests, including gas chromatography, would be negative.

The Investigation: The NTSB dispatched investigators to the rural crash site. Although the aircraft had burned, the NTSB was able to determine that the landing gear had been down and locked. All engines were producing power at impact. Investigators noted:

> [Burned] fuselage sound insulating material and burned paint were found for about 200 yards back along the approach path prior to the principal tree impact area. *[and also]* A search . . . back along the aircraft's approach path failed to disclose tree [impacts] prior to where the burned debris [trail] began.

The long trail of burned debris revealed that the C-54 was on fire *before* it hit the power line and trees. A young farmer told investigators that, awakened by the sound of the engines, he had run onto his front porch 300 yards from the crash site. Through the fog he had seen the Skymaster on fire in flight.

A retired schoolteacher who lived one-half mile from the crash site related that she had been in her kitchen and had heard the craft droning around and around in the dark. The instant before she heard the impact with the trees, her home lost electrical power when the C-54 clipped the power line. Her electric clock stopped at 0610 Hours, pinpointing the time of the crash.

In the tangled wreckage the investigators discovered a treasure trove of information. Sections of the newspaper *El Tiempo* from Bogota, Colombia, were found unburned in the cabin. Yet, the key sources of information were pulled from the charred cockpit:

A sectional aeronautical chart on which bearings from three VOR radio stations were plotted, indicating the location of the [landing] strip, was recovered from the wreckage. Detailed plans for the flight, weather conditions, turning on lights, landing, and unloading the aircraft were also recovered.

Plotted on the charts was a secret airstrip in a remote area of rural McCormick County. The NTSB took many photographs of the landing area. NTSB "Photograph No. 2" offers an excellent aerial view of the clandestine sod airstrip. The pilots had been on final approach on a heading of 265 degrees:

The aircraft was heading toward a sod landing area when it crashed. The landing area was about 3 1/2 miles from the crash [site] and about 5,000 feet long by 150 feet wide.

The NTSB delved into ownership of the C-54. Because of the nature of the cargo, the paper trail was understandably murky:

The aircraft remained registered to Westair International at the time of the crash, but an aircraft Bill of Sale was on file with [the] FAA, indicating Tiburon Aircraft, Inc., as the purchaser.

Tiburon Aircraft was headquartered in Corrales, New Mexico. A principal at Tiburon confirmed that he had hired the two now-deceased pilots to ferry the plane from Colorado Springs, Colorado, to San Jose, Costa Rica. The principal maintained that if the plane had flown to any place other than Costa Rica, it was stolen:

A ferry permit authorizing a flight from Oshkosh, Wisconsin, to Colorado Springs [Colorado] was issued by [the] FAA 10-5-79. The permit expired 10-29-79. A ferry permit for the flight from Colorado Springs to San Jose, Costa Rica, was not issued.

The media enjoyed a brief field day. One newspaper headlined the "Pot Plane" crash and alleged a street value of over six million dollars for the cargo. Another newspaper article included an aerial photograph of the clandestine landing area. Yet another included a photograph of the local sheriff standing amid the charred rubble.

Probable Cause: The NTSB wrapped up its investigation on 22

February 1980. This "General Aviation" accident was reported in a manner unlike that used for scheduled airline accidents. The NTSB detailed the final flight of the C-54 Skymaster in Aircraft Accident Report No. MIA80FA012 and additional documents. With regard to the in-flight fire, the dilemma confronting the pilots was almost identical to that which would face the pilots of another vintage piston-powered Douglas transport six years later:

On 31 December 1985 a Douglas DC-3, registration N711Y, would fly entertainer Eric "Ricky" Nelson and his entourage toward Dallas, Texas, for a New Year's Eve concert. Fire broke out in the cabin in flight. Burned paint and insulation fell along the flight track. The two pilots had to land **somewhere** *without delay. They clipped a power line as they tried to make an emergency landing in a farm field. Incapacitated by smoke, Mr. Nelson and all the passengers perished in the blazing DC-3.*

For the C-54 Skymaster pilots in South Carolina, in addition to the in-flight fire the NTSB noted "ground fog" at the accident site and weather conditions "below minimums." For the ***Probable Cause*** of this accident the NTSB found, in part:

Pilot in command misjudged distance, speed, or altitude [in the] fog. . . . [The aircraft] collided with trees on rising terrain near [the] sod airstrip . . . 15,000 lbs [of] marijuana aboard . . . .

And, of course, the aircraft was on fire. The pilots had to land *somewhere*, and land *immediately*. They faced three obstacles: (1) the blanket of fog, (2) the illicit nature of their cargo, and (3) the urgent necessity to land. In concert, these circumstances snared the pilots in a web of misfortune from which there was no escape.

Postscript: The aforementioned principal at Tiburon Aircraft had spent his childhood in Atlanta, Georgia. He later moved to Albuquerque, New Mexico, where he invested millions in shopping malls, condominium complexes, and other business ventures in the early 1980s. Law enforcement agents arrested him at his office in 1986. Along with 11 other defendants he eventually pled guilty in U.S. District Court in Scranton, Pennsylvania, to charges related to trafficking in illegal drugs over a period of several years. He was sentenced to serve 15 years in a federal prison.

Air New Zealand Flight 901

Douglas DC-10, registration ZK-NZP
28 November 1979, on Mt. Erebus, Antarctica
257 aboard, 257 killed

Overview: A Douglas DC-10 full of aerial sightseers flew over Ross Island, Antarctica, at an altitude of 1,500 feet. The forward visibility was 40 miles, but the pilots stumbled into a "white-out" environment -- no depth perception, no horizon, merely an opaque white cocoon. The airliner crashed into invisible rising terrain on Mt. Erebus, killing the 257 people on board.

The Flight: At 0817 Hours on 28 November 1979, summertime in the southern hemisphere, Air New Zealand Flight 901 soared skyward from Auckland, New Zealand. Although the destination was the continent of Antarctica, the 237 sightseers aboard all wore light clothing, for their flight was not scheduled to land on the frozen continent. Instead, they would fly over the South Pacific Ocean and make landfall on the northern coast of Victoria Land. From there the aerial excursion would continue southeast over McMurdo Sound to the Ross Ice Shelf. The projected track would then take the flight over New Zealand's Scott Base and the United States' McMurdo Station. Antarctica's ice-covered Mt. Erebus, an active volcano jutting 12,450 feet into the sky, would be one of the many visual splendors of the flight:

> There was an official flight commentator on the [DC-10] who was experienced in Antarctic exploration.

One of New Zealand's polar adventurers would serve as the tour commentator. Seated on the flight deck, he would use the airliner's public address system to explain the scenic wonders below as the flight cruised over the frozen continent. The airline intentionally had kept many seats vacant on the jumbo-jet, allowing passengers to move around the cabin and enjoy the view.
The Douglas DC-10 chosen for this flight, registration ZK-NZP,

had been manufactured in the United States and delivered new to Air New Zealand in 1974. It had accumulated 20,763 flying hours. For the trip to Antarctica it had been filled to capacity with the fuel needed to power its three General Electric engines during the long 11 hour flight. Air New Zealand had hand-picked an experienced captain. For "relief" purposes on the lengthy flight there were two first officers and two flight engineers for the cockpit, and 15 flight attendants for the cabin.

Armed with charts and a computerized flight plan the DC-10 sped south. As it approached the polar continent the pilots radioed McMurdo Center. The U.S. Navy manned this ATC facility at its base on Antarctica. ATC services over Antarctica were intended for military aircraft only, but they were available for use by civilian aircraft "at their own risk."

At landfall the crystal clear sky over Victoria Land allowed the passengers a stunning scenic view. The airliner arced high over Cape Hallett, then turned south over the sea toward the American base at McMurdo Station.

Trouble Ahead: Cruising south over McMurdo Sound, the big DC-10 flew over a low layer of solid clouds. The sea below was no longer visible. The captain turned back to a clear area and then descended in VMC weather:

> The DFDR showed that the aircraft carried out 2 descending orbits . . . while descending from 5,800 feet [and] finally leveling out at 1,500 feet above mean sea level.

Flight 901 proceeded south again, this time under the cloud layer. With no clouds below the aircraft, passengers *presumably* would have an unobstructed view of the wonderland below when they reached Ross Island.

The portion of the CVR transcript, below, begins *before* the flight descends to 1,500 feet. The first officer talks with McMurdo Center, and the captain is flying the DC-10. Meanwhile the dutiful flight engineer monitors the aircraft systems and performance:

Capt: . . . . . Captain, Flight 901
FO: . . . . . . First Officer, Flight 901
FltEngr: . . . Flight Engineer, Flight 901

UnidCrew: . . Unidentified crewmember, Flight 901
Tour: . . . . . Tour Commentator, Flight 901
GPWS: . . . . Ground Proximity Warning System, Flight 901
Radio-: . . . . (prefix) Radio transmission, Flight 901
PA-: . . . . . . (prefix) Public Address system, Flight 901
Center: . . . . McMurdo Center (ARTCC on Antarctica)

Radio-FO: . . . we are VMC and we'd like to let down . . . and proceed visually to McMurdo [Station]. (1342:01)

Center: New Zealand niner-zero-one, maintain VMC, keep us advised of your altitude as you approach McMurdo, over. (1342:15)

Radio-FO: Roger, nine-zero-one, we'll maintain VMC. (1342:24)

Capt: Well, we're just going VMC to McMurdo, and then [we'll] come back in. (1342:27)

Center: New Zealand niner-zero-one, report ten [miles] DME from McMurdo. (1342:34)

Radio-FO: Ah, roger, nine-zero-one to report ten DME McMurdo.

*[over 2 minutes pass with routine conversation; the First Officer responds to Center as **the flight descends**]*

Radio-FO: Affirmative, we are now at six-thousand, descending to two-thousand, and we're VMC. (1345:00)

Center: Nine-zero-one, roger. (1345:08)

PA-Tour: This is [the tour commentator] speaking again, folks, I still can't see very much . . . [I'll] keep you informed soon as I see something that gives me a clue as to where we are. (1346:02)

PA-Tour: We're going down in altitude now, and it won't be long before we get a quite a good view. (1346:19)

*[the Flight Engineer **voices concern** about the location of Mt. Erebus (which towers to 12,450 feet), somewhere nearby]*

FltEngr: Where's Erebus in relation to us? (1346:39)

UnidCrew: Left, do you reckon? Well, I don't know -- I think -- I've been looking for it. (1346:43)

FltEngr: I'm just thinking of [avoiding] any high ground in the area, that's all. (1346:48)

Tour: I think it'll be left, yes -- no, no -- I don't really know -- that's the edge --. (1347:02)

[41 seconds pass, routine cockpit conversation]

Capt: We might have to pop down [lower] to fifteen-hundred [feet] here, I think. (1347:43)

FO: Yes, OK, [we'll] probably see, farther in, anyway. (1347:47)

Tour: Ross Island [is] there -- Erebus should be here. (1348:10)

FO: Terrain, fifteen-hundred. (1348:12)

Capt: Actually, these conditions don't look very good at all -- do they? (1348:46)

Tour: No, they don't, you're down to [unintelligible] are you?

Capt: [I'm down to] fifteen-hundred [feet]. (1348:51)

Tour: That looks like the edge of Ross Island there. (1349:08)

FltEngr: I don't like this. (1349:24)

Capt: We'll have to climb out of this. (1349:30)

FO: It's clear on the right and well ahead. (1349:33)

Capt: Is it?

FO: Yes, you're clear to turn right, there's no high --. (1349:38)

Capt: No, negative.

FO: No high ground if you do a one-eighty [degree turn].

*[the aircraft flies over the **invisible up-slope of Mt. Erebus**; the GPWS senses the decreasing height above the terrain]*

GPWS: *Whoop whoop, pull up, whoop whoop . . . . (1349:44)*

[the Flight Engineer sees the radio altimeter winding down]

FltEngr: Five-hundred feet! (1349:48)

[the following "overlapped" in the final frantic 2 seconds]

GPWS: *Whoop whoop, pull up . . . .*

FltEngr: Four-hundred feet!

GPWS: *Whoop whoop . . . .*

UnidCrew: Pull up!

GPWS: *Whoop whoop . . . .*

Capt: Go-around power, please.

GPWS: *Whoop whoop, pull --.*

[sound of impact; end of the CVR tape at 1349:50]

[the pilots had never reported to Center (as instructed) that they had reached 2,000 feet; Center begins trying to recontact the flight at 1351, but there is no response]

The Accident: Over McMurdo Sound at an altitude of 1,500 feet, under a solid white overcast, the DC-10 had flown toward the Ross Ice Shelf. Once the aircraft began overflying the shelf the snow below and the white overcast above visually blended together in classic "white-out" conditions:

The surface definition at the time [was] poor . . . . Mountain tops in the area were covered in cloud.

Unable to see the rising terrain ahead, the pilots slammed into the snow-covered slope of Mt. Erebus at an altitude of 1,467 feet. The impact at 267 knots ripped the aircraft apart. Fragmented wreckage careened in all directions. Most people on board were "ejected" (in the subsequent words of the formal report) from the wreckage during the breakup sequence. Fed by fuel from the ruptured tanks, an inferno consumed most of the fuselage.

The next day the crew of a U.S. Navy C-130 Hercules spotted the wreckage. At 1256 Hours the military pilot radioed Center:

Center, we have located the wreckage. There appear to be no survivors. I say again, there appear to be no survivors.

Potential rescuers rushed to the scene, but the crash had killed all 257 people on Flight 901. Many bodies had fallen into deep crevasses and could not be recovered. Of the remains found, 213 were eventually identified. Postmortem examinations revealed that impact trauma, not the subsequent fire, caused all the deaths.

The Investigation: The DC-10 airframe and engines had been manufactured in the United States. Therefore, representatives from the American NTSB, the FAA, McDonnell Douglas (airframe) and General Electric (engines) were dispatched to participate in the investigation by the Air Accidents Investigation division of New Zealand's Ministry of Transport.

Analysis soon ruled out aircraft system failures as possible causes of the accident, so investigators began delving into the flight planning process. For the leg of the flight inbound to McMurdo Station, Air New Zealand had specified an IMC minimum descent altitude of 16,000 feet. If VMC conditions existed the flight would have been allowed to descend to 6,000 feet. Yet, the FDR and CVR both made it clear that the pilots had descended all the way down to a mere 1,467 feet.

Investigators zeroed in on meteorological conditions over the Ross Ice Shelf. A U.S. Air Force C-141 had flown over the area shortly after the airliner vanished. The military pilot reported:

> As we approached McMurdo we noted that Ross Island was obscured by clouds, ***no terrain was visible** [emphasis added]*.

As the DC-10 had flown over the ice and snow the pilots had entered "white-out" conditions. Below them lay an unbroken blanket of white snow. Above was a solid white overcast. The white clouds above visually merged with the white snow below. The pilots had no visible horizon, no depth perception. There were no shadows. There was no contrast, and no terrain features were visible. The pilots had looked into a featureless, dimensionless, monocolored white void. There had been considerable glare, and it seemed to come from all directions. The crew was unable to see snow-covered Mt. Erebus straight ahead, for it blended into the sea of white. They were unable to detect the rising white terrain below them. With regard to the captain's decision to fly at only 1,500 feet the ministry offered the following opinion:

> The pilot probably assumed that he would be able to see any and all obstacles clearly with a 2,000 foot cloud base and 40

miles visibility below the clouds. It is not likely that the potential white-out hazard . . . was appreciated by the crew.

Probable Cause: Six months after the accident the Ministry of Transport released the Aircraft Accident Report, No. 79-139, on 31 May 1980. The ministry report noted a host of factors which led to the accident, including planning shortcomings on the part of the airline, Air New Zealand. The ministry found that the airline's briefing for the crew contained "omissions and inaccuracies." The ministry also pointed out that the airline had given the crew faulty navigation information, and the charts prepared for the crew were deemed to be inadequate. Yet, the ministry noted that the pilots elected to descend far below the specified minimum safe altitude of 16,000 feet:

> The captain initiated a descent to an altitude below both the IMC (16,000 feet) and VMC (6,000 feet) minima . . . in contravention of the [Air New Zealand] briefing and outside the sector approved for the descent.

After dropping all the way down to 1,500 feet the pilots were unable to see (1) the surface of the ice and snow below or (2) the high terrain dead ahead. In these total "white-out" conditions they zoomed along at low altitude. They knew that lofty Mt. Erebus was somewhere close by. They looked for it, but they could not see it. They flew deeper and deeper into the dimensionless white void ahead. They could not determine their position in relation to topography they could not see. Flying blind, they impacted the invisible up-slope of Mt. Erebus. Consequently, the ministry found the *Probable Cause* of this accident to be:

> the decision of the captain to continue the flight at low level toward an area of poor surface and horizon definition when the crew was not certain of their position, and the subsequent inability to detect the rising terrain which intercepted the aircraft's flight path.

Air Florida Flight 90

Boeing 737, registration N62AF
13 January 1982, at Washington, DC
79 aboard, 74 killed (plus 4 killed on the ground)

Overview: A Boeing 737 took off from Washington National Airport at Washington, DC, during a snowstorm. After liftoff the airliner lost airspeed, stalled, struck a bridge, and crashed into the Potomac River. There were 79 people aboard, and 74 perished from impact trauma or drowned in the submerged cabin.

The Flight: Moderate to heavy snow fell in Washington, DC, on the cold 13th day of January 1982. Beginning at 1338 Hours, Washington National Airport closed for snow removal. One of the many flights waiting for the airport to reopen was Air Florida Flight 90. Aboard the small airliner were 74 passengers, including three infants, and the crew of five who were ready to head south toward sunny Tampa and Fort Lauderdale, Florida.

Air Florida had obtained the Boeing 737, registration N62AF, from United Airlines two years earlier. For the relatively short flight down to Florida the tanks had been loaded with 26,000 pounds of fuel. The two Pratt & Whitney turbofan engines each could provide 14,500 pounds of thrust. On this small airliner the takeoff weight had been calculated at 102,300 pounds, several tons below the maximum authorized takeoff weight.

The two young Air Florida pilots, ages 34 and 31, each held an ATP certificate, and both had the proper qualifications. They had logged a total of 11,653 flying hours. Yet, looking at their flying experience with the benefit of hindsight, one trait stands out. They were "warm weather" pilots:

> The Safety Board found that . . . the captain . . . had flown eight takeoffs or landings in which precipitation and freezing or near-freezing conditions occurred . . . [and] the first officer had flown two takeoffs or landings in such conditions.

The airport finally reopened. Runway 36 had been plowed and sanded, but the rest of the airport was covered with over three inches of snow, and more was falling. The captain requested deicing of his airplane. In the snowstorm at an air temperature of 24 degrees the deicing vehicle began applying a mix of glycol and water to the airfoil surfaces around 1445 Hours.

Trouble Ahead: Soon a tug arrived. It tried to push Flight 90 back from the ramp, but it got stuck in the snow and ice. The pilots started the engines and used reverse thrust, but the airliner still refused to budge. Finally a tug equipped with snow chains arrived, and Flight 90 successfully "pushed back" at 1535 Hours. Ahead of it, nine airliners and seven general aviation aircraft were already awaiting departure in the falling snow. Flight 90 fell 17th in line behind a New York Air DC-9. The first officer remarked: "It's been a while since we've been deiced." The pilots discussed the weather and the deicing process, and the first officer opined:

> This is a losing battle here on trying to deice these [planes], it gives you a false sense of security, that's all it does.

The portion of the CVR transcript, below, begins as the pilots wait in line for takeoff clearance. The first officer has the controls. In accordance with a standing agreement with the FAA, the ATC controllers use "Palm" as the call-sign for all Air Florida flights:

Capt: . . . . . Captain, Flight 90
FO: . . . . . . First Officer, Flight 90
FltAtt(A): . . Head Flight Attendant, Flight 90
FltAtt(B): . . Another Flight Attendant, Flight 90
Radio-: . . . . (prefix) Radio transmission, Flight 90
PA-: . . . . . . (prefix) Public Address system, Flight 90
Tower: . . . . Washington National Airport Control Tower

FO: Boy, this is [expletive], it's probably the [expletive] snow I've seen. (1539:29)

Capt: [Unintelligible] go over to the hangar and get deiced.

FO: Yeah, definitely.

[sound of laughter]

FO: That Citation *[a small corporate jet]* over there, that guy's about ankle deep in [the snow]. (1541:24)

[sound of laughter; two Flight Attendants enter the cockpit]

FO: Hello, Donna. (1541:47)

FltAtt(A): I love it out here . . . I love it, the neat way the tire tracks [go in the snow]!

FO: See that Citation over there, looks like he's up to his knees.

FltAtt(B): Look at all the tire tracks in the snow!

FltAtt(A): Huh?

FltAtt(B): The tire tracks in the snow!

[normal cockpit conversation; over 4 minutes pass]

Capt: [I'll] tell you what, my windshield will be deiced, don't know about my wing. (1546:21)

FO: Well, all we really need is the inside of the wings anyway, the wing tips are gonna speed up by eighty [knots] anyway, they'll shuck all that other stuff. (1546:27)

[routine conversation; 1 minute and 39 seconds pass]

FO: It's impressive that these big old planes get in here with the weather this bad . . . it never ceases to amaze me when we break out of the clouds, there's the runway anyway, [don't] care how many times we do it, God, we [do it] good! See those icicles on the back there and everything? (1548:08)

Capt: Yeah.

[the flight waits in line for another 10 minutes]

Tower: Palm ninety, taxi into position and hold, be ready for an immediate [takeoff]. (1558:55)

Radio-FO: Palm ninety, position and hold. (1558:58)

PA-Capt: Ladies and gentlemen, we have just been cleared on the runway for takeoff, Flight Attendants, please be seated. (1559:06)

[the pilots complete their takeoff checklist]

FO: Flight Attendant alert. (1559:15)

Capt: Given. (1559:16)

FO: Bleeds. (1559:16)

Capt: They're off. (1559:17)

FO: Strobes, external lights. (1559:18)

Capt: On.

FO: Anti-skid. (1559:19)

Capt: On.

FO: Transponder. (1559:21)

Capt: On.

FO: Takeoff [checklist is] complete. (1559:22)

Tower: Palm ninety, cleared for takeoff. (1559:24)

Radio-FO: Palm ninety, cleared for takeoff. (1559:26)

Tower: No delay on departure if you will, traffic's two-and-a-half [miles] out for the runway. (1559:28)

Radio-FO: OK. (1559:32)

Capt: Your throttles. (1559:45)

   *[sound of engines spooling up; **the takeoff roll begins**]*

Capt: Holler if you need the wipers. (1559:49)

Capt: [The engines are] spooled. (1559:51)

Capt or FO: Hooo -- whhhooo -- really cold here. (1559:53)

Capt: Real cold, real cold. (1559:56)

FO: God, look at that thing! (1559:58)

FO: That don't seem right, does it? (1600:02)

FO: Ah, that's not right -- well --. (1600:05)

Capt: Yes it is, there's eighty [knots]. (1600:09)

FO: Naw, I don't think that's right. (1600:10)

FO: Aaahhh, maybe it is. (1600:19)

Capt: Hundred-and-twenty [knots]. (1600:21)

FO: I don't know --? (1600:23)

Capt: V-one. (1600:31)

Capt: Easy! (1600:33)

Capt: V-two. (1600:37)

[the aircraft lifts off at 147 knots at 1600:37]

[the stick-shaker activates at 1600:39 and remains activated]

*[the aircraft climbs to 240 feet, but **airspeed decreases**]*

Tower: Palm ninety, contact Departure Control. (1600:41)

Capt: Forward! Forward! (1600:45)

Capt: We only want five-hundred [feet of altitude]. (1600:48)

Capt: Come on! Forward! (1600:50)

[altitude decreases; airspeed falls to 130 knots]

Capt: Forward -- just barely climb! (1600:53)

Capt or FO: We're stalling *[or, falling]*. (1600:59)

FO: Larry! We're going down, Larry! (1601:00)

Capt: I know it. (1601:01)

[sound of impact, immediately followed by the end of the CVR tape at 1601:01]

The Accident: Nose high, mushing downward, the Boeing 737 sank toward the ground. At 1601:01 Hours it struck the top of the traffic-filled northbound span of the 14th Street bridge over the Potomac River. The impact destroyed seven occupied vehicles and 41 feet of the bridge wall. The aircraft tore across the bridge and then nosed down into the ice-covered river below. Within seconds only the vertical fin was visible, protruding above the surface:

The remainder of the wreckage sank in the Potomac River in about 25 to 30 feet of water.

Because of the snowstorm the tower controller had not been able to see the aircraft lift off. Yet, watching his radar display, he knew that the flight got airborne. He radioed instructions for the pilots to contact Departure Control. No response. He watched as the radar return from the flight dimmed, then vanished.

Soon a host of law enforcement, fire, and EMS agencies flocked to the site of the crash. From the riverbanks the potential rescuers helplessly watched six survivors in the water. They were clinging to the only thing protruding out of the river, the vertical stabilizer. There was no way rescuers could reach the injured survivors far out in the ice-choked Potomac:

> For the six occupants who escaped from the aircraft, [the] temperature, both water and air, was the major factor which affected their survival.

At 1622 Hours, 21 minutes after the crash, a U.S. Park Police helicopter arrived. The Bell 206 JetRanger hovered over the water, dropped ropes, and dragged three nearly-frozen survivors to the safety of the riverbank. A crewman crawled out on the skid of the helicopter and dragged another survivor to safety. With only two people still alive in the river, a bystander decided to wait no longer. He dove into the water, swam out through the ice, and swam back to the bank with one more debilitated survivor. One last person still clung to the vertical fin of the Boeing 737, but before he could be rescued he slipped below the surface and disappeared forever.

With regard to the 73 people who were unable to escape from the sunken aircraft, the medical examiner would later report:

> Seventeen passengers received injuries not considered to be immediately fatal. However . . . all suffered *incapacitating [emphasis added]* injuries due to secondary impact forces, making escape [from the submerged aircraft] impossible.

Of the five survivors who were plucked from the icy water, four were passengers and one was a flight attendant. The remaining passengers and crewmembers died from the trauma of the impact or drowned in the submerged wreckage. The accident also killed four people on the bridge and seriously injured four others.

The Investigation: The NTSB reconstructed the fatal flight. On takeoff Flight 90 should have accelerated to 145 knots in 30 seconds while using 3,500 feet of runway. However, the CVR and FDR showed that the aircraft actually took 45 full seconds to accelerate, and it used 5,400 feet of runway in the process. After liftoff, instead of continuing to accelerate and climb, the aircraft slowed down and stalled.

Investigation revealed that Flight 90 took off with snow and ice on its airfoil surfaces. This determination was based upon the statements of numerous witnesses, the four surviving passengers, and the content of the CVR tape. The snow and ice degraded the aerodynamic performance of the wings. Lift decreased. Parasitic drag increased. Stall speed increased. In addition the Boeing 737 airliner has a known penchant to "pitch up" when the wings are contaminated with snow or ice:

> Departing and arriving flight crews and others who saw Flight 90 before and during takeoff stated that the aircraft had an unusually heavy accumulation of snow and ice on it.

The NTSB discovered that the deicing procedure had not been conducted properly. Neither engine inlet plugs nor pitot/static covers were installed during the deicing process. Further, neither an Air Florida maintenance representative nor the captain checked to see that the aircraft was free of ice before push-back from the ramp. Thereafter the airliner waited for about an hour in moderate to heavy snowfall before getting clearance to take off. As recorded on the CVR, the pilots were aware of snow and ice on the wings. At one point they had tried to deice their aircraft by positioning it near the exhaust of the aircraft ahead in line for takeoff.

Both engines on the Boeing 737 are equipped with a thermal engine anti-ice system that uses heated engine "bleed" air. The CVR revealed that the pilots switched the anti-ice function "off":

> The engine inlet pressure probe on both engines became blocked with ice before initiation of takeoff.

When the pilots moved the throttles forward for takeoff, they set the thrust by reference to the EPR gauges. Unfortunately, because the probes were blocked with ice the gauges gave faulty readings. The thrust achieved was only 75 percent of what it should have been. Investigators noted:

> Although the first officer expressed concern that something was "not right" to the captain four times during the takeoff [roll], the captain took no action to [abort] the takeoff.

Probable Cause: The NTSB adopted the Aircraft Accident Report for Flight 90, NTSB-AAR-82-8, on 10 August 1982. The board found that the aircraft had been unable to sustain flight for two reasons. First, the snow and ice on the airfoil surfaces degraded aerodynamic lift, increased drag, and increased the stall speed. In addition the takeoff attempt was made with lower than normal thrust due to the erroneous EPR indications. With either condition alone, flight would have been possible. However, with both conditions together, the crash was inevitable. The board found that the *Probable Cause* of this accident was threefold:

> [First was] the flightcrew's failure to use engine anti-ice during ground operation and takeoff.

> [Second was the crew's] decision to take off with snow/ice on the airfoil surfaces of the aircraft.

> [Third was] the captain's failure to reject the takeoff during the early stage when his attention was called to anomalous engine instrument readings.

The board found three factors that *contributed* to the accident:

> [First was] the prolonged ground delay between deicing and the receipt of [the] ATC takeoff clearance during which the airplane was exposed to continued precipitation.

> [Second], the known inherent pitch-up characteristics of the [Boeing] 737 aircraft when the leading edge [of the wing] is contaminated with even small amounts of snow and ice.

> [Third was] the limited experience of the flight crew in jet transport winter [weather] operations.

Pan Am Flight 759

Boeing 727, registration N4737
9 July 1982, at New Orleans, Louisiana
145 aboard, 145 killed (plus 8 killed on the ground)

Overview: A Boeing 727 took off during a violent storm at New Orleans, Louisiana. Just after liftoff in torrential rain the aircraft flew into microburst-induced windshear. The airliner crashed into tall trees almost a mile from the airport. The impact and fire killed the 145 people on board and 8 people on the ground.

The Flight: On the hot and stormy afternoon of 9 July 1982, Pan American World Airways (Pan Am) Flight 759 taxied from the gate at New Orleans International Airport in Louisiana. The medium range airliner and its human cargo were headed for Las Vegas, Nevada. The 138 passengers and the crew of 7 presumably looked forward to sunny dry skies at their destination, the famed resort and gaming Mecca of the Western World.

The Pan Am captain, age 45, held an ATP certificate and had amassed 10,595 flight hours in the Boeing 727 series aircraft. He had qualified as a captain on the trusty "three-holer" over 10 years earlier. His young first officer, age 32, held a Commercial Pilot certificate and had logged 6,127 hours in the air. Their flight engineer had 14 years of experience documented in his logbook. Four flight attendants staffed the cabin of the Boeing airliner, and a non-revenue passenger rode in the cockpit jumpseat. The big Boeing 727 aircraft, registration N4737, had been delivered new to National Airlines in 1978 before Pan Am acquired National. Three Pratt & Whitney engines, each rated at 14,000 pounds of thrust, powered the swept-wing craft.

Trouble Ahead: As the aircraft taxied toward the approach end of Runway 10, wind and rain lashed the airport. Halfway down the runway much heavier rain was falling. The portion of the CVR transcript, below, begins as Flight 759 nears the runway. Per an agreement between Pan Am and the FAA, the ATC controllers use the call-sign "Clipper" to identify Pan Am flights. The first officer has the controls:

Capt: . . . . . . Captain, Flight 759
FO: . . . . First Officer, Flight 759
FltEngr: . . . . Flight Engineer, Flight 759
Radio-: . . . . . (prefix) Radio transmission, Flight 759
PA-: . . . . (prefix) Public Address system, Flight 759
GPWS: . . . . . Ground Proximity Warning System, Flight 759
Tower: . . . . . New Orleans Airport Control Tower
GndControl: . . New Orleans Ground Control

Radio-FO: What are your winds now? (1603:33)

GndControl: Winds now zero-seven-zero degrees at one-seven and peak gusts [at] two-three, and we have low level windshear alerts all quadrants, appears the frontal [system is] passing overhead right now, we're right in the middle of everything. (1603:37)

Capt: Let your airspeed build up on takeoff. (1603:57)

Capt: Leo, you want to do a no-packs *[meaning, air conditioning packs off]* takeoff on this thing? (1604:23)

FltEngr: No packs, OK. (1604:26)

Capt: The winds are going to be off to the left too. (1604:46)

PA-Capt: Good afternoon, ladies and gentlemen . . . we'd like to ask you to please ensure that your seatbelts are all buckled . . . after takeoff we'll be maneuvering around, circumnavigating some, aaahhh, some little thundershowers out there, so we would like to ask you folks to please remain in your seats. (1605:20)

[routine takeoff preparations for 1 minute and 2 seconds]

Radio-FO: Clipper seven-fifty-nine is ready. (1606:22)

Tower: Clipper seven-fifty-nine, maintain two-thousand, fly [the] runway heading, cleared for takeoff, Runway one-zero. (1606:24)

[the First Officer acknowledges the clearance at 1606:30]

Capt: OK, [do] we have the pre-taxi [checklist] and the taxi checklist complete? (1606:35)

FO: Yes. (1606:39)

Capt: Takeoff checklist. (1606:40)

FO: Takeoff check, transponders and DME on . . . . (1606:41)

Capt: We got 'em. (1606:45)

FO: Engineer's check. (1606:48)

FltEngr: Complete. (1606:49)

FO: Configuration check. (1606:50)

FltEngr: Anti-skid. (1606:53)

Capt: 'Skid is on. (1606:54)

FltEngr: Speed brake. (1606:56)

Capt: Forward. (1606:57)

FltEngr: Stabilizer trim. (1606:58)

Capt: It's set. (1606:59)

[the flight deck crewmen complete their checklist]

FltEngr: Takeoff check complete. (1607:25)

Capt: Lights are on, engines spooling up, Leo. (1607:33)

FO: We're cleared for takeoff. (1607:50)

FltEngr: Looking good. (1607:52)

FO: Takeoff thrust. (1607:59)

*[the engines spool up to full thrust; **the takeoff roll begins**]*

FO: [I] need the wipers. (1608:04)

[sound of windshield wipers begins at 1608:06]

Capt or FO: Eighty knots. (1608:16)

[sound of click; windshield wiper speed increases at 1608:27]

Capt: V-r. (1608:33)

[the First Officer rotates for takeoff at 1608:34]

[6 seconds later the aircraft lifts off and climbs at 1608:40]

<u>Capt</u>: Positive climb. (1608:41)

<u>FO</u>: Gear up. (1608:42)

<u>Capt</u>: V-two. (1608:43)

*[the aircraft flies into **horizontal windshear** and a **downdraft**; airspeed and altitude begin to decrease]*

<u>Capt</u>: Come on back [on the control column], you're sinking, Don! Come on back! *[spoken in an <u>alarmed</u> voice]* (1608:45)

<u>Tower</u>: Clipper seven-fifty-nine, contact Departure [Control on] one-two-zero-point-six, so long. (1608:51)

<u>GPWS</u>: Whoop whoop, pull up, whoop whoop, pull up, whoop whoop, pull up, whoop whoop --. (1608:57)

[sound of first impact with tall trees at 1609:00]

<u>Capt or FO</u>: [Expletive]! (1609:02)

[sound of second impact with the trees at 1609:04]

[sound of third impact; end of the CVR tape at 1609:05]

The Accident: The airliner lifted off in a normal manner about 7,000 feet down the runway. Wings level, it began to climb as it entered an area of exceptionally heavy rainfall. The ascent stopped only 95 feet above the ground. With the three engines at full power the aircraft began to sink downward as it screamed over the rooftops of New Orleans.

At a height of 50 feet above the ground the left wing clipped tall trees 2,376 feet beyond the end of the runway. Three-hundred feet farther along its flight path the aircraft tore through the tops of more trees. The impacts tore away pieces of the left wing leading edge devices and the trailing edge flaps.

Fatally wounded, the aircraft rolled to the left. It crashed into a residential area in the New Orleans suburb of Kenner, Louisiana, 4,610 feet beyond the departure end of the runway. All 145 people on the aircraft died in the crash and the fuel-fed pyre that followed.

The accident also took the lives of eight people on the ground and injured nine others. The impact and fire destroyed six homes and seriously damaged several more. Later adding to the death toll, the coroner of Jefferson Parish would issue a "Certificate of Death" for a fetus carried by one of the adult female victims.

The Investigation: Although the aircraft had been incinerated in the post-crash fire, investigators were able to eliminate aircraft anomalies as potential factors in the loss of Flight 759. The experts rapidly zeroed in on *microburst-induced windshear*, the assassin of the aircraft and its human cargo. An explanation is in order for non-flying laymen:

> *A microburst is a rapidly descending column of air sometimes found beneath a thunderstorm. As this shaft of air approaches the ground it spreads laterally in all directions -- like water poured from a glass onto a flat surface. An aircraft flying low toward a microburst first flies into a **headwind** as it meets the lateral outflow of air. However, as the aircraft transverses the microburst, the outflow on the other side (in the opposite direction) becomes a **tailwind** to the aircraft. This sudden change in wind direction is called windshear.*

Armed with reams of data the technical experts reconstructed the flight. As the Boeing had lined up for takeoff, radar had "painted" convective weather echoes over the departure end of Runway 10. Similar storm cells were located over and adjacent to the departure path beyond the end of the runway. Four other pilots who saw these thunderstorms would later testify that they appeared to be "level three" or higher cells:

> Clipper 759's takeoff began in light rain, [and the airliner] encountered increased rain during the takeoff roll and even heavier rain after liftoff.

Flight 759 had begun its takeoff roll in light rain. However, meteorologists calculated that at liftoff the aircraft flew into extremely heavy precipitation that approximated a rate of 5.7 inches per hour. Within this heavy downpour an invisible microburst was centered near the departure end of the runway.

Flight 759 entered the outflow as it approached the shaft of the microburst. The aircraft lifted off at 138 knots, aided by a 16 knot *headwind*. The FDR revealed that the aircraft then climbed to 95 feet above ground level while accelerating to V-2, 151 knots.

Then the flight passed beneath the shaft of the microburst and encountered the outflow on the other side, a strong *tailwind*. The sudden horizontal windshear stole *38 knots* of crucial airspeed. At the same time a vicious 25 foot per second *downdraft* snared the aircraft. Despite full power on the engines the airliner sank toward the treetops. The investigators would later note:

> Vertical winds showed a steadily increasing downdraft from the 35 feet AGL point to about 5 seconds before impact. At this point the downdraft remained at about 25 fps until tree impact.

Torrential rain obscured all visual cues outside the cockpit as the airliner screamed along only 95 feet above the ground. This forced the pilots to rely solely on their flight instruments for airspeed, rate of climb or descent, and pitch attitude. Low and slow, caught in the downdraft, the aircraft sank earthward. Nose high, mushing forward, desperately trying to regain flying speed, the pilots fought against the horizontal windshear and the downdraft. Mother Nature and her fury won the brief fight. With the synthetic voice of the GPWS blaring in the cockpit the aircraft sank lower and lower, hit the trees, crashed, and burned.

Within the 10 minute period before Flight 759 took off, ATC had transmitted nine separate windshear advisories. Yet, when the pilots began their takeoff roll at 1608 Hours the last such advisory contained information that was four minutes old:

> The windshear which affected Clipper 759's takeoff was not detected by the LLWSAS *[Low Level Windshear Alert System]* until after Clipper 759 began its takeoff.

Based upon the new windshear information, ATC broadcast an updated advisory at 1609:03 Hours. Ironically, it came too late to help the pilots on Flight 759, for their airliner had clipped the top of the first tree three seconds earlier.

Probable Cause: The NTSB adopted its Aircraft Accident Report, NTSB-AAR-83-02, on 21 March 1983, eight months after the crash. The board pointed out that the presence, location, and magnitude of a microburst can not be predicted in advance. The board found that "the captain's decision to take off was reasonable in light of the information that was available to him." The board found the *Probable Cause* of this accident to be:

the airplane's encounter, during the liftoff and initial climb phase of flight, with a microburst-induced windshear which imposed a downdraft and a decreasing headwind, the effects of which the pilot would have had difficulty recognizing and reacting to in time for the airplane's descent to be arrested before its impact with [the] trees.

The board noted that a *contributing* cause of the accident was:

the limited capability of current ground based low level windshear detection technology to provide definitive guidelines for controllers and pilots for use in avoiding low level windshear encounters.

Postscript: Microbursts can array three invisible weapons against an aircraft: (1) horizontal windshear, (2) updrafts and downdrafts (often called vertical windshear), and (3) turbulence. An aircraft is most vulnerable to these hazards when it is flying low and slow near the ground.

The airlines and the FAA took the lessons learned from the Flight 759 tragedy to heart. The industry emphasized more pilot training and a need for improved windshear detection technology. Despite the training and the detection efforts, microburst-induced windshear would strike again 37 months later in August 1985. A big jumbo-jet would be snatched from a stormy afternoon sky near Fort Worth, Texas (see the chapter, "Delta Airlines Flight 191").

Korean Airlines Flight 007

Boeing 747, registration HL7442
1 September 1983, shot down over Sakhalin Island, Russia
269 aboard, 269 killed

Overview: A Boeing 747 took off from Anchorage, Alaska, and headed for Seoul, South Korea. It strayed hundreds of miles off course and flew deep into Soviet Union airspace. Believing the "target" to be an American spyplane, a Soviet fighter-interceptor shot it down. All 269 persons on board were killed.

The Flight: On 1 September 1983, Korean Airlines Flight 007 took off from Anchorage, Alaska, and headed west over the Pacific Ocean toward Seoul, South Korea. Aboard were 246 passengers and a crew of 23. The pilots planned to take the customary R-20 commercial aviation route across the ocean.

The big Boeing 747, registration HL7442, cruised effortlessly westward. It left the radar coverage area of Anchorage ATC about 27 minutes after takeoff. For the next three hours the pilots would navigate with blind reliance upon their onboard inertial navigation system. In the dark, as the hours and minutes ticked away, the flight deck crew had little to do except chat idly. Flight 007 began drifting off course, far to the north and west of R-20:

> The pilots did not notice that they were 500 kilometers off course and violating Soviet [Union] airspace.

The errant heading would eventually take the airliner across the Soviet Union's Kamchatka Peninsula, then over the Okhotsk Sea toward Sakhalin Island. There the Soviet Union maintained an ultra-secret military base.

Trouble Ahead: Roughly three and one-half hours into the flight, Soviet air defense radar "painted" the high-flying Boeing 747. As Flight 007 overflew the Kamchatka Peninsula, six Soviet MIG-23 fighters scrambled to intercept it. However, before the intercept could be made Flight 007 left Soviet airspace while flying over the Okhotsk Sea. The six fighters returned to their base.

Now the Soviets were forewarned and ready. As the airliner neared Soviet airspace over Sakhalin Island the Soviet Air Defense Command radar picked it up. The Soviets scrambled two SU-15 fighter-interceptors from Sokol Airfield on Sakhalin Island. The two fighters soon caught up with Flight 007, and this time the interceptors were within Soviet airspace. Following instructions, a Soviet pilot switched on all his external lights. No response from the target. He fired warning shots into the night and rocked his wings. Still no response. The Soviet pilot then got a direct order from his ground command center:

> The target is military . . . arm your weapons. The target has violated the state border. Destroy the target.

Years later, after the end of the Cold War, the government of the former Soviet Union would allow access to the CVR and FDR tapes. The CVR and ATC transcript (UCT) allows insight into the final minutes of Flight 007. The cockpit crew casually talks about plans for exchanging currency in Seoul. The transcript does not identify the member of the flight crew who is speaking:

UnidCrew: . . . Unidentified crewmember, Flight 007
Radio-: . . . . . (prefix) Radio transmission, Flight 007
PA: . . . . Public Address system, Flight 007
Center: . . . . . Tokyo Center (ARTCC in Japan)

UnidCrew: I have heard that there is [a] currency exchange at your airport. (1811:27)

UnidCrew: Yes, in the airport currency exchange. What kind of money? (1811:30)

UnidCrew: Dollar to Korean money. (1811:33)

UnidCrew: That's in the domestic building too (1811:39)

UnidCrew: Domestic [building]? Where? (1811:40)

UnidCrew: That's the Cho-Hung Bank in the domestic building.

UnidCrew: Can I exchange in Cho-Hung Bank? (1811:43)

UnidCrew: What kind of money do you wish to exchange? Dollar to Korean money is all right. (1811:49)

Radio-UnidCrew: Tokyo, Korean Air zero-zero-seven. (1814:59)

Center: Korean Air zero-zero-seven, Tokyo. (1815:30)

Radio-UnidCrew: Korean Air zero-zero-seven [is] requesting a climb [to flight level] three-five-zero. (1815:07)

Center: [You are] requesting three-five-zero? (1815:13)

Radio-UnidCrew: That is affirmative, [we are] now at [flight level] three-three-zero. (1815:15)

Center: Korean Air zero-zero-seven, stand by. (1815:19)

[Flight 007 reenters Soviet airspace at 1816]

Center: Korean Air zero-zero-seven, [your] clearance: Tokyo ATC clears Korean Air zero-zero-seven, climb and maintain flight level three-five-zero. (1820:21)

Radio-UnidCrew: Tokyo, roger. (1820:28)

[Flight 007 begins to climb immediately after 1820:28]

[the Soviet pilot is ordered to "destroy the target" at 1822]

[the Soviet pilot launches two air-to-air missiles at 1826]

*[sound of a **loud explosion** at 1826:02]*

UnidCrew: What's happened? What? (1826:06)

UnidCrew: Retard throttles! (1826:10)

UnidCrew: Engines are normal! (1826:11)

UnidCrew: Landing gear? (1826:14)

[sound of automated altitude deviation warning at 1826:18]

UnidCrew: Altitude is going up. Altitude is going up. (1826:23)

UnidCrew: Speed brake is coming out. (1826:25)

UnidCrew: What? What? (1826:26)

UnidCrew: Check it out! (1826:29)

UnidCrew: I am not able to drop altitude now, unable. (1826:33)

PA: Attention, emergency descent, attention . . . . (1826:34)

UnidCrew: Altitude is going up. (1826:38)

UnidCrew: This is not working! This is not working! (1826:40)

UnidCrew: Manually. (1826:41)

UnidCrew: Cannot do manually! (1826:42)

PA: Attention, emergency descent, attention . . . . (1826:42)

[sound of autopilot disconnect warning]

UnidCrew: Not working manually, also! (1826:43)

UnidCrew: Engines are normal, sir! (1826:45)

PA: Put out your cigarette, this is an emergency descent . . . . *[spoken in English, Korean, and Japanese].* (1826:46)

UnidCrew: Is it power compression? Is that right? Is that right?

PA: Put the mask over your nose and . . . . (1826:55)

Radio-UnidCrew: Tokyo Radio, Korean Air zero-zero-seven!

Center: [This is] Tokyo, Korean Air zero-zero-seven. (1826:57)

Radio-UnidCrew: Roger, Korean Air zero-zero-seven is -- ah -- [unintelligible] we are experiencing decompression, descending to one-zero-thousand! (1827:04)

PA: Attention, emergency descent, attention . . . . (1827:19)

UnidCrew: Now . . . we have to set this. (1827:20)

Center: Korean Air zero-zero-seven, [unintelligible] radio check on one-zero-zero-four-eight. (1827:21)

PA: Attention, emergency descent, attention . . . . (1827:23)

UnidCrew: Speed -- stand by, stand by, stand by, stand by -- set!

PA: Put out your cigarette, this is an emergency descent, put the mask over your nose and mouth, adjust the . . . . (1827:33)

UnidCrew: Altitude!

UnidCrew: Get ready!

[end of the CVR tape at 1827:46]

[10 minutes later Flight 007 crashes into the ocean]

The Accident: After his missile hit Flight 007 the fighter pilot radioed his command center: "The target is destroyed":

[The airliner] was hit by at least one of two air-to-air missiles fired from a USSR SU-15 interceptor aircraft.

The airliner was damaged, but not immediately destroyed. The crew did not know what had caused the explosion. The pilots radioed Tokyo, reported the decompression, and stated that they were in an emergency descent. Several times one of the pilots said that the engines were "normal." The CVR stopped operating 1 minute and 44 seconds after the missile struck, but the FDR showed that the airliner kept flying.

After descending to a level where the air was more dense, the aircraft flew straight and level for four minutes. American military radio intercepts revealed that the Soviet Air Defense Command ordered another missile attack. That would not be necessary, for the damaged airliner soon began a spiraling descent. It impacted the sea 12 minutes after the missile strike.

Pieces of human remains washed ashore on Hokkaido Island, although only two intact bodies were found. Small fragments of the Boeing 747 were found floating on the surface of the water, but all else had been swallowed up by the ocean. There had been 269 people on board, and no one survived.

The Investigation: By the following morning it was clear that the Soviets had shot down a civilian airliner. The shoot-down could not have happened at a worse time. The world's two nuclear superpowers, the Soviet Union and the United States, were engaged in an unprecedented global military and political struggle. Tension between the two adversaries had never been higher:

The era of "detente" was long gone. Uri Andropov, the Soviet General Secretary, was the feared former KGB chief. Ronald Reagan, the U.S. President, viewed the struggle against Soviet expansionism as a noble crusade against an "evil empire." Both nations feared a nuclear "first strike" by their avowed enemy. In a military cat-and-mouse game, American RC-135 spyplanes daily skirted Soviet airspace, often making brief inroads to test the response of Soviet forces. A powder keg?

The Soviet Union and the United States used the shoot-down to trumpet their political causes. The Soviets maintained that the commercial flight was a transparent cover for American espionage. They produced an *edited* version of their Air Defense Command tapes to "prove" their claim. The United States created an *edited* version of its clandestine listening post tapes and claimed that the Soviets had knowingly shot down a civilian airliner. Cool heads fortunately prevailed, and the crisis gradually subsided.

The search for answers began. Why had Flight 007 drifted so far off course? It was far outside both Japanese and American radar coverage areas, so ATC did not know its location. Ironically, pilots of other airliners on the R-20 route were joking about the weather conditions that Flight 007 routinely reported by radio. Because the flight was hundreds of miles off course, its weather observations did not agree with the weather on the R-20 route:

The failure to detect the aircraft's deviation from its assigned track for over five hours indicated a lack of situational awareness and flight deck coordination [by] the crew.

Moments before painting Flight 007, Soviet radar operators had been tracking a U.S. Air Force RC-135, a military variant of the Boeing 707. This four-engine reconnaissance plane had been skirting Soviet airspace. The Soviets *assumed* that Flight 007 was the same aircraft. No foreign civilian aircraft, they knew, would dare to over-fly Mother Russia without permission. The Soviets therefore identified the intruder as "target 6065":

The proximity of an RC-135 (a United States intelligence aircraft) and [the airliner] northeast of Kamchatka Peninsula resulted in confusion and the assumption by USSR Air Defense that the aircraft proceeding towards the USSR was an RC-135.

When the Soviet fighter caught up with the "target" the military pilot radioed a description to his command center. As documented by American military listening posts, he described a large four-engine jet transport (a good description of either a military RC-135 spyplane or a Boeing 747 airliner). It was flying straight and level with its navigation and anticollision lights on. In the dark, from a half-mile behind the target, the fighter pilot had no way to know that he had intercepted a commercial airliner.

When ordered to do so, the fighter pilot turned on his external lights. However, he was in an *attack* position behind Flight 007 and could not have been seen by its crew. The Soviet command then instructed its pilot to fire warning shots. The SU-15 pilot fired his guns, but "Murphy's Law" prevailed:

> Contrary to instructions the interceptor had only armor-piercing ammunition and no tracer [ammunition] that would have been [visible at night].

The Soviet command considered trying to contact the target by radio, but on what frequency? In what language would the Soviet fighter pilot have spoken? If no action was taken the target soon would cross over Sakhalin Island and enter international airspace again. Should they allow it to *escape* once more?

Tragically, just at the moment when the Air Defense Command had to make a decision, the crew of Flight 007 unwittingly made that crucial choice easy for the Soviets. At 1620:28 Hours, Flight 007 began to climb, a planned altitude change approved by Tokyo ATC. The Air Defense Command saw it differently. Obviously their target was climbing and heading for international waters in an attempt to *escape*. Therefore, it had to be destroyed.

Probable Cause: An ICAO investigation was finalized ten years later in 1993. It revealed that Flight 007 erroneously maintained a heading of 246 degrees from climbout at Anchorage until the missile strike. The *most plausible* explanation was the:

> crew's failure to note that the autopilot had either been left in a heading mode or had been switched to INS when the aircraft was beyond the range for the INS to capture the desired track.

The pilots did not use any of several routine procedures that would have alerted them to their error. The faulty navigation took the flight deep into Soviet Union airspace:

The deviation from its assigned track resulted in [the flight] penetrating USSR sovereign airspace over Kamchatka Peninsula and Sakhalin Island and the surrounding territorial waters.

The crew of Flight 007 was (1) unaware of its navigation error, (2) unaware that it was in Soviet airspace, and (3) unaware of the presence of the Soviet fighter-interceptor aircraft. Soviet military aircraft tried to identify the "target." ICAO investigators concluded that Soviet military forces:

> assumed that [Flight 007] was a United States RC-135 [military] reconnaissance aircraft before they ordered its destruction.

The ICAO found that Soviet air defense forces ordered the target to be destroyed when it was inside Soviet airspace. The ICAO found that the loss of Flight 007 was the result of *"human error."*

Postscript: The destruction of Flight 007 remains the last great crisis of the Cold War era. The large loss of life prompted a storm of protest worldwide. Many years later in Russia, the Yeltsin administration declassified the "black box" transcripts and other records relating to the shoot-down of the airliner.

Some die-hard conspiracy theorists still believe the truth has yet to be told. Many claim that the "007" flight number is "proof" that the Americans, or the British, or the Japanese, or South Koreans, or *someone* turned the airliner into a clandestine "James Bond" spyplane. Others believe that the 269 people aboard the flight survived and were shipped off to a Siberian gulag as slave laborers. Some say that the Soviets killed everyone aboard because they had "targeted" a passenger, an unnamed covert double agent.

Conspiracy theories will never end, but there is one eternal and undeniable truth. The 269 innocent people on Flight 007 must be added to the list of victims of the long Cold War.

> *Note: Five years later, in a similar case of mistaken identity, the U.S. Navy would shoot down a civilian airliner (see the chapter, "Iran Air Flight 655").*

Delta Airlines Flight 191

Lockheed L-1011 TriStar, registration N726DA
2 August 1985, near Fort Worth, Texas
163 aboard, 134 killed (plus 1 killed on the ground)

Three years earlier a Boeing 727 had flown into microburst-induced windshear on takeoff, and it crashed a mile from the airport (see the chapter, "Pan Am Flight 759"). Now, nature's microburst fury would swat a big jumbo-jet from the sky.

Overview: A Lockheed L-1011 TriStar was on final approach near Fort Worth, Texas. Flying beneath a thunderstorm, the airliner encountered a microburst. Horizontal and vertical windshear tossed the big aircraft like a rag-doll. The TriStar flew into the ground a mile short of the runway, killing 134 of the 163 people aboard.

The Flight: On 2 August 1985 at Fort Lauderdale, Florida, 152 passengers and a crew of 11 boarded a big Lockheed L-1011 TriStar. The tri-jet, Delta Airlines Flight 191, took off and headed toward an en route stop at Dallas-Fort Worth International Airport. As they neared New Orleans the pilots took a more northerly route to avoid stormy weather along the Gulf Coast. They had no way to know that the worst weather lay ahead of them in Texas. They would fly into a meteorological monster at their destination:

The microburst diameter was 3.4 kilometers. The horizontal windshear across the microburst was 72 knots; the maximum updrafts and downdrafts were 25 fps and 49 fps, respectively.

The captain, age 57, held an ATP certificate and had amassed 29,300 hours of experience in his logbook. Over the years he had built a reputation as a meticulous by-the-book pilot who would cautiously circumvent thunderstorms. His first officer, age 42, held a Commercial Pilot certificate and had logged 6,500 hours in the air. The flight engineer, like the two pilots, had been characterized by his peers as professional. He had been flying in the L-1011 for five years and had logged 4,500 hours in the aircraft. Backing up the cockpit crew were eight flight attendants who ranged from 23 to 35 years of age.

The L-1011 TriStar chosen for this flight, registration N726DA, had been delivered new to Delta in 1979. Since then it had logged 20,555 hours in the air. On this trip it left Fort Lauderdale with a relatively light load of passengers and fuel, putting it far below its maximum takeoff weight of 430,000 pounds. Three Rolls-Royce engines, one slung under each wing and another mounted in the vertical stabilizer, powered the big wide-body airliner. Each engine could produce over 41,000 pounds of thrust.

Trouble Ahead: Fort Worth Center cleared Flight 191 to begin its descent at 1735 Hours. The controller vectored the flight around thunderstorms that had mushroomed in the hot and humid Texas afternoon. After skirting around one ominous looking weather cell the captain casually remarked to his first officer at 1748 Hours:

> I'm glad we didn't have to go through that mess, I thought sure [the controller] was going to send us through it.

ATC cleared the pilots for an approach to Runway 17L. The TriStar captured the ILS localizer and glideslope at 1803:11 Hours, and the aircraft rode down the invisible electronic rails in the sky toward the runway. Dead ahead, between the aircraft and the airport, a severe thunderstorm lashed the approach path.

The portion of the CVR transcript, below, begins with the aircraft on final approach after Approach Control has handed the flight off to the tower. The first officer is flying the TriStar:

Capt: . . . . . Captain, Flight 191
FO: . . . . . . First Officer, Flight 191
FltEngr: . . . Flight Engineer, Flight 191
GPWS: . . . . Ground Proximity Warning System, Flight 191
Radio-: . . . . (prefix) Radio transmission, Flight 191
Tower: . . . . Dallas-Fort Worth Airport Control Tower

Radio-Capt: Tower, Delta one-ninety-one heavy [is] out here in the rain, feels good. (1803:58)

Tower: Delta one-ninety-one heavy, [this is the] regional tower,

Runway one-seven left, cleared to land, wind zero-nine-zero at five [knots], gusts to one-five. (1804:01)

Radio-Capt: Thank you, sir. (1804:06)

FO: Before landing check. (1804:07)

FltEngr: Landing gear. (1804:08)

Capt: Down, three green. (1804:10)

FltEngr: Flaps, slats. (1804:11)

Capt: Thirty-three, thirty-three, green light. (1804:12)

FO: Lightning [is] coming out of that [thunderstorm]. (1804:18)

Capt: What? (1804:19)

FO: Lightning [is] coming out of that one. (1804:21)

Capt: Where? (1804:22)

FO: Right ahead of us. (1804:23)

Capt or FO: [The rain will] wash [us] off a little bit. (1805:04)

Capt: A thousand feet. (1805:05)

Capt: I'll call [altitude and airspeed] out to you. (1805:12)

FO: All right. (1805:13)

[an invisible microburst has formed beneath the thunderstorm]

*[754 feet above the ground the aircraft flies into a strong and **sudden headwind**; airspeed increases; the First Officer pulls the throttles back to flight idle at 1805:14]*

Capt: Watch your speed. (1805:19)

*[the headwind suddenly changes to a **strong tailwind**; airspeed drops; an **extreme downdraft** grips the aircraft at 1805:19]*

[sound of heavy rain begins at 1805:20]

Capt: You're gonna lose it all of a sudden! There it is! (1805:21)

Capt: Push [the throttles] up. Push it way up! (1805:26)

Capt: Way up! (1805:27)

Capt: Way up! (1805:28)

Capt: Way up! (1805:29)

[sound of high engine rpm at 1805:29]

Capt: That's it. (1805:30)

[a windshear vortex rolls the aircraft to the right at 1805:31]

Capt: Hang on to the [expletive]! (1805:36)

FO: What's the vee-ref? (1805:39)

*[caught in the grip of the strong downdraft, the aircraft begins a **rapid descent** at 1805:42]*

GPWS: Whoop whoop, pull up, whoop whoop . . . . (1805:44)

[the Captain puts the flight director in TOGA mode at 1805:45]

Capt: TOGA! (1805:45)

[sound of the radio altimeter alert at 1805:46]

GPWS: Whoop whoop, pull up, whoop whoop . . . . (1805:46)

Capt: Push it way up! (1805:47)

GPWS: Whoop whoop, pull up, whoop whoop . . . . (1805:48)

[sound of the stick-shaker activating at 1805:48]

*[sound of initial **"touchdown"** in a **plowed field** at 1805:52]*

Capt or FO: [Expletive]! (1805:53)

*[sound of **impact with a car** on a highway at 1805:55]*

Capt or FO: Oh, [expletive]! (1805:55)

Tower: Delta, go around! (1805:56)

*[sound of the **impacts with two water towers**; end of the CVR tape at 1805:58]*

The Accident: Flight 191 had flown into horizontal and vertical windshear in a microburst. A sudden tailwind had stolen crucial airspeed, and a 49 foot per second downdraft pushed the TriStar earthward. Gear and flaps down, slats extended, nose high, wings level, engines spooling up to full power, the airliner mushed toward the ground. The pilots were *almost* able to arrest the descent:

> The airplane touched down initially . . . 6,336 feet north of the runway threshold in a plowed field in a wings level [and] nose-high attitude.

The main landing gear left tracks 240 feet long and 8 inches deep in the field. Undamaged, the aircraft struggled back into the air, then settled again. Because of the tailwind from the microburst there was little airspeed, but the L-1011 had over 200 knots of ground speed. Later, investigators would determine:

> The main gear . . . finally touched down [again] just before [reaching] the north edge of State Highway 114. The nose gear touched down in the westbound lane of the highway.

The main landing gear struck a car, crushing and killing the driver instantly. Tearing through several light poles along the roadside, the aircraft began to break apart. It skidded 1,700 feet, sideswiped one water tower, then scored a direct hit on a second water tower. The empennage and the rear of the cabin ripped off from the rest of the fuselage. Many occupants were flung from the aircraft as it tumbled to a stop and erupted into flames.

Firefighting vehicles from the three airport fire stations sped to the burning wreckage. They soon were joined by firefighting crews from around the Fort Worth area, and within 10 minutes they quenched the flames. There had been 163 people on board, and 134 of them died in the crash and fire.

Burned survivors crawled from the tangle of torn aluminum that had once been the aft section of the passenger cabin. It had broken free from the rest of the fuselage, allowing it to escape the flames that roared through most of the wreckage. The injured survivors, 3 flight attendants and 26 passengers, collapsed onto the ground in the driving wind and rain.

The Investigation: What had gone wrong? Investigators poured over records of the weather through which Flight 191 had flown on final approach. They quickly found that the airliner had tangled with both vertical and horizontal windshear.

The experts reconstructed the flight. In landing configuration, low and slow, the aircraft had flown into a rainshaft under a severe *level four* thunderstorm. Below the boiling cumulonimbus cloud an invisible **microburst** had formed (non-flying laymen may refer to a previous chapter, "Pan Am Flight 759," for the description of a microburst and its impact on aircraft during the landing or takeoff phase of flight). The investigators found:

> Flight 191 entered the microburst at 1805:14 [Hours] and crashed at 1805:52 [Hours]. During that 38 seconds it encountered a horizontal windshear of about 72 knots.

Windshear of 72 knots! Approaching the runway at 150 knots, the Tri-Star had flown into outflowing winds from the invisible monster at 1805:14 Hours. A sudden headwind caused the airspeed to jump to 173 knots. In response the first officer pulled the throttles to flight idle and pushed the nose down to remain on the ILS glideslope.

Five seconds later at 1805:19 Hours the aircraft flew into severe horizontal windshear. The headwind was almost instantly replaced by a strong tailwind. The airspeed quickly fell by an incredible 53 knots -- from 173 knots to 120 knots. Almost simultaneously a swirling windshear vortex rolled the aircraft to the right. Then a violent 49 foot per second downdraft gripped the aircraft, driving it down toward the ground. Meteorologists learned:

> Flight 191 entered a microburst which the pilot was unable to traverse successfully. *[and also]* The flight encountered a second severe disturbance subsequently identified as the vortex ring, consisting of large variations in wind components along all three axes of the airplane.

The first officer found himself in grave peril. He was low and slow. His engines had spooled down to flight idle. His craft was descending rapidly, caught in an aerodynamic vice. He firewalled his throttles. He needed both *time and altitude* to recover, but unfortunately he had neither.

The first officer pulled his control column far back, desperately trying to stop the descent. The angle-of-attack increased to 23 degrees. The stick-shaker signaled imminent disaster. On the brink of a stall with no airspeed or altitude to spare, snared by the strong downdraft, the aircraft mushed down onto the plowed field.

Probable Cause: Just over a year after the loss of Flight 191 the NTSB adopted NTSB-AAR-86-05 on 15 August 1986. The board found that the pilots had no specific information that could have enabled them to identify the presence of extreme windshear on their approach course. Windshear is invisible, and its existence can not always be predicted in advance.

Yet, the board noted that the pilots had sufficient information to know that they were flying into, or beneath, a thunderstorm on final approach. Faced with visible evidence of this severe weather, their decision to continue the approach violated their employer's weather avoidance procedures, as explained by the board:

> The Delta Flight Operations Procedures Manual states that below 10,000 feet, thunderstorms are to be avoided by 5 miles. Furthermore, the Delta company publication *Up Front* . . . stated in part, "Microbursts occur from [thunderstorm] cell activity. Do not take off or land directly beneath a cell."

The board reported: "The captain should have been well aware of the volatility of these storms." Yet, the board pointed out that he never voiced a desire to execute a missed approach until seven seconds before the touchdown in the plowed field. The board found that the *Probable Cause* of this accident was threefold:

> [First was] the flight crew's decision to initiate and continue the approach into a cumulonimbus cloud which they observed to contain visible lightning.

> [Second was the] lack of specific guidelines, procedures, and training for avoiding and escaping from low-altitude windshear.

> [Third was the] lack of definitive real-time windshear hazard information which resulted in the aircraft's encounter at low altitude with a microburst-induced severe windshear from a rapidly developing thunderstorm located on the final approach course.

Arrow Air Flight 1285

Douglas DC-8, registration N950JW
12 December 1985, at Gander, Newfoundland, Canada
256 aboard, 256 killed

Overview: Soldiers of the 101st Airborne Division, U.S. Army, headed for home two weeks before Christmas on a charter flight. After a refueling stop at Gander, Newfoundland, the Douglas DC-8 roared down the runway for the trip to Fort Campbell, Kentucky. The aircraft mushed into the air, stalled, then crashed and burned. The impact and fire killed all 256 people on board.

The Flight: In the volatile Middle East a multinational military force performed "peacekeeping" duty in the Sinai Desert. Many soldiers of the 101st Airborne Division, U.S. Army, who had been assigned to this force were scheduled to return to their base at Fort Campbell, Kentucky, at the end of 1985. Their commanders vowed to get them "home before Christmas."

Chartered by the U.S. Army, Arrow Air Flight MF1285R (Flight 1285) took off from Cairo, Egypt, with 248 soldiers who were headed for Fort Campbell. The DC-8, registration N950JW, had been built in 1969 and had accumulated 50,861 flying hours. For this flight it was loaded well under its maximum takeoff weight of 355,000 pounds. The airliner stopped in Cologne, Germany, to refuel. Then it took off and flew westward over the Atlantic Ocean at night, and at 0534 Hours the pilots made another refueling stop at Gander, Newfoundland, in Canada.

At Gander in the pre-dawn darkness on 12 December 1985 the soldiers of the 101st Airborne Division looked forward to the final leg of their trip home to Fort Campbell. Their families, relatives, and friends anticipated their arrival around midmorning. The military brass had planned a festive "Welcome Home" ceremony. The band would play, the crowd would cheer, children would wave small American flags, and family members would rush to embrace the returning warriors.

The experienced Arrow Air captain on this flight, age 45, held an ATP certificate and had logged 7,001 flight hours. The previous year he had been appointed Vice President and Director of Flight Operations at Arrow Air. His first officer, also age 45, held a Commercial Pilot certificate and had logged 5,549 flight hours. The flight engineer had gained the necessary experience, and a contingent of five flight attendants staffed the cabin.

Trouble Ahead: Before daylight in freezing rain and snow the DC-8 lined up for takeoff on Runway 22 at Gander. The first officer was flying the airliner. He advanced the four throttles and released his brakes at 0645:06 Hours:

> For several hours . . . light precipitation in the form of snow, snow grains, and freezing drizzle had been falling.

Fifty-one seconds after the start of the takeoff roll, 8,000 feet down the runway, the airliner lifted off at 167 knots. Still in ground effect, the DC-8 accelerated to 172 knots. However, as the first officer attempted to climb, the DC-8 decelerated. Airspeed dropped all the way down to 142 knots. The airliner shuddered and mushed downward. The CVR would prove to be inoperative, so there would be no voice transcript.

The Accident: Twenty seconds after liftoff, nose high, right wing low, yawed to the right, the DC-8 flew into the treetops 2,975 feet beyond the end of the runway. The aircraft tore apart as it cut a 1,300 foot long swath through the trees. Two engines broke away, and the empennage ripped off at the aft pressure bulkhead. The wings and cockpit then tore off, and the remains of the fuselage tumbled down into a ravine.

A severe fuel-fed fire erupted. Airport firefighting crews arrived at the site about 10 minutes after the crash, and they quickly were joined by crews from the town of Gander. They extinguished the main fires within 45 minutes, although spot fires continued to burn for 23 hours. The 256 people in the aircraft had perished.

Assisting Canadian authorities, the Armed Forces Institute of Pathology in the United States conducted autopsies on the bodies of the soldiers and the aircraft crew. These examinations verified the manner of death for 247 of the 256 people on board. The medical examiner determined that 175 of the victims died as a direct result of impact related trauma. An additional 41 victims succumbed to the combined effects of impact trauma and inhalation of combustion products. For the remaining victims, the examiner ruled that "impact injuries played no role in their deaths." Trapped inside the mangled and burning wreckage in the dark, they died due to inhalation of toxic gasses from the fire.

The Investigation: Canadian investigators began reconstructing the flight. The FDR showed that, following an apparently normal ground roll and takeoff, the aircraft failed to achieve a normal rate of climb. Airspeed fell, angle-of-attack increased to 21 degrees, and the aircraft stalled. Investigators searched for the cause of the performance degradation, and they discovered:

> As determined from the FDR, the aircraft stalled within 10 seconds of liftoff. . . . The aircraft stalled at an airspeed between 15 and 24 knots above the predicted stall speed.

Prior to takeoff the pilots had computed the gross takeoff weight to be 330,625 pounds. However, they used the standard airline guide of 170 pounds per passenger. Considering the all-adult and all-male soldiers plus their heavy baggage, investigators estimated that the actual takeoff weight was 344,540 pounds. The takeoff "bug" airspeeds should have been slightly higher. Nonetheless, by itself, the (1) weight increase and (2) bug speed errors would not have had a major effect on takeoff and climb performance.

Examination of the wreckage revealed that the No. 4 engine was producing less than normal power at impact. This could have been caused by a number of factors, including the high angle-of-attack as the aircraft stalled, or foliage ingestion as the aircraft plowed through the trees. In any event, computer analysis confirmed that this condition alone would not have played a significant role in the accident:

> The performance of the aircraft after liftoff . . . was consistent with the reduced aerodynamic efficiency and resultant high drag associated with *wing ice contamination* [emphasis added].

Experts knew that seemingly insignificant amounts of ice on an aircraft's wings can seriously degrade flight performance. This *roughening* of the airfoil surface is most severe when sleet or snow freezes atop a layer of ice. The rough surface alters the otherwise smooth flow of air over the wing. Drag and stall speed soar. Lift decreases. Calculations showed that on the ill-fated DC-8:

> The increase in drag and decrease in lift production were consistent . . . with wing surface roughness elements of [only] 0.03 inches, or an amount of leading edge ice contamination with equivalent effects.

A Boeing 737 had taken off right before the accident, and its pilots reported moderate icing. A PA-31 had landed shortly after the crash, and the pilot reported that icing obscured his vision through the windshield. Weather conditions at the airport had included freezing drizzle combined with light snow -- the precise conditions conducive to *maximum roughening* of the wings. The airport at Gander had deicing equipment available, but the pilots on Flight 1285 had declined to utilize it.

Probable Cause: On 28 October 1988, almost three years after the crash, the Canadian Aviation Safety Board finally released its Aviation Occurrence Report, No. 85-H50902. The board noted that the investigators had been "severely hampered" by the absence of a functional CVR. In addition, a more modern FDR would have documented engine performance, control surface movement, and other parameters that would have been of great assistance.

The board discovered *no smoking gun*, no tangible physical evidence that could explain the crash. Wreckage analysis by the Royal Canadian Mounted Police Central Forensic Laboratory turned up no evidence of a pre-impact explosion. There was no indication of mechanical failure or pre-impact fire. Consequently, the board turned to known phenomena that would leave no trace, phenomena that could logically account for the performance degradation exhibited by the DC-8. The board found *Causes* as follows:

> The Canadian Aviation Safety Board was unable to determine the exact sequence of events which led to this accident. The board believes, however, that the weight of evidence supports the conclusion that, shortly after liftoff, the aircraft experienced an increase in drag and reduction in lift which resulted in a stall

at low altitude from which recovery was not possible. The most probable cause of the stall was determined to be ice contamination on the leading edge and upper surface of the wing. Other possible factors such as a loss of thrust from the number four engine and inappropriate takeoff reference speeds may have compounded the effects of the [ice] contamination.

Postscript: Beginning shortly after dawn on 12 December 1985 at Fort Campbell, hundreds of wives, parents, children, brothers, sisters, and friends had gathered to greet the returning soldiers. The huge crowd had been festive and merry, waiting for the arrival of the heroes who answered the call of Their Country. Everyone present had been eager for the big DC-8 to swoop down and land. Scores of children waved small American flags. The members of the band gathered, ready to play.

Military commanders at Fort Campbell got the sobering news in a series of telephone calls. Initial reports were sketchy. However, as the hours slipped away the magnitude of the tragedy became obvious. Commanders then tackled the gut-wrenching task of telling the waiting families that there would be no Welcome Home ceremony. Flight 1285 and all aboard had been lost.

Four days later Ronald Reagan, President of the United States, and his wife, Nancy, flew to Fort Campbell. The president spoke at length at a somber memorial service, and he explained:

You do not grieve alone. We grieve as a nation, together.

The loss of Flight 1285 was the worst military aviation disaster in the history of the United States. Today a monument stands at "Gander Grove" at Fort Campbell, and it is officially known as the Task Force 3-502 Memorial. On this memorial are inscribed the names of the 248 Screaming Eagles of the 101st Airborne Division who died in the crash of Arrow Air Flight 1285. They are the warriors who *almost* made it home for Christmas.

NASA Space Shuttle
Challenger

NASA Space Shuttle *Challenger*, mission 51-L
28 January 1986, over the Atlantic Ocean, near Florida
7 aboard, 7 killed

One could argue that the National Aeronautics and Space Administration (NASA) space shuttle transports are not airliners and should not be addressed in this book. Yet, the commercial aviation industry has much to learn from the United States' space exploration program.

Overview: On the cold morning of 28 January 1986, NASA launched the winged reusable space shuttle *Challenger*. Only 72 seconds into the flight, leaking propellent gas caused a structural failure. Supersonic aerodynamic forces then destroyed the launch vehicle and shuttle. The seven astronauts on board were killed.

The Flight: NASA began the "space shuttle" program in the early 1970s. The goal of this ambitious project was creation of a reusable transport to ferry cargo and passengers into low-Earth orbit above the atmosphere. The first such transport to be built, *Columbia*, launched in 1981.

The following year *Challenger* rolled off the assembly line. Named after an 1870s British research vessel, *HMS Challenger*, the latest shuttle completed its first flight in April 1983. The new winged vehicle followed that maiden flight with eight more successful research trips into orbit. By the end of 1985 the four NASA shuttles then in service (*Columbia, Challenger, Discovery,* and *Atlantis*) had completed 24 such flights.

Challenger prepared for another launch on 28 January 1986. Designated as Mission 51-L, this flight would involve a host of technical endeavors. A satellite would be deployed and Halley's Comet would be studied, among other things. Plus, in a unique effort to generate more public enthusiasm and government funding for the NASA program, a schoolteacher from New Hampshire would inaugurate the new Teacher in Space Program.

Early in the morning the seven astronauts, including the teacher, rode the crew elevator to the top of launch pad 39-B at the Kennedy Space Center in Florida. They strapped themselves into their seats, ready to go.

Trouble Ahead: However, not everyone was "ready to go." The temperature had dipped below freezing during the night. The cold weather alarmed engineers from Morton Thiokol, the manufacturer of the two solid-fuel booster rockets:

> The ambient air temperature at launch was 36 degrees Fahrenheit . . . . This temperature was 15 degrees colder than that of any previous launch.

The engineers pleaded with NASA management for a launch delay. They knew that cold temperature would make the booster rocket O-ring seals too brittle. Unfortunately NASA management dismissed the engineers' concern.

The portion of the transcript from the Operational Recorder voice tape, below, begins 30 seconds before liftoff. Instead of a time-of-day cue, this transcript uses seconds before-and-after liftoff. The transcript includes the radio transmissions from *Challenger* and conversation in the crew module, but it excludes NASA radio transmissions from the ground to *Challenger*:

> Cmdr: . . . . . . Commander, Mission 51-L
> Pilot: . . . . . . Pilot, Mission 51-L
> Spec-2: . . . . . . Mission Specialist No. 2, Mission 51-L
> UnidCrew: . . . . Unidentified crewmember, Mission 51-L

Cmdr: Thirty seconds [until launch] down there. (T-30)

Pilot: Remember the red button . . . . (T-25)

Cmdr: I won't do that, thanks a lot. (T-23)

Cmdr: Fifteen [seconds until launch]. (T-15)

[at T-07 seconds the three space shuttle liquid-fuel engines fire and throttle-up to 100 percent thrust]

Cmdr: There they go, guys, three [engines] at a hundred. (T-06)

Spec-2: All right! (T-06)

[the two big booster rockets fire; the launch vehicle begins to ascend at T+00]

Spec-2: Aaalll rrriiight! (T+00)

Pilot: Here we go. (T+01)

Cmdr: Houston, *Challenger* roll program. (T+07)

Pilot: Go, you mother! (T+11)

Spec-2: [Expletive] hot! (T+15)

Cmdr: Ooohhh-kkkaaay! (T+16)

Pilot: Looks like we've got a lotta wind here today. (T+19)

Cmdr: Yeah. (T+20)

Cmdr: It's a little hard to see out my window here. (T+22)

Pilot: There's ten-thousand feet and Mach point-five. (T+28)

Cmdr: [Mach] point-nine. (T+35)

Pilot: There's Mach one. (T+40)

Cmdr: Going through nineteen-thousand [feet]. (T+41)

Cmdr: OK, we're throttling down. (T+43)

[the launch vehicle momentarily reduces power, as planned, in the region of maximum dynamic air pressure]

Cmdr: [We are] throttling [back] up. (T+57)

Pilot: Throttle-up. (T+58)

Cmdr: Roger. (T+59)

Pilot: Feel that mother go! (T+60)

UnidCrew: Wwwooo-hhhooo! *[an exultation]* (T+60)

Pilot: [We are at] thirty-five-thousand [feet], going through [Mach] one-point-five. (T+62)

<u>Cmdr</u>: Reading four-eighty-six on [my airspeed indicator]. (T+65)

<u>Pilot</u>: Yep, that's what I've got too. (T+67)

<u>Cmdr</u>: Roger, go at throttle-up. (T+70)

[a strut on the right solid rocket booster fails due to heat damage; the right booster rocket breaks free at T+72]

<u>Pilot</u>: Uh-oh! (T+73)

[loss of all telemetry data; end of the transcript at T+73]

The Accident: Disaster struck 72 seconds into the flight as the shuttle sped upward through Mach 1.92 at 46,000 feet. The right booster rocket broke free from the massive external tank. The ruptured tank allowed liquid hydrogen and liquid oxygen to mix and ignite, creating an aerial fireball:

> Within milliseconds there was a massive . . . burning of the hydrogen streaming from the failed tank bottom and the liquid oxygen breach in the area of the intertank.

Supersonic aerodynamic forces broke *Challenger* into several sections. The intact crew module containing the seven astronauts cleared the fireball. Within 25 seconds, inertia carried the module on upward to about 65,000 feet. From there it began a long free-fall toward the Atlantic Ocean below. Another 2 minutes and 25 seconds later it hit the surface of the sea at about 181 knots. The force of the impact was roughly 200 G's, and this far exceeded the survivability limits of the crew.

The shuttle and launch vehicle, valued at three billion dollars, were totally destroyed. The seven astronauts died while strapped in their seats with harnesses locked. A salvage operation would recover the crew module and its human remains from the floor of the ocean 40 days later.

The Investigation: Ronald Reagan, President of the United States, set up a task force to investigate the loss of *Challenger*. He picked William Rogers, former U.S. Secretary of State, to head the presidential commission.

What destroyed Challenger? Enhanced photographic data

showed that, less than one second into the launch, a strong puff of grey smoke spurted from the aft field joint on the right solid rocket booster.   Computer analysis of film from various viewpoints revealed that the smoke came from the 270 to 310 degree sector of the joint.   Within slightly over two seconds, eight more puffs appeared.   This told investigators what was happening:

Grease, joint insulation, and rubber O-rings in the joint seal were being burned and eroded by the hot propellent gasses. *[and also]* Vaporized material streaming from the joint indicated that there was not complete sealing within the joint.

The first flickering *flame* appeared 58 seconds into the flight. It grew into a well-defined plume within one second.   Telemetry then showed a lowering of the pressure in the right booster rocket, confirming a significant leak of the hot propellent gas.   The supersonic slipstream deflected the flame onto the external tank. The flame also impinged on the lower strut that attaches the solid rocket booster to the huge external tank.   At 64 seconds into the flight the flame breached the tank:

There was an abrupt change in the shape and color of the plume. This indicated that it was mixing with leaking hydrogen from the External Tank.

The breach in the external tank was confirmed by telemetry which showed dropping tank pressure.   The growing conflagration became a bright glow visible between the external tank and the belly of *Challenger*.   The launch vehicle struggled futilely against the forces trying to destroy it.   At 72 seconds into the flight the heat-weakened lower strut finally broke free from the tank:

The lower strut linking the Solid Rocket Booster and the External Tank was severed or pulled away from the weakened hydrogen tank, permitting the right Solid Rocket Booster to rotate around the upper attachment strut.

The launch vehicle and shuttle yawed violently.   At just under Mach 2, aerodynamic forces ripped at the unstreamlined vehicle. Structural disintegration took less than one second.   The aft dome of the hydrogen tank ripped away, and the liquid oxygen tank ruptured.   Within milliseconds the two volatile fuels combined and ignited, creating a massive aerial burn. Sideways in the violent supersonic slipstream, *Challenger* succumbed and broke apart.

When did the astronauts die? Video footage of the destruction of the shuttle and the launch vehicle was played and replayed by the scandal-hungry news media. To the layman this *suggested* that the seven astronauts died in a tremendous "explosion." However, analysis available to the commission revealed that the crew, in all likelihood, was not killed when *Challenger* broke apart. The launch vehicle did not actually "explode."

Both booster rockets continued to produce thrust. Out of control, they spiraled and corkscrewed skyward as video footage confirmed. The mixing of liquid fuels from the ruptured external tank, and the ruptured tanks on the shuttle, created a gigantic fireball in the upper atmosphere. This was an aerial "burning." It was *not* the violent "explosion" repeatedly referenced by the news media. The shuttle broke apart due to *aerodynamic* forces, not because of the fire. The crew module remained intact and hurtled beyond the fireball, and NASA scientists reported:

> The forces on the Orbiter at break-up were too low to cause death or serious injury, but were sufficient to separate the crew [module] from the forward fuselage. *[and also]* The probability of major injury to crewmembers is low [at this time].

Were the astronauts conscious during the long fall? The commission could not make an absolute determination. A team of medical specialists and engineers reported:

> It is possible, but not certain, that the crew lost consciousness due to an in-flight loss of cabin pressure.

The impact with the sea crushed the crew module. Investigators could not determine, to a certainty, if pressure had been lost prior to impact. Yet, they had a vital telltale clue. The helmet of each astronaut was connected to a Personal Egress Air Pack (PEAP). Each PEAP contained compressed air that the astronaut could breathe in an emergency. Four of the PEAPs were recovered from the crushed crew module. Three of them had been *manually* activated. In other words, after the break-up, three of these four astronauts still had the presence of mind -- and the ability -- to understand their dilemma and switch on their PEAP.

Probable Cause: On 6 June 1986 the *Report of the Presidential Commission on the Space Shuttle Challenger Accident* was made public. The commission relied on reams of data, records, civilian contractors, and various government agencies in establishing its conclusions, failure scenarios, and causative factors. The consensus of the commission and the participating investigative agencies was that *The Cause of the Accident* was as follows:

> The loss of the Space Shuttle *Challenger* was caused by a failure in the joint between the two lower segments of the right Solid Rocket Motor. The specific failure was the destruction of the seals that are intended to prevent hot gasses from leaking through the joint during the propellant burn of the rocket motor. The evidence assembled by the Commission indicates that no other element of the Space Shuttle system contributed to this failure.

In simple language, a rubber O-ring seal failed. Under extreme pressure, white-hot gasses from the rocket motor leaked through the joint. The searing flames (in effect, a blow-torch) penetrated the massive external tank and caused the lower strut to fail. Structural disintegration followed. The commission pointed out:

> The decision to launch the *Challenger* was flawed.

The manufacturer of the solid rocket booster had cautioned NASA, in writing, that it was unsafe to launch with a temperature below 53 degrees. Colder temperatures made the O-ring seal too brittle and subject to burn-through. Yet, NASA management had deemed the risk "acceptable."

AeroMexico Flight 498 and a General Aviation Aircraft

AeroMexico Flight 498
Douglas DC-9, registration XA-JED
31 August 1986, mid-air collision over Cerritos, California
64 aboard, 64 killed (plus 15 killed on the ground)

General Aviation Aircraft
Piper PA-28 Cherokee, registration N4891F
31 August 1986, mid-air collision over Cerritos, California
3 aboard, 3 killed

Overview: A Douglas DC-9 descended to land at Los Angeles, California. Meanwhile, a small Piper PA-28 Cherokee plodded through the Los Angeles Terminal Control Area without clearance from ATC. In clear weather the two aircraft collided over Cerritos, California. The collision and crashes killed all 64 people on the DC-9, the 3 occupants of the Piper, and 15 people on the ground.

The AeroMexico Flight: On 31 August 1986, Aeronaves de Mexico (AeroMexico) Flight 498 left Mexico City, Mexico, and headed for Los Angeles, California. The twin-jet Douglas DC-9, registration XA-JED, swooped down for an intermediate stop at Tijuana, Mexico. Then the aircraft took off at 1120 Hours for the short trip to Los Angeles. High over the congested urban sprawl of southern California the 58 passengers and 6 crewmembers fell under the guiding hands of Los Angeles Approach Control.

The DC-9 captain, age 46, held two ATP certificates. One was issued by the government of Mexico, and the other had been issued by the FAA in the United States. The captain had logged 10,641 flying hours, almost half of which were in the DC-9. His young first officer, age 26, held a Commercial Pilot certificate issued by Mexico and another issued by the FAA. He had logged a total of

1,463 hours, the vast majority of which were in the DC-9.

The General Aviation Flight: The General Aviation aircraft was piloted by its owner. He and two passengers took off from Torrence, California, at 1141 Hours on a flight to Big Bear, California. Although he never activated it, he had filed a VFR flight plan with a local flight service station. At 9,500 feet the proposed route would take the small airplane to Long Beach, then to the Paradise VORTAC, and then to Big Bear.

The owner-pilot, age 53, held a Private Pilot certificate issued by the FAA. He was properly qualified to make this flight, although he had logged only a relatively meager 231 flying hours. The Piper PA-28 Cherokee, registration N4891F, was a small single-engine airplane with fixed landing gear.

Trouble Ahead: The Piper drifted off course and blundered into the Los Angeles TCA. The Piper was not equipped with a CVR, and the pilot did not contact any air traffic control facility.

The portion of the CVR transcript from the DC-9 and the ATC transcript, below, begins as Flight 498 first contacts Los Angeles Approach Control. The first officer is flying the DC-9:

> Capt: . . . . Captain, Flight 498
> FO: . . . . First Officer, Flight 498
> Radio-: . . . . (prefix) Radio transmission, Flight 498
> AppControl: . . . . . Los Angeles Approach Control
> American 333: . . . American Airlines Flight 333

Radio-Capt: Los Angeles Approach [Control], good morning, this is AeroMexico four-ninety-eight . . . seven-thousand. (1147:38)

AppControl: AeroMexico four-ninety-eight, [this is] Los Angeles Approach, depart Seal Beach three-two-zero [for] vector [to] ILS [for Runway] two-five left, final approach. (1147:39)

Radio-Capt: Affirmative, two-five-left [is the] runway. (1147:46)

Capt: Course two-four-nine, flight director up. (1148:15)

FO: Flight director up. (1148:16)

[1 minute and 49 seconds pass]

<u>AppControl</u>: AeroMexico four-ninety-eight, reduce speed to two-one-zero [knots]. (1150:05)

<u>Radio-Capt</u>: [Reduce] to two-one-zero, four-ninety-eight. (1150:08)

*[in the clear sunny sky, each aircraft is now within the others' field of vision; **both will remain visible** until the collision]*

<u>AppControl</u>: AeroMexico four-ninety-eight, reduce speed to one-niner-zero, then descend and maintain six-thousand. (1151:03)

<u>Radio-Capt</u>: [Reduce speed to] one-niner-zero and then descend and maintain six-thousand. (1151:09)

<u>AppControl</u>: AeroMexico four-ninety-eight, maintain your present speed. (1151:46)

<u>Radio-Capt</u>: Roger, AeroMexico four-ninety-eight, uuuhhh, what speed do you want? We're reducing to one-niner-zero. (1151:48)

<u>AppControl</u>: OK, you can hold what you have, sir, and we have a change in plans here, stand by. (1151:57)

*[at 6,560 feet **the DC-9 and the Piper collide** at 1152:09]*

<u>Capt</u>: Oh, [expletive], this can't be! (1152:10)

[the controller does not know the two aircraft have collided; he makes a routine radio call to Flight 498]

<u>AppControl</u>: AeroMexico four-ninety-eight, expect the ILS two-four right approach, localizer frequency is . . . . (1152:12)

[there is no response]

[the radar return from Flight 498 fades off the controller's scope; the airliner impacts the ground at 1152:32]

<u>AppControl</u>: AeroMexico four-ninety-eight, turn left [to] heading two-eight-zero. (1152:58)

<u>AppControl</u>: AeroMexico four-ninety-eight, turn left [to] heading two-eight-zero. (1153:03)

<u>AppControl</u>: AeroMexico four-ninety-eight, turn left [to] heading two-eight-zero. (1153:08)

AppControl: AeroMexico four-ninety-eight, [this is] Los Angeles Approach. (1153:24)

[between 1153:43 and 1155:16 the controller makes four more attempts to contact Flight 498, but there is no response]

AppControl: American three-thirty-three heavy, I want you to look around at eleven o'clock and about five miles, I just lost contact with a DC-9, let me know if you see anything. (1156:05)

American 333: What altitude? (1156:17)

AppControl: He was last assigned to six-[thousand feet], he's no longer on my radar scope. (1156:21)

American 333: OK, I see a -- uuuhhh -- very large smoke screen off on the left side of [my] aircraft, abeam the nose of [my] airplane, right off our left. It is a very large smoke -- uuuhhh -- column -- uuuhhh -- coming from it, emanating from the ground. And at our altitude, eight-thousand feet, [we can see] another smoke column . . . . (1156:26)

The Accident: At 1152:09 Hours in a cloudless sunny sky with a reported visibility of 14 miles, the two aircraft collided. The impact tore the vertical stabilizer and horizontal stabilizer off the Douglas airliner. Collision damage was confined to the tail and its control surfaces. The passengers and crew survived the collision, but their aircraft nosed over and plunged down toward the ground a mile below. The DC-9 dove into a residential area of Cerritos, California, and exploded:

The airplane cockpit and passenger cabin were destroyed by massive impact forces and [a] post-crash fire. Although the occupants of the DC-9 survived the mid-air impact, this was an unsurvivable [ground impact].

The crash of Flight 498 killed all 64 people on the aircraft and another 15 people on the ground. The impact and the fire totally destroyed five homes and seriously damaged many others. The bodies of the two pilots were too "fragmented" to allow an autopsy or toxicological testing. The Los Angeles Country Coroner ruled that all occupants died from "multiple blunt force trauma."

The small Piper aircraft, wings level, had flown straight into the vertical stabilizer of the DC-9. The Piper engine and fuselage tore completely through the airliner structure. The top of the Piper fuselage peeled away, decapitating the pilot and his two passengers. The heavy engine and propeller unit separated from the rest of the airframe, and the fuselage fell to earth in a schoolyard about 1,700 feet from the DC-9 wreckage.

The Piper did not burn upon impact. The coroner would ascribe the deaths of the three Piper occupants to "multiple trauma due to, or as a consequence of, blunt force." Fragments of human remains from the Piper occupants were found embedded in the wreckage of the horizontal stabilizer of the DC-9 almost a half-mile away.

The Investigation: Accident reconstruction experts from the NTSB poured over a wealth of technical information. Recorded ATC radar data showed that the DC-9 had been flying northeast. The Piper had been flying southeast on a track perpendicular to the track of the DC-9:

> The airplanes collided at a 90 [degree] angle at an altitude of 6,560 feet, and in visual meteorological conditions.

The Piper flew straight into the left side of the vertical stabilizer of the DC-9. Even though the Piper was a much smaller and lighter aircraft, its heavy engine and propeller unit had torn through the main support structure of the airliner's vertical fin. Both the vertical and horizontal stabilizers ripped off of the airliner, and further controlled flight was not possible:

> The evidence was conclusive that the collision occurred within the Los Angeles TCA; that the Piper pilot had entered the TCA without having been cleared to do so; that the controller did not advise Flight 498 of the position of the Piper; and that neither pilots tried to perform any type of evasive maneuver.

The radar track of the Piper revealed that it had flown almost directly to the scene of the collision after taking off from Torrence. The Piper was equipped with a transponder, and it had been set to Code 1200. The transponder displayed only position information, not altitude, on the ATC radar display. The controller testified that he never saw the radar return from the Piper.

The NTSB conducted an exhaustive cockpit visibility study. It revealed that each aircraft had been within the other's field of vision for at least 1 minute and 13 seconds before the collision. The Piper had been visible through the center windshield of the airliner. The airliner had been visible through the right windshield of the Piper. The visibility study concluded:

> The AeroMexico flight crew should have had an almost unobstructed view of the Piper PA-28. *[and also]* The Piper pilot had an 80 percent probability of seeing the DC-9.

Probable Cause: The NTSB adopted its Aircraft Accident Report, NTSB-AAR-87-07, on 7 July 1987. In the VFR conditions inside the Los Angeles TCA, the FAA regulations required the pilots in both aircraft to "see and avoid" each other. Yet, there was no evidence to indicate that any of the pilots saw the other aircraft heading toward them. Neither aircraft tried to avoid the other, for both were in straight and level flight when they collided.

The board found that the Piper was not cleared to enter the Los Angeles TCA, but that the entry was inadvertent. The presence of the Piper in the TCA was a "casual factor" to the accident. The board determined that the radar return from the Piper "may not have been displayed, or may have been displayed weakly" on the controller's display.

The board found that the ***Probable Cause*** of this accident fell upon the shoulders of the ATC system in the United States. The board found that the accident resulted from:

> the limitations of the Air Traffic Control system to provide collision protection through both air traffic control procedures and automated redundancy.

The board found two factors that ***contributed*** to the accident:

> [First was the] inadvertent and unauthorized entry of the [Piper] PA-28 into the Los Angeles TCA.

> [Second were the inherent age-old] limitations of the "see-and-avoid" concept to ensure traffic separation [during VMC flight].

Southern Air Transport Flight 15

Lockheed L-382 Hercules, registration N15ST
4 October 1986, at Kelly Air Force Base, Texas
3 aboard, 3 killed

Overview: A Lockheed L-382 Hercules attempted to take off from Kelly Air Force Base, Texas, at night on a contract military cargo flight. After liftoff the aircraft climbed, rolled inverted, and crashed because of an ironic oversight. All three members of the crew died in the crash.

The Flight: Southern Air Transport earned a rich history. The company was born during the turmoil of World War II:

The then-shadowy airline and its mercenary pilots and ground crews flew passengers and cargo for the U.S. Armed Forces in the Pacific Theater and in Southeast Asia. Most people who do not have an aviation background know nothing about Southern Air Transport, but they have heard of "Air America." If they visit the Air America Memorial in Dallas, Texas, they will find that Southern Air Transport is also honored.

In recent years Southern Air Transport (SAT) has concentrated on domestic military cargo contracts. In the predawn darkness on 4 October 1986 one of its "freighters" was loaded at Kelly Air Force Base at San Antonio, Texas. SAT was scheduled to fly the Air Force cargo, which included military explosives, to Warner Robbins Air Force Base in Georgia.

The Lockheed L-382 Hercules, registration N15ST, was a civil "stretched" version of the military C-130 Hercules workhorse. This four-engine turboprop cargo hauler had accumulated 45,621 flight hours since its manufacture in 1971. SAT had acquired the aircraft only three weeks earlier on a lease option.

The captain, age 52, was a former U.S. Air Force pilot, and he held the customary ATP certificate. He had over 7,000 hours in his logbook and around 1,400 hours in the C-130/L-382 type of aircraft. His first officer had been employed by SAT for less than a week, but he was an experienced pilot. However, although ATP rated, he was new to the L-382. Backing the two pilots up in the cockpit was the flight engineer, also a former military pilot. He had logged over 6,000 hours in the L-382.

Trouble Ahead: At 0405 Hours, Kelly Tower cleared the flight for takeoff on Runway 15. Yet, a combination of circumstances would cut the flight short. Slightly over two minutes after getting their takeoff clearance the three crewmembers would be dead.

The portion of the CVR transcript, below, begins before takeoff. The captain has the controls. The first officer contacts Kelly Ground Control and reports that he is ready for his ATC clearance and ready to taxi. Controllers use the radio call-sign "LogAir" for all Southern Air Transport flights:

Capt: . . . . Captain, Flight 15
FO: . . . . First Officer, Flight 15
FltEngr: . . . . . Flight Engineer, Flight 15
Radio-:   . . . . . . (prefix) Radio transmission, Flight 15
GPWS: . . . . . . Ground Proximity Warning System, Flight 15
GndControl: . . . Kelly Air Force Base Ground Control
Tower: . . . . . . Kelly Air Force Base Control Tower

GndControl: LogAir one-five, cleared to Warner Robbins as filed, except change route to read Jay one-thirty-eight Seeds, direct [to] Lufkin, on departure fly runway heading, climb and maintain one-three-thousand, expect flight level two-three-zero one-zero minutes after departure, departure frequency will be one-two-five-point-seven, squawk two-four-seven-two, taxi to Runway one-five, wind one-four-zero at five, altimeter two-niner-niner-four. (0400:37)

[the First Officer reads back the clearance at 0401:12]

GndControl: LogAir one-five, read-back is correct. (0401:28)

[the aircraft taxis out toward the runway; the pilots go through their checklists for 3 minutes; then the First Officer announces]

FO: We be all set. (0404:27)

FO: I'm going to flip over to [the Kelly Air Force Base] Tower and tell 'em we're ready. (0404:58)

Capt: OK.

Radio-FO: Ah, Tower, LogAir one-five's ready. (0405:02)

Tower: LogAir one-five, last one-thousand feet [of the runway is] closed, wind one-five-zero at four, cleared for takeoff. (0405:24)

Radio-FO: [LogAir] one-five, roger. (0405:33)

FO: Transponder's on. (0405:36)

Capt: OK, before takeoff check. (0405:39)

FltEngr: OK, whenever you're ready for one and four, Captain.

Capt: One and four normal. (0405:44)

FO: Off at [zero-four]-zero-five. (0405:50)

Capt: Yeah.

FltEngr: Before takeoff check is complete. (0405:59)

FltEngr: Lights are out.

Capt: Set max power [on the engines for takeoff]. (0406:45)

Capt: Airspeed's alive. (0406:48)

FO: Sixty knots. (0406:55)

Capt: My yoke. (0406:59)

FO: Your yoke. (0407:00)

FO: V-one. (0407:08)

FO: Rotate. (0407:10)

*[as the aircraft rotates, **the control column jams** in the aft position; the aircraft takes off and **climbs much too steeply**]*

[the Captain desperately tries to push the control column forward; he pleads with the First Officer to help him]

Capt: [Expletive]! Help me on my yoke! (0407:12)

Capt: Help me on the yoke! God! Help, push forward! (0407:16)

FO: I can't get it down! (0407:19)

*[the Captain sees the problem, a "**control block**"]*

Capt: You got this [expletive] thing in here! (0407:21)

[the Flight Engineer sees that the control column must be pulled back, slightly, to allow removal of the control block]

FltEngr: Come on. Pull it. Pull it back a little. Pull it back a little. Did you pull it back? (0407:23)

Capt: OK, let me roll it into a bank. (0407:27)

FO: What's the airspeed doing? (0407:32)

Capt: [Expletive] it! OK, come on, get it over! (0407:34)

FO: We're dead! (0407:36)

Capt: Lots of rudder! Lots of rudder! (0407:38)

FltEngr: OK, it's clear now. (0407:41)

*[the control block has been removed, but the aircraft is **inverted** only a few hundred feet above the ground]*

GPWS: Whoop whoop, pull up, whoop whoop . . . . (0407:42)

Capt, FO, or FltEngr: Oh, [expletive]! (0407:42)

[sound of impact; end of the CVR tape at 0407:45]

The Accident: Even though it was dark, during takeoff the aircraft was visible to Kelly Tower because of background lighting. The controllers watched the aircraft rotate after a normal takeoff run of about 4,500 feet. A few seconds after liftoff it was obvious that something had gone awry. The aircraft pitched up to an *extreme nose high* attitude in excess of 40 degrees and climbed to about 700 feet above the ground.

Airspeed decreased, and the Hercules began a slow roll and a descending turn to the left. The roll continued until the aircraft became inverted. With the gear still extended and the flaps still at 50 degrees, Flight 15 dove into the ground between two aircraft hangers. Full of fuel, and with the cargo of military explosives, it exploded upon impact.

The impact threw debris and pieces of the Hercules as far as 1,666 feet from the crash site. Two aircraft hangers sustained fire and impact damage. The crash also destroyed an Air Force bus, two vans, two trucks, an aircraft tug, and three privately owned vehicles. The L-382, valued at eight million dollars, and its cargo were destroyed. The three men aboard died instantly.

The Investigation: A brief explanation is necessary:

Like its military cousin, the C-130 Hercules, cargo is loaded into the L-382 via a rear ramp under the horizontal stabilizer and elevator at the back of the aircraft. To make sure that the elevator is not hanging down and damaged during loading operations, some cargo airlines used an elevator control block. This device would be installed in the cockpit to hold the control column to the rear, raising the elevator.

NTSB investigators offered their own explanation:

The elevator control block was non-approved and was used to hold the elevator control surface in a faired to slightly trailing-edge-up position in order to prevent damage to the elevator control surface during cargo loading operations.

Sifting through the rubble of what had once been the cockpit of Flight 15, investigators found a control block. The first officer on the *previous* flight confirmed that he installed the control block prior to leaving the aircraft. He acknowledged that it did not have a "Remove Before Flight" warning banner attached to it.

Investigators found that it was a common *unwritten* practice for a SAT first officer to install the control block after completing a flight. When entering the cockpit in preparation for another flight, the new first officer would remove the control block and store it behind the bunk in the rear of the cockpit. Although this was a common practice, it was not officially approved. The Lockheed Maintenance Manual prohibited use of control blocks, and they were not included on checklists used by pilots. SAT training did not address use of a control block.

Although he was an experienced pilot, the first officer on the fatal flight was new to SAT. He had been hired only six days before the accident. Investigators found that there was no control block on the aircraft in which he took his transition training, and the use of such a device was not covered in his ground training classes. The investigators determined:

> The captain and flight engineer were aware of the use of an elevator control block, and the first officer was not aware of the [existence or use of the] device.

In reconstructing the accident, investigators found that the control block had fallen to the floor of the cockpit near the rudder pedals. Score marks in the metal revealed that it became lodged against the rudder pedal shroud, jamming the control column to the rear. This effectively locked the elevator in the nose-up position.

Probable Cause: The NTSB issued its Aircraft Accident Report, NTSB-AAR-87-04, on 9 April 1987. The board pointed out that the new first officer was not aware of the control block. Yet, at SAT it had been an "unwritten practice" for first officers to remove and store the device before flight.

The FAA was aware of the unauthorized use of control blocks by some cargo-hauling airlines, but it had not issued cautions against such use. Lockheed also was aware of the use of these devices. Lockheed had printed precautions against their use in the aircraft Maintenance Manual, but these precautions were not printed in the Flight Manual used by pilots. SAT had no written policy concerning these devices. The NTSB determined that the *Probable Cause* of this accident was:

> the use by the carriers of a non-approved device, designed to raise the elevator during loading operations, which was not properly stowed by the flight crew and which lodged in the controls, preventing the flight crew from controlling the airplane during takeoff.

BAC-111: The British Aircraft Corporation (BAC), later British Aerospace, began design work in the late 1950s on an airliner that would evolve into the BAC-111. Spurred on by an order from British United Airways, the new twin-jet craft first flew in 1963. During the flight testing program at a high angle-of-attack, one prototype entered a deep stall. The T-tail concept was relatively new, insufficient pitch control prevented recovery, and the crash killed the entire crew. Engineers soon corrected the deep stall problem, and the BAC-111 entered airline service in 1965. The intermediate range airliner could be configured to seat up to 119 passengers. A total of 235 were built in the United Kingdom, and nine more rolled off an assembly line in Romania.

An in-flight fire caused by a malfunctioning valve resulted in the loss of a BAC-111 and all aboard in Pennsylvania in 1967 (see the chapter, "Mohawk Airlines Flight 40").

Photograph: Copyright 1985 Donnie L. Head

Boeing 707: The most famous airliner in the world is, arguably, the Boeing 707. Boeing designed a predecessor for military and commercial use, and it flew in 1954. The U.S. Air Force ordered a larger version which became the RC-135 electronic surveillance aircraft and the KC-135 tanker. Boeing then built a commercial version which evolved into the famed Boeing 707. As the years passed stretched variants, re-engined variants, and pure freighters entered airline service. The aircraft depicted above, registration HK-2016, ran out of fuel and crashed while trying to land in New York (see the chapter, "Avianca Airlines Flight 052").

The production of military versions of the Boeing 707 continued for over three decades. For example, the E-3 Sentry (AWACS) is a state-of-the-art electronic warfare command and control platform that remains at the point-of-the-spear.

Boeing 727: The popular Boeing 727 was the first airliner to incorporate the rear tri-jet concept. Design began in 1956 on the medium range transport. Three engines offered enhanced safety, better climb performance than a twin, and better economics than a four-engine design. In addition, the installation of all engines at the rear of the fuselage eliminated engine-out asymmetric thrust concerns inherent in engine-on-wing designs.

The prototype flew in 1963, and the aircraft entered passenger service with Eastern the following year. Further development of the basic design resulted in higher gross weight options, a stretched fuselage, and freighter configurations. New engines increased performance and range, and they enabled the aircraft to meet more restrictive noise abatement requirements.

Photograph: Copyright 1983 Donnie L. Head

Boeing 747: Following development of the wildly successful Boeing 707, the Boeing engineers vied for a contract to build the proposed U.S. Air Force ultra-large strategic transport. However, Lockheed won that contract with its huge C-5 Galaxy. Undaunted, Boeing relied upon its plans for the military aircraft and built the enormous Boeing 747 commercial transport.

The first flight took place in 1969, and Pan Am began line service early in 1970. The Boeing 747 was far bigger and more complex than any other airliner; it revolutionized intercontinental air travel. On long-haul routes the seat cost per mile was far lower than anything else the market could offer. Later versions could seat over 500 passengers, and maximum takeoff weights gradually increased to over 900,000 pounds. The massive Boeing 747 wide-body transport remained the world's largest commercial airliner for 35 years. It relinquished that title to the new "super-jumbo" Airbus A-380 in early 2005.

Airbus Industrie A-320: A consortium of European countries developed the versatile Airbus A-320 in the mid-1980s. Air France took delivery of the first new airliner in 1988. The Airbus family of airliners introduced the fly-by-wire control concept (meaning, pilot input is transmitted to the flight controls via electrical wiring) in modern commercial transports. A new side-stick replaced the conventional control column, and integrated EFIS "glass cockpit" displays replaced the old needle-and-gauge instruments.

The twin-jet A-320 is a short to medium range transport, and it has proven to be a technological trailblazer. Computer protection, added to the flight control system, makes it almost impossible for pilots to inadvertently exceed operating limits such as speed, pitch attitude, and G force. Over the past decade the family of Airbus transports has outsold its Boeing counterparts.

Lockheed L-1049 Super Constellation: Most aviation pundits agree that the Lockheed L-1049 Super Constellation is the most beautiful transport aircraft ever to fly. The graceful dolphin-like fuselage and distinctive triple-tail empennage make the original "Connie" and subsequent "Super-Connie" unique aviation icons.

The Connie was designed to the specifications of the eccentric aviation entrepreneur and airline owner, Howard Hughes. In 1944, Hughes piloted a Connie while setting a new transcontinental speed record of 7 hours and 3 minutes. Four huge Wright Cyclone 18-cylinder twin-row radial engines powered the speedy behemoth, the first pressurized airliner in widespread use. Over 60 years later in 2004 the design and production of the Connie were highlighted in the motion picture, *The Aviator*.

In 1956, high over the Grand Canyon in Arizona, a Connie was involved in one of the worst mid-air collisions in history when it collided with a Douglas DC-7 (see the chapter, "TWA Flight 2 and United Airlines Flight 718").

Lockheed L-188 Electra: In the early 1950s, American Airlines identified the need for a short to medium range airliner that would seat 75 to 100 passengers. Lockheed designed the L-188 Electra in response, and the prototype flew in 1957. Lockheed soon had orders for 144 of the swift four-engine turboprop aircraft.

Eastern Airlines inaugurated passenger service with the Electra in 1959, and the flying public fell in love with the sleek speedy airliner. However, this infatuation rapidly waned after two Electras disintegrated in flight, killing all aboard and raising grave doubts about the L-188 design (see the chapters, "Braniff Airways Flight 542" and "Northwest Airlines Flight 710"). Lockheed modified the wings and eliminated the problem, but damage to the airliner's image lingered. Most airlines converted their passenger Electras into freighters, and production ended in the early 1960s.

Lockheed L-382 Hercules: An ageless wonder! Long, long ago in 1951 the U.S. Air Force specified a requirement for a turboprop freighter. In response Lockheed built the military C-130 Hercules, and it first flew in 1954. It featured a rear drive-on loading ramp for vehicles and cargo. Refinements and fuselage stretches evolved over the years. An astounding 51 years later in 2005, Lockheed is still manufacturing new cargo and tanker variants (the J-model) of the versatile Hercules -- the longest production run in history.

Lockheed developed a commercial version of the Hercules, the L-382, in the 1960s. The new L-382 features an improved cargo handling system and the same rear ramp as its military cousin. Composite six-blade propellers, new engines, and a "glass cockpit" make the latest L-382 an efficient freighter. Over 2,600 military and commercial variants of the venerable Hercules have been built.

Lockheed L-1011 TriStar: After American Airlines announced a need for a large capacity and medium range airliner, Lockheed developed the L-1011 TriStar. Three engines, one under each wing and another atop the rear of the fuselage, would power the new aircraft. With an initial maximum takeoff weight of 430,000 pounds, the big TriStar first flew in 1970 and began passenger service with Eastern and Delta in 1972. Later models carried greater loads and held more fuel. The TriStar became famous for reliability, economy, and a low noise signature.

The most tragic accident involving a TriStar had nothing to do with the mechanical health of the aircraft. On final approach near Fort Worth, Texas, the airliner encountered microburst-induced windshear. The sudden unexpected change in wind direction stole an incredible 53 knots of airspeed, and the TriStar mushed down onto the ground (see the chapter, "Delta Airlines Flight 191").

ATR-42: France and Italy joined forces and established Avions de Transport Regional (ATR) to build turboprop regional airliners. The ATR-42 (depicted above) first flew in 1984 and entered airline service the following year. The aircraft was designed to seat 42 passengers on short-haul routes. ATR later introduced a stretched version with seating for 72 passengers, the new ATR-72. Both cargo and convertible versions were available, and the economical transport found a home with airlines throughout the world.

Tragically, the ATR design had a secret Achilles' heel. In icing conditions the deicing boots kept the leading edge of the wing free of ice. Unfortunately, a ridge of ice could build up *behind* the boots. As angle-of-attack increased, this ice ridge could cause the smooth flow of air over the ailerons to suddenly separate, leading to a total loss of control. Ice quickly became a *four-letter-word* for ATR pilots (see the chapter, "American Eagle Flight 4184").

Douglas C-54 Skymaster: The United States entered World War II as the Douglas DC-4 rolled down the assembly line. To further the war effort, the U.S. government commandeered the production of the transports and gave the aircraft a military name, the C-54 Skymaster. Four 14-cylinder twin-row Pratt & Whitney radial engines gave the craft transoceanic range. After the war, Douglas continued to manufacture military and commercial variants. Later outfitted as freighters, a handful were still in service worldwide at the start of the Third Millennium in the year 2000.

One C-54 freighter, registration N8060C, swooped low over the southeastern United States during the pre-dawn darkness on 19 November 1979. Loaded with over seven tons of illicit marijuana, the transport headed for an improvised sod airstrip in western South Carolina. Unfortunately an in-flight fire broke out. The big C-54 crashed on approach, before daylight, while attempting to land in blinding fog (see the chapter, "Clandestine Marijuana Flight").

Douglas DC-8: In the early 1950s, Douglas reigned as the premier airliner manufacturer in the world. In 1955 the company outlined plans to build the DC-8, a large four-engine jet transport. Yet, this announcement came a year *after* Boeing had already flown the innovative aircraft that would evolve into the Boeing 707.

The DC-8 first flew in 1958, certification followed a year later, and United and Delta began flying the new transport late in 1959. By this time the earlier Boeing design had gained a strong foothold in the market, and sales of the DC-8 remained slow for a number of years. Nonetheless, the DC-8 gradually proved its worth as a reliable and economical transport for passengers and cargo.

The Arrow Air transport depicted above, registration N345JW, is similar to an Arrow Air DC-8 that crashed in Newfoundland while trying to take off with ice and snow on its wings (see the chapter, "Arrow Air Flight 1285").

Douglas DC-9: After the long range four-engine DC-8 became economically viable, Douglas began designing a new short range domestic airliner to complement it. The much smaller DC-9 was an original design. With its distinctive T-tail and twin turbines mounted at the rear of the fuselage, the DC-9 became an instant success story. The airliner first flew in 1965, and stretched re-engined variants soon followed. Over 2,400 have been built.

Perhaps the most unique DC-9 accident involved the unexpected fury of Mother Nature. The pilots encountered tornadoes, severe thunderstorms, and extreme turbulence. Massive amounts of rain and hail caused both engines to fail, and the pilots tried to glide down and land on a narrow two-lane road. The DC-9 disintegrated and burned as it tumbled into the rural community of New Hope, Georgia (see the chapter, "Southern Airways Flight 242").

<u>Douglas DC-10</u>: American Airlines announced a need for a large capacity and medium range airliner in the late 1960s. In response, Douglas engineers designed a widebody tri-jet, and the DC-10 first flew in 1970. Grasping the potential in the marketplace, Douglas produced both transcontinental and intercontinental variants. A total of 386 such commercial airliners were built, and 60 additional KC-10 military models were delivered to the U.S. Air Force.

In the 1970s a series of tragic accidents clouded the reputation of the DC-10. Perhaps the most infamous accident occurred at Chicago, Illinois, when an engine and pylon ripped off during the takeoff. Hydraulic damage caused the outboard slats on the left wing to retract. The resulting asymmetric stall killed all aboard. Such accidents cast grave doubts on the design of the aircraft. On the other hand, when a DC-10 crashed into Mt. Erebus, Antarctica, the cause had nothing to do with the mechanical health of the aircraft (see the chapter, "Air New Zealand Flight 901").

<u>Embraer EMB-120 Brasilia</u>: The Brazilian manufacturer first flew the prototype of the EMB-120 in 1983, and the regional twin turboprop entered airline service two years later in 1985. The new airliner offered a blend of reliability, high speed, and economy. The EMB-120 carries a flight crew of two, and with three abreast seating it can carry 30 passengers. Extended range and cargo variants also are available. The twin turbines have been mated to four-blade Hamilton Standard composite propellers, and roughly 400 of these aircraft have been delivered worldwide.

In 1995 a flawed inspection procedure caused a unique accident near Atlanta, Georgia. A fatigue crack in a propeller was not detected, and over time the crack slowly grew larger. Ultimately the EMB-120 "chunked a prop" in flight. The resulting structural damage made level flight impossible, and the aircraft crashed in rough terrain (see the chapter, "ASA Flight 529").

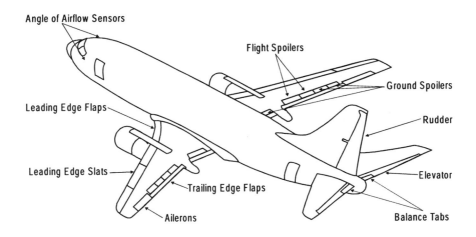

Flight Control Surfaces: This illustration identifies the flight control surfaces on a modern-day Boeing 737 transport. The three basic control surfaces on any aircraft are (1) the rudder, which controls yaw; (2) the elevator, which controls pitch; and (3) the ailerons, which control roll.

Spoilers, as the name implies, may be deployed to *spoil* the smooth flow of air over the wings. They are deployed immediately after touchdown to decrease lift generated by the wings. This puts more weight on the landing gear and tires, which increases the effectiveness of the aircraft's brakes. When spoilers are deployed in flight they dramatically increase aerodynamic drag, and in this capacity they are called "speed brakes."

Slats and flaps, when extended, change the *shape* of the wing; they increase the curvature of the airfoil. This (1) increases lift and (2) decreases the stall speed. Thus enabled, an aircraft can take off or land at lower airspeeds and use shorter runways.

On 16 August 1987 the pilots on a Douglas DC-9 tried to take off at Detroit, Michigan. Tragically, they forgot to extend their flaps and slats. The aircraft mushed into the air but was not able to climb. It clipped a light pole and an office building a half-mile beyond the airport. The resulting crash killed 154 of the 155 people aboard (see the chapter, "Northwest Airlines Flight 255").

Illustration: Courtesy of NTSB

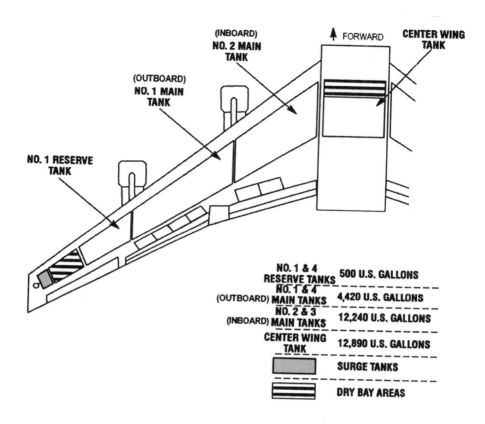

Fuel Tanks: The initial Boeing 747-100 and -200 models have three fuel tanks in the left wing and three more in the right wing. Another tank is located in the wing structure beneath the fuselage. These seven tanks hold the necessary fuel to give the airliner its long range. In the illustration, above, only the three fuel tanks in the left wing and the center wing fuel tank are shown. Later models have a greater fuel capacity than shown above.

On 17 July 1996 a Boeing 747 took off from JFK Airport in New York and headed out over the Atlantic Ocean on a flight to Paris, France. Only 12 minutes after takeoff an electrical short circuit ignited flammable fuel-air vapor in the center wing tank. The explosion destroyed the airliner and killed the 230 people aboard (see the chapter, "TWA Flight 800").

Illustration: Courtesy of NTSB

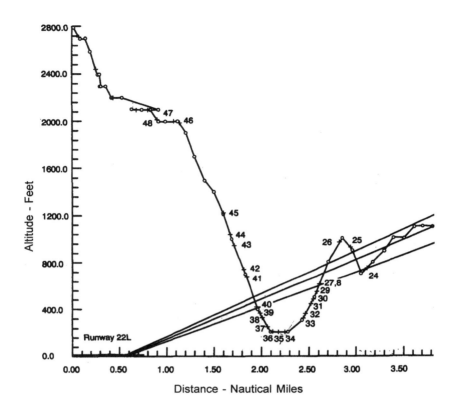

Tracking the Glideslope: Inbound from South America at night and desperately low on fuel, a Boeing 707 made an ILS approach to JFK Airport in New York. The illustration, above, graphically depicts information from the Flight Data Recorder. It shows the airliner's descent down the glideslope, flying from right to left.

The aircraft rose above the glideslope at locations No. 25 and 26. Windshear then drove the aircraft far below the glideslope at locations No. 34 through 36. Only 200 feet above the ground and unable to see the runway lights, the pilots executed a missed approach and climbed to 2,800 feet.

ATC tried to vector the pilots 15 miles from the airport to intercept the ILS localizer for another approach. The airliner ran out of fuel and crashed (see the chapter, "Avianca Flight 052").

Illustration: Courtesy of NTSB

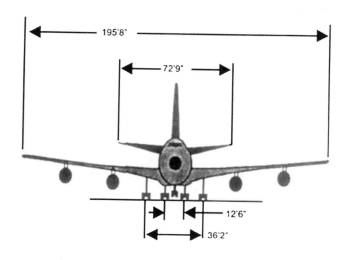

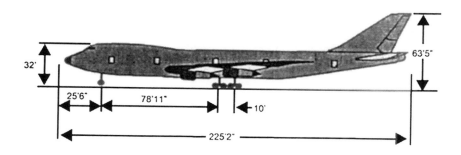

Exterior Dimensions: The illustration, above, includes the exterior dimensions of the Boeing 747-100 and -200 models. Some more recent models have a longer wingspan, longer fuselage, greater range, and maximum takeoff weights of up to 910,000 pounds.

Boeing identified a market for a high capacity "jumbo-jet" in the mid-1960s, and the initial flight of the Boeing 747 took place in 1969. The aircraft, far larger than any commercial transport then flying, revolutionized air travel. The Boeing 747 was the first widebody airliner and the first to use new fuel efficient and high bypass turbofan engines. Often called the "Queen of the Skies," the Boeing 747 remained the world's largest airliner for 35 years. It was surpassed in size by the Airbus A-380 in April 2005.

Illustration: Courtesy of NTSB

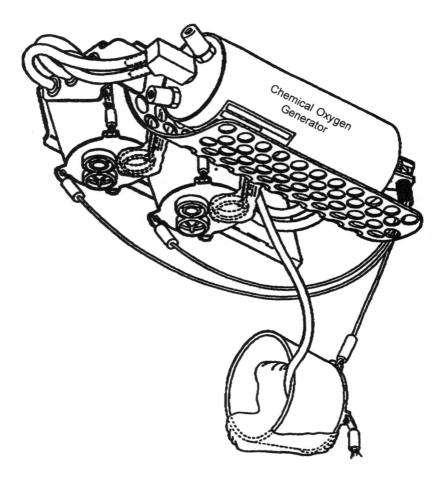

Oxygen Generators: The illustration, above, depicts an installed and shielded Chemical Oxygen Generator. These devices are used on some airliners to provide emergency oxygen for passengers in the cabin. When activated, a chemical reaction in the oxidizer core releases oxygen gas, but it also produces extreme heat.

In May 1996 a Douglas DC-9 took off with Chemical Oxygen Generators improperly carried in the cargo hold. The volatile devices activated. The extreme heat caused a raging fire, which was sustained by oxygen gas generated by the devices. All 110 persons on board were killed when the aircraft, out of control, dove into the Everglades (see the chapter, "ValuJet Flight 592").

Illustration: Courtesy of NTSB

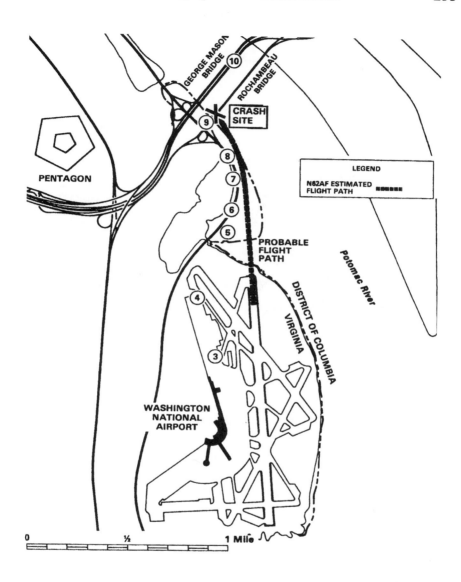

Crash after Takeoff: A Boeing 737 took off from Washington, DC. The flight lasted 24 seconds. The airliner struck a bridge and crashed into the ice-covered Potomac River. There were 79 people aboard, and 74 perished from impact trauma or drowned in the submerged cabin (see the chapter, "Air Florida Flight 90").

Illustration: Courtesy of NTSB

American Airlines Flight 587: The big Airbus Industrie A-300 accelerated down the runway at JFK International Airport in New York for a planned flight to the Dominican Republic. Soon after liftoff the pilots retracted their landing gear and enhanced lift devices, and they continued a normal climb.

At 250 knots, climbing through 2,000 feet, the Airbus flew into wake turbulence from a heavy Boeing 747 that had taken off from the same runway several minutes before. A wingtip vortex rolled the Airbus to the left. The first officer countered the roll with a series of hard alternating aileron and rudder deflections. Dynamic air pressure caused the vertical stabilizer to rip off of the fuselage, and the aircraft tumbled earthward, out of control. It crashed into a residential area of Belle Harbor, New York, killing all 260 people on board the French-built craft.

The photograph, above, depicts recovery of the vertical stabilizer from the waters of Jamaica Bay almost a mile from the main crash site (see the chapter, "American Airlines Flight 587").

Photograph: Courtesy of NTSB

Aloha Airlines Flight 243: A Boeing 737 twin-jet airliner flew at flight level 240 toward Honolulu, Hawaii. Cabin pressurization caused a fatigue crack to suddenly enlarge and rip open. Explosive decompression blasted the entire upper section of the cabin off of the aircraft for a longitudinal distance of 18 feet. One occupant would later explain: "There was blue sky where the First Class ceiling had been."

Prior to the structural failure all passengers were seated, and the seat belt sign was illuminated. Unfortunately the First Class flight attendant was standing in the isle, and the sudden decompression swept her out of the airliner. Although many other occupants sustained severe injuries, the First Class flight attendant was the only fatality. Her remains were never found.

The damaged aircraft made an emergency landing at the airport on the island of Maui, Hawaii. The photograph, above, depicts the tremendous hole in the upper fuselage. Damaged beyond repair, the Boeing 737 was dismantled at the airport and sold for parts and scrap. Readers should note that a chapter detailing this accident is *not included* in this book.

Photograph: Courtesy of NTSB

*The page of text, below, applies to the **two photographs on the following page**. These two photographs depict the wreckage of a McDonnell Douglas MD-82 which overran the runway and crashed at Little Rock, Arkansas.*

American Airlines Flight 1420: A McDonnell Douglas MD-82 with 145 people aboard droned toward Little Rock, Arkansas, at night. The pilots knew the weather there would be rough. Their corporate weather advisory called for thunderstorms along the route of flight, and the National Weather Service had forecast severe storms. As the MD-82 neared the airport the controller warned the pilots that a severe thunderstorm was nearing Little Rock. Surface winds were already gusting to 44 knots, and lightning was snapping and crackling across the night sky.

The pilots were not able to keep the airport lights in sight because of the intensity of the storm. Yet, in torrential rain, they managed to touch down on the runway, but they had *forgotten* to arm their spoilers. A 25 knot crosswind with a tailwind component whipped across the landing area. Without extended spoilers, which would have put more weight on the landing gear and tires, brakes and reverse thrust could not stop the airliner as it fishtailed down the runway. The pilots ran out of asphalt at 97 knots. Hurtling forward, the aircraft tore through a chain link security fence and careened over a rock embankment. Shedding its engines and landing gear, the MD-82 plowed through the heavy steel framework of the Runway 22L approach lighting structure. The long slide tore open the fuselage and ejected many occupants from the cabin.

The tower controller never saw the airliner because of the intensity of the rain, and radio contact with the airliner was lost. Rescue personnel drove through "blinding wind and rain" that limited visibility to 100 feet. After 12 minutes of searching they stumbled upon the burning wreckage. The *miracle* of the accident was that only 11 people died, although over 100 others suffered serious injuries (see the chapter, "American Airlines Flight 1420").

The photographs on the next page depict the MD-82 wreckage the next day. The top photograph, taken from the air, shows the burned-out fuselage. The lower photograph shows remnants of the fuselage entangled in the demolished approach light structure.

<u>Photographs</u>: Courtesy of NTSB

Delta Airlines Flight 191: A Lockheed L-1011 TriStar jumbo-jet approached Fort Worth, Texas, and rode down the electronic rails of the ILS toward Runway 17L. Dead ahead, between the aircraft and the runway, a thunderstorm lashed the approach path. Beneath the thunderstorm raged an invisible monster, a microburst.

Flying at approach speed, gear and flaps down, the TriStar first flew into the microburst outflow, a headwind. Then it transited the shaft of the microburst and flew into the outflow on the other side, a sudden tailwind, horizontal windshear of an incredible 72 knots. In addition to the loss of airspeed, a vicious downdraft within the microburst snared the airliner. Nose high, engines at full power, it mushed to the ground over a mile short of the runway.

The photograph, above, depicts the rear of the passenger cabin and empennage, which broke off from the rest of the aircraft. The accident killed 134 of the 163 people aboard the TriStar (see the chapter, "Delta Airlines Flight 191").

Photograph: Courtesy of NTSB

United Flight 811: A Boeing 747 took off from Hawaii and headed out over the Pacific Ocean. A cargo door opened in flight, and explosive decompression ripped a hole 15 feet high and 13 feet wide in the side of the fuselage. Nine passengers seated near the hole were sucked out of the airliner, and their bodies were never found. Two engines ingested debris and failed, but the airliner was able to flounder back to the airport and land safely.

The photograph, above, shows the huge hole in the side of the fuselage (see the chapter, "United Airlines Flight 811").

Photograph: Courtesy of NTSB

*The page of text, below, applies to the **two photographs on the following page**. These two photographs depict a Boeing 727, with its damaged right wing ablaze, arcing down toward the ground after a mid-air collision.*

<u>PSA Flight 182</u>: A Boeing 727 descended to land at Lindbergh Field in San Diego, California. The weather was clear and sunny, and the pilots had reported the airport in sight. The controller cleared the flight for a *visual approach* to Runway 27.

Meanwhile a small single-engine Cessna 172 was practicing ILS approaches at the airport. Lindbergh Tower instructed the Cessna pilots to *maintain VFR conditions*.

ATC issued four traffic *advisories* to the airline pilots. The pilots said they had the Cessna in sight, but then they lost visual contact with it. Tragically, as the airliner maneuvered to land the Cessna was dead ahead. Both aircraft were flying in the same direction, and the big airliner was overtaking the much slower and smaller Cessna from behind. A subsequent cockpit visibility study would conclude that the Cessna would have been visually centered on the windshield of the Boeing 727.

The airline pilots saw the Cessna directly in front of them two seconds before impact. Too late! The inboard right wing of the airliner slammed into the small aircraft, and the collision caused massive damage to the wing. Several leading edge devices were totally ripped away. A large part of the leading edge, back to the front spar, had been bashed in. The raging fire trailing back from ruptured wing fuel tanks made it impossible to photographically (see the two photographs) analyze damage to the trailing edge devices. Out of control, trailing fire and smoke, the airliner arced down into a residential area, and the crash instantly killed all 135 people on board (see the chapter, "PSA Flight 182").

By happenstance a professional photographer, Hans Wendt, was covering an event nearby. He heard the noise of the collision, looked up, and quickly took the two <u>photographs shown on the next page</u>. The <u>upper photograph</u> depicts the stricken airliner, right wing damaged and on fire, moments after the mid-air collision. The <u>lower photograph</u> shows the airliner several seconds later, a moment before it dove out of sight behind the roof of a building.

Take a Break!
Happy Hour for Aviators!

Aviators live in a regimented world foreign to laymen. They comprehend the intricacies of their profession in a way outsiders will never understand.

When aviators gather they talk about flying, and they speak a mystical language unlike that spoken by non-practitioners. Their verbiage is filled with acronyms: ATIS, VASI, VOR, IFR, VMC. They talk about radials, slats, spoilers, ground effect, and pucker factor. When they speak of their "clean machine" they are not thinking of a wash job, and their "flight director" is not made of flesh and blood. Fixed-wing drivers understand when their rotary-wing brothers dwell on the nuances of "translational lift" and "vortex ring state" or bemoan their HIGE versus HOGE capability. They understand, but not because they studied these principles in a book. They understand because they *lived* them.

Aviators also revel in their unique brand of camaraderie. Often it is "gallows humor," tongue-in-cheek references to the perils of flight or commercial aviation industry malaise. This **Happy Hour for Aviators** extolls the aeronautical humor in three sub-chapters:

1. Dubious Aviation Predictions
2. Trouble in Airline Paradise?
3. Murphy's Laws for Aviation

-- Dubious Aviation Predictions --

Listed below, in approximate chronological order, are many of the world's most dubious predictions about man's ability in the field of aviation and aeronautics:

It is not impossible for human beings to fly, but it so happens that God did not give them the knowledge of how to do it.
[Roger Bacon (1214-1294), English scholar and philosopher]

What can you conceive more silly and extravagant than to suppose a man racking his brains and studying day and night how to fly?
[William Law, *A Serious Call to a Devout and Holy Life*, 1728]

It is entirely impossible for man to rise into the air. For this you would need wings of tremendous dimensions, and they would have to be moved at three feet per second. Only a fool would expect such a thing to be realized.
[Joseph de Lalande, French astronomer, in *Journal de Paris*, 1782]

Is it not demonstrated that a true flying machine, self-raising, self-sustaining, self-propelling, is physically impossible?
[Joseph Le Conte, in *Popular Science Monthly*, 1888]

Heavier-than-air flying machines are impossible.
[Lord Kelvin, President of the Royal Society, 1895]

As a means of rapid transit, flying could not begin to compete with the railroad.
[*Popular Science*, 1897]

Flight by machines heavier than air is unpractical and insignificant, if not utterly impossible.
[Simon Newcomb, American scientist and mathematician, 1902]

Aerial flight is one of that class of problems with which man will never be able to cope.
[Simon Newcomb, American scientist and mathematician, 1903]

The [aeroplanes] may even carry mail in special cases, but the useful load will be very small. [The aeroplanes] are not to be thought of as commercial carriers.
[Octave Chanute, American engineer, 1904]

Could any nation afford to wage war upon any other with such a hazard *[that is, airplanes dropping bombs]* in view?
[John Brisbane Walker, in *Cosmopolitan*, 1904]

All attempts at artificial aviation are not only dangerous to life but

[are] doomed to failure from an engineering standpoint.
[Editor, *The Times*, 1905]

It is complete and utter nonsense to believe that flying machines
will ever work.
[Sir Stanley Mosley, philosopher, 1905]

A one-man machine without a float and favored by a wind, say, of
fifteen miles an hour, might succeed in getting across the Atlantic.
But such an attempt would be the height of folly. *[and also]* No
flying machine will ever fly from New York to Paris [because] no
known motor can run at the requisite speed for four days without
stopping.
[Orville Wright, American aviation pioneer, 1908]

A popular fallacy is to expect enormous speed to be obtained [by
aeroplanes]. There is no hope of competing for racing speed with
either our locomotives or our automobiles. *[and also]* Another
popular fallacy is to suppose that flying machines could be used to
drop dynamite on an enemy in time of war.
[William H. Pickering, American astronomer, *Aeronautics*, 1908]

I confess that in 1901 I said to my brother, Orville, that man would
not fly for fifty years.
[Wilbur Wright, American aviation pioneer, 1908]

I do not think a flight across the Atlantic will be made in our time,
and in our time I include the youngest readers.
[Charles S. Rolls, co-founder of Rolls-Royce, 1908]

We soon saw that the helicopter had no future, so we dropped it.
The helicopter does, with great labor, only what the balloon does
without labor. The helicopter is no more fitted than the balloon for
rapid horizontal flight. If its engine stops it must fall with deathly
violence, for it can neither glide like the aeroplane nor float like
the balloon. The helicopter is easier to design than the aeroplane,
but it is utterly worthless.
[Wilbur Wright, American aviation pioneer, 1909]

The popular mind often pictures gigantic flying machines speeding across the Atlantic, carrying innumerable passengers. It seems safe to say that such ideas must be wholly absurd.
[William H. Pickering, American astronomer, 1910]

We do not consider that aeroplanes will be of any possible use for war purposes.
[Report of the British Secretary of State for War, 1910]

To affirm that the aeroplane is going to "revolutionize" naval warfare of the future is to be guilty of the wildest exaggeration.
[*Scientific American*, 1910]

Aviation is fine as a sport. But as an instrument of war, it is worthless. *[and also]* Aeroplanes are interesting toys, but are of no military value.
[Gen. Ferdinand Foch, Marshall of France, 1911]

The aeroplane is an invention of the Devil. It will never play any part in the defence of the nation, my boy!
[Sir Sam Hughes, Canadian Minister of Defence, 1914]

What's the matter? Do you think that perhaps I will not return?
[Baron Capt. Manfred von Richthofen ("The Red Baron", 80 kills in World War I), German Flying Service, to the mechanic who asked for his autograph before his final and fatal flight, 1918]

Airmail [is] an impractical sort of fad and [has] no place in the serious business of postal transportation.
[Col. Paul Henderson, U.S. Assistant Postmaster General, 1919]

It is highly unlikely that an airplane, or a fleet of them, could ever sink a fleet of navy vessels under battle conditions.
[Franklin D. Roosevelt, 32nd President of the United States, 1922]

Recently a man asked whether the business of flying ever could be regulated by rules and statutes. I doubt it.
[Walter Hinton, American aviator, in *Liberty Magazine*, 1926]

This fellow Charles Lindbergh will never make it. He's doomed.
[Harry F. Guggenheim, aviation enthusiast and financier, 1927]

The helicopter has never achieved much success and . . . may be classed with the ornithopter as obsolete.
[Maj. Oliver Stewart, Royal Air Force, 1928]

There is no hope for the fanciful idea of reaching the moon because of unsurmountable barriers to escaping the Earth's gravity.
[Forest R. Moulton, American astronomer, 1932]

Scientific investigation into the possibility of [jet engines] has given no indication that this method can be a serious competitor to the airscrew-engine combination.
[British Under-Secretary of State, 1934]

There is not in sight any source of energy that would be a fair start toward that which would be necessary to get us beyond the gravitative control of the Earth.
[Forest R. Moulton, American astronomer, 1935]

No enemy bomber can reach the Ruhr. If one reaches the Ruhr, my name is not Goering.
[Hermann W. Goering, German Marshall of the Reich, 1939]

The Americans can not build airplanes.
[Hermann W. Goering, German Marshall of the Reich, 1940]

To place a man in a multi-stage rocket and project him into the controlling gravitational field of the moon . . . constitutes a wild dream. I am bold enough to say that such a man-made voyage will never occur regardless of all future advances.
[Lee De Forest, American inventor, 1957]

-- Trouble in Airline Paradise? --

Modern airline transportation is often deemed a showcase for man's technological prowess. Sleek aluminum craft, the product of engineering ingenuity and manufacturing excellence, can whisk passengers or cargo to virtually any spot on Earth.

Yet, dog-eat-dog competition, government deregulation, and cutthroat economics often bring disaster. Many within the industry have decried the financial chaos:

These days one can not make money in the [expletive] airline business. The economics represent sheer Hell.
[Cyrus R. Smith, CEO of American Airlines]

You can not get one nickel for commercial flying.
[Inglis M. Uppercu, President of Aeromarine West Indies Airways]

People who invest in aviation are the biggest suckers in the world.
[David G. Neeleman, CEO of JetBlue Airways, in *Business Week*]

If we went into the funeral business, people would stop dying.
[Martin R. Shugrue Jr., President of Continental Airlines]

If the Wright Brothers were alive today, Wilbur would have to fire Orville to reduce costs. *[and also]* It takes nerves of steel to stay neurotic.
[Herbert D. "Herb" Kolleher, CEO of Southwest Airlines]

This is a nasty, rotten business.
[Robert L. Crandall, CEO of American Airlines]

You [expletive] eggheads! You don't know [expletive]. You can't deregulate this industry, you're going to wreck it. You don't know a [expletive] thing!
[Robert L. Crandell, CEO of American Airlines]

Once you get hooked on the airline business, it's worse than dope.
[Ed Acker, President of Air Florida]

I really don't know one plane from another. To me they are just marginal costs with wings.
[Alfred E. Kahn, airline economist]

Maybe it's sex appeal, but there's something about an airplane that drives investors crazy.
[Alfred E. Kahn, airline economist, speaking of aviation financiers]

The money that has been made since the dawn of aviation by all this country's airline companies was zero -- absolutely zero.
[Warren Buffett, billionaire investor]

Today we are literally hemorrhaging money. Clearly this bleeding has to be stopped, and soon, or United will perish.
[James Goodwin, Chairman of United Airlines]

No one expects Braniff [Airways] to go broke. No major U.S. carrier ever has. *[Ooops!]*
[*The Wall Street Journal*]

I can't imagine a set of circumstances that would produce Chapter Eleven for Eastern. *[Ooops again!]*
[Frank Lorenzo, CEO of Eastern Airlines and corporate raider]

Air transport is just glorified bus operation. *[and also]* Code-sharing, alliances, and connections are all about, "How do we screw the poor customer for more money?"
[Michael O'Leary, CEO of Ryan Air]

If the pilots were in charge, Columbus would still be in port.
[Robert L. Crandall, CEO of American Airlines]

The state of our airline industry is a national embarrassment. Things were in turmoil and chaos and out of control.
[Tom Plaskett, Chairman of Pan Am]

There has always been a certain romanticism associated with the airline business. We must avoid its perpetuation at Eastern.
[Frank Borman, former astronaut and CEO of Eastern Airlines]

I did not fully understand the dread term "terminal illness" until I saw Heathrow [Airport] for myself.
[Dennis Potter, English dramatist, in *The Sunday Times*]

It's not a testosterone-driven business any longer. Success [lies in] making money, not in the size of the airline.
[Gordon Bethune, CEO of Continental Airlines]

A recent White House panel on security concluded that [the FAA] software was so out of date that no one could possibly hack into it.
[*Aviation Week and Space Technology*]

If you would look up bad labor relations in the dictionary, you would [see] an American Airlines logo beside it.
[Joe Kendall, Judge, U.S. District Court]

. . . and, on the lighter side . . . .

There are only two reasons to sit on the back row in an airplane. Either you have diarrhea, or you're anxious to meet people who do.
[Henry Kissinger, American diplomat]

The Devil himself [had] probably redesigned Hell in light of information he had gained from observing airport layouts.
[Anthony Price, English author, *The Memory Trap*]

Hell, as every frequent traveler already knows, is in Concourse D of O'Hare Airport.
[David D. "Dave" Barry, *There is no Concourse D at O'Hare*]

When the art of radio communications between pilots and ATC is improved, the result will be vastly increased areas of significant misunderstanding.
[Robert E. Livingston, *Flying the Aeronca*]

United hired gentlemen with the expectation of training them to become pilots. Northwest hired pilots, hoping to train them to become gentlemen. To date, despite their best efforts, neither carrier can be considered successful.
[Edward Thompson, aviation pundit]

If forced to fly on an airplane, try and get in the [cockpit] with the Captain so you can keep an eye on him and nudge him if he falls

asleep or point out any mountains looming ahead.
[Mike Harding, *The Armchair Anarchist's Almanac*]

Now I know what a dog feels like watching TV.
[an airline pilot who was trying to transition to the new "glass cockpit" Airbus A-320]

-- Murphy's Laws for Aviation --

In 2003 the author published a tongue-in-cheek military book, MURPHY'S LAWS OF COMBAT. Hidden behind the veil of humor, readers discovered a wealth of military wisdom. They found that the subtitle was right on target: "The American Warrior's Guide to Staying Alive in Battle."

Most principles that apply to military aviation also apply to commercial aviation. Therefore, from MURPHY'S LAWS OF COMBAT, excerpted below are a few aeronautical gems of wisdom which the wise aviator will read and heed:

. . . first, a few Aeronautical Admonitions:

When in doubt, climb! No one ever collided with the sky.

Remember, you can only *tie* the record for flying low.

If you absolutely must fly low, do not fly slow.

Airspeed, Altitude, Brains. You need at least two at all times.

Pilots who hoot with the owls by night must not try to soar with the eagles by day.

In time of aerial crisis, do not forget your priorities: (1) aviate, (2) navigate, (3) communicate.

Do not crash while trying to fly the radio. Aircraft fly because of the principle discovered by Bernoulli, not Marconi.

If you deviate from a rule, make your performance flawless (for example, if you fly under a bridge, try not to hit the bridge).

When swooping around VFR, avoid the pretty little fluffy clouds, for mountains often lurk in them.

Never, never, never let your aircraft take you somewhere your *brain* did not get to five minutes earlier. Remember that you fly your aircraft with your *brain*, not with your hands.

If something in the cockpit is (1) red, (2) yellow, or (3) dusty, do not touch it without a lot of forethought.

Simultaneously running out of (1) airspeed, (2) altitude, (3) luck, and (4) bright ideas will ruin your day.

In aviation you start with (1) a bag full of luck and (2) an empty bag of experience. The trick is to fill your bag of experience before you empty your bag of luck.

. . . *next, priceless* <u>*Aeronautical Philosophy:*</u>

Gravity never loses. The best you can hope for is a draw.

Although fuel is a limited resource, gravity is forever.

The only time you have too much fuel is when you are on fire.

In the battle between (1) aircraft going hundreds of knots, and (2) mountains going zero knots, the mountains have yet to lose.

If you don't know who the world's greatest pilot is, it is not you.

While flying, you usually do not know what you do not know.

Assumption is the mother of most crashes.

If all you can see out of the cockpit window is the ground, going round and round, and all you can hear is screaming in the cabin, something likely is amiss.

When returning to Earth at high speed, the probability of survival is *inversely* proportional to the angle of arrival (large angle of arrival, small probability of survival, and vice versa).

Exemplary pilots use their exemplary judgment to avoid situations where they might have to use their exemplary skills.

A pilot lives in a world of perfection -- or not at all.

The seven most totally useless things in aviation:

1. The Approach Charts you did not bring.
2. The NOTAMs you did not check.
3. The fuel you have burned.
4. The airspeed you had.
5. The runway behind you.
6. The altitude above you.
7. A tenth of a second ago.

. . . *finally, a few* **Aeronautical Ironies:**

Flying is not dangerous. *Crashing* is what is dangerous.

Flying is not like a video game. When flying, you can not push a button and start over.

When things go wrong it is always better to be (1) on the ground, wishing you were flying, than to be (2) flying, wishing you were on the ground.

In time of crisis it is much better to (1) break ground and head into the wind, than to (2) break wind and head into the ground.

The farther you fly over the ocean at night, the stronger the strange fuselage vibrations will become.

Objectivity is a great virtue (for example, if it requires over 90 percent power to taxi, perhaps you have landed gear-up).

A smooth landing is *mostly luck*, two in a row is *all luck*, and three in a row is *lying*.

There are three simple and easy-to-understand rules for making smooth landings. Of course, no one knows what they are.

A thunderstorm usually is not as bad on the inside as it looks on the outside. It is worse.

The two worst things in the world that can happen to an old aviator:

1. One sunny day he will walk out to his aircraft, **knowing** that this will be his last flight.

2. One sunny day he will walk out to his aircraft, **not knowing** that this will be his last flight.

Northwest Airlines Flight 255

Douglas DC-9, registration N312RC
16 August 1987, near Detroit, Michigan
155 aboard, 154 killed (plus 2 killed on the ground)

Overview: In a suburb of Detroit, Michigan, a Douglas DC-9 tried to take off with its flaps and slats retracted. The aircraft mushed into the air and climbed to a height of only 37 feet. It clipped a light pole a half-mile beyond the airport, tore into the roof of an office building, skidded down a road, hit a railroad embankment, and disintegrated. Of the 155 people on the aircraft, a young child was the only survivor.

The Flight: Northwest Airlines Flight 255 taxied out to take off from Detroit Metropolitan Wayne County Airport in Michigan on 16 August 1987. The twin-jet airliner was packed full with 149 passengers, 2 pilots, and 4 flight attendants, all bound for Phoenix, Arizona. Counting the passengers, fuel, crew, and the baggage, the aircraft weighed 144,047 pounds. The Douglas DC-9, registration N312RC, had been manufactured six years earlier. Each of its two engines could pump out 20,000 pounds of thrust.

The experienced captain, age 57, and his first officer, age 35, had logged a total of 28,903 hours of flight time during their careers. Both had years of line experience in the DC-9, but in the twilight they missed their designated turn-off on Charlie Taxiway. They also missed a frequency change directive. In the midst of all this confusion ATIS broadcast windshear alerts, and the tower supervisor changed the active runway. The new runway was the shortest on the airport, so the pilots had to review their manual to make sure their weight was within prescribed limits for takeoff.

Trouble Ahead: With all that was going on the pilots somehow failed to complete their taxi checklist. One of the items on that checklist -- vital for the coming takeoff -- called for extending the flaps and slats on the wings.

The portion of the CVR transcript, below, begins as the captain is taxiing toward the runway. For the aircraft's gross weight and the *assumed* flap and slat configuration, the crucial takeoff speeds are: V-1, 142 knots; V-r, 144 knots; V-2, 153 knots:

Capt: . . . . Captain, Flight 255
FO: . . . . First Officer, Flight 255
Radio-: . . . . . . (prefix) Radio Transmission, Flight 255
PA-: . . . . (prefix) Public Address system, Flight 255
Tower: . . . . . . Detroit Airport Control Tower
GndControl: . . . Detroit Ground Control

Radio-FO: Ah, Ground [Control], Northwest two-fifty-five, I guess we went by Charlie [Taxiway], we're going to [Runway] three center, right? (2038:01)

GndControl: Northwest two-fifty-five, Ground, affirmative, make a right turn on Hotel, a left turn at Foxtrot, and follow the heavy jet and contact Ground on one-nineteen-forty-five. (2038:03)

Radio-FO: OK, we'll follow that heavy [jet and contact Ground Control on] one-nineteen-forty-five, so long. (2038:10)

FO: [The tower] just changed runways. (2038:18)

GndControl: Northwest two-fifty-five, are you on this frequency?

Radio-FO: Yeah, we are, nobody turned us over [to you] until just now when I called him back. (2038:34)

GndControl: Northwest two-fifty-five, roger, taxi to Runway three center via Taxiway Foxtrot and Juliet . . . windshear alerts are in effect and the altimeter is two-niner-eight-five. (2038:40)

[3 minutes and 31 seconds pass, routine takeoff preparations]

Tower: Northwest two-fifty-five, Metro Tower, roger, I need you to make a -- aaahhh -- disregard, Northwest two-fifty-five, Runway three center, taxi into position and hold . . . . (2042:11)

Capt: If we need to pull up in this taxiway, we will, and back around and take our turn. (2042:21)

Radio-FO: Position and hold, Northwest two-fifty-five. (2042:22)

Capt: No, [we're] not holding up for that [expletive] Continental [Airlines DC]-ten. (2042:31)

PA-FO: Ladies and gentlemen, ah, we're currently number one for departure, [we] should be rolling in a couple of minutes, we got two minutes in trail separation, Flight Attendants, please be seated, thank you. (2042:36)

Capt: It's blacker than [expletive] out there. (2042:57)

FO: A little rain out there. (2043:00)

FO: Transponder is set and on, annunciator. (2043:04)

Capt: Checked. (2043:09)

FO: Ignition. (2043:11)

Capt: On. (2043:12)

Capt: Well, we ain't going left. (2043:38)

FO: Nope. (2043:40)

Tower: Northwest two-fifty-five, Runway three center, turn right heading zero-six-zero [after takeoff], cleared for takeoff. (2044:04)

Radio-FO: Right to zero-six-zero, [we're] cleared to go, Northwest two-fifty-five. (2044:08)

[sound of the engines spooling up at 2044:21]

Capt: [The autothrottle] won't stay on. (2044:28)

FO: [It] won't go on. (2044:30)

Capt: But they won't stay on. (2044:31)

FO: OK, power's normal. (2044:32)

[the autothrottle engages at 2044:38]

FO: They're on now. (2044:42)

FO: Hundred knots. (2044:45)

Capt: OK. (2044:46)

FO: V-one. (2044:57)

<u>FO</u>: Rotate. (2044:58)

*[at **168 knots** the aircraft **finally lifts off** at 2045:04]*

[sound of the stick-shaker begins at 2045:05 and continues until the end of the recording]

[sound of the Supplemental Stall Recognition System (SSRS) at 2045:09 and again at 2045:11]

<u>Capt or FO</u>: Right up to the vee-bar! (2045:11)

[sound of SSRS starts again at 2045:14]

<u>Capt or FO</u>: Aaahhh, [expletive]! (2045:15)

[sound of SSRS at 2045:17]

[sound of first and second impacts with light poles at 2045:19]

[sound of third impact at 2045:22]

<u>Capt or FO</u>: [Unintelligible]. (2045:22)

[sound of fourth impact at 2045:23]

[sounds of fifth, sixth, and seventh impacts at 2045:24]

[end of the CVR tape at 2045:24]

The Accident: Acceleration through V-r had been normal during the takeoff roll. The DC-9 should have lifted off after V-r, 144 knots, with between six and eight degrees of nose-up pitch, but the aircraft stayed glued to the runway. The captain pulled the nose all the way up to 12 degrees. The aircraft finally lifted off at 168 knots, two knots under the "clean wing" stall speed.

The stick-shaker began sending its warning of impending peril. Nose pulled high into the air, the aircraft zoomed past the end of the runway only 10 feet above the ground. The SSRS blared out its warning in the cockpit. Slowly gaining speed, rolling right, then rolling back left, the DC-9 mushed forward.

The aircraft *almost* gained adequate flying speed. Almost! Over a half-mile beyond the end of the runway the airliner screamed over a parking lot. The left wing clipped the top of a light pole 37 feet above the ground. The NTSB would later explain:

After impacting the light pole, Flight 255 continued to roll to the left, continued across the car lot, struck [another] light pole in a second rental-car lot, and struck the roof of the auto rental facility . . . . It impacted the ground on a road outside the airport boundary. The airplane continued to slide along the road, struck a railroad embankment and disintegrated as it slid along the ground. Three occupied vehicles on the road and numerous vacant vehicles in the auto rental parking lot . . . were destroyed by impact forces and fire.

The crash left a scattered trail of wreckage 3,000 feet long in the Detroit suburb of Romulus, Michigan. Law enforcement agencies and dozens of fire trucks converged on the scene. They found a passenger from the aircraft, a girl four year of age, crying amid the rubble under a highway overpass. She turned out to be the sole survivor. The remaining 154 passengers and crewmembers were killed. The crash and fire also killed two people on the ground and injured six others. With regard to passengers and crewmembers who died the Wayne County Medical Examiner reported:

> Autopsies on the victims were not performed in view of obvious injuries which caused instantaneous death. . . . all fire injuries were postmortem. The survivor, a 4 year old female child, sustained third degree burns, a skull fracture, fractures of the left femur and clavicle, and multiple lacerations, abrasions . . . .

The Investigation: The CVR recording disclosed that the pilots never completed their taxi checklist, which included extension of the flaps and slats. Data from the FDR confirmed that the flaps and slats remained fully retracted.

Trailing edge *flaps* and leading edge *slats* are lift augmentation devices on the wings. When extended they alter the contour of the wing to increase lift at low airspeeds for takeoff and landing. The position of the flaps and slats is controlled by moving a "flap handle" in the cockpit. The DC-9 flaps may be set to one of six incremental positions, from "Up/Retracted" to fully extended at 40 degrees. The slats are automatically activated by the same flap handle, and they have three positions: fully retracted, mid-range, and fully extended. Investigators recovered the burned flap handle mechanism from the wreckage. They found that the handle was in the "Up/Retracted" position at impact.

The airliner's Central Aural Warning System (CAWS) provides (1) warning sounds (horn, bell, chime, etc.) and (2) synthetic voice warnings for 12 unsafe operating conditions. The NTSB explained:

> If the slats are not set for takeoff and the slat takeoff light is not illuminated, the warning system will state the word "slats"; if the flap handle is not in agreement with the value set in the flap window of the takeoff condition computer, the warning system will state the word "flaps."

On Flight 255 the CAWS should have sounded a warning and synthetically stated "flaps" and "slats." The CVR revealed that the system did not do so. Investigation determined that the CAWS did not activate because electrical power to the unit had been lost. The reason for the power loss was never identified.

Probable Cause: Nine months after the loss of Flight 255 the NTSB adopted its report, NTSB-AAR-88-05, on 10 May 1988. The board concluded that the flight crew (1) did not accomplish the taxi checklist, (2) did not extend the flaps and slats, and (3) did not check the aircraft configuration. The board found that the aircraft took off with its flaps and slats fully retracted. The CAWS was inoperative and did not warn the pilots of the unsafe condition.

The board found that climb performance was "severely limited" by the improper wing configuration. Also, the rolling near-stall condition of the aircraft further degraded climb performance. Tests revealed that, with the slats *alone* extended, the aircraft would have cleared the top of the light pole by 400 to 600 feet. The board found that the *Probable Cause* of this accident was:

> the flightcrew's failure to use the taxi checklist to ensure that the flaps and slats were extended for takeoff.

The board took note of a *contributing* cause:

> Contributing to the accident was the absence of electrical power to the airplane [CAWS] system which, thus, did not warn the flight crew that the airplane was not configured properly for takeoff.

Iran Air Flight 655

Airbus A-300, registration EP-IBU
3 July 1988, shot down over the Strait of Hormuz
290 aboard, 290 killed

Five years earlier in a tragic example of mistaken identity, a Soviet Union warplane shot down a commercial airliner (see the chapter, "Korean Airlines Flight 007"). Now the same scenario would be repeated, and this time the mistake would be made by the United States.

Overview: A big Airbus A-300 took off from Bandar Abbas in southern Iran. On course and on schedule, the airliner flew over the Strait of Hormuz, the entrance to the Persian Gulf. By chance its flight path took it directly toward a U.S. Navy warship which was engaged in a battle with Iranian gunboats. The warship crew believed the airliner was an attacking Iranian F-14 fighter, and they shot it down. All 290 people on board were killed.

The Flight: On Sunday morning, 3 July 1988, the captain aboard Iran Air Flight 655 radioed the tower at Bandar Abbas in southern Iran. He was ready to copy his ATC clearance for the twice-weekly 150 mile flight to Abu Dubai in the United Arab Emirates. The flight plan for the short 28 minute trip had been pre-filed on the Aeronautical Fixed Telecommunications Network (AFTN) and was available worldwide to civil and military authorities. It called for the usual direct route on commercial airway Amber 59 over the Strait of Hormuz and the Persian Gulf.

The captain, age 38, had been trained in the United States. His daughter, age five, had been born there, and his sister-in-law still lived in Norman, Oklahoma. In his aviation career he had logged over 7,000 flying hours.

At 1013 Hours the Airbus A-300, registration EP-IBU, with 290 people on board and a calculated takeoff weight of 287,000 pounds, began to lumber toward Runway 21. Powered by General Electric

CF6 jet engines, the Airbus rumbled down the runway and pointed its nose skyward into the haze at 1017 Hours. The pilots radioed Bandar Abbas Approach Control (which performed the duties of Departure Control) and also checked-in with Tehran Center.

The flight proceeded exactly as planned. Seven minutes after takeoff the captain said goodbye to Approach Control at 1024:11 Hours. Neither he, nor his crew, nor his passengers had any inkling that they had only 29 seconds left to live.

Trouble Ahead: The Iran-Iraq War raged on land hundreds of miles away. The battle often raged in the Persian Gulf too. A brief explanation will synopsize the military crisis in the gulf:

The previous day Iraq had conducted more airstrikes against Iranian shipping. Iran countered by attacking more merchant ships bound for Iraq. In response to this ongoing struggle, United States warships had entered the gulf to protect tankers registered under the U.S. flag. One of these warships was the USS Vincennes. She had steamed into the Strait of Hormuz, the narrow entrance to the gulf. The United States and Iran were not officially at war, but frequent sea clashes between their military forces had become routine.

Flight 655 climbed toward its cruising altitude of 14,000 feet while tracking along the centerline of Amber 59. Meanwhile the *Vincennes* was steaming at 30 knots directly below the airway. The ship was at "General Quarters" and firing its five-inch guns at gunboats manned by the Iranian Revolutionary Guard.

Search radar on the *Vincennes* detected Flight 655 one minute after it took off. It was flying directly toward the warship. In the ship's Combat Information Center (CIC), its windowless electronic war room, radar specialists saw the "unidentified bogey" closing the range. Friend or foe? Was it a commercial airliner? Was it an Iranian warplane? Was it climbing? Was it descending to attack? Seven times the warship radioed a verbal warning on VHF and UHF aviation distress frequencies, but there was no response.

The *Vincennes* soon "identified" the bogey as an Iranian F-14 in the typical attack profile. It headed straight for the warship and closed the distance to nine miles, well within range of its Maverick air-to-surface missiles. The *Vincennes* waited no longer. It fired two Standard Missile-2 (SM-2) surface-to-air missiles.

A portion of the intercepted ATC radio traffic is quoted below. It begins while Flight 655 is still on the ground at Bandar Abbas. There is no CVR tape and no record of intracockpit conversation:

Iran 655: . . . . . Iran Air Flight 655
Tower: . . . . . . Bandar Abbas Airport Control Tower
AppControl: . . . Bandar Abbas Approach Control
Center: . . . . . . Tehran Center (ARTCC)

Tower: Iran Air six-fifty-five, [are you ready to] copy your ATC clearance? (1013:19)

Iran 655: Go ahead. (1013:24)

Tower: Iran Air six-fifty-five is cleared to destination Dubai via flight plan route, climb and maintain flight level one-four-zero, after takeoff follow [a straight ahead climb] squawking Apha six-seven-six-zero. (1013:25)

[one of the pilots reads back the clearance at 1013:41]

Tower: Squawk six-seven-six-zero, Iran Air six-fifty-five, that is correct, call when ready for departure. (1013:53)

Iran 655: [We will] call you for departure. (1013:59)

[1 minute and 31 seconds pass as the pilots prepare for takeoff]

Iran 655: Iran Air six-fifty-five [is] ready for takeoff. (1015:30)

Tower: Iran Air six-fifty-five, cleared for takeoff, Runway 21, wind calm, after departure contact Approach Control [on] one-twenty-four-point-two, have a nice flight. (1015:34)

Iran 655: Six-fifty-five [is] cleared for takeoff [on Runway] twenty-one, after takeoff [we'll contact] Approach [Control], thank you very much, good day. (1015:43)

[the Airbus takes off at 1017; radar on the USS Vincennes "paints" the "unidentified bogey" 1 minute later at 1018]

Iran 655: Good morning, [this is] Iran Air six-fifty-five, airborne out of three-thousand-five-hundred feet. (1019:18)

AppControl: Iran Air six-fifty-five, good morning to you, continue as cleared, next report at Mobet, and [we are] standing by for your estimate. (1019:24)

[at 1019:33 the pilots give ATC their ETA at Mobet]

AppControl: Iran Air six-fifty-five, roger. (1019:43)

[the pilots exchange radio messages with their airline dispatch office at Bandar Abbas; then they radio Tehran Center]

Iran 655: [Unintelligible]. (1020:54)

Center: Station calling Tehran, [say again]? (1020:59)

Iran 655: Iran Air six-fifty-five from Bandar Abbas to Dubai, out of [flight] level seven-zero for one-four-zero, estimating Fir [at] fifty-eight, Dubai . . . . (1021:04)

Center: Roger, report maintaining [flight level] one-four-zero and passing Darax. (1021:20)

Iran 655: Roger. (1021:26)

Center: Confirm you are squawking six-seven-six-zero. (1021:28)

Iran 655: Affirmative. (1021:30)

[the pilots recontact Bandar Abbas Approach Control]

Iran 655: Six-fifty-five, [we are passing] position Mobet, out of [flight level] one-two-zero. (1024:00)

AppControl: Iran Air six-fifty-five, roger, contact Tehran [Center on] one-three-three-point-four, have a nice flight. (1024:07)

Iran 655: Thank you, good day. (1024:11)

[8 seconds later, in the Strait of Hormuz below the Airbus, the USS Vincennes launches two SM-2 missiles at 1024:19]

[21 seconds later the missiles destroy Flight 655 at 1024:40]

The Accident: Flight 655 was climbing through 13,500 feet at 380 knots, eight miles from the ship, when the missiles detonated. The high explosive warheads sent 12,000 steel projectiles ripping out in all directions. The left wing and empennage of the Airbus tore away. The fuselage ripped open, and the wreckage tumbled down in flames toward the sea. The fall took 82 seconds, and the 290 people on board the Airbus were killed.

By noon Iranian helicopters and boats began a search for the bodies, and the recovery effort continued for a month. Eventually the remains of 192 victims were recovered, but few bodies were in one piece. One-hundred-eighty of them were identified, most by circumstantial evidence:

The political war of words, fueled by the mindless mercenary media rabble, reached fever pitch. The pompous talking heads on television babbled incessantly. At the United Nations, Iran compared the "intentional slaughter" and "barbaric massacre" to the Soviet shoot-down of a Korean airliner in 1983 and vowed to "avenge the blood of our martyrs." Meanwhile the President of the United States called the shoot-down a "terrible human tragedy." He did not apologize for the "tragic accident," but he offered condolences to the families of the victims. The United States addressed the U.N. Security Council and claimed that (1) the Vincennes was in international waters, that (2) the Airbus was outside the commercial air corridor, that (3) it was descending and accelerating in an attack profile, and that (4) it ignored repeated warnings to turn away. The United States maintained that the Vincennes fired in "assumed" self defense.

The Investigation: For the non-military layman an explanation of the *Vincennes'* capability is necessary:

The "star wars" warship, launched in 1984, was a Ticonderoga class Aegis (the shield of Athena in Greek mythology) cruiser with a state-of-the-art computerized surveillance and weapons system. She had been optimized for "blue water" defense of an aircraft carrier battle group against the Soviet Navy, part of the global maritime strategy of the United States. Her darkened electronic war room, looking much like a luxury video arcade, could process, interpret, and display data from a complex air battle extending over hundreds of miles. She could track over 200 targets simultaneously and (1) identify, (2) analyze, and (3) prioritize each threat. Plus, the automated Aegis fire control system could fire her weapons automatically, independent of human involvement, if such a mode was selected.

What really happened? Armed with the electronic data trail from the Aegis system, the shoot-down was not hard to reconstruct. At 1018 Hours the Aegis radar detected an "unidentified bogey" 55 miles away, climbing out from Bandar Abbas. Because that airport serves both civilian airliners and Iranian warplanes, the bogey was "assumed hostile" until proven otherwise.

The Aegis computer flashed an electronic query to the bogey's transponder. The response came back immediately: Mode III, Code 6760. This indicated the bogey was a commercial airliner, called "ComAir." The next task fell to a human, not a computer. Within the CIC in "Air Alley" a petty officer manually checked the list of airline flights over the gulf that morning:

Flight 655 was on the list but the petty officer did not see it, most likely because of the four times zones in the gulf.

The *Vincennes* had found no record of an airline overflight, and the bogey was headed straight for the warship. At 1019 Hours the "talker" radioed a standard challenge on the international VHF and UHF aviation distress frequencies:

Unidentified aircraft *[emphasis added]*, you are approaching a United States naval warship in international waters . . . .

No response. The bogey, now only 32 miles away, continued to close the range. Was it an Iranian military plane rushing to assist the Iranian gunboats battling the warship? The *Vincennes* was tracking an Iranian Air Force P-3 patrol plane zipping down the coast. Was it coordinating an attack by the bogey?

Air Alley queried the bogey's transponder again, and this time the response was different: Mode II, Code 1100. A warplane!

*The Air Alley operator had forgotten to **reset the range** for the query. Consequently, the query triggered the transponder on an Iranian military aircraft still at the airport.*

The talker again transmitted the challenge. Still no response. At 1020 Hours a CIC officer shouted: "Possible Astro!"

Astro was the code name for an Iranian F-14. The Iranian Air Force had moved three of them to Bandar Abbas on 25 June to supplement their older F-4 fighters. An Iranian F-14 and its

Maverick air-to-surface missiles (which could be fired within 13 miles of their target) would be lethal against the Vincennes.

The alarm *rocketed* through the CIC. The commanding officer (CO), seated in front of his big blue display, planned to shoot down any hostile aircraft that closed within 20 miles. Nonetheless, not everyone in Air Alley was sure they were tracking an Iranian F-14. An officer shouted: "Possible ComAir!" The electronic warfare specialists watched as the bogey climbed through 7,000 feet, too high for the normal attack profile. Yet, at 380 knots the bogey was zooming a mile nearer to the warship each 10 seconds. The talker radioed a different warning, more dire than the original:

> *Iranian fighter [emphasis added]*, you are steering into danger and you are subject to United States defensive measures . . . .

Four more times the talker radioed the same final warning. No response. Each second counted, for the bogey continued to scream toward the ship. In Air Alley everyone was shouting. Most were hollering: "Astro!" A few still yelled: "Possible ComAir!" Time was running out.

Chaos reigned in the high-tech CIC. The cruiser's big five-inch guns hammered away at the gunboats. At 30 knots the ship heeled hard over in a turn to starboard. Loose papers and anything not nailed down skidded across the CIC deck. Those not seated had to hold on in order to stand erect. Everyone was yelling to be heard. The bogey still bored in toward the ship, refusing to veer away, rapidly closing the range:

> *For an Air Alley specialist to document a bogey's speed or its altitude, he must "punch up" that information. It is displayed on a small and separate 12 inch monitor. Crucially, it does not display the rate of change. The analyst must calculate the rate of change in his head or on scratch paper.*

Suddenly two officers in Air Alley alerted the CO. The bogey had accelerated to 455 knots, they yelled. Even worse, they shouted that it was descending straight toward their ship -- the lethal F-14 attack profile!

In the heat of battle, sinister scenario fulfillment had taken control. The electronic data trail would later show that the bogey was neither accelerating nor descending. Instead, it was climbing through 12,000 feet at 380 knots.

The "attacking F-14" had closed within range to fire its deadly Maverick missiles. The CO could wait no longer. He switched on the key to arm his missile battery. A petty officer in Air Alley pressed the firing button at 1024:19 Hours. Two supersonic and deadly SM-2 surface-to-air missiles whooshed skyward at Mach 2.5 speed. Twenty-one seconds later, eight miles away, they detonated and blew Flight 655 out of the sky:

Prior to missile launch no one on the ship had visual contact with the bogey high overhead because of the haze over the gulf.

On the ship's bridge a sailor filmed debris as it rained down from the sky. The audio track on the film captured jubilation from those watching: "Comin' down! -- Direct hit! -- Dead on!"

Yet, something was wrong. The falling wreckage was much bigger than the expected pieces of an F-14 fighter plane. An entire Airbus wing fluttered down, then huge sections of the fuselage. Slowly an awful and eerie silence settled over the bridge. No one uttered a word. The guns ceased fire. The *Vincennes* turned south and steamed out of Iranian waters.

Probable Cause: Several entities, including the U.S. Navy, have conducted "investigations" into this aviation disaster. Each had its own axe to grind, and the findings of each are therefore flawed. However, this chapter is predicated upon unbiased *independent* technical reports.

Although the players, location, and hardware had changed, this accident mirrored the Soviet Union shoot-down of Korean Airlines Flight 007 in 1983. In both instances military authority, under life-and-death pressure, fell prey to *scenario fulfillment*. As with the proverbial "bump in the night," in time of actual or perceived peril one's mind perceives what it fears most. One sees his worst nightmare, what he dreads most, the greatest evil.

The professional men in the CIC found themselves overwhelmed by technology and user interface human failures. The CO got well intended but faulty information from his crew. Yet, given the information in hand and the need to act immediately, he had no choice. His paramount duty was to defend his ship and his crew. His written Rules of Engagement stated in part:

> If a potentially hostile contact persists in closing after you warn him away and if, in your judgment, the threat of attack is imminent, it is an inherent right and responsibility to act in self defense. We do not want, nor intend, to absorb a first attack.

The mighty Aegis computer system had been caught in a murky quasi-fight for which it was not designed. Yet, it functioned perfectly. The interface failures were human, not electronic. When seconds counted and with lives on the line, the professionals on the *Vincennes* fell prey to simple human errors, emotional frailty, and cruel illusion. The philosophy that best explains the tragedy was espoused by retired Gen. William T. Sherman (1820-1891), who cautioned young men on 12 August 1880:

> There is many a boy here today who looks on war as all glory. But, boys, war is Hell.

As for Flight 655, the tragedy probably should be attributed to simple *bad luck*. Iranian military commanders had not warned Iran Air about their gunboat plans, as they had done in the past. Had the Airbus captain been informed he would have circumvented the area. However, he did not know, and he flew directly toward a warship engaged in battle.

Many allege that the Airbus pilots were at fault for not turning away, for *ignoring* seven warnings. In reality, they probably did not. The pilots were busy with almost simultaneous radio contacts with Bandar Abbas Approach Control, Tehran Center, the Iran Air dispatcher, plus the pending contact with Emirates Center. Amid all the ATC radio chatter and their many cockpit duties they most likely never heard, or understood, the warship talker.

Yet, even if the pilots did hear the warnings, they had no way to know they were directed at them. The first two warnings were for an "unidentified aircraft." Which unidentified aircraft? Where? The last five radio warnings were directed to an "Iranian fighter," not a commercial airliner.

The Airbus pilots merely flew to the (1) wrong place, at the (2) wrong time, under the (3) wrong circumstances. For them, chalk the tragic shoot-down up to *bad luck* -- the misfortunes of war.

Pan Am Flight 103

Boeing 747, registration N739PA
21 December 1988, over Lockerbie, Scotland
259 aboard, 259 killed (plus 11 killed on the ground)

This project makes no attempt to document the conduct or results of criminal investigations, or judicial mandates, which stemmed from the loss of Pan Am Flight 103. This project is limited in scope to the aeronautical aspects of the flight and the Department for Transport investigation which followed.

Overview: A Boeing 747 took off from London, England, and headed for New York. En route a bomb detonated in the forward cargo hold, causing the aircraft to break apart in flight. Wreckage fell in and around the town of Lockerbie, Scotland. All 259 people on board, plus 11 more on the ground, were killed.

The Flight: Four nights before Christmas on 21 December 1988, Pan American World Airways (Pan Am) Flight 103 waited at the gate at Heathrow Airport in London, England. While baggage and cargo handlers loaded the cavernous cargo holds, passengers bound for New York joined the crewmembers and filed down the ramp into the aircraft. At 1804 Hours the flight pushed back from the gate and lumbered out toward Runway 27R.

The captain, age 55, and the first officer, age 52, both held ATP certificates, and they had accumulated a total of 22,765 hours of flight time. Their flight engineer had logged 8,068 hours in the air. In the cabin the 13 flight attendants were responsible for the care of 243 paying passengers.

The Boeing 747, registration N739PA, had been delivered new to Pan Am in 1970 and had amassed 72,464 hours of flying time. The fuselage consisted of conventional skin, stringer, and frame construction, but the interior had modifications not apparent to the untrained eye. The cabin had been built with heavier decking so that it could carry "special purpose" military cargo as part of the

Civil Reserve Air Fleet (CRAF). In a national emergency the seats could be removed, and military freight containers could be loaded onto the strengthened deck for delivery anywhere in the world.

Trouble Ahead: At a takeoff weight of 713,002 pounds the big jumbo-jet clawed its way skyward into the cold and rainy night at 1825 Hours. ATC cleared the pilots to climb to their planned cruising altitude at flight level 310. At 1858 Hours the pilots checked-in with Shanwick Oceanic Control (ARTCC), and there was no hint of trouble. The controller asked if the pilots were ready to copy their transatlantic clearance, and one of the pilots replied: "Ready to copy." Those three words became the epitaph for 259 people, for no one heard from Flight 103 again:

> The [CVR] tape ended . . . with a sudden loud sound on the CAM channel, followed almost immediately by the cessation of recording whilst the crew were copying their transatlantic clearance from Shanwick ATC.

At 1902:50 Hours the CVR documented the *loud sound*. The CVR recording stopped milliseconds later, and the FDR stopped at the same time. Eight seconds later the ATC radar signature from the flight fragmented into four separate returns. Then it fragmented into several more, all drifting downwind.

The Accident: The Boeing 747 had self-destructed in the air. Residents of the town of Lockerbie, Dumfriesshire, Scotland, heard a loud rumbling noise like faraway thunder. The rumble steadily grew louder and louder, reaching a deafening crescendo that forced many residents to cover their ears. Then pieces of what once had been a modern airliner began screaming down into the town:

> The wings impacted at the southern edge of Lockerbie . . . creating a fireball, setting fire to neighboring houses, and carrying aloft debris which was then blown downwind for several miles . . . . Major portions of the aircraft, including the engines, also landed on the town of Lockerbie, and other large parts . . . landed in the countryside to the east of the town.

At a speed of between 440 and 500 knots the primary structure of the wing knifed down tip-first into the Sherwood Crescent section of Lockerbie. The impact blasted out a tremendous crater 155 feet long and threw over 500 cubic yards of earth into the air. A 60 foot long section of the fuselage fell into a housing estate 1,800 feet away. The forward fuselage and cockpit landed in a field two miles from the town. Free-falling at about 260 knots, the four engines plummeted to earth in Lockerbie. Human bodies also rained down from the night sky:

> Examinations of the victims indicated that the majority had experienced severe multiple injuries . . . consistent with the in-flight disintegration of the aircraft and ground impact.

All 259 people on Flight 103 had perished. Within minutes it was clear that a disaster of almost biblical proportions had befallen the residents of Lockerbie. Human remains and jagged remnants of the aircraft had fallen helter-skelter into the town. Flames roared skyward, fed by ruptured gas mains and by the 239,997 pounds of fuel carried in the Boeing 747 tanks. Twenty fire trucks converged on Lockerbie. At 1937 Hours the first of many ambulances loaded with injured residents sped toward Dumfries, 12 miles away, and toward the Galloway Royal Infirmary.

By dawn on 22 December the firefighters had brought most of the fires under control. In addition to the dozens of homes that had been destroyed by falling debris or fire, 21 others had to be demolished because of irreparable damage. Eleven residents of Lockerbie had been killed by direct impact trauma from falling debris or by the resulting fires. Scores of others were injured:

> Lighter debris from the aircraft was strewn as far as the coast of England over a distance of 130 kilometers.

The identity of 10 persons known to have been aboard the flight could not be linked to any of the bodies, or parts of bodies, that were found. Investigators *theorized* that these 10 people had fallen to earth inside a small part of the cabin that had remained attached to the wing. The inferno in the crater, fueled by a quarter-million pounds of jet fuel, had melted the metal structure and burned all human remains into unidentifiable ash.

The Investigation: Teams of experts from the Air Accident Investigation Branch, Department for Transport, began arriving in

Lockerbie before dawn on 22 December. Within a few days a host of technical analysts arrived from Canada, Germany, France, and the United States. Twenty-two civil and military organizations pitched in to help.

Why had Flight 103 broken apart in mid-air? The investigators first turned to the CVR and FDR. What was *not* found told them that the death of the airliner had been sudden. The FDR revealed that the craft had been cruising at flight level 310. The routine data trail suddenly stopped at 1902:50 Hours. Turning to the CVR, analysts found that it had recorded normal cockpit conversation and radio messages. Then, at the identical time when the FDR had stopped, the CVR tape ended with a mysterious *loud sound*.

Over 90 percent of the wreckage was recovered and laid out in a two dimensional reconstruction. Examination of torn edges of fuselage skin did not reveal any evidence of pre-existing cracks or defects. The position of the controls and switches in the cockpit was indicative of normal cruising flight.

Investigators then found airframe damage consistent with an *explosion*. Metallurgists determined that the blast occurred inside a metal cargo container in the forward cargo hold. Forensic scientists from the Royal Armaments Research and Development Establishment found remnants of a radio-cassette player in the explosive "shatter zone." Analysis of residue on fragments of this device confirmed that it had contained an IED:

> Detonation of an IED *[meaning, improvised explosive device]* loaded in a luggage container [in] the forward cargo hold directly caused the loss of the aircraft.

The powerful blast and the explosive decompression created a "star burst" hole 5 feet long and 17 feet high in the fuselage. From this jagged hole the high intensity shock wave caused cracks to propagate around the circumference of the fuselage. From that moment on, the aircraft and everyone aboard were doomed:

> The initial explosion triggered a sequence of events which effectively destroyed the integrity of the forward fuselage.

Over the cargo hold the shock wave buckled the cabin floor beams. This jammed the flight control cables, forcing the aircraft to *violently* pitch down and roll left. Forward of the blast hole and the cracks in the fuselage skin, the (1) pitch change and (2) left roll caused the weakened airframe to twist to the right. The cracks widened, then spread all the way around the fuselage:

> The movement of the forward fuselage relative to the remainder of the aircraft was an initial twisting motion to the right, accompanied by a nose-up deflection.

Within three seconds the entire front of the fuselage ripped away. As this part of the craft tore off, the 434 knot slipstream whipped it rearward. It struck the number three engine and pylon, tearing both off the right wing. The debris swept on rearward, slamming through the vertical and horizontal stabilizers.

With the cockpit and forward fuselage gone and the flight controls jammed nose-down, the rest of the aircraft "tucked under" and dove earthward. At around 19,000 feet the dive became vertical. The damaged tail surfaces ripped away, and the remainder of the aircraft began to disintegrate. One by one the remaining three engines broke free. Then the fuselage tore apart, throwing passengers and crew out into the cold night. The heaviest pieces of wreckage and most of the bodies fell in and around the town of Lockerbie. Light pieces of debris fluttered down as far away as the North Sea, 78 miles to the east.

Probable Cause: The Department for Transport adopted the Aircraft Accident Report, No. 2-90 (EW/C1094), over a year after the loss of Flight 103. The department confirmed that an IED caused the loss of Flight 103 when explosive forces created a large hole in the fuselage. Cracks propagated from the hole as a result of the explosive pressure differential. Buckling of the structure jammed the flight control cables, causing the aircraft to *violently* pitch down and roll left. This twisting motion, combined with the cracks, caused the forward section of the aircraft to tear away. The rest of the aircraft disintegrated as it fell to earth. The department synopsized the *Cause* of the accident in one sentence:

> The in-flight disintegration of the aircraft was caused by the detonation of an improvised explosive device located in a baggage container on the left side of the forward cargo hold.

United Airlines Flight 811

Boeing 747, registration N4713U
24 February 1989, over the Pacific Ocean, near Hawaii
355 aboard, 9 killed

Overview: A Boeing 747 took off from Hawaii and headed south over the Pacific Ocean. A cargo door ripped open at 23,000 feet, and explosive decompression tore a huge hole in the fuselage. Nine passengers were sucked out of the cabin and "lost in flight."

The Flight: Shortly after midnight on 24 February 1989 the passengers began shuffling aboard United Airlines Flight 811 at Honolulu, Hawaii. The three members of the flight deck crew, the 15 flight attendants, and 337 passengers on this red-eye flight were headed for Auckland, New Zealand, an en route stop on the way to Sydney, Australia. Their aircraft left Gate 10 at 0133 Hours and taxied out toward Runway 8R.

The Boeing 747 chosen for this trip, registration N4713U, was one of 31 Boeing 747s in the United fleet. For this flight the airliner had a calculated takeoff weight of 697,900 pounds. The two pilots and flight engineer had amassed an amazing total of 62,500 hours of airline flying experience.

The tower cleared Flight 811 for takeoff at 0152 Hours. The jumbo-jet accelerated down the runway and arced up into the cold and rainy Pacific night. Shortly after takeoff the captain began to circumvent a line of thunderstorms. Because they might encounter turbulence from the cells, he elected to leave the seat belt sign illuminated until they left the storms behind. For some passengers this minor aggravation would prove to be a lifesaving coincidence.

Trouble Ahead: There was no indication of impending peril. The portion of the CVR transcript, below, begins as the pilots discuss the thunderstorms along their route. The captain is flying the airliner as it climbs through 23,000 feet:

Capt: . . . . . Captain, Flight 811
FO: . . . . . . First Officer, Flight 811
FltEngr: . . . Flight Engineer, Flight 811
Radio-: . . . . (prefix) Radio transmission, Flight 811
Tower: . . . . Honolulu Airport Control Tower
Center: . . . . Honolulu Center (ARTCC)

FO: [The storm] ends out there to the right, doesn't it? (0208:37)

Capt: Yeah. (0208:47)

FO: You're gettin' a hole right here on the radar. (0208:50)

Capt: Yup. (0208:52)

FltEngr: You guys take the quickest way around it. (0208:53)

[sound of a "thump" at 0209:07]

Capt: What the [expletive] was that? (0209:07)

FO: I don't know. (0209:08)

*[sound of a **loud explosion** at 0209:09]*

[a cargo door has "blown out;" decompression has ripped a huge hole in the fuselage and swept 9 passengers out of the aircraft; the pilots do not know this; they only know the aircraft has experienced explosive decompression]

[loss of electrical power to the CVR for 22 seconds]

Radio-FO: . . . looks like we've lost number three engine, and we're descending rapidly, coming back [to Honolulu]. (0209:31)

Center: United eight-eleven, roger, keep Center advised. (0209:38)

Capt: Emergency descent. (0209:53)

Radio-FO: [Center, this is] United eight-eleven heavy, we're doing an emergency descent. (0209:56)

Center: United eight-eleven heavy, roger. (0209:59)

[1 minute and 10 seconds pass; the descent continues]

Center: United eight-eleven heavy, say your altitude. (0211:09)

Radio-FO: Ah, United eight-eleven heavy, we're out of fifteen-point-five *[meaning, 15,500 feet]*. (0211:13)

Capt: We don't have any fire indications. (0211:53)

FltEngr: I don't have -- no, I don't have anything. (0211:56)

Capt: OK, we lost number, aaahhh, three [engine]. Let's, aaahhh, shut it down. (0211:59)

[the crew shuts down the No. 3 engine; 44 more seconds pass]

FltEngr: [We have] lots of fuel, should we dump? Want me to start dumpin'? (0212:43)

Radio-FO: Honolulu [Center], United eight-eleven heavy, we're gonna level at nine-thousand [feet] here while we assess our problem, and, ah, we're comin' back, direct Honolulu. (0213:17)

Center: United eight-eleven heavy, roger, keep the Center advised . . . when able, forward the souls on board and fuel. (0213:27)

[1 minute and 2 seconds pass; the pilots explore their problem]

Capt: What are ya dumpin' down to? We've got a [expletive] of a control problem here, I've got almost full rudder. (0214:29)

FO: You dumping as quick as you can? (0214:41)

FltEngr: I'm dumping everything. (0214:43)

Capt: We got a problem with number four engine too. (0214:54)

FO: Can you maintain two-[hundred]-forty [knots]? (0215:13)

Capt: Yeah, just barely. (0215:15)

FO: Yeah, but we're losin' altitude. (0215:18)

FltEngr: We're down to . . . seventy-thousand [pounds of fuel] now, we're dumping five-thousand pounds a minute. (0215:21)

Radio-FO: Ah, Center, United eight-eleven heavy, ah, do you have a fix on us? (0215:22)

Center: Affirmative, sir, I have you on radar. (0215:27)

Radio-FO: OK, it appears that we've lost number three engine, and we've lost -- we're not getting full power out of number four, we're not able to hold altitude right now, we're dumping fuel, so, aaahhh, I think we're gonna be able to . . . . (0215:30)

Center: United eight-eleven heavy, roger, I show you six-zero miles south of Honolulu at this time. (0215:48)

> *[unable to contact the Flight Attendants via the ICS, the Captain instructs the Flight Engineer to go back into the cabin and check for damage; 1 minute and 51 seconds pass]*

Capt: We got a fire in [engine] number four, go through the procedure, shut down the engine. (0217:39)

FO: We're not gonna be able to hold altitude on two. (0217:44)

> *[the pilots shut down the No. 4 engine; both engines on the right wing now have been shut down]*

> *[the Flight Engineer returns from his inspection; he exclaims]*

FltEngr: The whole right side! The right side is gone! (0217:53)

Capt: What da ya mean? (0218:07)

FltEngr: Looks like a bomb [caused the damage], the fuselage, it's just open! (0218:08)

Capt: The whole right side is gone? . . . Anybody hurt? (0218:15)

FltEngr: Some people are probably gone *[meaning, sucked out of the aircraft]*, I don't know. (0218:22)

Capt: We've got a real problem here. (0218:24)

Radio-FO: Center, United eight-eleven heavy, you've got to give us a vector, direct Honolulu, we're losin' the VOR. (0218:30)

Center: [Turn to] zero-three-zero [degrees]. Can you maintain heading now, and altitude? (0218:32)

Radio-Capt: Ah, not really, we shut down number four, we're on [only] two engines. (0218:34)

> *[14 minutes and 43 seconds pass; slowly losing altitude, powered only by the two engines on its left wing, the wounded airliner flounders back to the airport at Honolulu and slips down*

the glideslope for Runway 8L]

FO: Two-hundred [knots] -- one-ninety-five -- half a dot high -- lookin' good -- one-ninety-two -- one-ninety-five. (0233:17)

Capt: Comin' off on the power. (0233:26)

FltEngr: One-hundred feet -- fifty feet. (0233:28)

Capt: Center the trim, center the trim. (0233:30)

FltEngr: Thirty [feet], ten . . . . (0233:31)

[sound of touchdown on the runway at 0233:35]

FO: We're on! (0233:37)

FltEngr: Gear's holding! (0233:38)

FO: No spoilers . . . one-[hundred]-seventy [knots] . . . one-sixty . . . one-forty . . . one-thirty . . . one-twenty . . . one-ten . . . lookin' good, one-hundred, pressure's holding . . . . (0233:39)

[the aircraft slowly brakes to a safe stop on the runway]

Capt: Shut 'em down, we're evacuating. (0234:19)

Radio-FO: [Tower], United eight-eleven heavy, we're evacuating the airplane. (0234:20)

Tower: United eight-eleven, you've got the airport. (0234:22)

The Accident: As the aircraft had climbed through 23,000 feet at 300 knots, the latching mechanism on the forward lower cargo door failed at 0209:09 Hours. The door blew open, ripping a huge hole in the right side of the fuselage. The pressure differential instantly blasted everything out of the cargo bay into the night sky:

> This accident was precipitated by the sudden loss of the forward lower lobe cargo door, which led to explosive decompression.

The new vacuum in the cargo bay buckled the cabin floor beams downward. The explosive force of the out-rushing air swept nine passengers out of the cabin through the hole in the fuselage. At 300 knots, sub-zero-temperature wind screamed through the cabin. Flying debris whipped and swirled everywhere. No one could hear anything except the deafening shriek of the wind.

The pilots began an emergency descent, dumping fuel to lighten the aircraft. The two engines on the right wing failed, and the heavily loaded aircraft was powered by only the No. 1 and No. 2 engines on the left wing. Losing altitude, the flight staggered back to the airport. Damage to the flaps and slats limited flap extension to five degrees, but the aircraft managed to land safely:

> The explosive nature of the decompression . . . swept nine of the passengers from the airplane.

The nine passengers who had been sucked out of the aircraft were officially "lost in flight." An intensive sea search involving over 1,000 people turned up no trace of their bodies.

The remaining 346 people aboard Flight 811 survived. Many who had been seated near the enormous hole in the fuselage *almost* had been sucked out into the night sky. Only their fastened seat belts, thanks to the pre-accident possibility of turbulence, held them inside the aircraft. Nonetheless, 38 people aboard suffered broken bones, lacerations, facial injuries, and barotitis (injury to the middle ear and sinuses due to a sudden air-pressure change) caused by the explosion and the flying debris.

The Investigation: Boeing 747 airliners have two lower cargo doors on the right side of the fuselage. The doors open outward, swinging up on a piano-hinge device to facilitate cargo loading. The doors are locked and unlocked by electrical power from the *ground handling bus*, and they can not be opened in flight. Ten latches, all electrically actuated by the ground handling bus, lock the cargo doors prior to flight:

> The cargo doors on the Boeing 747 have a master lock handle installed on the exterior of the door. The handle is opened and closed manually.

When the cargo door on Flight 811 broke open it tore a hole 13 feet long and 15 feet high in the side of the aircraft. Through the hole in the fuselage, sections of the cabin floor and some of the passenger seats had been sucked out of the aircraft. Investigation determined that flying debris from the explosion damaged large sections of the right wing, plus the right horizontal stabilizer and vertical stabilizer. Debris ingested by the No. 3 and No. 4 engines, below the right wing, caused them to fail:

> The loss of power from the Nos. 3 and 4 engines was caused by foreign object damage when debris [was] ejected from the cabin and cargo compartment during the explosive decompression.

The deep-sea submersible *Sea Cliff* located and recovered the missing cargo door from the floor of the Pacific Ocean, 14,000 feet below the surface. Evidence indicated that the door itself did not fail. It was intact when it separated from the aircraft. Further, evidence clearly showed that loss of the door was not caused by a failure of the surrounding structure.

Investigators determined that the door latches had been fully closed, and the locking handle was in the stowed position. Unfortunately, the latch cams were in the nearly *open* position. Wear patterns on the latch pins revealed that the door had been out-of-rig for an extended period of time.

Probable Cause: Over three years after the accident the NTSB adopted its Aircraft Accident Report, NTSB-AAR-92-02, on 18 March 1992. The board found that the Boeing design did not provide the intended "fail-safe" locking and indicating systems for the door. The board also pointed out that, following a previous cargo door incident, Boeing and the FAA did not immediately provide cam position view-ports on the cargo doors. The board found the *Probable Cause* of this accident to be:

> the sudden opening of the forward lower lobe cargo door in flight and the subsequent explosive decompression. The door opening was attributed to a faulty switch or wiring in the door control system which permitted electrical actuation of the door latches toward the unlatched position . . . .

The board found two factors that *contributed* to the accident:

> [First], a deficiency in the design of the cargo door locking mechanisms which made them susceptible to deformation.

> [Second], a lack of timely corrective actions by Boeing and the FAA following a [previous] cargo door opening incident.

Avianca Airlines Flight 052

Boeing 707, registration HK2016
25 January 1990, at Cove Neck, New York
158 aboard, 73 killed

Overview: A big Boeing 707 approached New York at night in horrible weather. Although low on fuel, the pilots loitered in holding patterns at three locations. They allowed ATC to sequence them with routine traffic. The pilots never declared an emergency, and the airliner ran out of fuel. The crash killed 73 of the 158 people on board.

The Flight: Avianca Airlines Flight 052 left Bogota, Colombia, on the sunny afternoon of 25 January 1990. The airliner made a short flight to the Jose Maria Cordova Airport near Medellin, Colombia. There it refueled and prepared for the long transatlantic trip north to New York in the United States.

The Boeing 707, registration HK2016, was a long range variant of the original Boeing design. When fully fueled it was capable of flying up to 6,000 miles. Avianca had bought the aircraft from another carrier 13 years earlier, and the transport had logged 61,764 hours of flying time. The flight plan for the trip to New York specified a takeoff weight of 254,430 pounds. The distance to the airport measured 2,067 miles, roughly one-third the range of the aircraft when it is fully fueled.

The captain held two ATP certificates, one issued by the FAA in the United States and another issued by the government of Colombia. He had flown to New York many times and had amassed 16,787 flight hours in his logbook. The captain also served as a military pilot in the Colombian Air Force Reserve. His young first officer, age 27, held a Commercial Pilot certificate issued by the United States and another issued by Colombia. His total flight time was 1,837 hours. He had recently transitioned to the Boeing 707 and had completed his initial line check the previous month. An experienced flight engineer and six flight attendants rounded out the Avianca crew.

At 1505 Hours the four Pratt & Whitney engines powered Flight 052 skyward over the Atlantic. At flight level 350 the aircraft overflew Bimini and continued north toward the United States.

Trouble Ahead: As Flight 052 cruised up the eastern seaboard the weather in the northeastern United States turned progressively more rotten. Air traffic was already "stacking up" over Philadelphia, Newark, New York, and Boston. ATC put Flight 052 into a holding pattern near Norfolk, Virginia, while controllers struggled to sequence hundreds of arriving flights down for safe landings.

Flight 052 eventually got clearance to proceed north again, but not for long. Over Atlantic City, New Jersey, ATC mandated another holding pattern. The extent of the bad weather had not been forecast, and the delays were not expected. The pilots knew that their aircraft did not have enough fuel to spend much more time droning around in holding patterns. Concerned, they cast anxious glances at their fuel gauges. They watched their fuel supply dwindle as the minutes slowly ticked away.

ATC finally cleared Flight 052 to head north again, but the aerial reprieve did not last. Only 39 miles from New York the pilots got bad news again. For the third time ATC placed them in a holding pattern. The NTSB would later note:

> The first officer incorrectly assumed that his request for priority handling by air traffic control had been understood as a request for *emergency [emphasis added]* handling.

To properly illustrate the pilots' dilemma, the portion of the CVR and ATC transcript quoted below is rather lengthy. It begins with the flight in its *third* holding pattern. As the minutes slip away the engines continue to gulp down precious fuel.

The captain, who is flying the airliner, has a communications problem. He can not hear radio messages from ATC, so he relies on his first officer to handle all radio communications:

Capt: . . . . . . Captain, Flight 052
FO: . . . . First Officer, Flight 052
FltEngr: . . . . Flight Engineer, Flight 052
Radio-: . . . . . (prefix) Radio transmission, Flight 052

GPWS: ..... Ground Proximity Warning System, Flight 052
Tower: ..... John F. Kennedy Airport Control Tower
Center: ..... New York Center (ARTCC)
AppControl: .. Kennedy Approach Control
DepControl: .. Kennedy Departure Control

Center: Avianca zero-five-two heavy . . . indefinite hold at this time . . . expect further clearance . . . . (2044:09)

Radio-FO: [This is Avianca] zero-five-two, well, I think we need priority, we're passing [unintelligible]. (2044:50)

Center: Avianca zero-five-two heavy, roger, how long can you hold and -- aaahhh -- what is your alternate [airport]? (2044:58)

Radio-FO: Yes sir, we'll be able to hold about five minutes, and that's all we can do . . . [our alternate is] Boston, but we can't [make] it now, we, we don't -- we will run out of fuel. (2045:03)

[26 minutes pass; Center finally clears the flight to the Kennedy Airport and instructs the pilots to contact Approach Control; the flight descends to 2,000 feet and gets vectors to the ILS]

AppControl: Avianca zero-five-two heavy, you are one-five miles from the outer marker, maintain two-thousand 'till established on the localizer, cleared ILS, [Runway] twenty-two left. (2111:07)

[4 minutes pass, routine cockpit conversation]

AppControl: Avianca zero-five-two, contact Kennedy Tower, one-one-niner-point-one, good day. (2115:08)

Radio-FO: One-one-niner-point-one, so long. (2115:12)

Tower: Avianca zero-five-two heavy, Kennedy Tower, [Runway] two-two left, you're number three [for landing]. (2115:23)

[2 minutes and 48 seconds pass; routine cockpit conversation]

FO: We are three miles [from] the outer marker now. (2118:11)

FO: Glideslope alive. (2118:32)

Capt: Lower the gear. (2119:09)

Capt: Give me forty [degrees of flaps]. (2119:21)

Tower: Avianca zero-five-two, [Runway] two-two left, wind one-nine-zero at two-zero [knots], cleared to land. (2119:58)

Radio-FO: Cleared to land, Avianca zero-five-two. (2120:00)

Capt: We are cleared to land, no? (2120:21)

FO: Yes sir, we are cleared to land. (2120:23)

[2 minutes and 21 seconds pass; the aircraft tracks the ILS]

FO: Below glideslope. (2122:44)

FO: Glideslope! (2122:52)

*[the aircraft flies into horizontal **windshear** and rapidly sinks below the ILS glideslope]*

FO: This is windshear. (2122:57)

FltEngr: Glideslope! (2123:08)

GPWS: Whoop whoop, pull up . . . . (2123:08)

FO: Sink rate -- five-hundred feet. (2123:10)

GPWS: Whoop whoop, pull up, whoop whoop . . . . (2123:11)

Capt: [Where are the runway] lights? (2123:13)

GPWS: Whoop whoop, pull up, whoop whoop, pull up, whoop whoop, pull up, whoop whoop . . . . (2123:14)

Capt: Where is the runway? (2123:20)

GPWS: Whoop whoop, pull up, whoop whoop . . . . (2123:21)

Capt: The runway! Where is it? (2123:23)

*[the aircraft is 1.3 miles from the runway, dangerously below the glideslope, **only 200 feet above the ground**]*

GPWS: Glideslope, glideslope . . . . (2123:25)

FO: I don't see it! I don't see it! (2123:27)

[the Captain decides to execute a missed approach]

Capt: Landing gear up, landing gear up. (2123:28)

<u>*GPWS*</u>: *Glideslope, glideslope. (2123:29)*

<u>Capt</u>: Request another traffic pattern. (2123:33)

<u>Radio-FO</u>: [Tower, we are] executing missed approach. (2123:34)

<u>Tower</u>: Avianca zero-five-two heavy, roger, climb and maintain two-thousand, turn left, heading one-eight-zero. (2123:39)

<u>Capt</u>: We don't have fu --! (2123:43)

<u>Capt</u>: I don't know what happened with the runway. I didn't see it. I didn't see it. (2124:00)

[the Captain stops the climb at 2,000 feet]

<u>Capt</u>: Tell them we are in [an] emergency! (2124:06)

<u>Radio-FO</u>: [Turning] to one-eight-zero on the heading, and we'll try [to land] once again. We're running out of fuel. (2124:08)

<u>Tower</u>: OK. (2124:15)

<u>Capt</u>: Advise him we are emergency, did you tell him? (2124:22)

<u>FO</u>: Yes sir, I already advised him. (2124:28)

*[the First Officer **never declares an emergency**; the Captain does not know this because of his radio problem]*

<u>Tower</u>: Avianca zero-five-two heavy, contact Approach [Control] on one-one-eight-point-four. (2124:39)

<u>Radio-FO</u>: Approach, Avianca zero-five-two heavy, we just missed an approach and we're maintaining two-thousand . . . . (2124:55)

<u>AppControl</u>: Avianca zero-five-two heavy, [this is] New York, good evening, climb and maintain three-thousand. (2125:03)

<u>Capt</u>: Advise him we don't have fuel! (2125:08)

<u>Radio-FO</u>: Climb and maintain three-thousand and -- aaahhh -- we're running out of fuel, sir. (2125:10)

<u>AppControl</u>: OK, fly a heading of zero-eight-zero. (2125:12)

<u>Capt</u>: Did you already advise that we don't have fuel? (2125:28)

<u>FO</u>: Yes sir, I already advised him. Hundred-and-eighty on the

heading. We are going to maintain three-thousand and he is going to get us back [to the ILS course]. (2125:29)

[1 minute and 6 seconds pass; the aircraft tracks outbound]

AppControl: Avianca zero-five-two heavy, turn left heading zero-seven-zero . . . I'm gonna bring you about fifteen miles northeast and then turn you back onto the approach, is that fine with you and your fuel? (2126:35)

Radio-FO: I guess so -- thank you very much. (2126:43)

Capt: What did he say? (2126:46)

FO: [He said] fifteen miles to get back to the localizer. (2126:47)

Capt: Zero-seven-zero on the heading, maintaining three-thousand feet. (2126:52)

Capt: Give me the Kennedy ILS in number one. (2127:03)

FO: The ILS or the VOR? (2127:08)

Capt: The VOR. (2127:11)

FO: It is not centered, the localizer, on the radial, no? (2127:29)

Capt: I'm going to follow this --. (2127:31)

[the jittery First Officer interrupts the Captain]

FO: We must follow the identified ILS! (2127:32)

[the Captain tries to calm his nervous First Officer]

Capt: To die? . . . Take it easy! Take it easy! (2127:36)

[1 minute and 35 seconds pass]

Radio-FO: [Tower, this is] Avianca zero-five-two -- aaahhh -- can you give us a final now? (2129:11)

AppControl: Avianca zero-five-two, affirmative, sir, turn left to heading zero-four-zero. (2129:20)

[1 minute and 12 seconds pass]

AppControl: Avianca zero-five-two, climb and maintain three-thousand. (2130:32)

Radio-FO: Negative, sir! We [are] running out of fuel! (2130:36)

Capt: No! No! Three-thousand, three-thousand! (2130:39)

Radio-FO: We -- OK -- three-thousand now, OK. (2130:41)

AppControl: OK, turn left heading three-one-zero, sir. (2130:44)

Radio-FO: [Heading] three-one-zero. (2130:47)

Capt: Set flaps fourteen. (2130:55)

AppControl: And Avianca zero-five-two, fly a heading of three-six-zero, please. (2130:55)

Capt: Tell me [the] heading -- what? (2130:58)

Radio-FO: OK, we'll maintain three-six-zero now. (2130:58)

AppControl: OK, and you're number two for approach, I just have to give you enough room so that you can [intercept the ILS] without having to come out again. (2131:01)

Radio-FO: OK, we're number two, flying three-six-zero. (2131:07)

AppControl: Thank you, sir. (2131:10)

[56 seconds pass; the aircraft flies toward the ILS course]

AppControl: Avianca zero-five-two heavy, turn left heading three-three-zero. (2132:06)

Radio-FO: Three-three-zero on the heading. (2132:11)

FO: *[speaking to the Captain]* Three-three-zero. (2132:14)

*[**the fuel tanks run dry**; the engines begin to fail at 2132:36]*

FltEngr: Flame out! Flame out on engine number four! (2132:39)

Capt: Flame out on it? (2132:42)

FltEngr: Flame out on engine number three! Essential [electrical load transferred] to number two and number one. (2132:43)

Capt: Show me the runway! (2132:49)

Radio-FO: [This is] Avianca zero-five-two, we just, aaahhh, lost two engines and -- aaahhh -- we need priority, please. (2132:49)

[the First Officer <u>still</u> does not use the word "emergency"]

AppControl: Avianca zero-five-two, turn left heading two-five-zero and intercept the localizer. (2132:54)

[the No. 1 and No. 2 engines flame out at 2132:56; the airliner begins to glide down toward the ground]

Capt: Select the ILS! Let's see --. (2133:00)

AppControl: Avianca zero-five-two heavy, you're one-five miles from the outer marker, maintain two-thousand until established on the localizer, cleared for ILS, [Runway] two-two left. (2133:04)

[the First Officer does not report that the flight is going down]

Radio-FO: Roger, [this is] Avianca. (2133:12)

Capt: That, no -- that! . . . Did you select the ILS? (2133:15)

[the aircraft impacts the ground at 2133:24]

[end of the CVR tape at 2133:24]

AppControl: Avianca zero-five-two, you have -- uuuhhh -- you have enough fuel to make it to the airport? (2134:00)

[there is no response]

AppControl: *[a phone call to the Tower]* We're not talking to Avianca any longer, he's fifteen [miles] north of Kennedy . . . we don't know what his altitude, what his problem was, he last reported losing an engine. (2134:16)

AppControl: Avianca zero-five-two, New York, over. (2134:36)

AppControl: *[a phone call to the Tower]* We lost radar contact fifteen [miles] northwest of Kennedy with Avianca. (2135:06)

AppControl: Avianca zero-five-two, radar contact lost. (2135:26)

The Accident: Fuel ran out. The four engines flamed out. The Boeing 707, now merely an expensive glider, sank toward the treetops in the town of Cove Neck, New York. The wings tore through big trees as the fuselage impacted a steep up-slope.

The cockpit and forward part of the fuselage broke away and

careened over the crest of the hill. The rest of the passenger cabin "dug in" on the hill and stopped within a mere 25 feet. A sudden stop! Both wings ripped off. The main fuel tanks ruptured, but there was no fuel left to ignite. There was no fire:

> Serious and fatal injuries were the result of blunt force trauma because of high vertical and longitudinal deceleration forces.

The three occupants of the cockpit died from extreme crushing forces. There had been 158 people aboard, and 73 were killed. Another 81 people on the airliner, including 8 infants, sustained severe incapacitating injuries during the crash.

The Investigation: Accident investigation experts from the NTSB dug through the wreckage and examined the fuel system and engines. They found no malfunction that could have caused increased fuel consumption or premature fuel exhaustion. The fuel supply on board had lasted as long as expected. The problem lay in the duration of the flight. The NTSB made it clear:

> The accident occurred when the airplane's engines lost power as the result of fuel exhaustion.

Prior to departure from Colombia the flight crew had not asked for, and was not given, the current weather forecast for the New York area. Even if they had obtained this information, the weather turned out to be worse than forecast in the northeastern United States. Investigators found no record to indicate that the crew had tried to obtain updated weather information during the flight. Also, at the time of departure the weather in Boston was not suitable for selection of that airport as the alternate:

> The alternate airport [in Boston] . . . did not meet the prescribed weather criteria for an alternate [airport] based on weather information provided to the crew.

The CVR and ATC tapes revealed that the first officer handled all radio contacts with ATC. Judging from the captain's questions, investigators realized that he could not hear, or understand, the radio transmissions from ATC. The captain repeatedly told his first officer to tell ATC that the flight had an "emergency":

The first officer . . . never used the word "emergency," [not] even when he radioed that two engines had flamed out.

At 2126:43 Hours, six minutes before the engines flamed out, ATC had queried the first officer. The controller explained that he planned to vector the flight out 15 miles for another ILS approach, and he asked: "Is that fine with you and your fuel?"

"I guess so, thank you very much," the first officer replied. That verbal exchange sealed the fate of all aboard the Boeing 707. The last chance to avoid disaster quietly slipped away.

Probable Cause: On 30 April 1991 the NTSB adopted its Aircraft Accident Report, NTSB-AAR-91-04. The board pointed out that, if the aircraft had been fully fueled prior to takeoff, it could have flown to New York with enough remaining fuel to fly another 3,900 miles. However, prior to departure the bad weather had not been given proper consideration, and the aircraft had not been loaded with enough fuel for the flight. The board found that the *Probable Cause* of this accident was:

> the failure of the flight crew to adequately manage the airplane's fuel load, and their failure to communicate an emergency fuel situation to air traffic control.

The board noted several factors which *contributed* to the accident:

> [First was] the flight crew's failure to use an airline operational control dispatch system to assist them during the international flight into a high-density airport in poor weather.

> [Second was] inadequate traffic flow management by the FAA and the lack of standardized understandable terminology for pilots and controllers for minimum and emergency fuel states.

> [Third], windshear, crew fatigue, and stress were factors that led to the unsuccessful completion of the first approach [at Kennedy Airport] and thus contributed to the accident.

Lauda Airlines Flight 004

Boeing 767, registration OE-LAV
26 May 1991, near Phu Toey, Suphan Buri Province, Thailand
223 aboard, 223 killed

Overview: A Boeing 767 took off from Bangkok, Thailand, on a night flight to Vienna, Austria. Fifteen minutes after takeoff, flying at Mach 0.78, the left thrust reverser deployed. The big airliner entered an uncontrolled inverted dive and disintegrated in the air, killing all 223 people on board.

The Flight: Lauda Airlines Flight 004 took off from Bangkok, Kingdom of Thailand, on the evening of 26 May 1991 at 2302 Hours. Bound for Vienna, Austria, eleven long hours away, this red-eye flight carried 213 passengers. Eight flight attendants in the cabin and two pilots on the flight deck rounded out the crew.

The Boeing 767, registration OE-LAV, had been manufactured to the specifications of Lauda Airlines only two years earlier. By the time of this final flight the airframe had accumulated 7,444 hours in the air. Two Pratt & Whitney turbofans, one slung on a pylon below each wing, powered the modern airliner.

The captain, age 48, held an ATP certificate issued by the FAA in the United States, and he had logged 11,750 hours of flight time. For his European employer, his FAA certificate had been validated under a Decree of Recognition from the government of Austria. The first officer, age 41, held an ATP certificate issued by the Department of Civil Aviation in Austria. His logbook reflected 6,500 hours of flight experience.

Trouble Ahead: Shortly after takeoff the pilots began to discuss an automated *alert* for a thrust reverser isolation valve. They checked their Quick Reference Handbook, and it stated that no immediate corrective action was necessary.

The portion of the CVR transcript, below, begins as the aircraft climbs toward its cruising altitude. The meddlesome thrust reverser alert light continues to flash on and off. The pilots debate the cause of the alert and what, if anything, they should do about it:

Capt: . . . . Captain, Flight 004
FO: . . . . . First Officer, Flight 004

Capt: That [light] keeps -- that's come on. (2307:48)

FO: We passed transition altitude one-zero-one-three. (2308:52)

Capt: OK, what's it say in [the Quick Reference Handbook] about that [light], just -- oh --. (2310:21)

FO: *[reading from the Quick Reference Handbook]* Additional system failures may cause in-flight deployment, expect normal reverse operation after landing. (2310:27)

Capt: OK -- just -- aaahhh -- let's see. (2310:35)

FO: Shall I [radio] the ground [maintenance] staff? (2311:43)

Capt: What's that? (2311:46)

FO: Shall I [radio] the technical men? (2311:47)

Capt: Oh, you can just tell 'em about it, just -- it's, it's -- it's just, ah, no -- ah, it's probably moisture or something, 'cause it's not just on, it's coming on and off. (2311:50)

FO: Yeah. (2312:03)

Capt: But, oh, you know, it's a -- it doesn't really, it's just an advisory thing, I don't -- aaahhh -- could be some moisture in there or somethin'. (2312:04)

FO: You need a little bit of rudder trim to the left. (2312:27)

Capt: What's that? (2312:30)

FO: You need a little bit of rudder trim to the left. (2312:32)

Capt: OK. (2312:34)

[at 2313:14 the First Officer begins verbally adding numbers to amuse himself; he continues this activity until 2316:33]

*[the left engine **thrust reverser deploys** at 2316:59]*

FO: Oh! -- Reversers deployed! (2317:01)

[the aircraft violently rolls to the left, then rolls inverted and pitches nose-down]

[sound of airframe "shuddering" begins at 2317:02]

[sound of metallic "snap" at 2317:04]

Capt: *[shouted name of the son of The Deity]* (2317:05)

[sound of metallic "snap" at 2317:06]

[sound of 4 automated caution tones at 2317:08]

[sound of siren warning alert begins at 2317:11]

[sound of metallic "snap" at 2317:17]

Capt: *[shouted in desperation]* Here! Wait a minute! (2317:17)

[sound of increasing wind noise at 2317:23]

[sound of severe vibration at 2317:25]

Capt: [Unintelligible]! (2317:27)

*[sounds of **structural break-up** begin at 2317:28]*

[end of the CVR tape at 2317:30]

The Accident: Ascending through 24,700 feet at Mach 0.78 with both engines at climb power, the left thrust reverser suddenly deployed. Instead of thousands of pounds of thrust pulling the left wing forward, the left thrust reverser in effect *hit the brakes.*

The aircraft yawed violently to the left, then rolled left, then pitched down. Flight 004 dove toward the mountains and jungle below. The airframe groaned and shuddered in protest. The rudder and left elevator tore away. Then the horizontal stabilizer broke free, and the pilots lost all hope of regaining control:

High speeds . . . during the descent indicate that the in-flight break-up most likely occurred at an altitude below 10,000 feet.

Extreme negative G force buckled the wings downward, and they broke away. Aerodynamic forces tore open the fuselage, and the remains of Flight 004 tumbled earthward in free-fall. Flaming wreckage rained down into the jungle three miles from the hamlet of Phu Toey in the mountains of Suphan Buri Province, Thailand. None of the 223 people on the aircraft survived the disintegration and the long fall to the ground 94 miles northwest of Bangkok.

A medical team from the Royal Thai Police Forensic Medicine Institute conducted postmortem examinations on the victims. Most had been flung out into the night sky during the break-up. The cause of death for each person was the same: "severe trauma."

The Investigation: The Thai Department of Aviation notified Austria, the country in which the airliner was registered. Thai authorities also informed the United States, the country where the aircraft had been manufactured. Both countries dispatched teams of technical experts to assist Thai authorities.

On all Boeing 767 aircraft, reverse thrust is designed for ground operation only. Boeing engineers had designed multiple electrical and hydraulic safeguards which *supposedly* made it impossible for the reversers to deploy in flight; however:

> Physical evidence at the crash site conclusively showed that the left engine thrust reverser was deployed.

Nonvolatile computer memory in the left engine control revealed that the reverser deployed while the engine was producing climb power. Analysis showed that the resulting "plume" of *forward* airflow disrupted the normal rearward flow of air over the left wing. This caused a 25 percent loss of lift on the left side of the aircraft, causing a rapid roll to the left. The aircraft rolled inverted and dove downward. Extreme aerodynamic forces, compounded by desperate flight control inputs by the pilots, exceeded the structural design limits of the airframe.

Investigators dug into Lauda Airlines maintenance records. They found that since August 1990, maintenance crews had worked on the left thrust reverser 13 times:

> The majority of the [repair efforts] involved removing and replacing valves or actuators and adjustments to the system.

Ten such "repairs" had occurred within the four months prior to the accident. The latest repair attempt had been completed the day before the aircraft crashed, when mechanics replaced a thrust reverser locking actuator.

Investigators found that the repair work had been prompted by automated warnings from the Propulsion Interface Monitor Unit (PIMU). Yet, no one had pinpointed the *cause* of the warnings, and now it was too late. The physical evidence, if it had existed, had been incinerated in the wreckage of Flight 004.

Probable Cause: On 21 July 1993, two years after the accident, the Aircraft Accident Investigation Committee of the Ministry of Transport and Communications in Thailand issued an exhaustive report on the loss of Lauda Airlines Flight 004. The committee conclusively excluded fire, sabotage, military action, and a host of other possible causes.

The committee determined that thrust reverser deployment was not the *immediate* cause of the in-flight structural failure. It was, however, the first step in the failure sequence. The deployment caused a loss of control. The resulting high speed dive exceeded the design limits of the airframe:

> The in-flight break-up did not occur immediately after the deployment of the thrust reverser, but rather during the subsequent high-speed descent.

The committee studied many hypothetical electrical and hydraulic causes of thrust reverser deployment. Yet, in the end it was forced to concede that "no specific component malfunction was identified." The committee -- after exhaustive input from Boeing, the NTSB, Lauda Airlines, and experts from the aviation industry -- specified the following *Probable Cause* of this accident:

> Uncommanded in-flight deployment of the left engine thrust reverser, which resulted in loss of flight path control. The specific cause of the thrust reverser deployment has not been positively identified.

USAir Flight 427

Boeing 737, registration N513AU
8 September 1994, near Aliquippa, Pennsylvania
132 aboard, 132 killed

Overview: A Boeing 737 descended for landing at Pittsburgh, Pennsylvania. Six miles from the airport the airliner yawed left, rolled inverted, and dove into the ground. The fiery crash killed all 132 people on board.

The Flight: At O'Hare International Airport at Chicago, Illinois, 132 people sauntered aboard USAir Flight 427 (USAir would later become US Airways) on 8 September 1994. Their destination was Pittsburgh, Pennsylvania, only 55 minutes to the east. Flight 427 lifted off from the runway at 1810 Hours and began climbing toward its cruising altitude at flight level 290.

The Boeing 737, registration N513AU, was a modern narrow-body airliner powered by two CFM International engines. The "glass cockpit" craft had been manufactured in 1987 and delivered new to USAir. Prior to the takeoff from Chicago the airliner had accumulated 23,846 hours of flight time.

The captain, age 45, had been a military pilot in the Air National Guard. He held the required ATP certificate and had logged over 12,000 hours in the air. His first officer, also ATP rated, had 9,119 hours of experience documented in his logbook. Three flight attendants were responsible for the 127 passengers in the cabin.

In the late afternoon in sunny clear weather, Cleveland Center handed the flight off to Pittsburgh Approach Control at 1857 Hours. With guidance from the controller the pilots continued a descent toward Pittsburgh. The flight attendants had completed their preparations for landing. The crew expected to be taxiing to the terminal in about 12 minutes.

Trouble Ahead: The first officer was flying the airliner as it descended toward the airport. The portion of the CVR transcript, below, begins as one of the female flight attendants enters the cockpit and casually converses with the pilots:

Capt: . . . . Captain, Flight 427
FO: . . . . First Officer, Flight 427
FltAtt: . . . . One of the Flight Attendants, Flight 427
PA-: . . . . (prefix) Public Address system, Flight 427
Radio-: . . . . . . (prefix) Radio transmission, Flight 427
Center: . . . . . . Cleveland Center (ARTCC)
AppControl: . . . Pittsburgh Approach Control

FltAtt: You guys need drinks here? (1853:37)

Capt: Uuuhhh -- I could use a glass of somethin', whatever's open, water -- uuuhhh -- water, [or] a juice. (1853:38)

FO: I'll split a -- yeah, a water, a juice, whatever's back there, I'll split one with him. (1853:44)

FltAtt: Okey-dokey. Do you want me to make you my special fruity juice cocktail? You wanna try it? (1853:48)

Capt: How fruity is it? (1853:56)

FltAtt: [Do you want to] try it? (1853:57)

FO: All right, I'll be a guinea pig. (1853:58)

[the Flight Attendant leaves; the cockpit door closes at 1854:02]

Center: USAir four-twenty-seven, cross Cutta [Intersection at] one-zero-thousand, two-five-zero knots. (1854:27)

Radio-Capt: Ten-[thousand feet], two-[hundred]-fifty [knots] over Cutta, USAir four-twenty-seven. (1854:30)

[the pilots discuss the clearance; almost 2 minutes pass]

Center: USAir four-twenty-seven, reduce speed to two-one-zero now, that's at the request of Pit[tsburgh] Approach, I'll take the speed first. (1856:16)

Radio-Capt: OK, speed back to two-ten, USAir four-twenty-seven, uh, we'll do our best to make the restriction. (1856:22)

[the pilots switch to Pittsburgh Approach Control at 1856:36]

[the cockpit door opens; the Flight Attendant reenters with "fruity juice cocktails" for the pilots at 1857:07]

FltAtt: Here it is. (1857:08)

FO: All right, thank you, thank you. (1857:09)

FltAtt: Now [unintelligible] if you don't like it, I didn't taste 'em, so I don't know if they came out right. (1857:10)

Capt: That's good. (1857:14)

FO: That is good! (1857:16)

FltAtt: It's good? (1857:17)

FO: . . . [would] be *real* good with some dark rum in it. (1857:17)

FltAtt: Yeah, right -- can I get you something else? (1857:20)

[routine radio contacts with Pittsburgh Approach Control]

Capt: There's a little grapefruit in it? (1857:47)

[sound of laughter at 1857:49]

FO: Cranberry? (1857:54)

FltAtt: Yeah, you saw that from the color. (1857:55)

[casual conversation continues until the Flight Attendant leaves the cockpit 34 seconds later at 1858:29]

AppControl: USAir four-twenty-seven, descend and maintain six-thousand [feet]. (1858:33)

Radio-Capt: Cleared to six, USAir four-twenty-seven. (1858:36)

[the pilots run through their checklists, preparing to land]

AppControl: USAir four-twenty-seven, turn left heading one-four-zero, reduce speed to one-niner-zero. (1900:15)

Radio-Capt: OK, one-four-zero heading, and one-ninety on the speed, USAir four-twenty-seven. (1900:20)

PA-FO: Folks, from the flight deck, we should be on the ground in 'bout ten more minutes -- uh -- sunny skies, little hazy, temperature, temperature's, ah, seventy-five degrees, wind's out of the west around ten miles per hour, [we] certainly 'preciate you choosing USAir for your travel needs . . . . (1900:44)

Capt: [Runway] two-eight right. (1901:10)

FO: Right, [Runway] two-eight right, that's what we planned on, autobrakes on one for it. (1901:11)

AppControl: USAir four-twenty-seven, turn left heading one-zero-zero. Traffic will be one-to-two o'clock, six miles, northbound Jetstream, climbing out of thirty-three for five-thousand. (1902:24)

Radio-Capt: We're looking for the traffic, turning to one-zero-zero, USAir four-twenty-seven. (1902:32)

FO: Oh, yeah, I see [the] Jetstream. (1902:54)

*[at 6,000 feet and 190 knots the CVR records the sound of three "thumps" at 1902:57; **the aircraft rolls left**]*

Capt: Sheeezzz! (1902:57)

[sound of another "thump" and a "clickety-click" at 1902:58]

Capt: Whoa! (1902:59)

[sound of another "clickety-click" at 1902:59]

Capt: Hang on, hang on. (1903:01)

[sound of engines spooling up and autopilot disconnect]

[sound of loud pilot "grunting" or "exertion" at 1903:01]

Capt: Hang on. (1903:03)

FO: Oh, [expletive]! (1903:04)

Capt: Hang on! (1903:05)

*[the aircraft continues to **roll left**; sound of the stick-shaker starts at 1903:07 and continues until the end of the recording]*

Capt: What the [expletive] is this? What the --! (1903:08)

[sound of altitude alert at 1903:08]

FO: Oh --! (1903:09)

Capt: Oh, God! -- Oh, God! (1903:10)

[on radar the controller sees the altitude of the flight rapidly decreasing, but he has no idea why]

AppControl: USAir four-twenty-seven, maintain six-thousand [feet], over. (1903:13)

*[the aircraft has pitched 85 degrees nose-down and has rolled **inverted** by 1903:13]*

Radio-Capt: Four-twenty-seven! Emergency! (1903:15)

FO: [Expletive]! (1903:17)

Capt: Pull! (1903:18)

FO: Oh, [expletive]! (1903:18)

[vertical acceleration force increases to 3.8 G's by 1903:18]

Capt: Pull! Pull! (1903:19)

FO: God! (1903:20)

[sound of unintelligible screaming at 1903:21]

[end of the CVR tape at 1903:22]

The Accident: The airliner, valued at 30 million dollars, and its priceless human cargo dove into a densely wooded area near the community of Aliquippa, Pennsylvania, six miles from the airport. In the words of the NTSB, the aircraft was "severely fragmented, crushed, and burned." Much of the wreckage was buried far underground beneath the main impact crater.

During the final dive both wings had torn off of the fuselage. The inverted empennage was found near the left wing. The cockpit, which had broken off from the rest of the fuselage, fell to the ground south of the main crater.

At the main crater an intense fire melted most of the remaining aircraft structure. Firefighting units from Hopewell Township and from Beaver and Allegheny Counties soon arrived. The fuel-fed fire in the crater raged for five hours, and thereafter it smoldered for several days. None of the people aboard the Boeing 737 had a chance at survival. The Beaver County Coroner ruled that the

132 persons aboard died from "blunt force impact trauma."

The Investigation: Investigators began collecting the crushed and melted remains of the airliner. Much of it had to be dug out of the ground beneath the crater. Accident reconstruction experts slowly began ruling out likely culprits: asymmetric flap or slat extension, mountain rotors, windshear, in-flight fire or explosion, structural failure, sabotage, mid-air collision, etc. For months the NTSB labored to identify the cause of the crash.

The FDR told investigators exactly *what* had happened, but not *why*. Without any input from the pilots the aircraft rudder had suddenly extended to its extreme left limit. This caused the aircraft to yaw left, roll left, pitch down, and crash. Yet, no one knew why the rudder had malfunctioned. Gradually the investigators began focusing on two similar incidents involving Boeing 737 airliners. Both incidents involved "uncommanded" rudder movement similar to the malady that caused the crash of Flight 427:

United Airlines Flight 585, also a Boeing 737, had been on final approach for landing at Colorado Springs, Colorado, on 3 March 1991. At 160 knots, gear and flaps down, it had almost reached the runway. Without warning it suddenly yawed left, rolled left, and dove into the ground, killing everyone aboard. Maintenance records showed a history of "uncommanded" rudder movements. After two years of investigation the NTSB had been unable to pinpoint the cause of the crash. Frustrated, the NTSB reported that it "could not identify conclusive evidence to explain the loss of United Airlines Flight 585."

Eastwind Airlines Flight 517, another Boeing 737, descended to land at Richmond, Virginia, on 9 June 1996 (while the USAir investigation was ongoing). The aircraft inexplicably yawed right, then rolled right. The pilots jammed in full left rudder to counter the roll, but it had no effect. However, they chanced to switch off the yaw damper. The aircraft returned to straight and level flight and landed without further difficulty.

In all three incidents the rudder had suddenly deflected to its extreme blowdown limit. Analysis revealed that this could be caused by a jam in the main rudder control unit. The rudder could jam in a direction *opposite* to that commanded by the pilots:

> The rudder had the potential to operate in a direction opposite to
> that commanded by the flight crew if the main rudder PCU
> primary slide became jammed to the secondary slide and pushed
> the secondary slide to its internal stop.

There was no redundancy built into the system.   A crude
analogy can be made to the steering mechanism on an automobile.
A driver turns the steering wheel to the *right* as he enters a curve
to the right.   But if the wheels and tires turn in the opposite
direction, to the *left*, disaster is certain to follow.

Probable Cause: Almost five years after the crash of Flight 427
the NTSB adopted Aircraft Accident Report NTSB-AAR-99-01 on
24 March 1999. The report includes the results of investigations
into the United Flight 585 accident and the Eastwind Flight 517
incident. Much of the report deals with exclusion of a host of
potential causes such as wake vortices, asymmetric flap or slat
extension, in-flight thrust reverser deployment, etc.
The board found that the rudder on Flight 427 deflected left to
its full blowdown limit. This caused the airliner to yaw left and
roll left. Under the circumstances the board found that the pilots:

> could not have been expected to [assess] the flight control
> problem and then devise and execute the appropriate recovery
> procedure for a rudder reversal.

The board pointed out that it is "possible" to counter such a
rudder reversal in "some instances," but the training had not been
developed and was not available to pilots. The NTSB found that
the ***Probable Cause*** of this accident was:

> a loss of control of the airplane resulting from the movement of
> the rudder surface to its blowdown limit. The rudder surface
> most likely deflected in a direction opposite to that commanded
> by the pilots as a result of a jam of the main rudder power
> control unit servo valve secondary slide.

American Eagle Flight 4184

ATR-72, registration N401AM
31 October 1994, near Roselawn, Indiana
68 aboard, 68 killed

Overview: On Halloween an ATR-72 droned toward Chicago, Illinois, in icing conditions. The ailerons suddenly slammed to the right-wing-down limit. The airliner rolled inverted and dove earthward. Extreme aerodynamic forces caused both wings to snap off, and the crash killed all 68 people on board.

The Flight: On Halloween, 31 October 1994, crewmembers and passengers boarded American Eagle Flight 4184 in Indianapolis, Indiana. The aircraft clawed its way skyward into cold and rainy skies and headed for Chicago, Illinois. The flight should have been a routine 45 minute trip at 16,000 feet and 190 knots.

The modern new transport was an Avions de Transport Regional, Model 72, commonly called an ATR-72. This pressurized twin turboprop, registration N401AM, had been manufactured eight months earlier in Toulouse, France. It received its Certificate of Airworthiness in the United States the following month and went into service with Simmons Airlines, d.b.a. American Eagle. At takeoff the airframe had accumulated 1,352 flight hours.

The young captain, age 29, held an ATP certificate and had logged 7,867 hours of flight time. His first officer, age 30, held a Commercial Pilot certificate and had logged over 5,000 hours, most of them in the ATR-72. Two young flight attendants staffed the cabin. Ironically, the junior flight attendant was a new-hire. The young woman had completed her American Eagle training, and this Halloween flight was her *very first* passenger trip.

Trouble Ahead: Nearing Chicago the pilots began a descent to 10,000 feet. Because of worsening weather, Chicago Center put the flight in a holding pattern with six other aircraft at 1524 Hours. Finding themselves in icing conditions, the pilots activated their

Level III deicing system. Deicing "boots" on the leading edge of the wings kept that part of the airfoils clear of ice.

The portion of the CVR transcript, below, begins as the ATR-72 drones around in the holding pattern, flaps extended to 15 degrees. The captain leaves the cockpit to use the rest-room. It is occupied. While he waits the captain uses the ICS to engage in "small talk" with the first officer, who is flying the airliner:

Capt: . . . . Captain, Flight 4184
FO: . . . . . First Officer, Flight 4184
GPWS: . . . Ground Proximity Warning System, Flight 4184
Radio-:   . . . (prefix) Radio transmission, Flight 4184
ICS-:   . . . . (prefix) ICS transmission, Flight 4184
Center: . . . Chicago Center (ARTCC)

ICS-Capt: Hey, bro! (1551:39)

ICS-FO: Yeah? (1551:39)

ICS-Capt: [I'm] gettin' busy with the ladies *[meaning, the Flight Attendants]* back here. (1551:40)

[sound of a Flight Attendant's "snicker" at 1551:43]

ICS-Capt: Yeah -- so if -- so if I don't make it up there within the next, say, fifteen or twenty minutes, you know why. (1551:45)

ICS-FO: I'll -- uuuhhh -- when we get close to touchdown I'll give you a ring. (1551:51)

ICS-Capt: There you go! (1551:53)

[the Captain stops the "small talk" and becomes serious]

ICS-Capt: No, I'll be up right [after I use the rest-room], there's somebody in [it], so . . . . (1551:55)

[2 minutes and 18 seconds pass; then the cockpit door opens and the Captain enters at 1554:13]

Capt: We have a brand new hombre! (1554:16)

[1 minute and 26 seconds pass; routine cockpit conversation]

FO: We still got ice. (1555:42)

Center: Eagle flight [four]-one-eighty-four, descend and maintain eight-thousand [feet]. (1556:27)

Radio-FO: [Descending] down to eight-thousand, Eagle flight [four]-one-eighty-four. (1556:31)

Center: Eagle flight [four]-one-eighty-four, should be about ten minutes, uh, 'till you're cleared in. (1556:44)

Radio-FO: Thank you. (1556:50)

FO: They say [it will be] ten more minutes. (1556:53)

Capt: Are we out of the hold? (1557:16)

FO: No, we're just goin' [down] to eight-thousand -- uuuhhh, ten more minutes, [the controller] said. (1557:17)

[because the flaps are extended, the overspeed warning starts at 1557:22 and continues for 4.6 seconds]

FO: . . . ooop! (1557:23)

Capt: We -- I knew we'd do that. (1557:26)

FO: I's trying to keep [the airspeed] at one-eighty. (1557:27)

*[as the aircraft descends through 9,130 feet the pilots retract the flaps; **the aircraft suddenly rolls right**]*

Capt: Oh! (1557:29)

FO: Ooops, [expletive]! (1557:32)

[the autopilot can not compensate for the roll, so it disconnects; sound of autopilot disconnect warning at 1557:33]

[the ailerons slam full right-wing-down; the roll accelerates]

FO: [Expletive]! (1557:33)

[sound of "heavy breathing" begins at 1557:37; the rate of roll increases to over 50 degrees per second]

Capt or FO: Oh, [expletive]! (1557:39)

Capt: OK -- all right, man -- OK, mellow it out! (1557:44)

[sound of overspeed warning starts at 1557:45; the aircraft

completes its first full 360 degree roll]

<u>Capt</u>: Mellow it out! (1557:47)

<u>FO</u>: OK! (1557:47)

<u>Capt</u>: Autopilot's disengaged! (1557:48)

<u>FO</u>: OK! (1557:49)

<u>Capt</u>: Nice and easy! (1557:52)

<u>GPWS</u>: *Terrain, whoop whoop . . . . (1557:54)*

<u>FO</u>: Aaawww, [unintelligible]! (1557:56)

[descent rate increases to 500 feet per second at 375 knots; sound of "crunching" in-flight break-up at 1557:56]

[end of the CVR tape at 1557:57]

The Accident: The aircraft dove earthward at 115 knots *over* its certified maximum airspeed. As it broke out of the cloud base at 1,700 feet the pilots saw the ground rushing up to meet them. They hauled back on their control columns. Overstressed, the outboard sections of both wings snapped off.

Nose down, inverted, the remains of Flight 4184 fell into a wet soybean field near Roselawn, Indiana. There were 64 passengers, 2 pilots, and 2 flight attendants on board, including the junior flight attendant on her maiden flight. No one survived.

Emergency response teams from the local sheriff's department, volunteer fire department, and the Indiana State Police soon arrived at the scene. Because of the in-flight structural failure and the high speed involved, they found the wreckage strewn over a wide area. They discovered that the French-built airliner had fallen prey to "catastrophic destruction." The NTSB would later state:

The majority of the fuselage [had] disintegrated into small unidentifiable pieces . . . .

The in-flight destruction of the aircraft complicated the recovery of human remains. According to the Newton County Coroner's report, those aboard the ill-fated Halloween flight had sustained "multiple anatomical separations."

The Investigation: Investigators recovered both the CVR and the FDR. The content of the tapes, combined with weather and icing analysis, allowed the investigators to reconstruct the flight.

The aircraft had been flying in icing conditions in the holding pattern at 10,000 feet with the flaps extended to 15 degrees. Deice boots kept ice off the leading edge of the wings, but a ridge of ice began building up -- larger and larger -- *behind* the boots.

The pilots retracted the flaps. To compensate for the loss of lift the autopilot increased the pitch of the aircraft, the "angle-of-attack" (AOA) of the wings through the air. Airflow over the wings was already unstable due to the ridge of ice, therefore:

> [As the] AOA increased through 5 degrees, the airflow in the area of the right aileron began to separate from the wing upper surface because of the ice ridge . . . causing a *reversal [emphasis added]* of the right aileron hinge moment characteristics [which caused] the ailerons to deflect rapidly to a right-wing-down position.

The aircraft rapidly rolled to the right. The autopilot tried to compensate, failed, and disconnected. The roll continued until the aircraft was inverted. Nose down, still rolling, the aircraft headed for the ground at an incredible rate of 24,000 feet per minute. The vertical force increased to an untenable 3.7 G's. Airspeed soared far beyond the maximum certified operating speed. The outer sections of the wings broke away, the horizontal stabilizer tore off, and the rest of the aircraft disintegrated in the air.

Probable Cause: The NTSB adopted Aircraft Accident Report NTSB-AAR-96-01, Volume 1, on 9 July 1996. The board found that Flight 4184 encountered a mixture of rime ice and clear ice from supercooled rain and drizzle in the clouds. The ice ridge *behind* the deice boots caused the smooth airflow over the wings to separate, and the aircraft entered an uncommanded roll:

> The [NTSB] concludes that the [ATR-72] can experience ice-induced aileron hinge moment reversals . . . and uncommanded rolls [when] operated in near-freezing temperatures.

The board discovered that the French manufacturer *knew* about this icing characteristic of the ATR 72 wing. The board reported that the manufacturer had not shared this information with airlines operating the ATR-72. Further, in the certification process the FAA had accepted the manufacturer's icing test results that were not comprehensive. Accordingly, the board pointed out: "The FAA effectively precluded any chance of identifying the phenomena that led to Flight 4184's ice ridge build-up." The NTSB found that the *Probable Cause* of this accident was a:

loss of control, attributed to a sudden and unexpected aileron hinge moment reversal that occurred after a ridge of ice accreted behind the deice boots because:

(1) ATR *[the manufacturer]* failed to completely disclose to operators . . . adequate information concerning *previously known [emphasis added]* effects of freezing precipitation on the stability and control [of the aircraft];

(2) [of the French] Directorate General for Civil Aviation's inadequate oversight of the ATR-72 and its failure to take the necessary corrective action to ensure continued airworthiness in icing conditions;

(3) [of the French] Directorate General for Civil Aviation's failure to provide the FAA with timely airworthiness information developed from previous ATR incidents and accidents in icing conditions.

The board found two factors that *contributed* to the accident:

[First was the] Federal Aviation Administration's (FAA's) failure to ensure that aircraft icing certification requirements . . . for flight into icing conditions, and FAA published icing information, adequately accounted for the hazards that can result from flight in freezing rain and other icing conditions . . . .

[Second was] the FAA's inadequate oversight of the ATR-72 to ensure continued airworthiness in icing conditions.

ATI Flight 782

Douglas DC-8, registration N782AL
16 February 1995, at Kansas City, Missouri
3 aboard, 3 killed

Overview: At Kansas City, Missouri, one engine on a Douglas DC-8 would not start. The crew attempted a three-engine takeoff to ferry the aircraft to a repair facility. The captain lost control and aborted the *first* takeoff attempt. On the *second* attempt the aircraft veered off the runway, staggered into the air, rolled inverted, and crashed. The three crewmembers died in the burning wreckage.

The Flight: On 16 February 1995 a four-engine Douglas DC-8 landed at Kansas City, Missouri. The aircraft was a scheduled cargo flight operated by Air Transport International (ATI). Freight handlers loaded the aircraft with cargo, but when the crew prepared to taxi the No. 1 engine would not start. Mechanics found that the engine gearbox drive gear had failed.

ATI management scheduled a three-engine ferry flight to their contract repair facility in Massachusetts. The freight handlers unloaded the cargo. Three-engine ferry flights are authorized under FAR Part 91, but they must not carry cargo or passengers.

The captain, age 48, had been type rated in the DC-8 for six years, and almost half of his 9,711 hours had been logged in that aircraft. He held an ATP certificate. The first officer, age 38, also held an ATP certificate, and he had logged 4,261 flying hours. The experienced flight engineer had begun his flying career in the U.S. Air Force. He had retired with over 4,000 hours logged as a C-141 flight engineer, and he had been flying the line as a DC-8 flight engineer with ATI for 5 months.

The DC-8, registration N782AL, was powered by four Pratt & Whitney turbofan engines mounted on pylons below the wings. For the coming three-engine takeoff there would be no computed V-1 speed, for one engine *already* was inoperative. Instead of V-1 the crew would use V-mcg (velocity, minimum control on ground).

The crew *erroneously* calculated bug speeds as follows: V-mcg, 107 knots; V-r, 123 knots; V-2, 140 knots.

The No. 1 engine, the outboard engine on the left wing, is inoperative. For non-flying laymen an explanation of the coming three-engine DC-8 takeoff technique is necessary:

> *When beginning the takeoff roll the throttle on the No. 4 engine can not be advanced to full thrust. If full power on all three engines is attempted, the asymmetric thrust (one engine pulling the left wing; two engines pulling the right wing) will cause the aircraft to veer off the runway to the left. Consequently, the pilot will begin by using full throttle on only the inboard engine on each wing (No. 2 and No. 3).*

> *As the aircraft gains speed the rudder will become effective. The pilot should **gradually** advance the throttle on the No. 4 engine, using the rudder to counter the asymmetric thrust. **After** the aircraft has accelerated to **crucial V-mcg**, full thrust on the No. 4 engine can be used. At and above V-mcg speed, the rudder will enable the pilot to counter full asymmetric thrust and maintain directional control on the runway and in flight.*

> *If full thrust is applied on the asymmetric engine **below** V-mcg, directional control will be lost.*

Trouble Ahead: At 2019 Hours the tower cleared Flight 782 for takeoff. The captain firewalled the throttles on the No. 2 and the No. 3 engines, and the DC-8 began rumbling down Runway 01L on its *first* takeoff attempt. As the aircraft accelerated the captain advanced the throttle on the No. 4 engine too rapidly, too soon. Despite full right rudder he could not maintain directional control. He pulled the throttles back to idle and hit the brakes. The DC-8 coasted off the runway onto a taxiway.

The portion of the CVR transcript, below, begins as the crew discusses the problem encountered on the first takeoff attempt. For the *second* takeoff attempt the captain agrees to allow the flight engineer to handle the throttles:

Capt . . . . Captain, Flight 782
FO: . . . . First Officer, Flight 782
FltEngr: . . . . . . Flight Engineer, Flight 782

Tower: . . . . Kansas City Airport Control Tower
GndControl: . . . . Kansas City Ground Control

FltEngr: . . . and then power went all the way up . . . it went up real fast. (2021:06)

Capt: Yeah, it jerked up. (2021:15)

FO: You brought it up too fast, it jerked up, or what? (2021:17)

Capt: It just came up too fast is what it did. (2021:19)

FltEngr: If you want to try it again, I can try addin' the power if you like. (2021:22)

Capt: OK, let's do it that way, yeah, aaahhh, tell 'em. (2021:24)

Radio-FO: Kansas City Ground, Air Transport seven-eighty-two's clear [of the runway], we'd like to taxi back and [try to take off on Runway] one left again. (2021:39)

GndControl: Air Transport seven-eighty-two heavy, roger, taxi [to Runway] one left. (2021:47)

FltEngr: OK, when do I have to have max power in on the outboard [No. 4] engine? (2022:17)

Capt: One-hundred-and-seven [knots]. (2022:21)

FltEngr: By V-mcg? (2022:23)

Capt: Yeah. (2022:24)

*[from their remarks, the crew does not understand that full power on the No. 4 engine is not required **by** V-mcg; it simply can not be applied **before** V-mcg -- a crucial difference]*

*[the First Officer **incorrectly** explains rudder control]*

FO: When we get near V-mcg, if we're using all our rudder authority, you might wanta consider abort, possibly, because once we get higher we're gonna be in even worse trouble. (2022:44)

*[the Captain **erroneously** concurs]*

Capt: That's correct, absolutely. (2023:01)

*[the Flight Engineer **corrects** the First Officer and Captain]*

FltEngr: No! Actually, above V-mcg your rudder has more authority, it's helping you more. (2023:07)

FO: I understand. (2023:11)

[the crew heads back toward the approach end of the runway, ready to try the takeoff again]

Radio-FO: Kansas City Tower, Air Transport seven-eighty-two, [we] be ready to go . . . three-engine takeoff. (2024:36)

Tower: Air Transport seven-eighty-two heavy, Tower, turn right [after takeoff to] zero-three-zero, cleared for takeoff. (2024:42)

[1 minute and 30 seconds pass; the crew completes all tasks on their takeoff checklist]

Capt: OK, we're cleared for takeoff, lights are extended and on, checklist is complete? (2026:12)

FltEngr: Checklist is complete. (2026:24)

[the Flight Engineer pushes the throttles on the No. 2 and the No. 3 engines to full thrust, the second takeoff roll begins]

FO: Airspeed's alive. (2026:59)

Capt: God bless it -- keep it goin'! (2027:01)

[sound of further increase in engine noise at 2027:06]

FltEngr: Keep it going? (2027:07)

Capt: Yeah. (2027:07)

FO: Eighty knots. (2027:07)

FO: Ninety knots. (2027:11)

FO: One-hundred knots. (2027:13)

Capt: OK. (2027:17)

[sound of the aircraft running off the left side of the runway at 103 knots at 2027:17]

FO: We're off the runway! (2027:20)

Capt: Go max power! (2027:21)

Capt: Max power! (2027:26)

*[the pitch angle increases to 17 degrees; **the DC-8 lifts off** and wallows into the air at 2027:27]*

FO: Get the nose down! (2027:27)

Capt: Max power! (2027:28)

FO: You got [max power]! (2027:29)

Capt, FO, or FltEngr: We're gonna go --! (2027:30)

[sound of the left wing impacting the ground at 2027:30]

[sound of screams at 2027:30]

[final impact; end of the CVR tape at 2027:32]

The Accident: Far below the computed rotation speed the DC-8 veered off the left side of the runway. The captain pulled the nose up, and the aircraft mushed into the air 5,174 feet beyond the runway threshold. Climbing to a height of about 100 feet, the aircraft rolled to almost a 90 degree left bank. The left wing scraped the ground, and fuel gushed out of the ruptured tanks and ignited. The doomed airliner crumpled to the earth and exploded upon impact.

The forward fuselage and cockpit separated from the rest of the airframe and came to rest inverted, totally crushed. Fire consumed most of the cabin and the rear of the aircraft. Fortunately the Kansas City Fire Department was holding a night training exercise on the airport premises. Hearing the explosion and seeing the orange inferno mushrooming skyward, firefighters rushed to the burning wreckage. They eventually doused the flames, but they could do nothing to save the three crewmen.

The Investigation: A three-engine takeoff procedure for DC-8 aircraft had been approved by the FAA. Investigators reconstructed the takeoff attempt to find out what had gone awry.

Analysis revealed that on the second takeoff roll, power on the No. 4 engine had been advanced even more rapidly than on the first failed attempt. The aircraft skewed off the left side of the runway, as documented by tire marks in the grass. At about 103 knots, 20 knots *below* the computed rotation speed, the captain pulled the nose up and tried to get airborne. After accelerating through the grass alongside the runway the DC-8 finally mushed into the air. Although airborne, the airspeed was too low, and the captain could not maintain directional control.

In addition, investigators found that the crew made an error when calculating the V-mcg speed. It should have been 116 knots, not the 107 knots the crew had computed. The NTSB explained why 116 knots was so crucial:

> If full power on the asymmetric [No. 4] engine is applied before 116 knots, it is impossible for the pilot to continually maintain runway centerline. *[and also]* Even with the proper application of asymmetric throttle during a three-engine takeoff, the margin of safety is quite small.

Under the best of circumstances a three-engine takeoff in a four-engine airliner is a tricky procedure. The inherent spool-up delay of turbine engines compounds the difficulty:

> *The throttle on the asymmetric engine must be pushed forward in advance of the need for thrust. **Timing is everything**. If the asymmetric engine spools up to full thrust before V-mcg, full rudder deflection will not keep the aircraft tracking straight down the runway. If the engine spools up too late, a longer takeoff roll is required, and the aircraft may run out of runway before getting airborne.*

ATI had authorized most of its crews to perform three-engine ferry takeoffs. Almost all other cargo airlines restricted such flights to "select" crews or to test pilots, and only in the daytime.

The NTSB dug through the captain's training records. On two occasions he received simulator training on three-engine takeoffs. Investigators found no record to indicate that he had been the pilot in command during a three-engine takeoff in a real airplane. With regard to the crash of Flight 782 the investigators concluded:

> The [much-too-rapid] rate of asymmetric throttle application by crewmembers in both the attempted takeoffs precluded successful completion of the maneuver[s].

Probable Cause: Seven months after the crash the NTSB adopted Aircraft Accident Report NTSB-AAR-95-06 on 30 August 1995. The board noted that the crew was suffering from fatigue at the time of the accident, having just returned from an international flight. The board highlighted the lack of adequate training for three-engine takeoff techniques. The board determined that it was "unlikely" the first officer and flight engineer had ever participated in a three-engine takeoff.

The board found that *the crew did not understand* the three-engine takeoff procedures, as evidenced by their comments on the CVR tape. Also, they did not properly analyze the reasons for loss of directional control after the first takeoff attempt. Further, they were operating under self-imposed pressure to complete the flight and get to their destination. The board found that the *Probable Cause* of this accident was threefold:

> [First], the loss of directional control by the pilot in command during the takeoff roll and his decision to continue the takeoff and initiate a rotation below the computed rotation airspeed, resulting in a premature liftoff, further loss of control, and collision with the terrain.

> [Second], the flightcrew's lack of understanding of the three-engine takeoff procedures, and their decision to modify those procedures.

> [Third was] the failure of [Air Transport International] to ensure that the flight crew had adequate experience, training, and rest to conduct the non-routine flight.

The board found a *contributing* factor to be:

> the inadequacy of FAA oversight of ATI and FAA flight and duty time regulations that permitted a substantially reduced flight crew rest period . . . .

ASA Flight 529

Embraer EMB-120, registration N256AS
21 August 1995, near Carrollton, Georgia
29 aboard, 8 killed

Overview: In Atlanta, Georgia, 29 people took off in an Embraer EMB-120. The twin-turboprop airliner "chunked" a propeller blade in flight. The resulting imbalance and structural damage caused an off-airport controlled crash into large trees. The impact and fire killed 8 of the 29 persons on board.

The Flight: At Atlanta, Georgia, the 26 passengers and the 3 crewmembers aboard Atlantic Southeast Airlines (ASA) Flight 529 got ready for their trip to Gulfport, Mississippi. The pilots planned to cruise at flight level 240 for the 1 hour and 26 minute flight. The airliner pushed back from the ramp at 1210 Hours, and 13 minutes later it took off and headed southwest.

The regional turboprop airliner was a Brazilian-manufactured Empresa Brasileira de Aeronautica-120, often called an "Embraer." Common usage shortened the moniker to EMB-120. The airliner, registration N256AS, had been certified in the United States in accord with a bilateral agreement between the Brazilian and United States aviation authorities. ASA took delivery of the aircraft in March 1989, and prior to this final flight it had accumulated 17,151 flight hours. Each of its two turbine engines was mated to a composite material four-blade Hamilton Standard propeller.

The pilots climbed on course in IMC weather toward Gulfport. The captain, age 45, held an ATP certificate and had logged 9,876 hours of flight time. His young first officer, age 28, had earned a Commercial Pilot certificate, and his logbook reflected 1,193 flight hours. The lone flight attendant, age 37, was responsible for the welfare of her 26 revenue passengers.

Trouble Ahead: The sleek T-tailed EMB-120 scratched its way upward toward its intended cruising altitude. The captain is flying the airliner, and there is no hint of trouble. The portion of the CVR transcript, below, begins as ATC clears the pilots to climb to flight level 240. ATC uses the radio call-sign "ASE" for Atlantic Southeast Airlines flights:

Capt: . . . . . . Captain, Flight 529
FO: . . . . First Officer, Flight 529
FltAtt: . . . . . . Flight Attendant, Flight 529
Radio-: . . . . . (prefix) Radio transmission, Flight 529
ICS-: . . . . . . (prefix) ICS transmission, Flight 529
GPWS: . . . . . Ground Proximity Warning System, Flight 529
Center: . . . . . Atlanta Center (ARTCC)
AppControl: . . Atlanta Approach Control

Center: ASE five-twenty-nine, climb and maintain flight level two-four-zero. (1242:40)

Radio-FO: Two-four-zero, ASE five-twenty-nine. (1242:44)

FO: [We are cleared to] twenty-four-[thousand feet]. (1242:50)

Capt: Twenty-four. (1242:51)

[the aircraft is climbing through 18,100 feet at 160 knots]

*[sound of loud **thuds** caused by the loss of a propeller blade and resulting structural damage, and the sound of various cockpit alarms at 1243:25]*

Capt: [Unintelligible] we got a left engine out, left power lever, flight idle -- left condition lever, left condition lever. (1243:34)

FO: Yeah. (1243:48)

Capt: Feather [the propeller]. (1243:49)

[a series of beeps similar to engine fire warning at 1243:51]

Capt: Yeah, [the left engine propeller is] feathered, left condition lever, fuel shutoff -- I need some help here! (1243:54)

[several cockpit warning tones at 1244:02]

Capt: I need some help on this. (1244:03)

Capt: You said [the propeller is] feathered? It's feathered? What the [expletive]'s going on with this thing? (1244:05)

*[the left propeller blades have **jammed in place**; they have **not feathered**, but the pilots do not yet know this]*

FO: I don't know, [we] got this detector inop. (1244:13)

Capt: I can't hold this thing -- help me hold it! (1244:20)

[the aircraft is nine degrees nose-down and descending rapidly at 5,500 feet per minute]

Radio-FO: Atlanta Center, ASE five-twenty-nine, declaring an emergency, we've had an engine failure, we're out of fourteen-[thousand]-two-[hundred feet] at this time. (1244:26)

Center: ASE five-twenty-nine, roger, turn left direct [to] Atlanta.

Capt: [Expletive]! (1244:33)

Radio-FO: Left turn [to] Atlanta, ASE five-twenty-nine. (1244:34)

[sound of heavy breathing at 1244:36]

Center: ASE five-twenty-nine, altitude descending to? (1245:10)

Radio-FO: We're out of eleven-[thousand]-six-[hundred feet] . . . ASE five-twenty-nine. (1245:12)

Capt: All right, it's getting more controllable here -- the engine -- let's watch our speed -- all right, we're trimmed . . . . (1245:17)

FO: I'll tell Robin *[the Flight Attendant]* what's going on.

[the First Officer activates the Flight Attendant call button]

ICS-FltAtt: Yes sir? (1245:45)

ICS-FO: OK, we had an engine failure, Robin. We declared an emergency, we're diverting back to Atlanta. Go ahead and brief the passengers, this will be an emergency landing . . . . (1245:46)

ICS-FltAtt: All right, thank you. (1245:55)

[the descent stabilizes at 1,000 to 2,000 feet per minute]

Center: ASE five-twenty-nine, say altitude leaving. (1245:58)

Radio-FO: ASE five-twenty-nine's out of ten-point-three . . . .

Center: ASE five-twenty-nine, roger, can you level off, or do you need to keep descending? (1246:03)

Capt: We can -- we're gonna need to keep descending -- we need an airport quick. (1246:09)

Radio-FO: OK, we -- uuuhhh -- we're going to need to keep descending, we need an airport quick. (1246:13)

Center: ASE five-twenty-nine, West Georgia, the regional airport, is at your ten o'clock position and about ten miles. (1246:20)

[the pilots turn toward West Georgia Regional Airport]

Capt: Let's get out the engine failure checklist, please. (1246:38)

FO: OK, I'll do it manually here -- OK, engine failure in flight.

Center: ASE five-twenty-nine, say heading. (1246:57)

Radio-FO: 'Turnin' to about three-ten right now. (1246:59)

Center: ASE five-twenty-nine, roger, you need to be on about a zero-three-zero heading for West Georgia Regional, sir. (1247:03)

Radio-FO: Roger, we'll try ta turn right, we're having -- uh -- difficulty controlling [the aircraft] right now. (1247:07)

FO: OK, condition levers, feather -- it did feather? . . . OK, electric, yeah . . . there's no fire. (1247:11)

Capt: All right. (1247:27)

FO: Main auxiliary generator of the failed engine, off. (1247:32)

Capt: OK, I got that. (1247:35)

[for 1 minute and 9 seconds the pilots continue toward West Georgia Regional Airport]

Radio-FO: What kind of runway's West Georgia Regional got?

Center: The runway is five-thousand feet [long]. (1248:58)

FO: OK, APU started, OK, prop sync off, prop sync comin' off.

Capt: OK. (1249:03)

FO: Fuel pumps, failed engine -- you want, uh, max on this?

Capt: Go ahead, please. (1249:07)

[for 1 minute and 31 seconds while the aircraft descends the pilots continue their emergency procedures; then the Captain looks back at the No. 1 engine]

Capt: Engine's exploded! It's just hanging out there! (1250:38)

[the pilots contact Atlanta Approach Control]

Radio-FO: Atlanta Approach, ASE five-twenty-nine. (1250:43)

AppControl: ASE five-twenty-nine, Atlanta Approach. (1250:45)

Radio-FO: Yes sir, we're with you, declaring an emergency.

[Approach Control vectors the aircraft toward the airport]

Capt: Where the [expletive] is [the airport]? (1251:28)

AppControl: ASE five-twenty-nine, say altitude leaving. (1251:29)

Radio-FO: We're out of nineteen-hundred at this time. (1251:31)

[the aircraft breaks out of the cloud base; the pilots can see the ground below them]

Radio-FO: OK, we're -- uuuhhh -- VFR at this time, give us a vector to the airport. (1251:36)

AppControl: ASE five-twenty-nine, turn left -- uh -- fly heading zero-four-zero, the airport's at your -- about ten o'clock and six miles, sir. Radar contact lost at this time. (1251:39)

[the pilots can not maintain level flight, and they do not have enough altitude left to reach the airport]

GPWS: *Five hundred . . . . (1252:07)*

GPWS: *Too low, gear, too low, gear, too low . . . . (1252:10)*

Capt: Help me! Help me hold it! Help me hold it! (1252:20)

[sound of aural stall warning at 1252:32]

[sound of the stick-shaker at 1252:32]

FO: Amy! I love you! (1252:37)

[sound of first impact at 1252:45]

[sound of second impact at 1252:46]

[sound of more impacts; end of the CVR tape at 1252:48]

The Accident: Unable to arrest the descent and reach the airport, the pilots tried to make a forced landing in an open farm field. They *almost* made it, but they ran out of altitude only 360 feet short of the field near Carrollton, Georgia. Avoiding a stall, they flew the wounded EMB-120 into the trees. The wings and fuselage cut a swath through the treetops. Then the airliner slammed down onto the ground in the farm field and slid 500 feet.

The mangled left engine propeller assembly ripped off of the aircraft shortly after impact with the trees. Still attached to the propeller hub were three blades and part of the fourth blade. The remainder of the fourth blade was missing. Most of the aircraft was destroyed by the impact with the trees and ground and by the raging fire that followed. The NTSB would later report:

> The captain and four passengers sustained fatal injuries. Three other passengers died of injuries [during] the following 30 days. The first officer, flight attendant, and 11 passengers sustained serious injuries, [but they survived].

The Investigation: NTSB investigators conducted interviews with those who survived the final flight of the EMB-120. The flight attendant recalled that she looked out the left side of the aircraft and saw "a mangled piece of machinery where the propeller and front part of the cowling was." Most of the survivors remembered hearing a loud noise, and they felt the aircraft shudder violently. Several of them saw two or three blades from the left propeller wedged against the front of the left wing:

> Investigators found the left engine propeller assembly early in the ground debris path. The propeller hub contained three complete blades, and about 1 foot of the inboard end of the fourth blade [was] protruding from the hub.

In aviation lingo, the No. 1 engine had "chunked a prop." One of the propeller blades had been *thrown off* in flight. The resulting imbalance ripped the propeller housing loose from its mounts. The three intact blades jammed against the wing, so there was no way the pilots could feather them and maintain level flight:

> The resulting loss of left engine thrust, increased drag from a deformed engine nacelle and the unfeathered blades . . . and added drag from external sheet metal damage degraded airplane performance [and made] a forced landing necessary.

Investigators soon found the reason for the loss of the propeller blade, a fatigue crack. The crack had originated in corrosion pits on the surface of the blade:

> The borescope inspection procedure developed and used by Hamilton Standard . . . was inadequate and ineffective.

Routine flight operations had caused the crack to spread and enlarge. During the flight from Atlanta to Gulfport the weakened blade suddenly snapped off because of routine centrifugal force and dynamic air pressure.

Probable Cause: On 26 November 1996 the NTSB adopted its Aircraft Accident Report, NTSB-AAR-96-06, for Flight 529. The board pointed out that structural damage to the aircraft prevented the pilots from reaching an airport. The board found that the *Probable Cause* of this accident was:

> the in-flight fatigue fracture and separation of a propeller blade . . . . The fracture was caused by a fatigue crack from multiple corrosion pits that were not discovered by Hamilton Standard because of inadequate and ineffective corporate inspection and repair techniques.

American Airlines Flight 965

Boeing 757, registration N651AA
20 December 1995, near Cali, Colombia
163 aboard, 159 killed

Overview: Five days before Christmas a Boeing 757 took off from Miami, Florida, on an international flight to Cali, Colombia. Nearing the airport, descending toward the wrong navaid at night, the airliner slammed into El Deluvio Mountain. The crash killed 159 of the 163 people on board.

The Flight: In Miami, Florida, American Airlines Flight 965 waited for 34 minutes at the gate for connecting passengers and baggage. After taxiing toward the runway the flight again had to wait, this time for 1 hour and 21 minutes due to airport congestion. At 1835 Hours the flight finally took off with 155 passengers, 6 flight attendants, and 2 pilots. Everyone aboard expected a routine 3 hour and 12 minute night flight south to Cali, Colombia.

The Boeing 757, registration N651AA, incorporated a state-of-the-art "glass cockpit" driven by a computerized flight management system (FMS). The FMS held a worldwide database of radio frequencies and coordinates of navaids and airports. In flight the FMS would display airplane attitude, flight path, navigation, and related information for the pilots.

N651AA had been operated by American Airlines since it rolled out of the factory in 1991. Powered by two Rolls-Royce turbofan engines, the modern airliner had accumulated 13,782 flight hours. The captain, age 57, had begun flying in 1963. He later joined the U.S. Air Force and flew both fighters and transports. After his military career he was hired by American Airlines. He had logged over 13,000 flight hours, and he had flown to Cali 13 times. The first officer, age 39, also was a U.S. Air Force veteran, and in 1985 he had been selected as "Air Force Instructor of the Year." He had logged 5,800 flying hours and had flown to many airports in South America, but never to Cali.

The pilots flew south through Cuban and Jamaican airspace toward Colombia. Nearing their destination, they contacted Bogota Center and got clearance to proceed direct to the Tulua VOR, 33 miles north of Cali. The pilots pulled the throttles back to flight idle, deployed the speed brakes, and started down.

Trouble Ahead: The airport at Cali is located in a long narrow valley surrounded by mountains that range up to 14,000 feet in height. A VOR/DME approach or an ILS approach is available, depending upon the runway chosen.

The portion of the CVR transcript, below, begins as the captain contacts Approach Control. The first officer is flying the airliner:

Capt: . . . . . . Captain, Flight 965
FO: . . . . First Officer, Flight 965
GPWS: . . . . . Ground Proximity Warning System, Flight 965
Radio-: . . . . . (prefix) Radio transmission, Flight 965
AppControl: . . Cali Approach Control

Radio-Capt: Cali Approach, American nine-six-five. (2134:40)

AppControl: American niner-six-five, good evening, go ahead.

Radio-Capt: Ah, buenos noches, senor, American nine-six-five leaving [flight level] two-three-zero, descending to two-zero-zero.

AppControl: The, uh, distance DME from Cali?

Radio-Capt: The DME is six-three [miles].

AppControl: Roger, cleared to Cali VOR, descend and maintain one-five-thousand feet, altimeter three-zero-zero-two . . . no delay expected for approach, report -- uuuhhh -- Tulua VOR.

Radio-Capt: OK, understood, cleared direct to Cali VOR, uh, report Tulua and altitude one-five, that's fifteen-thousand, [and altimeter] three-zero-zero-two. Is that all correct, sir?

AppControl: Affirmative.

Capt: [I have] put Cali direct for you in [the FMS]. (2135:28)

AppControl: Sir, the wind is calm, are you able to [execute the VOR/DME] approach [to] Runway one-niner? (2136:21)

[the pilots had planned on an ILS approach to Runway 01]

Capt: Would you like to shoot the one-nine straight in? (2136:38)

FO: Yeah, we'll have to scramble to get down, we can do it.

Radio-Capt: Uh, yes sir, we'll need a lower altitude right away.

AppControl: Roger, American nine-six-five is cleared [for a] VOR/DME approach [to] Runway one-niner, Rozo number one arrival, report Tulua VOR.

Radio-Capt: Cleared [for] the VOR/DME [approach] to Runway one-niner, Rozo one arrival, will report the VOR, thank you, sir.

Radio-Capt: [Approach], can American Airlines, uh, nine-six-five go direct to Rozo and then do the Rozo arrival, sir? (2137:29)

AppControl: Affirmative, take the Rozo one and Runway one-niner, the wind is calm.

Radio-Capt: All right, Rozo, the Rozo one to [Runway] one-nine, thank you, [this is] American nine-six-five.

AppControl: . . . [and] report Tulua and, eh, twenty-one miles, ah, five-thousand feet, American nine, uh, six-five.

Radio-Capt: OK, [we will] report Tulua, twenty-one miles, and five-thousand feet, American nine-six-five.

*[after passing Tulua VOR the pilots turn left, **off course**, and fly east toward what they <u>assume</u> is the Rozo radio beacon]*

*[the First Officer soon realizes that **something is wrong**; they are flying in the wrong direction, not toward the airport]*

FO: Uh, where are we? (2138:49)

[the Captain does not respond]

FO: Where are we headed? (2138:58)

Capt: I don't know. What happened here?

[the pilots debate their position relative to the Tulua VOR; they do not know why the radio beacon (which they <u>assume</u> is Rozo) is not where they expected it to be]

FO: So you want a left turn back around to [Tulua]? (2139:30)

Capt: Naaawww. [Expletive] no, let's press on.

FO: Well -- press on to *where*, though?

Capt: Tulua.

FO: That's a right [turn].

Capt: Where're we going? Come to the right, let's go to Cali first of all -- let's -- We got [disoriented] here, didn't we!

FO: Yeah!

[the pilots turn right to return to the VOR approach path]

Radio-Capt: American [nine-six-five is] thirty-eight miles north of Cali, and you want us to go [to] Tulua and then do the Rozo, uh, to, uh, the runway, right to Runway one-nine? (2140:01)

AppControl: You can . . . land Runway one-niner, you can use Runway one-niner. What is [your] altitude and DME from Cali?

Radio-Capt: OK, we're thirty-seven DME at ten-thousand feet.

AppControl: Roger, report, uh, five-thousand [feet] and, uh, final to one . . . Runway one-niner. (2140:25)

Capt: It's that [expletive] Tulua I'm not getting for some reason, see, I can't get -- OK now -- no. Tulua's [expletive] up, but I can put it in the box *[the FMS]* if you want it. (2140:40)

FO: I don't want Tulua, let's go to the extended centerline of --.

Capt: Why don't you just go direct to Rozo, all right? (2140:56)

FO: OK, let's --.

Capt: I'm gonna put that over for you.

[Approach Control requests the flight's altitude at 2141:02]

Radio-Capt: Nine-six-five [is at] nine-thousand feet.

AppControl: Roger, distance now? (2141:10)

[the expected reply is preempted by the wail of the GPWS]

GPWS: Terrain, terrain, whoop whoop . . . . (2141:15)

Capt: Oh, [expletive]!

[the pilots jam the throttles forward and raise the nose]

Capt: Pull up, baby!

GPWS: Whoop whoop, pull up, whoop whoop, pull up . . . .

[sound of the stick-shaker activating]

[sound of impact; end of the CVR tape at 2141:28]

The Accident: Ten miles off course at an altitude of 8,900 feet, nose high, engines at full power, the aircraft flew into tall trees near the summit of a ridge on El Deluvio Mountain about 35 miles east of Cali. Shedding wings and engines and breaking apart, the wreckage tumbled over the top of the ridge and stopped about 400 feet on the other side of the mountain.

Cali Approach Control lost radio contact with the flight, and the airplane never arrived at the airport. The controller notified search and rescue authorities around 2150 Hours. Shortly after daylight the following morning a helicopter crew spotted the smoldering remains of Flight 965. Rescue teams converged on the scene. Probing through the mangled wreckage, they found five critically injured passengers who were still alive.

Helicopters rushed the injured people to a local hospital, where one of them soon died. The remaining four turned out to be the only survivors. Postmortem examinations of the victims attributed their deaths to extreme "deceleration trauma."

The Investigation: The Colombian government dispatched a team of investigators to the accident site the morning after the tragedy. They soon learned that a complex combination of circumstances interacted and led to the loss of Flight 965.

The CVR showed that the pilots anticipated an ILS approach to Runway 01, and they entered that approach into their automated FMS. However, the CVR confirmed that the captain and first officer later accepted the controller's offer; they agreed to land on Runway 19. This change in landing direction would require a non-precision VOR/DME approach, not an ILS approach. The pilots needed to complete several tasks to facilitate the different approach. Investigators determined that some of these tasks were "performed improperly or not at all."

The pilots tried to tune their ADF receiver to the Rozo radio beacon at Cali. Seeing the "R" designation for this navaid on the approach chart, they entered "R" into their FMS. They did not know that the "R" pre-programmed into FMS memory was not *Rozo*. Instead, it was the *Romeo* radio beacon near Bogota, 132 miles away. To tune to Rozo the pilots would have had to input the complete navaid name, R-O-Z-O:

> The flightcrew was not informed . . . that the "R" identifier that appeared on the approach [chart for the airport at Cali] did not correspond to the "R" identifier that they entered and executed as an FMS command.

The pilots never reported passing Tulua VOR, as requested by ATC. Believing that they were homing on the Rozo radio beacon at Cali, the pilots were confused. The navaid was not where they expected it to be. Nonetheless they turned left, off course, and flew toward the wrong radio beacon:

> The incorrect FMS entry led to the airplane departing the inbound course to Cali and turning toward the city of Bogota.

The pilots knew *something* was wrong. Their confusion was obvious from their "Where are we?" and "Where are we headed?" and "What happened here?" and "Where are we going?" questions. Within minutes they turned right to return to the VOR approach course. Too late. Their erroneous turn toward Bogota had taken them out of the valley and into the mountains.

When the GPWS alert sounded in the cockpit the first officer pulled the nose up and rammed the throttles forward to full power. However, the speed brakes had been extended early in the descent, and neither pilot retracted them. Performance studies revealed that, if the pilots had retracted the speed brakes, the aircraft *might have* cleared the top of the ridge.

Probable Cause: Aeronautica Civil of the Republic of Colombia adopted an Aircraft Accident Report in September 1996, nine months after the tragedy. The board acknowledged assistance from the NTSB, the Allied Pilots Association, American Airlines, the aircraft manufacturer, and the engine manufacturer.

Cali Approach Control, located in the control tower, was not equipped with surveillance radar. The controller was dependent upon the pilots in order to determine the position, heading, speed, and altitude of the flight. He used manual flight progress strips to keep track of each aircraft in his airspace.

From a technical standpoint the controller handled Flight 965 in accordance with ICAO policy. However, the board noted that the controller "lacked the English language fluency needed to . . . learn the extent of [the pilots'] difficulties." The controller explained to investigators that he would have asked the pilots more detailed questions if they had spoken Spanish.

ATC messages and CVR content revealed that the pilots were unsure of the controller's instructions. They also were unsure of their location relative to the VOR approach path. The board believed that they likely developed "cognitive tunnel vision" and considered no alternatives to continuing the approach. The board found that the *Probable Cause* of this accident was fourfold:

[First was] failure of the flightcrew to adequately plan and execute the approach to Runway 19.

[Second was] failure of the flightcrew to discontinue the approach into Cali despite numerous cues alerting them of the inadvisability of continuing the approach.

[Third was] the lack of situational awareness of the flightcrew regarding vertical navigation, proximity to terrain, and the relative location of critical [navaids].

[Fourth was] failure of the flightcrew to revert to basic radio navigation at the time when FMS-assisted navigation became confusing . . . in a critical phase of the flight.

The board found several factors that *contributed* to the accident. Among those factors was the "FMS-generated [navaid] information that used a different naming convention from that published in navigation charts."

ValuJet Airlines Flight 592

Douglas DC-9, registration N904VJ
11 May 1996, in the Everglades near Miami, Florida
110 aboard, 110 killed

Overview: A Douglas DC-9 lifted off from the runway at Miami, Florida. A raging fire began in the forward cargo compartment and burned through into the cabin. Before the pilots could return to the airport the airliner, out of control, dove into the Everglades. The near-vertical impact killed all 110 people on board.

The Flight: The 105 passengers and 5 crewmembers walked down the ramp at Miami, Florida, and entered ValuJet Flight 592. The aircraft was scheduled to whisk them to Atlanta, Georgia. The airliner pushed back and taxied out toward Runway 9L, and ATC cleared the pilots for takeoff at 1403 Hours. The aircraft rolled down the runway, rose, and began climbing in sunny VFR weather toward its intended cruising altitude at flight level 350.

The DC-9, registration N904VJ, had been delivered new to Delta Airlines in 1969. ValuJet purchased the airliner in 1993. At the time of the accident the popular T-tailed twin-jet craft had logged 68,400 hours in the air.

The young captain, age 35, held an ATP certificate. She had become a DC-9 captain two years earlier and had 8,928 hours of experience in her logbook. Her older first officer, age 52, held an ATP certificate and had 6,448 hours of flight time, including 2,148 hours in the DC-9. Three flight attendants staffed the cabin of the airliner, and two of them were only 22 years of age.

Trouble Ahead: Unknown to the passengers and crew the 4,109 pounds of cargo aboard included volatile "hazardous material" (HAZMAT) that should not have been aboard. ValuJet's contract maintenance company had stuffed five cardboard boxes full of unexpended ***chemical oxygen generators***. Safety caps were not installed over the percussion caps, and neither the boxes nor the shipping labels bore a HAZMAT warning.

Chemical oxygen generators, properly shielded, are used on some airliners to provide emergency oxygen for passengers in the cabin. When activated, a chemical reaction in the oxidizer core releases oxygen gas. The reaction also produces extreme heat:

> The chemical reaction is exothermic, which means that it liberates heat as a byproduct of the reaction . . . temperatures typically reach 450 to 500 [degrees Fahrenheit].

The portion of the CVR and ATC transcript, below, begins two minutes after takeoff. The captain is flying the aircraft. In keeping with an agreement between ValuJet and the FAA the controllers use "Critter" as the call-sign for ValuJet flights:

Capt: . . . . Captain, Flight 592
FO: . . . . First Officer, Flight 592
FltAtt: . . . . . . Flight Attendant, Flight 592
UnidCabin: . . . Unidentified persons in the cabin, Flight 592
Radio-: . . . . . . (prefix) Radio transmission, Flight 592
DepControl: . . . Miami Departure Control

FO: Gear's up and checked, flaps up, lights out, spoilers disarmed, the ignition is off, fuel pumps are set . . . . (1406:29)

Capt: Thank you. (1406:40)

DepControl: Critter five-ninety-two, turn left [to] heading three-three-zero. (1406:50)

Radio-FO: Three-three-zero, five-ninety-two. (1406:53)

[routine cockpit conversation for 3 minutes and 10 seconds]

*[the aircraft is climbing through 10,634 feet at 260 knots when the CVR records a loud **unidentified sound** at 1410:03]*

Capt: What was that? (1410:07)

FO: I don't know. (1410:08)

Capt: [Are we] 'bout to lose [an electrical] bus? (1410:12)

Capt: We got some electrical problem. (1410:15)

FO: Yeah, that battery charger's kickin' in -- ooohhh, we gotta --.

Capt: We're losing everything! (1410:20)

DepControl: Critter five-nine-two, contact Miami Center on one-thirty-two-forty-five, so long. (1410:21)

Capt: We need -- we need to go back to Miami. (1410:22)

[sound of shouting from the passenger cabin at 1410:23]

UnidCabin: Fire! Fire! Fire! Fire! (1410:25)

UnidCabin: We're on fire! We're on fire! (1410:27)

DepControl: Critter five-ninety-two, contact Miami Center, one-thirty-two-forty-five. (1410:29)

Capt: [Unintelligible] to Miami. (1410:30)

*[the pilots begin an **emergency descent** at 1410:31]*

Radio-FO: Uh, five-ninety-two needs immediate return to Miami.

DepControl: Critter five-ninety-two, uh, roger, turn left heading two-seven-zero, descend and maintain seven-thousand. (1410:35)

[sound of shouting from the cabin subsides at 1410:36]

Radio-FO: Two-seven-zero, seven-thousand, five-ninety-two.

DepControl: What kind of problem are you havin'? (1410:41)

Capt: Fire. (1410:44)

Radio-FO: Uh, smoke in the cock -- smoke in the cabin. (1410:46)

DepControl: Roger. (1410:47)

Capt: What altitude [are we cleared to]? (1410:49)

FO: Seven-thousand [feet]. (1410:49)

[sound of cockpit door opening at 1410:52]

FltAtt: We need oxygen -- we can't get oxygen back there -- is there a way we could test them? (1410:58)

DepControl: Critter five-ninety-two, when able turn left heading two-five-zero, descend and maintain five-thousand. (1411:07)

[sound of more shouting from the cabin at 1411:10]

FltAtt: Completely on fire! (1411:12)

[sound of shouting from the cabin subsides at 1411:14]

FO: [We are] outta' nine-[thousand feet]. (1411:19)

[sound of "loud rushing air" at 1411:21]

Radio-FO: [This is] Critter five-ninety-two, we need the -- uh -- closest airport available. (1411:38)

DepControl: Critter five-ninety-two, they're gonna be standing -- standing by for you. (1411:42)

[the CVR temporarily stops recording at 1411:45; the ATC tape is not affected]

Radio-Capt or FO: We need radar vectors. (1411:50)

[there will be no more radio messages from Flight 592]

DepControl: Critter five-nine-two, turn left heading one-four-zero.

DepControl: Critter five-ninety-two, keep the turn around, uh, heading, uh, one-two-zero. (1412:45)

[the CVR resumes recording at 1412:57]

[sound of "loud rushing air" at 1412:57]

DepControl: . . . contact Miami Approach on, correction, you, you, you, keep on my frequency. (1412:58)

DepControl: Critter five-ninety-two . . . turn left heading one-zero-zero and join the Runway one-two localizer at Miami. (1413:18)

DepControl: Critter five-nine-two, descend and maintain three-thousand. (1413:27)

[sound of "louder rushing air"]

*[the DC-9 **dives into the Everglades** at 1413:42]*

DepControl: Opa Locka airport's about twelve o'clock at fifteen miles. (1413:43)

[there is no response]

The Accident: The FDR tape stopped when the aircraft was at 7,200 feet, 260 knots, heading 218 degrees. The transponder still functioned, and it allowed ATC to track the position and altitude of the stricken airliner. Flight 592 completed a 180 degree turn to the left and headed back toward the airport at Miami.

Two witnesses fishing in the Everglades saw the aircraft flying low in a steep turn. The nose dropped, and the DC-9 dove almost vertically into the muck. The terrified fishermen described a "great explosion" and a "huge cloud of water and smoke" upon impact. They sped to the site of the crash in their boat and found that the airplane "seemed to have disappeared" beneath the Everglades. No wreckage or victims were visible:

> The primary impact area was identified by a crater in the mud and sawgrass.

A layer of limestone rock lies about seven feet below the surface of the Everglades. Atop this permeable rock lies a bed of mud and a thick layer of sawgrass, roots, and thatch. The DC-9 had dived vertically down into this muck and had blasted on down through the soft layer of rock. It had *vanished*, swallowed whole by the Everglades. No one on board had a chance at survival. The crash instantly snuffed out the lives of all 110 people on the airliner:

> Human remains were recovered from the accident site over [a period of] approximately 7 weeks.

Scraps of human tissue would eventually be fished up with the wreckage. Because of reports of an in-flight fire the NTSB would try to identify the carbon dioxide and hydrogen cyanide levels in the remains. The Dade Country Medical Examiner reported that the scraps of tissue were "unsuitable for testing."

The Investigation: Because of the force of the impact and the submerged wreckage the NTSB faced a daunting challenge. The expense of the long recovery effort would eventually total over 10 million dollars. The salvage workers slowly pulled the crushed debris from the Everglades, piece by piece. Investigators loaded the shattered remnants of Flight 965 onto airboats for transport to a decontamination station.

The NTSB checked records of the cargo aboard the DC-9. The

ValuJet contractor confirmed that ***chemical oxygen generators***, erroneously described as "Oxy Cannisters [sic] - Empty," had been packed inside cardboard boxes. These volatile oxygen generators were full, not empty. The employee who loaded the boxes into the forward cargo compartment remembered hearing the loose contents shifting and "clinking" around. Pilots and other ValuJet employees were trained to reject cargo shipments with HAZMAT labels, but the boxes bore no such labels. Also in the cargo compartment were baggage, U.S. Mail, and three inflated aircraft tires mounted on rims. None of this cargo had been tied down.

In the wreckage, investigators found 28 pieces of the oxygen generators. Most generators had been damaged by fire, and some generators had activated:

> 9 generators had indentations in their percussion caps consistent with indentations caused by the activation mechanism.

The tires carried in the cargo compartment also showed damage from fire. One of them had blown-out after 9 of its 12 plies had burned through. Analysis revealed that the "unidentified sound" on the CVR tape at 1410:03 Hours was the noise of the blow-out. Near the cargo compartment the analysts discovered more evidence of fire. Burn patterns were consistent with heat from an external source, not from electrical arcing:

> Heat and fire damage was observed on many of the wire bundles and cables that ran adjacent to the forward cargo compartment.

The oxygen generators would have created the heat necessary to initiate combustion. The cargo compartment was not equipped with smoke detection devices. It was designed to suppress a fire by oxygen starvation, and for this purpose the compartment liner was virtually airtight. However, the actuated oxygen generators would have fed any fire with the oxygen necessary to sustain combustion. The crew had no tools with which to fight the resulting fire. Their only recourse was to land as soon as possible. Unfortunately the intensity of the fire prevented a landing:

> [The crew] had no way of detecting the [fire] until smoke and fumes reached the passenger cabin . . . [and] no means to extinguish or even suppress the fire.

Probable Cause: The NTSB adopted its Aircraft Accident Report, NTSB-AAR-97-06, on 19 August 1997. The board opined that the loss of Flight 965 was the result of:

> a fire in the class D cargo compartment that was initiated by the actuation of one or more oxygen generators being improperly carried as cargo.

The fire had burned through the wall of the cargo compartment and into the passenger cabin. The board concluded that the loss of control most likely resulted from flight control failure caused by "extreme heat and structural collapse." Yet, the board could not totally exclude the possibility that the pilots might have become "incapacitated by smoke or heat in the cockpit."

The board pointed out: "Improper maintenance activities and *false entries [emphasis added]* pose a serious threat to aviation safety." The contractor had improperly labeled the boxes that contained unexpended chemical oxygen generators. The board found that the *Probable Cause* of the accident was:

> [First], the failure of [the contractor] to properly prepare, package, and identify unexpended chemical oxygen generators.

> [Second], the failure of ValuJet to properly oversee its contract maintenance program.

> [Third], the failure of the Federal Aviation Administration to require smoke detection and fire suppression in class D cargo compartments.

The board found three *contributing* causes of the accident:

> [First was the] failure of the FAA to adequately monitor ValuJet's heavy maintenance programs.

> [Second was the] failure of the FAA to adequately respond to prior chemical oxygen generator fires.

> [Third was] ValuJet's failure to ensure that both ValuJet and contract maintenance facility employees were aware of the [airline's] "no-carry" hazardous materials policy.

TWA Flight 800

Boeing 747, registration N93119
17 July 1996, over the Atlantic Ocean near New York
230 aboard, 230 killed

Overview: A Boeing 747 left New York on a transatlantic flight to France. Twelve minutes after takeoff a catastrophic fuel tank explosion ripped the airliner apart. Wreckage tumbled down into the Atlantic Ocean, and the 230 people on board were killed.

The Flight: At New York's JFK Airport, 212 passengers boarded Trans World Airlines (TWA) Flight 800. This international flight was scheduled to span the Atlantic Ocean at night and deposit the paying customers in Paris, France. Two glitches, concern about a possible passenger and baggage mismatch, and a disabled piece of ground equipment, delayed the flight for 59 minutes. These minor problems eventually sorted themselves out, and the aircraft pushed back from the gate at 2002 Hours.

The Boeing 747, registration N93119, had been built a quarter-century earlier in 1971. Four Pratt & Whitney turbines provided the necessary thrust to power the jumbo-jet. The captain, age 58, and the first officer, age 57, had been employed by TWA for over 30 years. These veteran pilots had logged a total of over 35,000 hours of flight time. The young flight engineer trainee, age 24, was backed up by a senior flight engineer. Fourteen experienced flight attendants staffed the cabin of the airliner.

The big Boeing accelerated down Runway 22R and lumbered out over the Atlantic Ocean. Turning north and climbing, the aircraft tracked along the usual international route toward Europe.

Trouble Ahead: Boston Center cleared the pilots to climb to 15,000 feet. The captain, who was flying the airliner in the clear twilight, acknowledged the clearance. This turned out to be the last radio transmission from Flight 800.

The portion of the CVR transcript, below, begins less than a

minute before disaster strikes. ATC transmissions and messages
from other aircraft are appended to the CVR transcript:

Capt: . . . . . . Captain, Flight 800
FO: . . . . First Officer, Flight 800
FltEngr: . . . . Flight Engineer, Flight 800
Radio-: . . . . . . (prefix) Radio transmission, Flight 800
Center: . . . . . . Boston Center (ARTCC)
Eastwind 507: . Eastwind Flight 507 (call-sign, "Stinger-Bee")
Alitalia 609: . . . Alitalia Flight 609
Virgin 009: . . . Virgin Atlantic Flight 009
UnidAircraft: . . Unidentified aircraft

Center: TWA eight-hundred, climb [to] and maintain one-five-
thousand [feet]. (2030:15)

Radio-FO: TWA eight-hundred heavy, climb and maintain one-
five-thousand, leaving one-three-thousand. (2030:19)

Capt: Ollie. (2030:24)

FltEngr: Huh? (2030:24)

Capt: Climb thrust. (2030:25)

Capt: Climb to one-five-thousand. (2030:28)

FltEngr: Power's set. (2030:35)

*[documentation of a **very loud sound** at 2031:12, and the end
of the CVR tape immediately thereafter]*

*[at 13,760 feet an **explosion** racks the aircraft; total structural
disintegration follows]*

Eastwind 507: [Boston Center], . . . we just saw an explosion out
here, [this is] Stinger-Bee five-oh-seven. (2031:50)

Center: Stinger-Bee five-oh-seven, I'm sorry, I missed it, you're
out of eighteen-[thousand], did you say something else?

Eastwind 507: Ah, we just saw an explosion up ahead of us here,
about sixteen-thousand feet or something like that, it just went
down in the water. (2032:01)

Alitalia 609: Alitalia six-oh-nine confirms [the explosion] just ahead of us. (2032:10)

<u>Virgin 009</u>: Boston, Virgin zero-zero-nine, I can confirm that out at my nine o'clock position . . . it looked like an explosion out there about . . . six miles away. (2032:25)

<u>Center</u>: An explosion six miles out at your nine o'clock position -- thank you very much, sir, contact New York Approach [on] one-two-five-point-seven. (2032:49)

[the controller sees that the radar return from Flight 800 has dropped off his scope; he tries to contact the pilots]

<u>Center</u>: TWA eight-hundred, Center. (2032:56)

<u>Center</u>: TWA eight-hundred, Center. (2033:04)

<u>Center</u>: TWA eight-hundred, if you hear, ident. (2033:09)

[there is no response]

<u>Center</u>: Stinger-Bee five-oh-seven, you reported an explosion, is that correct, sir? (2033:17)

<u>Eastwind 507</u>: Yes sir, about five miles at my eleven o'clock.

<u>Center</u>: Alitalia six-oh-nine, contact Boston now on one-two-four-point-five-two. (2033:31)

<u>Alitalia 609</u>: . . . and just for your information, sir, we are just overhead [of] the explosion, right overhead at this time, now a hundred-and-three miles from JFK [Airport]. (2033:36)

<u>Eastwind 507</u>: [Center], we are directly overhead the site where that airplane -- or whatever it was -- just exploded and went down into the water. (2033:48)

<u>Center</u>: Roger that, thank you very much, sir. (2034:01)

<u>Center</u>: TWA eight-hundred, if you hear Center, ident. (2034:05)

[there is no response; 38 seconds of silence pass]

<u>UnidAircraft</u>: I think that was him. (2035:43)

<u>Center</u>: I think so. (2035:45)

<u>UnidAircraft</u>: God bless him. (2035:48)

[1 minute and 17 seconds of silence pass]

Eastwind 507: [This is] Stinger-[Bee] five-oh-seven, anything we can do for ya before we go? (2037:05)

Center: Well, I just want to confirm that you saw the splash in the water approximately twenty [miles] southwest of Hampton, is that right? (2037:11)

Eastwind 507: Ah, yes sir. It just blew up in the air, and then we saw two fireballs go down into the water . . . . aaahhh, you know, so I saw him, and then it blew. (2037:20)

Center: Roger that, sir. That was a [Boeing] seven-forty-seven out there. You had a visual on that. Anything else in the area when it happened? (2037:40)

Eastwind 507: I didn't see anything. He seemed to be alone.

The Accident: At 2031:12 Hours a violent explosion had racked Flight 800. The Boeing 747 buckled. Within seconds the cockpit and forward section of the fuselage ripped away from the rest of the aircraft and tumbled down toward the sea. With the wings still intact and the front of the airplane lightened by roughly 80,000 pounds, the fuselage pitched up and climbed for about 38 seconds, reaching 16,000 feet. Then the wings began to fail, and complete disintegration followed. The NTSB would later report:

> Witnesses . . . stated that they saw and/or heard explosions, accompanied by a large fireball over the ocean, and observed debris, some of which was burning, falling to the water.

Pieces of the aircraft hit the water along a path four miles long off the coast of Long Island, New York, near Moriches Inlet. All through the night a flotilla of privately owned boats converged on the scene to search for survivors. They found none, for all 230 people aboard the airliner had perished.

During the first 24 hours the searchers found 99 bodies floating on the surface of the sea. Recovery of the other human remains floating on the surface, lying on the seabed, and entombed inside the wreckage would take many months. The last remains were pulled to the surface by a fishing trawler on 22 May 1997. The

Suffolk County Medical Examiner reported that all injuries were "consistent with in-flight break-up and subsequent water impact."

The Investigation: Because of the widespread distribution of the wreckage the aircraft obviously had fallen prey to some type of catastrophic in-flight structural break-up. The NTSB examined several broad "cause scenarios." The 1996 Olympic Games were in progress in the United States at the time. Many felt certain that terrorists had made an Olympic *statement* by somehow destroying the airliner.

Dozens of witnesses described what they believed was a missile streaking toward the aircraft. Surely the flight had been shot down, they reported. Consequently, agents from the Federal Bureau of Investigation and specialists from the Bureau of Alcohol, Tobacco, and Firearms joined the investigation. Interviews with hundreds of witnesses, backed up by laboratory analysis of recovered debris, gradually discounted the popular missile theory:

> Physical evidence indicated that a missile did not strike the airplane. *[and also]* Witness observations of a streak of light were not related to a missile, [but instead to] burning fuel from the accident airplane in crippled flight. *[and also]* Observations of one or more fireballs were of the airplane's burning wreckage falling toward the ocean.

Using laser-line scanning equipment, divers, remote-controlled undersea vehicles, and trawlers the NTSB eventually recovered 95 percent of the wreckage from the seabed. Metallurgists examined the remains of Flight 800 in detail. None of the small fatigue cracks and fractures they found would have led to major structural failures. A lightning strike? A meteorite? Perhaps fire migration through the vent system? Maybe static electricity? An uncontained engine failure with its accompanying deadly shrapnel? A flight control failure? Slowly the NTSB examined these and dozens of other potential causes, then eliminated them:

> It was clear from the wreckage recovery locations that the first pieces to depart the airplane were from the area in and around the airplane's wing center section.

Analysis of the wreckage revealed that an "over-pressure event" (technical words for an *explosion*) had occurred in the center wing tank. The temperature of fuel vapor in the tank had been between 101 to 127 degrees Fahrenheit. The fuel-air mixture was within the flammable range. Gradually NTSB investigators began to unmask the assassin of TWA Flight 800.

Probable Cause: It took over four years, but the NTSB finally adopted Aircraft Accident Report NTSB-AAR-00-03 on 23 August 2000. Terrorists, missiles, lightning, metal fatigue, and the like were not to blame. An electrical short circuit had produced excess voltage, and the flammable fuel-air mixture in the center wing tank ignited. The violent detonation ripped open the tank and destroyed the aircraft. The board explained the dangerous principle:

> Operating transport-category airplanes with flammable fuel-air mixtures in their fuel tanks presents an *avoidable risk [emphasis added]* of an explosion.

Experience had shown that accepting fuel tank flammability is not appropriate because all possible ignition sources can not be predicted and eliminated. The board found that the *Probable Cause* of this accident was:

> an explosion of the center wing fuel tank resulting from ignition of the flammable fuel-air mixture in the tank. The source of ignition energy for the explosion could not be determined with certainty, but, of the sources evaluated by the investigation, the most likely was a short circuit outside of the CWT that allowed excessive voltage to enter it through electrical wiring associated with the fuel quantity indicating system.

The board concluded that *contributing* causes of the accident were:

> [First, the flawed] design . . . concept that fuel tank explosions could be prevented solely by precluding all ignition sources.

> [Second], the design and certification of the Boeing 747 with heat sources located beneath the CWT with no means to reduce the heat transferred into the CWT or to render the fuel vapor in the tank non-flammable.

United Express Flight 5925 and a General Aviation Aircraft

United Express Flight 5925
Beechcraft 1900, registration N87GL
19 November 1996, runway collision at Quincy, Illinois
12 aboard, 12 killed

General Aviation Aircraft
Beechcraft A-90 King Air, registration N1127D
19 November 1996, runway collision at Quincy, Illinois
2 aboard, 2 killed

Overview: A Beechcraft 1900 airliner landed at Quincy, Illinois, in clear weather at night. At the same time a Beechcraft A-90 King Air was taking off on an intersecting runway. The two aircraft collided at the runway intersection, and a post-impact fire killed all 14 people aboard both planes.

The United Express Flight: United Express Flight 5925 took off from O'Hare Airport in Chicago, Illinois, on the clear afternoon of 19 November 1996. The pilots made a quick stop at Burlington, Iowa. After an exchange of passengers and baggage they took off again at 1637 Hours and headed toward Quincy, Illinois. There were 2 pilots and 10 passengers aboard.

The small airliner, a Beechcraft 1900 (Beech 1900), registration N87GL, had been manufactured in 1989 and configured with 19 passenger seats. Powered by Pratt & Whitney turbines mated to Hartzell propellers, the speedy little twin turboprop was operated by Great Lakes Aviation, d.b.a. United Express. The captain, age 30, held an ATP certificate and had logged about 4,000 hours of flight time, 700 of which were as pilot-in-command in the Beech 1900. She had begun flying for Great Lakes Aviation three years earlier as a first officer and had upgraded to captain nine months before this final flight. Her young first officer, age 24, held a Commercial Pilot certificate and had been flying for Great Lakes for 14 months. He had accumulated 1,950 flight hours.

The General Aviation Flight: Meanwhile at Quincy, a Beechcraft A-90 King Air was preparing to take off on Runway 4. The King Air pilot, age 63, was a retired TWA captain who had logged an impressive 25,647 flight hours. However, during his last year with TWA he had been downgraded to flight engineer because of poor performance. Also, six months before this fatal accident he had been involved in a gear-up landing incident. His young copilot, age 34, worked as a ground instructor at Flight Safety International. She held a Commercial Pilot certificate.

The King Air taxied into position on Runway 4, but it did not take off. The copilot radioed in the blind on the common traffic advisory frequency (CTAF), stating that the King Air was "holding short" on the runway.

Trouble Ahead: There was no control tower at Quincy. As Flight 5925 neared the uncontrolled airport the captain transmitted in the blind on the CTAF. She reported that the airliner was 30 miles north of the airport and inbound for landing on Runway 13. Meanwhile the King Air was holding on Runway 4. The two runways intersected near the middle of the airport.

The portion of the Beech 1900 CVR transcript, below, begins as the captain transmits on the CTAF. The first officer is flying the airliner. The flight operates under a code-sharing agreement with United Airlines and uses the radio call-sign, "Lakes Air 251":

<u>Capt</u>: . . . . . Captain, "Lakes Air 251"
<u>FO</u>: . . . . . . First Officer, "Lakes Air 251"
<u>Radio-</u>: . . . . (prefix) Radio transmission, "Lakes Air 251"
<u>King Air</u>: . . . Beechcraft A-90 King Air
<u>Cherokee</u>: . . . Piper PA-28 Cherokee

Radio-Capt: . . . two-fifty-one is a Beech airliner, just about thirty miles to the north of the field, inbound for landing, Runway one-three at Quincy, any traffic in the area, please advise. (1652:07)

[there is no response; 3 minutes and 12 seconds pass]

[on a taxiway at Quincy the young female copilot in the King Air transmits in the blind]

King Air: Quincy traffic, King Air one-one-two-seven delta's taxiing out [for] takeoff on Runway four [at] Quincy. (1655:19)

FO: [She] sounds like a little kid. (1655:26)

Capt: She's a little baby, an Elmer Fudd girl. (1655:29)

[a small Piper PA-28 Cherokee is taxiing far behind the King Air, and the Cherokee pilot transmits on the CTAF]

Cherokee: Quincy traffic, Cherokee seven-six-four-six juliet, back-taxi -- uuuhhh -- taxiing to Runway four, Quincy. (1655:40)

Capt: They're both using [Runway] four. (1655:48)

FO: [The airport is] in sight. (1656:13)

Capt: Okey-dokey. (1656:16)

Capt: [We will be] landing on [Runway] one-three, right? You're planning on [Runway] one-three still, right? (1656:42)

FO: Yeah, unless it doesn't look good, then we'll just do a downwind for four, but right now plan on one-three. (1656:46)

[the Lakes Air 251 Captain again transmits on the CTAF]

Radio-Capt: Quincy area traffic, Lakes Air two-fifty-one is a Beech airliner currently ten miles to the north of the field. We'll be inbound to enter on a left base for Runway one-three at Quincy, any other traffic, please advise. (1656:56)

[there is no response; 2 minutes and 7 seconds pass]

King Air: Quincy traffic, King Air one-one-two-seven delta, holding short of Runway four, [we'll] be takin' the runway for departure and [then] heading southeast [from] Quincy. (1659:03)

Capt: . . . she's takin' Runway four right now? (1659:14)

FO: Yeah. (1659:22)

[the Lakes Air 251 Captain again transmits in the blind]

Radio-Capt: Quincy area traffic, Lakes Air two-fifty-one is a

Beech airliner, currently just about to turn about a six mile final for Runway one-three . . . at Quincy. (1659:29)

Capt: Landing gear? (1659:52)

FO: Down, three green. (1659:52)

FO: Flaps approach. (1659:57)

Capt: Full [flaps] indicated. (1659:59)

Radio-Capt: Quincy traffic, Lakes Air two-fifty-one's on short final for Runway one-three. The aircraft gonna hold in position on Runway four, or [are] you guys gonna take off? (1700:16)

*[instead of a response from the King Air, which was on Runway 4, a response comes from **the Cherokee**, which was **not on the runway** and not ready to take off]*

Cherokee: Seven-six-four-six juliet -- uuuhhh -- holding -- uuuhhh -- for departure on Runway four . . . . (1700:26)

[the Lakes Air 251 Captain <u>thinks</u> she is talking to the King Air]

Radio-Capt: OK, we'll get through your intersection in just a second, sir, we appreciate that. (1700:37)

[the King Air pilots do not see the Beech 1900 and do not know it is about to land; without radioing their intentions on the CTAF they begin their takeoff roll]

Capt: Landing gear's down, three green, flaps are at landing, your yaw damp is off, finals are complete. (1700:42)

[Lakes Air 251 touches down on the runway at 1700:59; the Captain sees the speeding King Air about 2 seconds later]

Capt: Max reverse! Oh, [expletive]! (1701:01)

FO: What? -- Oh, [expletive]! (1701:03)

Capt: Oh, [expletive] me! (1701:07)

*[**the 2 aircraft collide** at the intersection of the 2 runways]*

[end of the CVR tape at 1701:08]

The Accident: The two aircraft collided at the intersection of Runway 13 and Runway 4. With their wings interlocked both planes skidded 110 feet to the edge of Runway 13. Both fuselages remained upright, still standing on their landing gear, but fuel from ruptured tanks leaked down onto the ground and ignited.

Three pilots at the airport terminal saw the collision and rushed to the site. The King Air was totally ablaze, but only a small fire burned on the right side of the Beech 1900. The potential rescuers ran to the front of the commuter airliner. The captain had her head and one arm out of the cockpit window, and she yelled to them in desperation: "Get the door open!"

> Witnesses who ran to the scene . . . stated that they heard sounds of life from within the cabin of the Beech 1900 and that the captain talked to them from the cockpit [window].

The rescuers ran to the forward air-stair door, the main entrance and exit on the Beech 1900. The exterior door handle was already in the unlocked position, and people inside were trying to open the door and get out. The rescuers could hear them shouting and yelling as they banged on the jammed door. Standing on the ground outside, one rescuer twisted the handle with all his strength. The door refused to open. Another rescuer gave it a try, but the door would not budge.

Slowly the fire grew more intense. The Beech 1900 cabin filled with jet-black smoke, then orange flames. Gradually the frantic screams of those trapped inside the small airliner fell silent.

The Quincy Fire Department, 10 miles away, dispatched two fire trucks and a firefighting contingent. By the time they arrived the conflagration had consumed both aircraft. Fireman quickly hosed down the flames, but they could not save the pilots and passengers. Everyone inside the Beech 1900 and the King Air was dead.

The Adams County Coroner performed an autopsy on the 14 victims. He found that the collision had not seriously injured any of them, but they all died in the post-crash fire:

> The cause of death for 10 occupants was carbon monoxide intoxication from inhalation of smoke and soot. The cause of death for [the remaining] occupants was inhalation of products of combustion.

The Investigation: NTSB investigators began by examining the physical evidence near the crash site. The pilots on both aircraft had tried to stop prior to the collision. The tires on the Beech 1900 airliner on Runway 13 had left skid marks for 475 feet leading to the point of the collision. The King Air skid marks on Runway 4 swerved to the right for 260 feet prior to the point of impact.

The Beech 1900 CVR documented the standard pre-recorded passenger briefing prior to takeoff from Burlington:

> There are four exits aboard this aircraft. There are three clearly marked over-wing exits, two over the right wing and one over the left wing. To open, pull down on the handle and pull the exit inward. The main cabin door through which you entered is also an emergency exit. To open, push the button next to the handle and then rotate the handle counterclockwise and push the door open.

According to the coroner the Beech 1900 occupants were "not incapacitated" by the collision. Yet, they had been unable to open the main cabin door. Also the two potential rescuers outside the aircraft had been unable to pull the door open. Investigation determined that the fuselage had been deformed slightly by the collision, jamming the door shut. There was no indication that the occupants tried to get out via the other three exits.

The NTSB conducted visibility studies to determine line-of-sight conspicuity of the Beech 1900 from the King Air cockpit. There were no physical obstructions to visibility. The study concluded that the pilots of the King Air should have been able to see the Beech 1900. Yet, the investigators concluded:

> The occupants of the King Air must have been unaware . . . that [the Beech 1900] airplane was about to land.

Radio transmissions revealed that the Beech 1900 captain made proper radio calls during the approach. Unfortunately she and her first officer mistook the Cherokee pilot's erroneous message (that he was *holding* for departure on Runway 4) as a reply from the King Air. Therefore, the Beech 1900 pilots assumed that the King Air was going to *hold* on Runway 4.

The pilot of the Cherokee had obtained a Private Pilot certificate nine months before the accident. He had logged a total of 80 hours of flight time. The board noted that his aircraft had *not* been on the runway and had *not* been in a position to take off. The board pointed out that his radio reply to the airliner was "unnecessary and inappropriate" and that it "reflected his inexperience."

Probable Cause: Seven months after the accident the NTSB adopted Aircraft Accident Report NTSB-AAR-97-04 on 1 July 1997. The board found that the failure of the King Air pilots to announce their intention to take off created the potential for the collision. The board also pointed out:

> It is clear that neither occupant of the King Air properly scanned for traffic.

The board concluded that the King Air pilots were "inattentive" and "distracted" from their duty to see and avoid other aircraft. Also, the board theorized that the King Air pilots never heard the radio transmissions from the Beech 1900 airliner.

The board members reasoned that, because of the Cherokee pilot's lack of experience, he did not realize that a collision was imminent and did not broadcast a warning. Nonetheless, the board concluded that the *Probable Cause* of this accident was the:

> failure of the pilots in the King Air A-90 to effectively monitor the common traffic advisory frequency [and] to properly scan for traffic, resulting in their commencing a takeoff roll when the Beech 1900 . . . was landing on an intersecting runway.

The board found two *contributing* factors:

> [First], the Cherokee pilot's [unnecessary] radio transmission. [It confused the Beech 1900 pilots. They believed it came from the King Air. Therefore, they believed that the King Air would not take off until after they cleared the runway.]

> [Second], contributing to the severity of the accident and the loss of life were the lack of adequate aircraft rescue and fire-fighting services, and the failure of the air-stair door on the Beech 1900 to open.

Korean Air Flight 801

Boeing 747, registration HL7468
6 August 1997, on Nimitz Hill, Guam, Mariana Archipelago
254 aboard, 228 killed

Overview: A Boeing 747 began a non-precision approach to the airport on the island of Guam in the vast South Pacific Ocean. The airliner descended prematurely and crashed into Nimitz Hill three miles short of the runway. There were 254 people aboard, and the impact and fire killed 228 of them.

The Flight: The tropical Mariana Archipelago lies 3,700 miles southwest of Honolulu and 2,100 miles southeast of Hong Kong. The largest island in the chain is Guam, the westernmost territory of the United States. Korean Air (formerly, Korean Air Lines) Flight 801, packed with vacationers, winged its way south over the Pacific Ocean toward the island on the night of 6 August 1997.

The Boeing 747, registration HL7468, had taken off from Seoul, South Korea, with 17 crewmembers and 237 revenue passengers. Normally the trip to Guam would have called for a smaller Airbus. However, on this flight the larger Boeing airliner was needed because of a large number of athletes headed for the Mini-South Pacific Games in American Samoa.

Before joining Korean Air the captain, age 42, had been a pilot in the Republic of Korea Air Force. He held an ATP certificate issued by the Ministry of Construction and Transport (MOCT) in Korea, and he had logged 8,932 hours in the air. The first officer, age 40, also a former pilot in the Korean Air Force, held an ATP certificate issued by the MOCT. In addition he had earned an ATP certificate from the FAA in the United States. Their flight engineer had been a military navigator before joining Korean Air. Fourteen flight attendants staffed the cabin of the airliner, and 12 of them were under 25 years of age.

After midnight in the clear sky the airliner entered airspace controlled by Guam Center, and at 0113 Hours the flight began a gradual descent toward Agana Airport. The combined Center and Approach Control facility on Guam is located on Andersen Air Force Base. This ATC facility handles military air traffic. It also handles commercial flights bound for nearby Agana Airport, the commercial air terminal. Each airport has its own control tower.

Guam Approach Control told the pilots that the ILS glideslope was out of service. The localizer would give the pilots directional guidance only. The captain pointed out to his crew that this should pose no problem, for the flight engineer had spotted the lights on Guam at 0126 Hours. From cruising altitude in the clear night sky the lights were visible over 100 miles away. The captain briefed his crew for the expected *visual* approach.

Trouble Ahead: The captain was flying the Boeing airliner, and he tracked down the localizer for Runway 6L. He discovered that this would not be the *visual* approach that he had expected, for a heavy rainstorm blocked the approach path.

The portion of the CVR transcript, below, begins with the flight on final approach. Pertinent sections of the ATC recording have been appended to the end of the CVR transcript:

Capt: . . . . . . Captain, Flight 801
FO: . . . . First Officer, Flight 801
FltEngr: . . . . Flight Engineer, Flight 801
GPWS: . . . . . Ground Proximity Warning System, Flight 801
Radio-: . . . . . (prefix) Radio transmission, Flight 801
AppControl: . . Guam Approach Control
Ramp: . . . . . . Agana Airport Ramp Coordinator
Agana Tower: Agana Airport Control Tower
AFB Tower: . Andersen Air Force Base Control Tower

Capt: Since today's glideslope condition is not good, we need to maintain one-thousand-four-hundred-forty, please set it. (0140:37)

Agana Tower: Korean Air eight-zero-one heavy, Agana Tower, Runway six left . . . cleared to land. (0141:01)

Radio-FO: Korean [Air] eight-zero-one, roger, cleared to land [on Runway] six left. (0141:14)

Capt: Flaps thirty. (0141:22)

FO: Flaps thirty. (0141:23)

Capt: Look carefully, set five-hundred-sixty feet. (0141:32)

FO: Set. (0141:35)

GPWS: One-thousand [feet]. (0141:42)

Capt: No flags, gear and flaps. (0141:43)

  [sound of altitude alert at 0141:45]

Capt: [Windshield] wipers on. (0141:48)

  [sound of the windshield wipers starts at 0141:53 and continues until the end of the CVR tape]

GPWS: Five-hundred [feet]. (0142:00)

FltEngr: Eh? *[spoken in an "astonished" tone]* (0142:02)

Capt: Oh, yes. (0142:04)

FltEngr: Auto-brake? (0142:05)

Capt: Minimum. (0142:07)

FltEngr: Minimum. (0142:07)

Capt: Landing gear down and green. (0142:08)

FltEngr: Gear down and green -- speed brakes armed. (0142:09)

GPWS: Minimums, minimums . . . . (0142:14)

GPWS: Sink rate . . . . (0142:17)

  *[nearing the ground, the airliner is **descending at 1,400 fpm**]*

FO: Sink rate OK. (0142:18)

FltEngr: Two-hundred. *[radio altitude]* (0142:19)

FO: Let's make a missed approach! (0142:19)

FltEngr: [Runway lights] not in sight! (0142:20)

FO: [Runway] not in sight, missed approach! (0142:21)

FltEngr: Go around! (0142:22)

Capt: [I'll] go around. (0142:23)

[sound of autopilot disconnect and increase in engine rpm]

FO: [Raise the] flaps. (0142:23)

GPWS: *One-hundred [feet]. (0142:24)*

GPWS: *Fifty [feet]. (0142:24)*

GPWS: *Forty. (0142:25)*

GPWS: *Thirty. (0142:25)*

GPWS: *Twenty. (0142:25)*

[sound of initial impact with the trees at 0142:25]

[the airliner momentarily staggers back into the air; sound of human "groans" at 0142:28]

[sound of more impacts; end of the CVR tape at 0142:32]

[2 minutes and 53 seconds pass; Agana Tower knows that the airliner should have landed by now]

Agana Tower: Korean Air eight-zero-one heavy, [Agana] Tower, how do you hear? (0145:25)

[there is no response; another 2 minutes and 40 seconds pass]

Agana Tower: Korean Air eight-zero-one, Agana Tower. (0148:05)

[there is no response; another 1 minute and 47 seconds pass]

[Agana Tower calls the Agana Airport Ramp Coordinator]

Agana Tower: . . . [did] Korean Air come up to you? (0149:52)

Ramp: Aaahhh, no. (0149:53)

[alarmed, Agana Tower queries Guam Approach Control]

Agana Tower: Approach, did Korean Air [contact] you? (0150:23)

AppControl: He checked-in with me, I cleared him to land, I don't know where he's at, [I] never did have him in sight. (0150:35)

Ramp: You never saw him? (0150:41)

AppControl: He didn't land? (0150:45)

Agana Tower: Negative. (0150:46)

AppControl: Oh, my God! (0150:50)

Agana Tower: I tried to get a-hold of him, he called me -- ah -- I cleared him to land -- I never had him in sight. (0151:06)

[Agana Tower calls Andersen Air Force Base Tower]

Agana Tower: Andersen Tower, Agana Tower . . . you didn't have a Boeing seven-forty-seven land up there, did you? (0151:17)

AFB Tower: Just now? (0151:35)

Agana Tower: Affirmative. (0151:36)

AFB Tower: Aaahhh -- aaahhh -- no. . . . I don't see any [airliners] out there. (0151:37)

Agana Tower: We're missing a Boeing seven-forty-seven.

[Agana Tower makes a final attempt to contact Flight 801]

Agana Tower: Korean Air eight-zero-one, Agana Tower. (0152:04)

[there is no response; 30 seconds pass]

AppControl: Well, he must have crashed. (0152:34)

The Accident: When the alarmed flight engineer announced the unexpected "two-hundred" feet read-out from the radio altimeter, he and the first officer called for a missed approach. The captain pulled back on his control column and pushed the throttles forward. Too late. Five seconds later at 0142:24 Hours the synthetic voice of the GPWS blared out its warning. Within two seconds the electronic sentry counted down the decreasing distance to the ground: "One-hundred [feet] -- fifty -- forty -- thirty -- twenty":

The airplane impacted hilly terrain at Nimitz Hill, Guam, about 660 feet msl and about 3.3 miles from the Runway 6L threshold.

The wings ripped through the tops of tall trees three miles from the airport. The airliner staggered skyward for a moment, then dropped back toward the ground. It plowed through trees and thick undergrowth, disintegrating along the way, and slid to a stop a half-mile from the initial point of impact.

One survivor would recall others screaming as "intense flames and heat" swept through the cabin. Many passengers had been thrown from the aircraft as it broke apart during the long slide. Those who survived the impact and the flames began extricating themselves from the burning wreckage in the dark.

The Boeing 747 never arrived at the airport. The controller tried to recontact the pilots by radio, but he was unable to do so. Meanwhile, Ryan International Flight 789 was winging its way toward Agana Airport. The tower controller asked the Ryan pilots if they had radio contact with the missing airliner. At 0156 Hours the Ryan captain responded:

> About fifteen minutes ago we saw . . . the clouds lit up . . . bright red. Uuuhhh, it was kinda weird, we thought it was just our eyes or something. Aaahhh! We [now see] a big fire on the hillside up here!

The Ryan captain spotted the pyre from Flight 801. Soon local emergency response teams began working their way toward the glow from the flames. The U.S. Naval Hospital on Guam sent medical teams, and they set up a triage center near the wreckage. Ambulances and helicopters began shuttling the injured to Guam Memorial Hospital and the U.S. Naval Hospital. All survivors had suffered grievous injuries.

The fire burned itself out after daylight. There had been 254 people on Flight 801, and the crash killed 228 of them. Human remains were taken to the Disaster Mortuary of Guam, where the medical examiner reported:

> Because many of the remains were fragmentary, the number of remains exceeded the number of fatalities. . . . the [deceased] airplane occupants died of blunt force trauma, thermal injuries, and carbon monoxide inhalation.

The Investigation: NTSB investigators began sorting through the wreckage of the Boeing 747. They found no mechanical or system anomalies that could have contributed to the crash. The keys to the loss of the aircraft would be found on the FDR and CVR tapes.

In reconstructing the accident, investigators found that the flight engineer had first seen the lights on Guam 16 minutes before the crash. However, an intense rainstorm was centered on the ILS approach course. Once the aircraft dropped down onto the final approach path the heavy rain blocked the pilots' view of the runway lights. Also, there were no lights on the ground below. In these "black hole" conditions the airliner skimmed low over the terrain, flying through torrential rain at night.

Without an electronic glideslope, non-precision approaches are conducted in a series of step-down altitudes. The FDR revealed that, with the autopilot engaged, the captain:

> twice commanded the entry of lower altitudes into the airplane's altitude selector before the airplane had reached the associated step-down fix, [and then he] improperly descended below the intermediate approach altitudes of 2,000 and 1,440 feet.

The CVR revealed no awareness by any crewmember that the aircraft was descending prematurely. The crew was confused, the investigators discovered, about the location of the DME transmitter on Nimitz Hill. The captain believed he was closer to the airport, and he began to descend too soon. The first officer and flight engineer never challenged the premature descent.

Probable Cause: Over two years after Flight 801 tore into Nimitz Hill the NTSB adopted NTSB-AAR-00-01 on 13 January 2000. The board found extensive problems with Korean Air's pilot training programs. Of special note was the ineffective training for missed approaches. With respect to the crash of Flight 801 the board concluded: "The captain lost awareness of [his] position on the ILS localizer-only approach." Members of the board found that the *Probable Cause* of this accident was:

> the captain's failure to adequately brief and execute the non-precision approach and the first officer's and flight engineer's failure to effectively monitor and cross-check the captain's execution of the approach.

SwissAir Flight 111

McDonnell Douglas MD-11, registration HB-IWF
2 September 1998, in the Atlantic Ocean near Nova Scotia
229 aboard, 229 killed

Overview: High over the Atlantic Ocean a fire broke out above the cockpit ceiling in a modern McDonnell Douglas MD-11. The pilots diverted toward Halifax, Nova Scotia. Before they reached the airport the fire destroyed numerous automated systems aboard the airliner. Out of control, it crashed into the ocean and killed all 229 people on board.

The Flight: After dark at 2018 Hours on 2 September 1998, SwissAir Flight 111 took off from JFK International Airport in New York. The 215 passengers, 12 flight attendants, and 2 pilots were bound for Geneva, Switzerland. Forty minutes after leaving New York, cruising at flight level 330, the pilots checked-in with Moncton Center. Exclusive of some light turbulence encountered earlier the flight had been flawless thus far.

The McDonnell Douglas MD-11 airliner, registration HB-IWF, had been manufactured in 1991 and delivered new to SwissAir. New cockpit automation allowed elimination of the former flight engineer's position, so only the two pilots manned the cockpit. Three big Pratt & Whitney engines, one slung under each wing and another embedded deep in the structure of the vertical stabilizer, powered the modern airliner:

> The McDonnell Douglas [MD-11] design project began in 1986. The MD-11 is structurally based on the . . . DC-10 design. The MD-11 was designed for more economical and efficient operation than the DC-10 by incorporating modern automated systems . . . thereby allowing for a two-crew cockpit.

The captain, age 49, and first officer, age 36, held Swiss ATP certificates. Prior to joining SwissAir both had been fighter pilots in the Swiss Air Force, and they had logged a total of 15,600 flight hours. In addition to his regular duties flying the line, the senior captain also was an instructor pilot in the state-of-the-art MD-11.

Trouble Ahead: At 2110 Hours, 52 minutes into the flight, the first officer told the captain that he smelled an unusual odor. Two minutes later the captain noticed traces of smoke in the cockpit. He summoned a flight attendant to the flight deck. She could not see any smoke, but she smelled *something* out of the ordinary.

The pilots theorized that the problem lay in the air conditioning system. However, by 2113 Hours both pilots again could detect small amounts of smoke. As a precautionary measure they donned their oxygen masks and diverted toward Halifax, Nova Scotia, the nearest suitable airport. Seven minutes later at 2120 Hours they talked to their passengers via the MD-11 public address system. They explained that the flight would make a precautionary landing at Halifax within 20 to 25 minutes.

The first officer is flying the McDonnell Douglas airliner. The portion of the *reconstructed* CVR and ATC transcript, below, begins as he detects the unusual odor in the cockpit:

Capt: . . . . . Captain, Flight 111
FO: . . . . . . First Officer, Flight 111
Radio-: . . . . (prefix) Radio transmission, Flight 111
Center: . . . . Moncton Center (ARTCC)

[the First Officer mentions an unusual odor at 2110:38]

Capt: Look [at the smoke]. (2110:57)

FO: [There is nothing more] up there. (2111:29)

[a Flight Attendant comes into the cockpit at 2112:06; she smells the unusual odor but can not see any smoke]

Capt: It's definitely smoke which came out. (2112:24)

Capt: [It's coming from the] air conditioning, is it? (2112:32)

FO: Yes. (2112:37)

[more smoke becomes visible to the pilots at 2113:14]

Capt: That's not doing well up there at all. (2113:53)

<u>Radio-Capt</u>: SwissAir one-eleven is declaring Pan, Pan, Pan. We have smoke in the cockpit, [we] request [an] immediate return to a convenient place -- I guess, uuuhhh, Boston. (2114:15)

<u>Center</u>: . . . would you prefer to go to Halifax? (2115:06)

[Halifax, Nova Scotia, is only 56 miles to the northeast]

<u>Radio-Capt</u>: Affirmative for SwissAir one-eleven heavy, we prefer Halifax from our position. (2115:36)

<u>Center</u>: SwissAir one-eleven, roger, proceed direct to Halifax, descend now to flight level two-niner-zero. (2115:41)

[the pilots begin donning their oxygen masks at 2115:56]

<u>Center</u>: . . . and SwissAir one-eleven, uh, can you tell me what your fuel on board is, and the number of passengers? (2116:50)

[the aircraft descends at 4,000 fpm with the speed brakes fully extended; the pilots switch to a different controller at Center]

<u>Radio-FO</u>: Moncton Center, good evening, SwissAir one-eleven heavy, flight level two-five-four, descending . . . . (2118:34)

<u>Center</u>: SwissAir one-eleven, good evening, descend to three-thousand, the altimeter is two-nine-seven-nine. (2118:46)

<u>Center</u>: . . . OK, can I vector you, uh, to set up for Runway zero-six at Halifax? (2119:12)

<u>Radio-FO</u>: Ah, say again [the] latest wind, please. (2119:17)

<u>Center</u>: OK, active runway [at] Halifax [is] zero-six. Should I start you on a vector for [Runway] six? (2119:20)

<u>Radio-FO</u>: Yes, vectors for [Runway] six will be fine. (2119:24)

<u>Center</u>: SwissAir one-eleven, roger, turn left [to a] heading of zero-three-zero, it's a back course approach for Runway zero-six. The localizer frequency [is] one-zero-niner-decimal-niner. You've got thirty miles to fly to the threshold. (2119:37)

<u>Radio-Capt</u>: Uh, we need more than thirty miles. (2119:50)

<u>Center</u>: SwissAir one-eleven, roger, you can turn left [to] heading three-six-zero to lose some altitude. (2119:57)

[using the public address system at 2120:14, the pilots announce that they will make a precautionary landing at Halifax]

Center: . . . SwissAir one-eleven, when you have time could I have the number of souls on board and your fuel on board, please, for emergency services? (2121:20)

Radio-Capt: Roger, at the time, uh, fuel on board is, uh, two-three-zero tons. We must dump some fuel. May we do that in this area during descent? (2121:27)

[the Captain has erroneously reported the gross weight of the MD-11 instead of the weight of the fuel; however, this will not be a factor in the fate of the flight]

Center: Roger, uh, turn to the left, uh, heading of two-zero-zero degrees, and advise me when you are ready to dump. It will be about ten minutes until you are off the coast. You are still within twenty-five miles of the airport. (2122:01)

[the aircraft turns south to dump fuel prior to landing; the pilots begin the smoke elimination checklist at 2123:45]

Center: . . . you will be staying within about thirty-five [to] forty miles of the airport if you have to get [there] in a hurry. (2123:53)

Radio-Capt: OK, that's fine for us. Please tell me when we can start to dump fuel. (2124:01)

*[sound of autopilot disconnect; **multiple systems failures** begin at 2124:09 and will continue for 92 seconds; multiple automated visual alerts and warning tones]*

Radio-FO: Ah, [this is] SwissAir one-eleven, at the time we must fly manually, are we cleared to fly between ten-thou -- eleven-thousand and niner-thousand feet? (2124:25)

Center: SwissAir one-eleven, you can block between five-thousand and twelve-thousand if you wish. (2124:36)

*[sound of additional **automated alerts** at 2124:41; both pilots excitedly declare an **emergency**]*

Radio-Capt: 'One-eleven is declaring an emergency! (2124:42)

Radio-FO: Roger, we are between, uh, twelve and five-thousand feet. We are declaring [an] emergency now! (2124:42)

[cabin electrical power is lost at 2124:46; Flight Attendants use flashlights to prepare for landing]

Radio-Capt or FO: 'Eleven heavy, we are starting [the fuel] dump now! We have to land immediately! (2124:53)

Radio-Capt or FO: . . . declaring an emergency now! (2125:02)

[cockpit altitude and airspeed indications are lost at 2125:07]

Center: SwissAir one-eleven, you are cleared to, ah, commence your fuel dump on that track and advise me when the dump is complete. (2125:16)

[the Captain says something is "burning already" at 2125:20]

[the First Officer's instrument displays all go dark at 2125:33]

[the FDR stops recording at 2125:40]

[the CVR loses power and stops recording at 2125:41]

[the crippled airliner remains airborne for another 5 minutes and 27 seconds]

[Center loses the radar return from Flight 111 at 2131:08]

*[out of control, the **airliner crashes into the sea**; seismographic recorders at Halifax document the impact at 2131:18]*

The Accident: At 2124:42 Hours the captain had declared an emergency. Electrical power had been lost in the cabin, and flight attendants were using flashlights to make preparations for landing. Up in the cockpit the automated systems began to fail, one after another. When the electronic displays lost power and died the pilots found themselves in deep, deep trouble. It was pitch black dark outside and totally dark in the cockpit. The pilots had no means to navigate electronically to the airport, no way to verify up and down, no instrument displays with which to verify the attitude of their aircraft.

Meanwhile the fire grew in intensity. Smoke, heat, and flames boiled down into the cockpit. One witness on the ground would report seeing "blue flames" trailing back from the aircraft. Twenty degrees nose down, in a 60 to 110 degree right bank at 300 knots, the airliner screamed down into the sea five miles from Peggy's Cove, Nova Scotia.

Royal Canadian Mounted Police, the Department of National Defense, the Canadian Coast Guard, and citizens in small boats flocked to the site of the crash. These potential rescuers found only fragmented human remains. Longitudinal impact forces on the order of at least 350 G's had instantly killed all 229 people aboard Flight 111. Postmortem examinations resulted in visual identification of one passenger. The other human remains were identified through dental records, fingerprint analysis, forensic radiography, and DNA protocols.

The Investigation: The water at the site of the crash was only 180 feet deep, but the recovery, salvage, and dredging operations lasted for 13 months. About 98 percent of the aircraft was pulled up from the seabed:

> The final phase of the wreckage recovery was conducted in the fall of 1999. It involved dredging the area of the debris field to a depth of about 1.5 meters to recover the remaining debris.

Investigators delved through the recovered wreckage. Heat damage revealed that a fire had started in the area over the cockpit ceiling. Heat signatures showed that temperatures of 900 to 1,000 degrees Fahrenheit existed in the avionics area and on the air diffuser structure above the cockpit ceiling. As the fire grew, molten insulation dribbled down into the cockpit onto or near the pilots, and flames began "encroaching on the pilot seat positions." The captain's seat was in the egress position at impact.

Investigators could not determine if the pilots were incapacitated by smoke, heat, flames, or the searing molten material bubbling down from the cockpit ceiling over their heads. The investigators would conclude:

> If the pilots were not incapacitated and were still attempting to control the aircraft, this suggests that in the last minute of flight they lost orientation with the horizon, [because] the aircraft was not in controlled flight.

The experts concluded that the fire "most likely started from [an electrical] wire arcing event." Thermal insulation blankets over the cockpit were flammable, and analysts calculated that this material was most likely the first to ignite. Silicone caps, hook-and-loop fasteners, adhesives, and acoustic insulation led to the spread and intensity of the fire. Ominously, examination of several MD-11 airliners revealed wiring discrepancies that held the potential for an identical wire arcing disaster. The board pointed out:

> There were no built-in smoke and fire detection and suppression devices in the area where the fire started . . . and [this] allowed the fire to propagate unchecked until it became uncontrollable.

Probable Cause: The Transportation Safety Board of Canada released Aviation Investigation Report No. A98H0003 on 27 March 2003. In the last minutes of flight the electronic displays in the cockpit had failed. In the dark this left the pilots without a means to navigate or determine the attitude of the airliner. With regard to *Findings as to Causes* the board determined:

> Flammable material propagated a fire that started above the [cockpit] ceiling. . . . The fire spread and intensified rapidly to the extent that it degraded aircraft systems and the cockpit environment, and ultimately led to the loss of control of the aircraft. *[and also]* Foams, adhesives, and thermal acoustic insulation splicing tapes contributed to the propagation and intensity of the fire.

The board found that the pilots made a wise decision to divert toward Halifax after noticing the smoke. Nonetheless, by the time they turned toward the airport it was *impossible* to arrive in time to land safely. In the dry words of the official report:

> From any point along the SwissAir Flight 111 flight path after the initial odor [was detected] in the cockpit, the time required to complete an approach and landing at the Halifax International Airport would have exceeded the time available before the fire-related conditions in the aircraft cockpit would have precluded a safe landing.

American Airlines Flight 1420

McDonnell Douglas MD-82, registration N215AA
1 June 1999, at Little Rock, Arkansas
145 aboard, 11 killed

Overview: During a severe thunderstorm a McDonnell Douglas MD-82 tried to land at Little Rock, Arkansas. After touchdown the airliner ran off the end of the runway. It tore into the ILS localizer array, careened down a rock embankment, smashed through a chain link fence, slammed through the steel approach lighting structure, broke into three pieces, and burned. The *miracle* of the accident was that only 11 of the 145 people on board were killed.

The Flight: American Airlines Flight 1420 took off from Dallas-Fort Worth at 2240 Hours on the night of 1 June 1999 and headed toward Little Rock, Arkansas. The pilots knew the weather there would be rough. Their corporate weather advisory warned them of thunderstorms along the route. Two advisories from the National Weather Service (NWS) forecast severe storms. Fourteen minutes after takeoff the American Airlines dispatcher urged the pilots to expedite the flight to "beat the thunderstorms."

The two pilots had earned impressive credentials. The captain, age 48, was a lieutenant colonel in the U.S. Air Force Reserve and had logged 10,234 flight hours. Five months earlier his employer had promoted him to the position of chief pilot at Chicago. Earlier, during a furlough he had worked as a nuclear engineer on submarine propulsion systems. The airline had hired the first officer, age 35, several months earlier. Prior to joining American he was an experienced corporate pilot and had risen to become director of operations for an air charter company.

The McDonnell Douglas MD-82, registration N215AA, had been delivered new to American Airlines in 1983. Based upon the older Douglas DC-9 design, the popular twin-jet airliner had accumulated 49,136 flying hours. On this trip it carried the 2 pilots, 4 flight attendants, and 139 trusting passengers.

Trouble Ahead: As the aircraft descended toward Little Rock at 2334 Hours the controller reported a severe thunderstorm nearing the airport. Winds were already gusting to 44 knots, he radioed. Five minutes later ATC issued a windshear alert, and it would not be the last. Flying through turbulence, with lightning illuminating the night sky, the pilots zeroed in on the airport.

The captain is flying the MD-82. The portion of the CVR transcript, below, begins as he and the first officer struggle to see the runway lights through the violent storm. A part of the ATC recording has been appended to the end of the CVR transcript:

Capt: . . . . . Captain, Flight 1420
FO: . . . . . . First Officer, Flight 1420
GPWS: . . . . Ground Proximity Warning System, Flight 1420
Radio-: . . . . (prefix) Radio transmission, Flight 1420
Tower: . . . . Little Rock Airport Control Tower
GndControl: . Little Rock Ground Control
AppControl: . Little Rock Approach Control
FireTruck: . . Airport fire truck, radio call-sign "Red Ball"

Capt: I don't [see] the airport. (2342:00)

FO: Yeah, there it is, I [see] the airport. (2342:13)

Capt: I don't see a runway. (2342:24)

AppControl: American fourteen-twenty, it appears we have, uh, [the] second part of this storm moving though, the winds now three-four-zero at one-six, gusts [to] three-four [knots]. (2342:27)

FO: You wanna accept a short approach, want to keep it tight?

Capt: Yeah, if you see the runway, 'cause I don't quite see it.

FO: Yeah, it's right here, see it? (2342:45)

Capt: You just point me in the right direction and I'll start slowing down here. Give me flaps eleven. (2342:48)

Radio-FO: [This is] American fourteen-twenty, we got the airport [in sight], we're going between clouds, I think [the airport is] right off to my -- uh -- three o'clock low, about four miles. (2342:59)

AppControl: American fourteen-twenty, that's it. Do you wanna shoot the visual approach, or you wanna go out for the ILS?

Radio-FO: I can -- well -- we'll start the visual, if we can do it.

Capt: We're losing it. I don't think we can maintain visual.

[like the Captain, the First Officer loses sight of the runway because of the storm; ATC vectors the pilots toward the ILS]

Capt: I hate droning around visual at night in [bad] weather without having some clue [as to] where I am. (2345:15)

FO: See how we're going right into this [storm]? (2345:29)

Radio-FO: Approach, American fourteen-twenty, I know you're doing your best, sir, we're getting pretty close to this storm, we'll keep it tight if we have to. (2345:47)

Capt: Aaawww, we're going right into this [storm]. (2346:52)

AppControl: American fourteen-twenty, right now we have, uh, heavy rain on the airport . . . visibility is less than a mile, Runway four right RVR is three-thousand. (2346:52)

AppControl: . . . cleared to land, the wind [is] three-five-zero at three-zero, gusts [to] four-five. (2347:08)

[the RVR drops farther; ATC issues another windshear alert]

AppControl: American fourteen-twenty, the Runway four RVR right now is one-thousand-six-hundred. (2348:12)

Capt: This is -- this is a can of worms! (2349:12)

FO: There's the runway off to your right, got it? (2349:24)

Capt: No. (2349:26)

FO: I got the runway in sight -- you're on course -- stay where you're at. (2349:27)

Capt: I got it. I got it. (2349:31)

[sound of the windshield wipers begins at 2349:41]

FO: Five-hundred feet. (2349:46)

Capt: [Bug airspeed] plus twenty [knots]. (2349:53)

Capt or FO: Aaawww, [expletive]! We're off course. (2349:56)

FO: We're way off [course]. (2350:00)

Capt: I can't see [the runway] -- yeah, I got it. (2350:01)

FO: Hundred feet. (2350:07)

GPWS: Sink rate, sink rate . . . . (2350:12)

FO: Fifty [feet]. (2350:13)

GPWS: Sink rate, sink rate . . . . (2350:14)

FO: Forty. (2350:14)

FO: Thirty. (2350:15)

FO: Twenty. (2350:17)

FO: Ten. (2350:18)

[sound of touchdown on the runway at 2350:20]

FO: We're down -- we're sliding. (2350:22)

Capt: [Two expletives]. (2350:26)

[the thrust reversers deploy for 7 seconds]

Capt or FO: On the brakes! Oh, [expletive]! (2350:31)

Capt or FO: [The] other one -- other one -- other one! (2350:35)

Capt or FO: Aaawww, [three expletives]! (2350:40)

[sound of the first impact at 2350:43]

Capt or FO: [Two expletives]! (2350:44)

[sound of several more impacts beginning at 2350:46]

[end of the CVR tape at 2350:48]

[the tower controller can not see the runway or the airliner through the blinding rain and hail; he <u>assumes</u> the airliner is still on the runway]

Tower: American fourteen-twenty, report [when you are] clear of the runway, please. (2350:54)

Tower: American fourteen-twenty, Tower. (2351:16)

Tower: American fourteen-twenty, Tower. (2351:31)

Tower: American fourteen-twenty, Tower. (2352:00)

[the alarmed controller phones the airport firefighting unit, then continues trying to get a radio response from Flight 1420]

Tower: American fourteen-twenty, Tower. (2353:22)

Tower: American fourteen-twenty, Tower. (2354:32)

FireTruck: Ground [Control], Red Ball one. . . . [Do] we have permission to proceed to Runway four right? (2354:51)

[because of the heavy rain the controller can not see the fire trucks; they go the <u>wrong end</u> of the runway; 5 minutes pass]

GndControl: Red Ball two, proceed on the runway, he was down at the *other end*, sir, he was at the *departure end* . . . . (0000:16)

[firefighters stumble onto the fire 3 minutes later]

FireTruck: Ground [Control], we [see] him off the end of the runway, we have sight of the fire . . . . (0003:16)

GndControl: Red Ball three, is he in the river? (0003:31)

FireTruck: He's off the end of the runway on the north end, burning. (0004:07)

[4 minutes and 27 seconds pass; the fire trucks have to take a circuitous route to reach the burning airliner]

FireTruck: We [see] survivors walking around! Get down here and get these people! [We see] many walking-wounded! (0008:34)

The Accident: Flight 1420 touched down 2,000 feet down the runway at 160 knots, sliding to the right. A 25 knot crosswind with a tailwind component whipped across the runway.

The pilots deployed the thrust reversers, had severe directional control problems, and quickly stowed them. They hit the brakes, but braking had little effect. They tried the thrust reversers again and ran into the same control problem. Once more they hit the brakes, but the airliner refused to stop. Surviving passengers would later explain that it "fishtailed" down the runway. The MD-82 ran out of asphalt at 97 knots, over 110 miles per hour. Hurtling past the end of the runway, it ripped through:

> the ILS localizer array . . . [tore] through a chain link security fence, [careened] over a rock embankment . . . and collided with the structure supporting the Runway 22L approach lighting.

With its inertia finally spent the broken remains of Flight 1420 slid to a stop in a flood plain 800 feet past the end of the runway. The impacts had torn off the left wing and broken the aircraft into three main sections. Parts of the steel approach light structure were embedded in the mangled wreckage. Fire broke out and consumed what was left of the passenger cabin.

Many occupants had been thrown out of the aircraft as it self-destructed during the long slide. Those who survived, plus others who managed to crawl out of the wreckage, found themselves at the mercy of the raging elements:

> Once outside the airplane the [survivors] encountered heavy rain, strong winds, and hail. Some passengers huddled in groups [for protection] and others reported sheltering themselves from the weather with bales of hay in a [nearby] field.

Firefighters described driving through "blinding wind and rain" that restricted visibility to 100 feet. Twelve long minutes after the crash, through the rain and hail they finally spotted the glow of the flames at 0003 Hours. Soon 13 fire trucks and 19 ambulances made their way to the site of the crash.

The captain and 10 passengers were killed. The Pulaski County Coroner reported that they succumbed because of traumatic injuries, thermal injuries, and smoke and soot inhalation. An additional 110 occupants of the aircraft sustained serious injuries.

The Investigation: The NTSB quickly pieced together the ill-fated flight of the MD-82. Analysts found no indication of any aircraft malfunction that could have played a role in the crash. The true tale of the tragedy was told by the FDR and CVR tapes.

The NWS had warned of thunderstorms with hail up to two inches in diameter and wind gusts up to 70 knots. Radar showed a severe thunderstorm approaching the airport:

NWS radar data indicated . . . a line of thunderstorms, with several areas of intense and extreme activity, was encompassing the Little Rock airport area and Runway 4R approach path.

Investigators pointed out that, with the second windshear alert, the pilots should have known that the maximum crosswind for landing had been far exceeded. Other concerns were mushrooming in the cockpit: heavy rain, lightning, hail, inability to keep the runway in sight, decreasing RVR, and windshear alerts. The NTSB stressed that the pilots should have abandoned the approach.

After touchdown the spoilers, crucial for obtaining maximum braking effectiveness, did not deploy. Investigators explained:

The spoilers did not deploy automatically because the spoiler handle was not armed by either pilot before landing. *[and also]* The captain failed to manually extend the spoilers when they did not deploy [automatically].

The pilots deployed their thrust reversers. They used excessive engine pressure ratios in doing so, and this led to severe directional control problems. As a consequence reverse thrust was not used continuously, and brakes alone could not stop the aircraft. The NTSB would explain the absence of effective braking:

The lack of spoiler deployment was the single most important factor in the flight crew's inability to stop the accident airplane within the available runway length.

Probable Cause: The NTSB adopted its Aircraft Accident Report, NTSB-AAR-01-02, on 23 October 2001, 28 months after Flight 1420 crashed and burned. The board found that the performance and decision-making of the pilots had been degraded by fatigue. Focus on expediting the landing and the information overload caused by the raging storm contributed to their poor performance. The board found that the *Probable Cause* of this accident was:

the flight crew's failure to discontinue the approach when severe thunderstorms and their associated hazards to flight operations had moved into the airport area, and the crew's failure to ensure that the spoilers had extended after touchdown.

EgyptAir Flight 990

Boeing 767, registration SU-GAP
31 October 1999, in the Atlantic Ocean near Massachusetts
217 aboard, 217 killed

Overview: Halloween was worse than spooky for the passengers and crew aboard a Boeing 767. Over the Atlantic Ocean, alone in the cockpit, the first officer shut down both engines. He chanted "I rely on God" and pushed the airliner into a steep dive. The craft dove into the sea and killed all 217 people on board.

The Flight: On Halloween, 31 October 1999, EgyptAir Flight 990 prepared to leave New York on an international flight to Cairo, Egypt. Because of the 10 hour flight time, two flight crews (two captains and two first officers) would be required. The "relief" pilots would replace the "command" pilots as necessary during the long flight to Egypt.

In the dark at 0120 Hours, Flight 990 took off from Runway 22R and headed out over the Atlantic. ATC cleared the pilots to climb to their cruising altitude at flight level 330. The Boeing 767, registration SU-GAP, had been delivered new to EgyptAir in 1989, and it had accumulated 33,354 hours in the air. It was configured to seat 10 first class passengers, 22 business class passengers, and 185 people in economy class. On this flight it carried the 4 pilots, 10 flight attendants, and 203 passengers.

The ***relief first officer***, age 59, would play the crucial role in the loss of Flight 990. EgyptAir hired him in 1987, twelve years before this final flight. He held a Commercial Pilot certificate issued by the government of Egypt, and he had logged 12,538 hours of flight time. Prior to joining EgyptAir he had been a major in the Egyptian Air Force, where he served as a military flight instructor. Later he transitioned to the civilian Flight Training Institute, which is sponsored by the government of Egypt, and there he rose to the position of chief flight instructor.

In the darkness, only 20 minutes into the flight, the relief first officer made an unusual demand. He told the command first officer that he would relieve him. Such a pilot switch usually did not take place until much later during the trip. The command first officer protested the early switch, but the relief first officer *insisted* on occupying the right seat immediately. Finally giving in, the command first officer vacated the cockpit, and the relief first officer replaced him at the controls.

Trouble Ahead: Once seated the relief first officer spoke to an unidentified crewmember, who also was in the cockpit. The relief first officer said that he had the writing pen of the command first officer. He asked the unidentified crewmember to leave the cockpit and return the pen. By chance, a moment later the command captain left to use the toilet. This left the relief first officer alone in the cockpit of Flight 990.

The portion of the CVR and ATC transcript, below, begins as the relief first officer is *demanding* that he be allowed to replace the command first officer immediately:

ComCapt: . . . . . . Command Captain, Flight 990
ComFO: . . . . Command First Officer, Flight 990
ReliefFO: . . . . . . Relief First Officer, Flight 990
UnidCrew: . . . . . . Unidentified crewmember, Flight 990
Center: . . . . New York Center (ARTCC)
Lufthansa 499: . . . Lufthansa Flight 499

ReliefFO: . . . I'm not going to sleep at all! (apx. 0140)

ComFO: But, I slept. I slept.

ReliefFO: You mean you're not going to get up? You *will* get up! Go and get some rest and come back [later]!

ComFO: You should have told me this . . . .

[the Command First Officer finally agrees to the early change]

ReliefFO: That's good!

ComFO: With your permission, captain? *[speaking to the captain]*

[with the Command Captain's concurrence the Command First Officer leaves the cockpit; the Relief First Officer takes his place

in the right seat]

[several minutes later the Relief First Officer also induces an unidentified crewmember to leave the cockpit]

ReliefFO: Look, here's the [command] first officer's pen, give it to him, please, God spare you. (0147:55)

UnidCrew: Yeah. (0147:58)

ReliefFO: . . . to make sure it doesn't get lost. (0148:01)

ComCapt: Excuse me . . . while I take a quick trip to the toilet, before it gets crowded, while they are eating, and I'll be back to you. (0148:03)

ReliefFO: Go ahead, please. (0148:08)

*[sound of the cockpit door opening and shutting; the Command Captain and the unidentified crewmember leave; the Relief First Officer is now **alone in the cockpit** at 0148:18]*

ReliefFO: I rely on God. *["Tawakkalt Ala Allah"]* (0148:39)

[the autopilot is <u>manually</u> disconnected at 0149:45]

ReliefFO: I rely on God. (0149:48)

[the throttles are <u>manually</u> pulled to flight idle at 0149:53]

*[there is an abrupt nose-down elevator movement at 0149:54; the aircraft begins a **steep descent**]*

ReliefFO: I rely on God. (0149:57)

ReliefFO: I rely on God. (0149:58)

[sound of the Master Caution aural beeper at 0149:58]

ReliefFO: I rely on God. (0150:00)

ReliefFO: I rely on God. (0150:01)

ReliefFO: I rely on God. (0150:02)

ReliefFO: I rely on God. (0150:04)

ReliefFO: I rely on God. (0150:05)

[struggling against negative G forces, the Command Captain manages to reenter the cockpit at 0150:06]

ComCapt: What's happening? *[shouted in a loud voice]* (0150:06)

ReliefFO: I rely on God. (0150:07)

[sound of numerous "thumps" and "clicks" for 15 seconds]

[at 0150:08 the diving aircraft exceeds its maximum operating airspeed; the hi-low aural Master Warning starts and continues until the end of the recording]

ReliefFO: I rely on God. (0150:08)

ComCapt: What's happening? *[shouted in a loud voice]* (0150:08)

ComCapt: What's happening, Gamil? What's happening?

*[rate of descent reaches **39,000 feet per minute** at 0150:19]*

[the Relief First Officer moves the engine start switches to the cutoff position at 0150:21]

ComCapt: What is this? What is this? Did you shut the engines?

ComCapt: [Did you] shut the engines? (0150:28)

ReliefFO: It's shut. (0150:29)

ComCapt: Pull [the control column back]! (0150:31)

ComCapt: Pull with me! (0150:32)

ComCapt: Pull with me! (0150:34)

[ATC loses the radar return from Flight 990 at 0150:34]

ComCapt: Pull with me! (0150:36)

[the engines spool down and cut off electrical power to the CVR; the recording ends at 0150:38; over 3 minutes pass]

Center: EgyptAir nine-ninety, radar contact lost, recycle [your] transponder, squawk one-seven-one-two. (0154:00)

[there is no response]

Center: EgyptAir nine-ninety, New York Center. (0154:19)

Center: EgyptAir nine-ninety, New York Center. (0154:42)

Center: EgyptAir nine-ninety, if you copy New York Center, squawk one-seven-one-two and ident. (0155:00)

Center: EgyptAir niner-niner-zero, this is New York Center on guard [frequency], contact New York Center on one-two-five-point-niner-two and squawk one-seven-one-two. (0157:49)

[there is no response; 8 minutes and 13 seconds pass]

Center: Lufthansa four-ninety-nine, New York Center, I could use your assistance, could you try calling EgyptAir niner-niner-zero on this frequency and see if he -- aaahhh -- checks in? (0206:02)

Lufthansa 499: OK, standby -- EgyptAir niner-niner-zero, this is Lufthansa four-ninety-nine, do you read? (0206:13)

Lufthansa 499: EgyptAir niner-niner-zero, this is Lufthansa four-ninety-nine, do you read? (0206:30)

Lufthansa 499: [Center], I am sorry, there is no reply. (0206:43)

The Accident: When the engines spooled down the CVR lost its electrical power. The CVR stopped operating at 0150:38 Hours. Yet, Flight 990 still had a chance to survive.

U.S. Air Force radar sites documented the altitude and heading of the flight. Military radar showed that the descent of the aircraft stopped momentarily. The airliner climbed for about 40 seconds and turned 60 degrees to the right. Then it began a second steep descent. It dove straight down into the ocean about 60 miles south of Nantucket, Massachusetts. The 217 people aboard were killed instantly by the impact with the water.

The Investigation: Under the provisions of the Convention on International Civil Aviation, investigation of an airplane crash in international waters falls under the jurisdiction of the country of registry. However, at the request of the Egyptian government the NTSB assumed full responsibility for this investigation.

Salvage operations recovered much of the wreckage, including the crucial FDR and CVR. Investigators found no mechanical or electrical problems that could account for the loss of Flight 990.

They examined a host of "anomaly scenarios," but none of them were consistent with the FDR documentation. Investigators poured over the CVR transcript, attempting to identify any indication of an in-flight malady that could explain the conduct and statements of the relief first officer. They found none:

> There were no sounds or events recorded by the flight recorders that would indicate an airplane anomaly or other unusual circumstance [had] preceded the relief first officer's statement, "I rely on God."

Examination of the engines revealed that they *could* have been restarted. The aircraft *could* have been returned to level flight. The relief first officer would have been aware of the downward pitch attitude and the negative load factor at the start of the dive. Nonetheless, the FDR showed that instead of attempting a recovery by pulling back on the control column, he continued to push it forward. Investigators pointed out:

> The relief first officer did not attempt to counter the dive by commanding nose-up elevator, a largely intuitive pilot response to initiate a recovery.

According to the CVR transcript the relief first officer never exhibited any audible surprise or anxiety during the fatal dive. He never called out for help. During the dive the captain managed to return to the cockpit and get into his left seat. He shouted several times to the relief first officer: "What's happening?"

In response the relief first officer merely repeated his passive and monotone phrase: "I rely on God."

The captain jammed the throttles forward. When the engines failed to respond the board *theorized* that the captain saw that both engine start switches were in the cutoff position. That would explain his question: "What is this, did you shut the engines?"

After that question the relief first officer made his only verbal response to the captain: "It's shut."

The FDR showed that the captain pulled back on his control column, desperately trying to halt the dive. He pleaded with the relief first officer: "Pull with me!" Yet, the FDR showed that the relief first officer continued to push forward:

The elevator surfaces [moved] in different directions, with the captain's control column commanding nose-up [elevator] movement and the relief first officer's control column commanding nose-down [elevator] movement.

The English language translation, "I rely on God," is based upon the words spoken in Arabic, "Tawakkalt Ala Allah." This phrase is routinely used by Egyptian laymen in day-to-day activities to beseech God's assistance for the task at hand.

Probable Cause: The NTSB adopted an Aircraft Accident Brief, NTSB-AAB-02-01, on 13 March 2002. The board found no relevant failure of any aircraft system. The board found that the aircraft movements during the accident sequence were the result of the relief first officer handling the controls:

The relief first officer was alone in the cockpit when he manually disconnected the autopilot and moved the throttle levers from cruise to idle.

The relief first officer's calm repetition of the monotone "I rely on God" phrase was not consistent with conduct expected from a pilot who encounters a hazardous flight condition. The board found that the actions of the relief first officer did not indicate an attempt to recover from the dive.

The board concluded that, when the captain returned to the cockpit, he initially *assumed* the relief first officer was trying to recover from a dive caused by some aircraft malfunction. The captain repeatedly shouted: "What's happening?" He desperately pulled back on his control column. The board found that the captain's actions and statements conclusively indicated a desire to (1) find out what had happened and (2) recover from the dive. The board found that the *Probable Cause* of this accident was:

the departure from normal cruise flight and subsequent impact with the Atlantic Ocean as a result of the relief first officer's flight control inputs. The reason for the relief first officer's actions was not determined.

Alaska Airlines Flight 261

McDonnell Douglas MD-83, registration N963AS
31 January 2000, in the Pacific Ocean near California
88 aboard, 88 killed

Overview: A McDonnell Douglas MD-83 left Mexico and headed north toward San Francisco, California. The horizontal stabilizer jammed in flight. Later the pitch trim jackscrew assembly failed. Without any pitch control the airliner dove into the Pacific Ocean and killed the 88 people on board.

The Flight: On the sunny afternoon of 31 January 2000, Alaska Airlines Flight 261 took off from Puerto Vallarta, Mexico. The 83 passengers, 2 pilots, and 3 flight attendants headed north toward Seattle, Washington. They had a planned intermediate stop in San Francisco, California, but they would never arrive.

The McDonnell Douglas MD-83, registration N963AS, traced its roots to the earlier Douglas DC-9 airliner which had entered service in 1965. The new McDonnell Douglas airplanes had been certified since 1980, and Alaska Airlines began flying them four years later. Powered by twin Pratt & Whitney turbofans, the airliner in use on this flight had been built in 1992 and was configured to carry 12 first class and 128 economy class passengers.

The captain, age 53, held an ATP certificate, and his logbook reflected 17,750 hours of flight time. His older first officer, age 57, also held an ATP certificate and had logged 8,140 hours.

Trouble Ahead: At 1349 Hours as the flight climbed through 23,000 feet at 331 knots, the horizontal stabilizer jammed in place. For laymen a basic MD-83 pitch control explanation follows:

*On the MD-83 the **horizontal stabilizer**, 40 feet long, is located atop the vertical fin in a T-tail configuration. The horizontal stabilizer is hinged near its trailing edge, allowing the leading edge to traverse up and down. The leading edge is connected* *to a jackscrew assembly consisting of an acme screw and nut, a torque tube, gearboxes, and trim motors. This pitch trim (also called longitudinal trim) system is designed to minimize pilot pitch control forces as the airplane transits various airspeeds and control surface configurations. The **elevator** is located on the trailing edge of the horizontal stabilizer. It is connected to the pilots' control columns via a mechanical linkage.*

After the jam the pilots continued the climb to cruising altitude at flight level 310 by using heavy back-pressure on their control columns. They could not get the horizontal stabilizer to budge. They tried every potential remedy they could think of and discussed the malady by radio with their maintenance experts. Nothing worked. The NTSB investigators would later confirm:

The pilots recognized that the longitudinal trim control system was jammed, but neither they nor Alaska Airlines maintenance personnel could determine the cause of the jam.

The captain decided to divert to Los Angeles. On the way there, trying to troubleshoot the problem, he disconnected the autopilot. The portion of the CVR and ATC transcript, below, begins as the autopilot is switched off. The first officer is flying the MD-83:

Capt: . . . . . Captain, Flight 261
FO: . . . . . . First Officer, Flight 261
Radio-: . . . . (prefix) Radio transmission, Flight 261
Center: . . . . Los Angeles Center (ARTCC)
AeroCom: . . Aero Commander "General Aviation" airplane
SkyWest: . . . SkyWest Airlines Flight 5154

Capt: This'll click [the autopilot] off. (1609:14)

[the Captain disconnects the autopilot]

*[the horizontal stabilizer suddenly un-jams and runs nose-down; the aircraft begins a **rapid descent**]*

Capt: Holy [expletive]! (1609:18)

Capt: You got it? -- [Expletive] me! (1609:21)

FO: What are you doin'? (1609:24)

Capt: I -- [the autopilot] clicked off. (1609:25)

Capt: [Our problem] got worse. (1609:26)

[sound of airframe vibration begins at 1609:30]

Capt: You're stalled. (1609:31)

Capt: No! No! Ya gotta release it, ya gotta release it! (1609:33)

Capt: Let's [unintelligible] speed brakes. (1609:42)

[the Captain takes over the flight controls]

Capt: Help me [pull] back! Help me [pull] back! (1609:52)

Radio-Capt: [Los Angeles] Center, Alaska two-six-one, we are -- in a dive here -- and I've lost control [of] vertical pitch. (1609:55)

[sound of overspeed warning begins at 1610:01 and continues for 33 seconds]

Center: Alaska two-sixty-one, say again, sir? (1610:05)

Radio-Capt: Yeah, we're out of twenty-six-thousand feet, we are in a vertical dive -- not a dive yet -- but -- uuuhhh -- we've lost vertical control of our airplane. (1610:06)

Capt: Just help me. Once we get the speed slowed, maybe we'll be OK. (1610:20)

Radio-Capt: We're at twenty-three-[thousand]-seven-hundred feet, request, uh -- yeah, we got it back under control here. (1610:28)

Radio-FO: No, we don't. (1610:34)

Center: [What is] the altitude you'd like to remain at? (1610:37)

FO: Let's take the speed brakes off, I'm --. (1610:45)

Capt: No, no, leave them there, it seems to be helping. (1610:46)

Capt: [Expletive] me! (1610:51)

Capt: OK, it really wants to pitch down. (1610:55)

[the pilots have pulled out of the dive by applying about 140 pounds of rearward force on their control columns; the elevator still works properly; the aircraft levels at 24,000 feet]

Capt: Don't mess with that. (1610:59)

FO: I agree with you. (1611:04)

Center: Alaska two-sixty-one, say your condition. (1611:04)

Radio-Capt: [Center, this is] two-sixty-one, we are at twenty-four-thousand feet, kinda stabilized -- we're slowing here and, uh, we're gonna do a little troubleshooting, can you gimme a block between, uuuhhh, twenty and twenty-five-[thousand feet]? (1611:06)

Center: Alaska two-sixty-one, maintain block altitude, flight level two-zero-zero through flight level two-five-zero. (1611:21)

Radio-Capt: [Center], Alaska two-sixty-one, we'll take that block, we'll be monitoring the freq. (1611:27)

FO: You have the airplane, let me just try [holding the control column back] . . . uh, how hard is it? (1611:31)

Capt: I don't know, my adrenalin's goin'. It was really tough there for a while. (1611:33)

FO: Yeah, it is, whatever we did is no good, don't do that again.

Capt: Yeah, it went down, it went full nose-down. (1611:44)

FO: Uh, it's a lot worse than it was? (1611:48)

Capt: Yeah, yeah, we're in much worse shape now. (1611:50)

[the pilots experiment with the flaps and slats; they contact their maintenance base again; they brief the Flight Attendants and the passengers; they slowly descend to 18,000 feet while holding heavy back-pressure on their control columns]

[6 minutes and 57 seconds pass]

Capt: What I'm -- what I wanna do is get the nose up -- and then let the nose fall through and see if we can stab it when it's unloaded. (1618:47)

FO: You mean -- use this again? I don't think we should -- if it can fly, it's like --. (1618:56)

Capt: It's on the stop now, it's on the stop. (1619:01)

FO: Well, not according to that, it's not -- the trim might be, and then it might be, uuuhhh, if something's popped [loose] back there.

Capt: Yeah. (1619:11)

FO: It might be [unintelligible] mechanical damage too. I think if it's controllable we oughta just try to land it. (1619:11)

Capt: You think so? OK, let's head for L.A. (1619:16)

[sound of "thumps" at 1619:21]

FO: You feel that? (1619:24)

Capt: Yeah. (1619:25)

Capt: OK, gimme si -- see, this is a bitch. (1619:29)

*[sound of an **extremely loud noise** at 1619:36]*

*[the acme screw torque tube has suffered a fatigue fracture and broken apart; the vertical stabilizer tip fairing brackets fail; the **aircraft pitches straight down**]*

[increase in background noise; sound of loose objects falling and banging around in the cockpit]

AeroCom: [Center, this is] five-zero-delta-xray, that plane *[Flight 261]* has just started to do a big huge plunge. (1619:39)

Center: A big huge plunge, ah, thank you. SkyWest fifty-one-fifty-four, the MD eighty-[three] is, ah, about two o'clock, about ten miles now, another pilot reports he's really looking pretty bad there ahead and to your right. Do you see him? (1619:43)

SkyWest: Yes sir. I concur. He -- I -- uuuhhh -- [he's] definitely in a nose-down, uuuhhh, position, descending quite rapidly.

FO: Mayday! *[spoken, but not transmitted on the radio]* (1619:43)

Capt: Push and roll! Push and roll! (1619:49)

Capt: OK, we are inverted! Now we gotta get it --! (1619:54)

Capt: Push! Push! Push! Push the blue side up! (1620:04)

Capt: Push! (1620:14)

FO: I'm pushing! (1620:14)

Capt: Let's kick rudder! Left rudder! Left rudder! (1620:16)

FO: I can't reach it! (1620:18)

Capt: OK, right rudder! Right rudder! (1620:20)

AeroCom: [Center], the plane's inverted, sir. (1620:20)

Capt: Are we flying? We're flying, we're flying! Tell 'em what we're doin'! (1620:25)

SkyWest: He's in sight, he [is] definitely out of control. (1620:29)

FO: Oh, yeah! Let me get [unintelligible]! (1620:33)

Capt: Gotta get it over *[meaning, right-side-up]* again -- at least upside-down we're flyin'! (1620:38)

SkyWest: He's inverted. (1620:39)

[sound of engine compressor stalls begins at 1620:49, followed by the sound of engines spooling down]

Capt: Speed brakes! (1620:54)

FO: Got it! (1620:55)

Capt: Aaahhh -- here we go! (1620:56)

[impact with the ocean; end of the CVR tape at 1620:57]

AeroCom: And, he just hit the water. (1620:59)

SkyWest: Ah, yes sir. He hit the water. He's down. (1621:03)

The Accident: During the final vertical plunge from 17,800 feet the aircraft rolled inverted. Because of structural failures in the empennage a recovery was not possible. No one survived the three-mile dive and impact with the ocean near Port Hueneme, California. The Ventura County Coroner would later rule that "blunt force impact trauma" instantly killed all 88 occupants of the ill-fated MD-83 airliner.

Recovery operations would continue through 15 March 2000. The NTSB used remotely operated undersea vehicles with side-scan sonar to search the ocean floor. In the late stages of the search the investigators utilized a commercial trawler to drag the seabed 700 feet below the surface. Eventually they recovered about 85 percent of the aircraft wreckage.

The Investigation: The FDR showed that the horizontal stabilizer had jammed as the aircraft climbed out from Puerto Vallarta. After the jam the pilots used the elevator alone to control pitch, continue the climb, and cruise north toward Los Angles.

The First Dive: Analysis would show that the acme screw and nut had remained jammed from climbout until the first dive at 1609:14 Hours. Investigators reconstructed that initial dive:

> The Safety Board concludes that the . . . initial dive from 31,000 feet began when the jam between the acme screw and nut was overcome [by] the primary trim motor. Release of the jam allowed the acme screw to pull up through the acme nut, causing the horizontal stabilizer leading edge to move upward, causing the airplane to pitch rapidly downward.

After diving from 31,000 feet to 24,000 feet the pilots recovered by applying 140 pounds of rearward force on their control columns. For almost 10 minutes thereafter the two pilots experimented with various slat and flap configurations. They briefed the three flight attendants and the passengers and made plans for an emergency landing in Los Angeles.

The Second Dive: The CVR recorded an "extremely loud noise" at 1619:36 Hours. Investigators determined that this noise was caused by the sudden structural failure of the torque tube:

> The Safety Board concludes that the cause of the final dive was the low-cycle fatigue fracture of the [acme screw] torque tube, followed by failure of the vertical stabilizer tip fairing brackets [which] caused an uncontrollable downward pitching of the airplane from which recovery was not possible.

Probable Cause: The NTSB adopted the Aircraft Accident Report for Flight 261, NTSB-AAR-02-01, on 30 December 2002 roughly two years after the accident. The NTSB analysts had examined the recovered jackscrew assembly and discovered that circular spirals of shredded metal clung like spaghetti to remnants of the screw threads. The NTSB determined:

> The excessive and accelerated wear of the jackscrew assembly acme nut threads was the result of insufficient lubrication. *[and also]* Approximately 90 percent of the thread thickness had worn away before the remainder of the threads sheared off.

There was *no* effective lubrication of the jackscrew assembly, and this caused the excessive wear. Alaska Airlines had extended the lubrication interval, and the FAA had approved the extension. The airline also had extended its "end-play" check interval, and the FAA had approved that extension too.

The board pointed out that a single jackscrew assembly driving a horizontal stabilizer does not provide necessary redundancy. The board stressed that single-point failure modes *must* be prohibited in all future aircraft designs.

The board noted that the "on-wing" end-play check procedure used by Alaska Airlines had low reliability. The board also found widespread deficiencies in the maintenance programs of Alaska Airlines, and the board pointed out that the FAA had not properly monitored the airline's maintenance operations for several years. The board found that the ***Probable Cause*** of this accident was:

> loss of airplane pitch control resulting from the in-flight failure of the horizontal stabilizer trim system jackscrew assembly's acme nut threads. The thread failure was caused by excessive wear resulting from Alaska Airlines' insufficient lubrication of the jackscrew assembly.

The board found several ***contributing*** factors:

> [First was the] Alaska Airlines' extended lubrication interval and the FAA approval of that extension . . . .

> [Second was] Alaska Airlines' extended end-play check interval and the FAA approval of that extension, which allowed excessive wear of the acme nut threads to progress to failure without the opportunity for detection.

> [Third was] the absence . . . of a fail-safe mechanism to prevent the catastrophic effects of total acme nut thread loss.

Emery Airlines Flight 17

Douglas DC-8, registration N8079U
16 February 2000, at Rancho Cordova, California
3 aboard, 3 killed

Overview: The Douglas DC-8 took off from Rancho Cordova, California, on a night cargo flight. A missing bolt caused a total loss of elevator pitch control. The aircraft crashed two minutes after takeoff and killed the three crewmembers aboard.

The Flight: The four-engine Douglas DC-8 had been certified in 1959. After hauling passengers worldwide for almost 40 years, most of the old workhorses had given way to a generation of more modern airliners. Yet, instead of getting put out to pasture, the majority of the reliable jet transports were converted into cargo haulers, commonly called "freighters."

The Emery Worldwide Airlines DC-8, registration N8079U, had been converted to a freighter in April 1993, and it had accumulated 84,447 hours of flying time. On the night of 16 February 2000 the aircraft, designated Emery Airlines Flight 17, was loaded with cargo at Sacramento Mather Airport in Rancho Cordova, California. Three crewmembers climbed aboard for the night flight to Dayton, Ohio. The 63,764 pounds of cargo and the 66,700 pounds of fuel brought the takeoff weight to 279,231 pounds. This relatively light load was well below the maximum takeoff weight. The flight engineer calculated the takeoff speeds: V-1, 126 knots; V-r, 146 knots; and V-2, 158 knots.

The captain, age 43, held an ATP certificate and had logged 13,329 hours of flight time, including over 2,128 hours as a DC-8 captain. The young first officer, age 35, held an ATP certificate and had logged 4,511 hours. The flight engineer also held an ATP certificate and had 9,775 hours of experience in his logbook.

The crew fired up the turbines at 1939 Hours and began taxiing out toward the runway. Because there was no control tower at the airport the first officer radioed Sacramento Departure Control. He reported that he was ready for takeoff and asked for the flight's IFR flight plan release. The controller responded: "You're released for departure, report airborne."

Trouble Ahead: Unknown to the pilots the mechanical health of the DC-8 was marred by a small, yet fatal, flaw. A crucial bolt had worked loose. The pilots would have no pitch control.

At 1948:15 Hours the engines began to spool up, and the DC-8 started rumbling down Runway 22L. The portion of the CVR transcript, below, begins as the engines go to full power. The first officer will be flying the aircraft:

Capt: . . . . . . Captain, Flight 17
FO: . . . . First Officer, Flight 17
FltEngr: . . . . Flight Engineer, Flight 17
GPWS: . . . . . Ground Proximity Warning System, Flight 17
Radio-: . . . . . (prefix) Radio transmission, Flight 17
DepControl: . . Sacramento Departure Control

FltEngr: Four [engines] spooled. (1948:24)

Capt: Airspeed's alive. (1948:44)

FO: [Airspeed's] alive here. (1948:44)

Capt: Eighty knots. (1948:50)

FO: Elevator checks. (1948:53)

[sound of a ratcheting noise and a "clunk" at 1948:55]

Capt: V-one. (1949:02)

Capt: Rotate. (1949:06)

[after rotation the aircraft continues to pitch up at a rate of 2 degrees per second, beginning at 1949:08]

[sound of stabilizer trim alert at 1949:09]

Capt: Watch the tail *[meaning, do not rotate so steeply]*. (1949:09)

Capt: V-two. (1949:13)

Capt: Positive rate [of climb]. (1949:14)

[the First Officer realizes the nose is pitching up too high]

FO: I got it. (1949:16)

Capt: You got it? (1949:17)

FO: Yep. (1949:17)

*[the nose still continues to pitch up; the First Officer realizes he has a **serious problem**]*

FO: We're going back [to the airport]. (1949:19)

FltEngr: What the [expletive]? (1949:20)

FO: CG's waaayyy out of limits! (1949:20)

FltEngr: Do you want to pull the power back? (1949:25)

[sound of decreasing engine rpm at 1949:27]

[sound of the stick-shaker at 1949:29]

FO: Oh, [expletive]! (1949:30)

Capt: Push forward! (1949:30)

Radio-Capt: Emery seventeen, emergency! (1949:36)

FO: Aaahhh, [expletive]! (1949:38)

DepControl: Emery seventeen, Sacramento Departure [Control], radar contact, say again? (1949:40)

FO: You steer, I'm pushing! (1949:40)

[the aircraft reaches a height of 1,037 feet, then descends]

Radio-Capt: Emery seventeen has an emergency! (1949:44)

FltEngr: We're sinking, we're going down, guys! (1949:44)

DepControl: Emery seventeen, go ahead. (1949:46)

[sound of increased engine rpm at 1949:46]

GPWS: Whoop whoop, pull up, whoop whoop, pull up, whoop whoop, pull up, whoop whoop . . . . (1949:47)

FO: Power! [Expletive]! (1949:47)

GPWS: *Whoop whoop, pull up, whoop whoop . . . . (1949:51)*

[the aircraft descends to 601 feet, then begins to climb again]

Capt: All right, all right . . . all right. (1949:52)

FO: Push! (1949:54)

FltEngr: OK, we're going back up -- there you go. (1949:54)

Capt: Roll out. (1949:58)

Radio-Capt: Emery seventeen, extreme CG problem. (1950:04)

DepControl: Emery seventeen, roger. (1950:06)

FltEngr: Anything I can do, guys? (1950:07)

Capt: Roll out to the right. (1950:11)

FO: OK . . . Push! (1950:12)

FO: Aaawww, [expletive]! (1950:18)

[the aircraft reaches a height of 1,087 feet, then descends again]

FltEngr: You got the [nose-down] trim maxed? (1950:26)

FO: Power! (1950:28)

FltEngr: More? (1950:28)

FO: Yeah. (1950:29)

GPWS: *Whoop whoop, pull up, whoop whoop . . . . (1950:29)*

FO: We're gonna have to land fast. (1950:32)

GPWS: *Whoop whoop, pull up, whoop whoop . . . . (1950:32)*

Capt: Left turn. (1950:36)

FO: OK, what I'm trying to do is make the airplane's position match the elevator, that's why I'm putting it in a bank. (1950:36)

Capt: All right. (1950:45)

FO: So we're gonna have to land it in, like, a turn. (1950:46)

[the aircraft continues a left turn back toward the airport]

Capt: Bring it around. *[meaning, continue the turn]* (1950:47)

    [sound of the stick-shaker at 1950:48]

Capt: Bring it around. (1950:49)

    [sound of human exertion at 1950:51]

FltEngr: [Expletive]! (1950:53)

FO: You [see] the airport? (1950:54)

Capt: Bring it around. (1950:56)

    [sound of a "snap" at 1950:56]

FO: Power! (1951:00)

GPWS: Whoop whoop, pull up, whoop whoop . . . . (1951:02)

FO: Power! Aaawww, [expletive]! (1951:07)

    [sound of initial impact at 1951:08]

    [final impact; end of the CVR tape at 1951:09]

The Accident: Left wing down, Emery 17 headed for the ground. With all four engines at high power settings, gear down, flaps at 15 degrees, the freighter could not regain level flight. The left wing clipped a masonry and steel column on a two story building. The aircraft then plowed into rows of cars in an automobile salvage yard and strewed wreckage along a path 1,500 feet long. The remains of the DC-8 and over 100 vehicles erupted into flame and smoke a mile east of the airport.

According to the coroner, the captain and flight engineer died as a result of traumatic injuries and also injuries sustained in the post-crash fire. The coroner discovered that the first officer survived the impact but succumbed to "thermal injuries and inhalation of combustion products."

The Investigation: The FDR would play a pivotal role in the NTSB investigation. The tape revealed that when the pilots moved the control column, the elevator did not move in response. The pilots had lost all pitch control, and investigators explained:

Examination of the . . . elevator control tab crank fitting lugs revealed evidence of repeated contact damage. *[and also]* The bolt . . . that normally secures the right elevator control tab pushrod to the tab crank fitting was missing.

Investigators reconstructed the takeoff of Flight 17. The loss of pitch control became obvious to the first officer soon after rotation speed when the nose of the DC-8 pitched up too far. The first officer pushed his control column forward, but the nose continued to pitch up, higher and higher. He added full nose-down trim, but the nose of the DC-8 still continued to rise.

Both pilots pushed their control columns forward in a desperate effort to lower the nose. They tried combinations of flight control inputs and engine power settings in an effort to bring the nose down. Despite their efforts the elevators remained in an extreme nose-up position, and recovery was not possible.

Probable Cause: Over three years after the loss of Flight 17 the NTSB adopted Aircraft Accident Report NTSB-AAR-03-02 on 5 August 2003. The board found that before the start of the takeoff roll the missing bolt "migrated" out of its fitting. This allowed the right elevator control tab crank fitting to disengage from its pushrod and shift to a trailing-edge-down position:

> As the airplane accelerated on its takeoff roll, the right elevator control tab crank fitting contacted the disconnected pushrod, restricting the control tab's further trailing-edge-up movement and leaving it in an extreme trailing-edge-down deflection.

The deflection caused the elevator surfaces to command an extreme nose-up pitch attitude. Despite desperate nose-down force on their control columns the pilots could not overcome the effects of the restricted right elevator control tab. The NTSB found that the *Probable Cause* of this accident was:

> a loss of pitch control resulting from the disconnection of the right elevator control tab. The disconnection was caused by the failure to properly secure and inspect the attachment bolt.

Air France Flight 4590

Aerospatiale/British Aerospace Concorde, registration F-BTSC
25 July 2000, at Paris, France
109 aboard, 109 killed (plus 4 killed on the ground)

Overview: In Paris, France, 109 people boarded the world's only supersonic airliner, the Aerospatiale/British Aerospace Concorde. They planned on a transatlantic trip to New York, but their flight would last only 1 minute and 10 seconds. After takeoff, trailing smoke and flames, the aircraft arced down toward the ground. All aboard perished in the fiery crash.

The Flight: Nothing was routine about the Aerospatiale/British Aerospace Concorde. Since the 1970s the sleek airliners had plied the airways between Europe and America. Passengers in the Concorde cabin endured tight and cramped conditions, but the needle-nosed flying machine had something no other passenger aircraft in the world could boast of, *supersonic speed*. For those who could ante up the money to go first class the Concorde, an engineering masterpiece, was the only way to fly.

On 25 July 2000 in the early afternoon, 100 passengers boarded their chartered Concorde at Charles de Gaulle Airport in Paris, France. The pilots aboard Air France Flight 4590 planned to outrace the sun across the Atlantic and deposit their human cargo at JFK International Airport in New York. The Concorde chosen for this flight, registration F-BTSC, had been in airline service since October 1979, over 20 years, and had amassed 11,989 hours of flying time. Despite her age, she and her sister Concordes were still the elite queens of the sky.

Flight 4590 carried nine crewmembers. The captain, age 50, held an ATP certificate and had logged 13,477 hours of flight time. His first officer, also age 50, had earned an ATP certificate and had 10,035 hours in his logbook. Their flight engineer, age 58, had documented 12,532 hours of experience in the air. In the cabin the five flight attendants would pamper the high-paying passengers under the supervision of a special "cabin services director."

For the flight to New York the Concorde had been loaded with 190,000 pounds of fuel. When the weight of the aircraft, fuel, the people aboard, and baggage were all taken into account they brought the gross takeoff weight to 375,200 pounds. Flight 4590 taxied out toward the runway shortly after 1437 Hours, and five minutes later the tower cleared the pilots onto Runway 26R. In aviation lingo the flight was in "position and hold."

Trouble Ahead: Concorde was ready to go. All of its systems would function perfectly, and the flight deck crew would make no errors. Yet, ironically, a mishap on a DC-10 that took off five minutes earlier would be a death sentence for the Concorde.

The takeoff bug airspeeds were calculated to be: V-1, 150 knots; V-r, 198 knots; and V-2, 220 knots. The captain will be flying the aircraft. The portion of the CVR transcript, below, begins as the tower clears the Concorde onto the runway:

Capt: . . . . Captain, Flight 4590
FO: . . . . . First Officer, Flight 4590
FltEngr: . . Flight Engineer, Flight 4590
GPWS: . . . Ground Proximity Warning System, Flight 4590
Radio-: . . . (prefix) Radio transmission, Flight 4590
Tower: . . . Charles de Gaulle Airport Control Tower

Tower: Four-five-nine-zero, line up on Runway twenty-six right.

Radio-FO: We line up and hold on [Runway] twenty-six right, [Air France] four-five-nine-zero. (1440:04)

Capt: Ready in the back? (1440:07)

FO: Let's go. (1440:10)

Capt: Prepare for takeoff -- pre-takeoff checklist. (1440:11)

Capt: How much fuel have we used? (1440:19)

FltEngr: We've got eight-hundred kilos there. (1440:23)

[almost 2 minutes pass; the pilots prepare for takeoff]

Tower: Air France four-five-nine-zero, Runway twenty-six right, wind zero-nine-zero [at] eight knots, cleared for takeoff. (1442:17)

Radio-FO: Four-five-nine-zero, takeoff [on] twenty-six right.

Capt: Is everybody ready? (1442:24)

FltEngr: Yes. (1442:26)

Capt: To one-hundred, V-one [is] one-hundred-fifty. (1442:26)

[all four engines go to full power; the takeoff roll begins]

FltEngr: We have four re-heats. (1442:43)

FO: One-hundred knots. (1442:54)

FltEngr: Four greens. *[meaning, four engine "go-lights"]* (1442:57)

FO: V-one. (1443:03)

*[While accelerating through 178 knots there is a **strange noise**, followed by a change in the background sound at 1443:10]*

[the No. 5 fuel tank has "blown out," causing a raging fuel-fire under the left wing; flames trail 275 feet behind the aircraft]

[at 1443:12 the "go-lights" for the No. 1 and No. 2 engines go out; those two engines lose thrust and the aircraft yaws left; still below V-r the Captain rotates the aircraft for takeoff]

FO: Watch out! (1443:13)

Tower: Concorde zero -- four-five-nine-zero, you have flames, you have flames behind you! (1443:13)

[the No. 1 engine temporarily increases thrust again, and its "go-light" temporarily comes back on at 1443:16]

Radio-FO: Roger. (1443:18)

FltEngr: Failure eng -- failure engine [number] two. (1443:20)

[at 205 knots the aircraft lifts off and climbs at 1443:21]

[sound of the fire alarm at 1443:22]

FltEngr: Shut down engine [number] two. (1443:24)

Capt: [Do the] engine fire procedure. (1443:25)

[airspeed drops to 200 knots at 1443:27]

FO: Watch the airspeed -- the airspeed -- the airspeed! (1443:27)

[sound of engine fire handle being pulled at 1443:29]

Capt: Gear on retract. (1443:30)

Tower: Four-five-nine-zero, you have strong flames behind you!

FltEngr: The [landing] gear! (1443:32)

[the smoke detector alarm activates at 1443:32]

Radio-FO: Yes, roger. (1443:34)

FltEngr: [Retract] the gear, Jean! (1443:34)

Tower: [Air France four-five-nine-zero,] do as you wish, you have priority for a return to the [airport]. (1443:37)

FltEngr: Gear! (1443:37)

Capt: Retract [the landing gear]! (1443:39)

[the fire alarm activates again at 1443:42]

[the Flight Engineer fires the fire extinguisher at 1443:44]

FltEngr: I'm firing it. (1443:45)

FO: I'm trying [to raise the landing gear]. (1443:45)

Capt: Are you shutting down engine two there? (1443:46)

FltEngr: I've shut it down. (1443:48)

FO: The airspeed! (1443:49)

[the No. 1 engine drops to flight idle -- two engines now have been lost]

FO: The gear isn't retracting! (1443:56)

[the fire alarm activates again, airspeed drops, and the aircraft begins to descend at 1443:58]

GPWS: Whoop whoop, pull up, whoop whoop . . . . (1443:59)

FO: The airspeed! (1444:00)

GPWS: Whoop whoop, pull up, whoop whoop . . . . (1444:02)

[at 1444:14 the First Officer urges the Captain to try to reach nearby Le Bourget Airport, ahead of them]

<u>FO</u>: Le Bourget! Le Bourget! (1444:14)

<u>Capt</u>: Too late! No time! (1444:16)

[angle-of-attack increases to 26 degrees; airspeed continues to drop; the left roll continues and can not be stopped]

<u>FO</u>: No! (1444:26)

[as the aircraft rolls left past 90 degrees, loose objects in the cockpit begin to slide and fall at 1444:27]

<u>Capt</u>: [Unintelligible]. (1444:29)

<u>Capt</u>: [Unintelligible]. (1444:30)

[sound of impact; end of the CVR tape at 1444:31]

The Accident: Full of fuel, with the two engines under the left wing inoperative, unable to maintain level flight, and with fire gnawing at the left wing, the Concorde arced down toward the ground. It crashed into a small hotel in the community of Gonesse just a few miles from the airport. On impact the hotel and the aircraft exploded in a gigantic fireball. So intense was the heat that man-made material in nearby buildings fused together.

Firefighting crews from Charles de Gaulle Airport (*aerodrome*, as the French call it) drove through crowded city streets toward the billowing column of jet-black smoke. However, the first firemen to arrive came from nearby Le Bourget Airport. Soon reinforced by firefighting crews from neighboring fire stations around Paris, the firemen brought the pyre under control after three hours. All 109 persons on the Concorde and another 4 persons on the ground perished in the crash and fire.

The Investigation: The day following the accident the Minister of Equipment, Transport, and Housing established a Commission of Inquiry. The French obtained assistance from experts in Germany, the United Kingdom, and the United States, and it did not take long for the investigative team to pinpoint the cause of the tragedy:

After V-1, the tyre on wheel No. 2 was cut by a metallic strip [that was lying] on the runway. The metallic strip came from the thrust reverser cowl door of engine [No.] 3 on a DC-10 that had taken off five minutes before the Concorde.

Records revealed that the metallic strip had been installed on the Douglas DC-10 in Houston, Texas, two weeks earlier. The DC-10 had begun its takeoff roll five minutes before the Concorde lined up for takeoff. During the takeoff roll the metallic strip had fallen off the Douglas airliner. Unnoticed by anyone this heavy strip of metal lay on the runway, right in the path of the Concorde.

Seven seconds after accelerating through the V-1 speed of 150 knots a tire on Concorde's left main landing gear struck the strip of metal. The tire blew out and exploded. Centrifugal force threw heavy pieces of the tire into the underside of the left wing. The tremendous impact caused a hydrodynamic pressure surge which ripped open the bottom of the No. 5 fuel tank.

Fuel gushed out and ignited. The No. 1 and No. 2 engines under the left wing began to fail due to ingestion of superheated gasses and debris from the fire. Concorde yawed hard to the left because of the asymmetric loss of thrust. Already beyond V-1, the captain applied right rudder and rotated for takeoff:

At 1443:21 [Hours the] takeoff was effective. The speed was 205 kt., the distance from the threshold was 2,900 meters, and the pitch attitude was +10 [degrees].

The pilots were obviously conscious of the lack of airspeed, for the captain had *slowly* rotated the nose, and the first officer made several "the airspeed" call-outs. Because of a fire alarm the pilots shut down the No. 2 engine. Then the No. 1 engine dropped back to flight idle. The Concorde had lost both engines on the left wing. Adding to their peril, the crew could not raise the landing gear and eliminate the associated drag:

Because of the incomplete opening of the left main landing gear doors, or the absence of detection of opening of these doors, the crew were unable to retract the landing gear.

Meanwhile the fuel-fed inferno was destroying the structural integrity of the left wing. Investigators found many pieces that had "burned off" of the wing and fallen along the flight path.

Concorde's highest airspeed had been 205 knots at takeoff, but thereafter the speed gradually dropped. Angle-of-attack slowly increased to an *unthinkable* 25 degrees. The aircraft began a roll to the left. The pilots could do nothing to stop the roll and nothing to gain altitude or airspeed. Investigators reported:

> Because of the lack of thrust and the impossibility of retracting the landing gear, the aircraft was in a flight configuration which made it impossible to climb or gain airspeed.

Probable Cause: The French government Bureau Enquetes-Accidents issued a voluminous report on the loss of Flight 4590. The board pointed out that no Concorde pilot was prepared to cope with failure of *two* engines on takeoff. Such an unlikely event had not been taken into account when the aircraft was certified, nor had it been covered during Air France pilot training. On 25 July the pilots suddenly found themselves in unknown territory: (1) they had lost two engines, (2) their airspeed had fallen far below the V-2 speed of 220 knots, (3) their landing gear would not retract, and (4) their aircraft was on fire. The analysts determined that recovery was not possible under these circumstances.

The board also reasoned that with only seconds to react "the crew had no way to grasp the overall reality of the situation." The board found the following *Probable Causes* of the accident:

> [First was the] high-speed passage of a tyre over a part *[the metal strip]* lost by an aircraft that had taken off five minutes earlier, and the destruction of the tyre.

> [Second], the ripping out of a large piece of [the fuel] tank [because of a] hydrodynamic pressure surge.

> [Third was] ignition of the leaking fuel . . . causing a very large fire under the aircraft's wing and severe loss of thrust on engine [number] 2, then engine [number] 1.

The board found that the "impossibility of raising the landing gear" *contributed* to the accident.

Gulf Air Flight 072

Airbus A-320, registration A40-EK
23 August 2000, in the Arabian Gulf near Muharraq, Bahrain
143 aboard, 143 killed

Overview: An Airbus A-320 twice attempted to land at Bahrain International Airport at night. After overshooting the runway on both approaches the Airbus flew into the dimensionless black void over the Arabian Gulf. The age-old aviation nemesis, spatial disorientation, took control. The captain dove the airliner into the sea, and none of the 143 people on board survived.

The Flight: Gulf Air Flight 072 took off from Cairo, Egypt, on a night flight to Bahrain International Airport at Muharraq in the Kingdom of Bahrain. Two pilots manned the flight deck and six flight attendants catered to the needs of the 135 passengers. The Airbus A-320, registration A40-EK, had been in service since 1994 and had amassed 17,370 hours in the air. Two CFM International turbofan engines powered the modern airliner:

> The A-320 employs a fly-by-wire flight control system. With this design all flight control surfaces are electrically controlled and hydraulically activated.

Gulf Air had hired the captain, age 37, as an engineer cadet. He progressed through the seniority ranks, and two months before this final flight Gulf Air promoted him to captain. Since this promotion he had logged 86 hours as a pilot-in-command. He passed his upgrade check-ride, although he got "D" ratings on two emergency procedures. His ATP certificate was issued by the Sultanate of Oman, and his logbook reflected 4,416 hours of fight time.

The young first officer, age 25, had been sponsored by Gulf Air during his initial training at Qatari Aeronautical College. Upon completion of that training he was hired by Gulf Air. He failed his initial proficiency check in the A-320 in 1999, getting "D" ratings in *seven* areas. Four months prior to the accident he had passed his initial line competency check. Captains who had flown with him described him as "timid, meek, mild, shy . . . ." Several felt that he was "too reserved to speak up or challenge a captain." The first officer had logged 608 flight hours. He held a Commercial Pilot certificate issued by the Sultanate of Oman.

Trouble Ahead: As the Airbus neared its destination in clear weather at night the captain planned for a simple VOR/DME non-precision approach to Runway 12. As it descended toward the runway the aircraft should have been configured to land: full flaps, gear down, target airspeed 136 knots. However, the Airbus was too high and far too fast, and its flaps were in position "one" instead of fully extended.

The captain was flying the Airbus. Just under a mile from the runway, 20 seconds from touchdown, he was still too fast to land. Standard operating procedure required him to climb straight ahead and execute a "missed approach." Instead, he tried to lose airspeed by making a steep 360 degree turn at low altitude. The portion of the CVR transcript, below, begins 1 minute and 21 seconds before the captain begins the turn:

<u>Capt</u>: . . . . . Captain, Flight 072
<u>FO</u>: . . . . . . First Officer, Flight 072
<u>PA</u>: . . . . . . Public Address system, Flight 072
<u>*GPWS*</u>: . . . . Ground Proximity Warning System, Flight 072
<u>Radio-</u>: . . . . (prefix) Radio transmission, Flight 072
<u>Tower</u>: . . . . Bahrain International Airport Control Tower

<u>Radio-FO</u>: Bahrain Tower, salam alaykom, Gulf Air zero-seven-two, eight [miles] DME established. (1926:04)

<u>Tower</u>: Gulf Air zero-seven-two, cleared to land, Runway one-two, wind zero-nine-zero [at] eight [knots]. (1926:08)

<u>Radio-FO</u>: [We are] cleared to land, Runway one-two, Gulf Air zero-seven-two. (1926:13)

<u>FO</u>: Speed checked, flaps [position] one. (1926:17)

<u>Capt</u>: [Put the landing] gear down. (1926:22)

[sound of landing gear extension at 1926:25]

FO: . . . checked, gear down. (1926:26)

Capt: OK, visual [contact] with airfield. (1926:37)

FO: Check -- gear down and flaps at [position] one. (1926:42)

Capt: Autopilot's coming off, flight director's off. (1926:47)

Capt: [We] have to be stabilized by five-hundred feet. (1926:51)

FO: Yes -- we're on [the VOR] radial. (1926:53)

PA: Ladies and gentlemen, the no smoking sign has now been illuminated. Please ensure that you carefully extinguish your cigarettes. No further smoking . . . . (1927:06)

[the Captain realizes that his airspeed is much too fast]

Capt: [Exclamation]! We're not gonna make it. (1927:08)

FO: Yeah. (1927:08)

Capt: Flaps two. (1927:09)

FO: Speed, check flaps [position] two. (1927:10)

Capt: We're not gonna make it. (1927:13)

Capt: Tell him [that we are going] to do a three-six-zero left.

[on short final approach, less than 1 mile from the runway, the Captain begins a low-level 360 degree turn at 1927:25]

Radio-FO: [Tower,] Gulf Air zero-seven-two, [we] request a three-six-zero [degree turn] to the left. (1927:25)

Tower: Approved, sir. (1927:29)

Radio-FO: [Turn] approved, Gulf Air zero-seven-two. (1927:31)

Capt: Flaps three. (1927:33)

FO: Speed checked, flaps three. (1927:34)

[sound of increasing engine rpm at 1927:38]

Capt: Flaps full. (1927:44)

FO: Speed check, flaps full -- flaps at full. (1927:45)

FO: And, seven-hundred [feet of altitude]. (1927:54)

Capt: Landing checklist. (1928:17)

FO: . . . landing checklist completed. (1928:28)

FO: Runway in sight -- three-hundred [feet]. (1928:47)

[the Captain completes only 270 degrees of the planned 360 degree turn; then he levels his wings and flies straight ahead]

Tower: Gulf Air zero-seven-two, cleared to land, Runway one-two.

Radio-FO: [We are] cleared to land, Runway one-two, Gulf Air zero-seven-two. (1928:52)

[the Airbus flies <u>perpendicular</u> to the runway and overflies the approach course, making a landing impossible]

Capt: We overshot [the runway]! (1928:57)

[sound of increasing engine rpm at 1928:59]

Capt: Tell [the tower we are] going around. (1929:07)

Radio-FO: Gulf Air zero-seven-two is going around. (1929:08)

[sound of increasing engine rpm at 1929:10]

Tower: I can see that, zero-seven-two. Sir -- uuuhhh -- would you like radar vectors for final again? (1929:11)

Capt: Go-around flaps. (1929:15)

FO: Go-around flaps set. (1929:17)

Radio-FO: We'd like radar vectors, Gulf Air zero-seven-two.

Capt: Gear up. (1929:22)

[sound of landing gear retracting at 1929:23; the Captain tries to circle over the Arabian Gulf and make yet another approach]

Tower: Roger -- uh -- fly heading three-hundred, climb [to] two-thousand-five-hundred feet, Gulf Air zero-seven-two. (1929:25)

Capt: Heading? (1929:33)

FO: Yes, three-hundred [degrees]. (1929:34)

[repetitive chime of overspeed warning at 1929:41]

FO: Speed, overspeed limit. (1929:42)

Tower: And contact Approach [Control on] one-two-seven-[point]-eight-five, sir. (1929:42)

*[at 1929:43 the Captain pushes his sidestick forward; the Airbus pitches nose-down and begins a **steep descent**]*

Capt: [Exclamation]! (1929:46)

Radio-FO: One-two-seven-[point]-eight-five. (1929:47)

FO: Speed check, flaps three. (1929:50)

GPWS: Sink rate, whoop whoop . . . . (1929:51)

Capt: Flaps up. (1929:52)

GPWS: Whoop whoop, pull up, whoop whoop, pull up, whoop whoop, pull up, whoop whoop . . . . (1929:52)

[the GPWS alert will continue until the end of the recording]

Capt: [Exclamation]! (1929:57)

FO: Gear's up, flaps --. (1929:58)

Capt: Flaps all the way [up]! (1929:59)

FO: Zero --. (1930:00)

GPWS: Whoop whoop, pull up, whoop whoop . . . . (1930:00)

[airspeed has increased to 282 knots]

[impact with the sea; end of the CVR tape at 1930:02]

The Accident: The tower controller watched the Airbus arc out over the Arabian Gulf. The turn looked very tight, tighter than anything he had seen before. He pointed to the aircraft and called out to his tower colleague: "Watch this!"

Accelerating out over the sea in the dark, the captain applied nose-down sidestick for 11 seconds. The aircraft pitched down. With the engines at full power the airspeed increased to 282 knots within seconds as the aircraft dove into the black void below. The

Airbus and its priceless human cargo flew into the sea, and the impact killed all 143 people on board.

The debris field was strewn three miles northeast of the airport in water about 10 feet deep. Salvage teams recovered almost every piece of the extremely fragmented aircraft. They took all human remains to the Forensic Science Laboratory at the Ministry of the Interior. Officially, 143 persons had been on the aircraft, but 144 severely battered bodies were recovered. Examination revealed that the extra body was that of a fetus "delivered" by the impact. Medical examiners specified "blunt force trauma" as the cause of death for each passenger and crewmember.

The Investigation: The day after the crash the High Supreme Council of the Government of Bahrain appointed an Accident Investigation Board. The investigation fell under the chairmanship of the Minister of Transportation.

Technical representatives from France, the United States, the Sultanate of Oman, and other countries assisted the board. The experts poured over the CVR and FDR tapes and reconstructed the flight. The FDR documented that the aircraft was much too fast during the first approach:

> Speed was 223 knots instead of [the required] 136 knots, the flap position was "one" instead of "full" . . . .

Standard procedure called for a "missed approach," a straight-ahead climb to 2,500 feet. Nonetheless, the captain tried to *salvage* the approach by losing airspeed in a low-level 360 degree turn. The captain hand-flew the aircraft. His altitude varied from 965 feet down to only 332 feet. Instead of completing the turn he rolled his wings level after turning 270 degrees. Consequently, instead of being aligned with the runway, the captain was flying perpendicular to it. Investigators surmised that perhaps the captain had mistaken the lights of the Shaikh Isa bridge and causeway for the runway lights.

For the *second time* the standard operating procedure called for a missed approach, but the captain began another low-level turn:

> There was no moon . . . in what is generally referred to in the aviation industry as a "dark night" condition. There were no

lights visible [to the pilots]. Thus, the horizon was unlikely to be distinguishable over the sea.

The pilots flew into a black dimensionless void over the Arabian Gulf. The attitude of the airliner could have been verified only by reliance upon the aircraft instruments. Yet, zipping along at low altitude over a surface he could not see, the captain attempted to *visually* fly the hazardous low-level turn at night:

The captain did not respond to either the initial GPWS "sink rate" alert or the subsequent "whoop whoop, pull up" warnings.

The FDR revealed that the captain applied nose-down control input and held it. The Airbus arced down toward the invisible sea below. The synthetic voice of the GPWS warned of the impending peril. Yet, instead of applying nose-up control input, the captain held the nose down and dove into the gulf.

Probable Cause: Twenty-three months after Gulf Air Flight 072 plunged into the sea the Accident Investigation Board adopted its report on 10 July 2002. The board found that the captain did not stabilize the Airbus during the first approach. He then attempted a (1) non-standard 360 degree turn (2) at night and (3) close to the ground with (4) gear down, (5) flaps down, and (6) with great variation in altitude, bank angle, and G force.

The board pointed out that the captain failed to line up with the runway for the second approach. He then attempted *another* low-level turn. The board noted that the captain -- inexplicably -- tried to fly *visually* during the turn at low altitude over the Arabian Gulf at night. The board explained the result of that course of action:

The aircraft was heading into an area of complete darkness conducive to the incidence of the somatogravic illusion. In this illusion, the absence of visual cues combined with rapid forward acceleration create a powerful pitch-up sensation.

The board reasoned that the captain was overwhelmed by spatial disorientation. He pushed the aircraft nose down to counter the *illusion* that the aircraft was pitching up. The captain did not use critical information provided by the aircraft instruments. Also, he did not consult his first officer in the decision-making process.

The board emphasized that in the final moments of the flight with the GPWS blaring in the cockpit, the crash could have been prevented. Under the circumstances, Gulf Air policy mandated that a first officer "assume the captain is incapacitated" and take control of the aircraft. The first officer failed to do this, and he never verbally warned or challenged the captain.

The board concluded that no single factor could be identified as the *Probable Cause* of this accident. The board found that the accident was the result of:

a fatal combination of many contributing factors, both at the individual and systematic levels.

The most crucial of these *contributing* factors are listed below:

[First], the captain did not adhere to a number of SOPs, such as: significantly higher than standard aircraft speeds during the descent and the first approach; not stabilizing the approach on the correct approach path; performing an orbit, a non-standard manoeuvre, close to the runway at low altitude; not performing the correct go-around procedure, etc.

[Second], in spite of a number of deviations from the standard flight parameters and profile, the first officer did not call them out or draw the captain's attention to them as required by SOPs.

[Third], it appears that the flight crew experienced spatial disorientation, [which] caused the captain to perceive (falsely) that the aircraft was pitching up. He responded by making a "nose-down" input . . . and flew into the shallow sea.

[Fourth], neither the captain nor the first officer perceived, or effectively responded to, the threat of increasing proximity to the [sea] in spite of repeated hard GPWS warnings.

[Fifth], a lack of training in [Cockpit Resource Management led to] the flight crew not performing as an effective team.

[Sixth], inadequacy in the airline's A-320 training programmes.

[Seventh], cases of non-compliance, and inadequate or slow responses in taking corrective actions to remedy them, on the part of the airline in some critical regulatory areas . . . .

The "9/11" Terrorist Attacks

*Because **four aircraft** were hijacked the **format** of this chapter will differ from that of other chapters.*

American Airlines Flight 11
Boeing 767, registration N334AA
11 September 2001, at the World Trade Center in New York
92 aboard, 92 killed (plus 2,621 killed on the ground)

United Airlines Flight 175
Boeing 767, registration N612UA
11 September 2001, at the World Trade Center in New York
65 aboard, 65 killed *(persons killed on the ground due to this crash at the World Trade Center are included, above)*

American Airlines Flight 77
Boeing 757, registration N644AA
11 September 2001, at The Pentagon in Washington, DC
64 aboard, 64 killed (plus 125 killed on the ground)

United Airlines Flight 93
Boeing 757, registration N591UA
11 September 2001, near Shanksville, Pennsylvania
44 aboard, 44 killed

Overview: Terrorists hijacked four airliners in the United States and took over the cockpits. They crashed two of the aircraft into the World Trade Center in New York. They crashed another into The Pentagon in Washington, DC. Passengers overwhelmed the terrorists on the fourth aircraft, and it plummeted to the ground near Shanksville, Pennsylvania. A total of 265 people were aboard the four airliners, and the crashes killed all of them. About 2,746 people on the ground also perished.

Quotations herein are excerpted from the report of the National Commission on Terrorist Attacks Upon the United States.

This project excludes the conduct and the results of criminal investigations by Law Enforcement agencies relative to the four hijacking incidents and subsequent homicidal attacks. This project is limited in scope to the aeronautical aspects of the four flights and the civil inquiry which followed.

Chronology: The time from the first takeoff until the last crash will span 2 hours and 4 minutes. All four airliners will be in flight *before* the first crash. This time-line will assist the reader:

<u>0759 Hours</u>: American Flight 11 takes off from Boston.
<u>0814 Hours</u>: United Flight 175 takes off from Boston.
<u>0820 Hours</u>: American Flight 77 takes off from Washington.
<u>0842 Hours</u>: United Flight 93 takes off from Newark.

The four airliners are now in the air. No one yet knows that they will become guided missiles.

<u>0846 Hours</u>: American Flight 11 hits the World Trade Center.
<u>0903 Hours</u>: United Flight 175 hits the World Trade Center.
<u>0937 Hours</u>: American Flight 77 hits The Pentagon.
<u>1003 Hours</u>: United Flight 93 crashes in rural Pennsylvania.

American Airlines Flight 11: The 11th day of September 2001 dawned warm and sunny along the eastern United States. It was ideal flying weather. Airport and airline operations geared up to accommodate the early morning increase in passenger flights.

American Airlines Flight 11 pushed back from the departure gate at Boston, Massachusetts. The Boeing 767, registration N334AA, carried a heavy load of fuel, for it was headed non-stop for Los Angeles, California. The twin-jet airliner carried a relatively light load of only 81 passengers. Nine flight attendants staffed the cabin, and two pilots manned the cockpit.

Flight 11 lifted off from the runway at 0759 Hours and began heading west under the guiding hand of ATC. Fifteen minutes later at 0814 Hours a controller at Boston Center cleared the pilots to climb to flight level 350. This clearance was never acknowledged. Most of what is known about the fate of Flight 11 would come via AT&T airphone calls from two Coach Class flight attendants.

At about 0814 Hours several male hijackers suddenly leaped up from their seats in First Class and stabbed two flight attendants. A passenger tried to assist the two wounded women, but the hijackers stabbed him too. Five hijackers commandeered the aircraft. They sprayed Mace or pepper spray to force all passengers and the seven uninjured flight attendants to the rear of the cabin.

Several hijackers "jammed their way" into the cockpit. Once inside they killed or incapacitated the two pilots. A flight attendant called American Airlines via an airphone and reported:

> The cockpit is not answering, [people are] stabbed in Business Class. . . . I think there's Mace, we can't breathe. . . . I don't know, I think we are getting hijacked.

At 0825 Hours one of the hijackers in the cockpit tried to speak to the passengers via the airliner's public address system. He obviously did not know how to use it. He keyed the radio, instead, and transmitted to Boston Center:

> We have some planes. Just stay quiet and you'll be OK. We are returning to the airport. Nobody move. Everything will be OK. . . . just stay quiet.

The hijackers turned south toward New York. One of the stabbed flight attendants lay on the floor, critically wounded, and was breathing emergency oxygen. One passenger's throat had been slashed. A flight attendant in the rear of the cabin kept American Airlines on the phone and explained events as they unfolded:

> We are flying low. We are flying very, very low. We are flying way too low. Oh, my God! We are way too low!

At 0846:40 Hours the telephone line went dead. At 430 knots Flight 11 slammed into the 93rd through 98th floors of the north tower of the World Trade Center in New York. The impact instantly killed the 92 people on board. Hundreds of people in the tower, plus hundreds more on the ground, perished in the crash, the ensuing fire, and the eventual collapse of the building.

United Airlines Flight 175: United Airlines Flight 175 left the gate at Boston at 0758 Hours. The big Boeing 767, registration N612UA, was scheduled for a non-stop flight to Los Angeles. The aircraft held an exceptionally slim load of only 56 passengers.

Seven flight attendants and two pilots constituted the crew. At 0814 Hours the airliner took off, and within 19 minutes it reached its planned cruising altitude at flight level 310.

Five hijackers struck sometime between 0842 and 0846 Hours. With the same tactics that were used on Flight 11 they brandished knives, sprayed Mace, and also claimed that they had a bomb. Information about the hijacking would come via telephone calls from passengers and flight attendants. On the phone, one of the flight attendants explained that hijackers had killed the two pilots, stabbed a flight attendant, and were "probably flying the plane."

At 0851 Hours the aircraft descended from its assigned altitude and turned south toward New York. Desperate radio queries from ATC were met with an eerie and awful silence. In a final phone call to his father at 0900 Hours a passenger related:

> It's getting bad, Dad. A stewardess was stabbed. . . . People are throwing up and getting sick. . . . I think we are going down. I think they plan to go to Chicago or someplace and fly into a building. Don't worry, Dad. If it happens it'll be very fast. My God! My God!

In the background a woman screamed, and then the telephone connection suddenly died. At 0903:11 Hours, left wing low at 485 knots, the airliner tore into the 78th through 84th floors of the south tower of the World Trade Center. The impact killed the 65 people on the airliner. Many hundreds of people in the building, plus many others on the ground, died in the crash and the inferno that followed, or in the subsequent collapse of the tower.

American Airlines Flight 77: Several hundred miles south of Boston and New York, American Airlines Flight 77 prepared to take off from Dulles International Airport near Washington, DC. The Boeing 757, registration N644AA, was bound non-stop for Los Angeles like the two previous flights. The aircraft clawed its way skyward at 0820 Hours. Two pilots, four flight attendants, and 58 passengers settled back for what each of them -- exclusive of five homicidal terrorists aboard -- assumed would be a routine trip. At 0851 Hours the pilots transmitted a message to ATC, and it proved to be the epitaph for Flight 77.

Sometime between 0851 and 0854 Hours the hijackers struck.

They used small knives, box-cutters, Mace, and the verbal threat of a bomb. They forced the passengers to the rear of the cabin and broke into the cockpit. No one knows what happened to the two pilots, for the passengers never heard from them again. Alerted by telephone calls from passengers and from ATC, American Airlines realized that another of its flights was in trouble:

At 0854 [Hours] the aircraft deviated from its assigned course, turning south. Two minutes later the transponder was turned off and even primary radar contact with the aircraft was lost.

Dulles Approach Control, west of the nation's capital, detected a primary target "tracking eastbound at a high rate of speed" at 0932 Hours. Within two minutes Reagan National Airport radar picked up an "unknown aircraft." It was streaking straight toward forbidden airspace over the White House in the heart of downtown Washington, DC. ATC alerted the Secret Service as the bogey bored in, only five miles away.

Aboard Flight 77 the hijacker-pilot veered away and made a slow 330 degree turn. At 0937 Hours he firewalled the throttles and dove the airliner into the western wall of The Pentagon at 460 knots. The impact and fire killed the 64 people on the aircraft plus 125 people in the United States military nerve center.

United Airlines Flight 93:   United Airlines Flight 93 took off from Newark, New Jersey, at 0842 Hours. The crew of two pilots and five flight attendants was not aware of the other hijackings. Their Boeing 757, registration N591UA, was scheduled for a flight to San Francisco, California. Fortunately for those who *could* have been aboard, most of the seats were empty. There were only 33 passengers and 7 crewmembers who intended to reach California. The remaining four, all hijackers, had other plans.

The first 46 minutes of the flight slipped by without incident. Information about the fate of Flight 93 would come via phone calls from 10 passengers and 2 flight attendants. Crucial information also would come from the CVR and FDR.

The hijacking began as the flight cruised over eastern Ohio at flight level 350. At 0928 Hours a controller at Cleveland Center heard a desperate "Mayday!" In the background he could hear the noise of a violent struggle, and then a pilot screamed: "Get out of here! Get out of here! Get out of here!"

The hijackers dragged one of the female flight attendants into the cockpit with them. The CVR recorded her tenacious fight with her assailants, who eventually killed her and the two pilots. At 0932 Hours the CVR captured the following message:

> Ladies and gentlemen, hear the captain. Please sit down. Keep remaining sitting. We have a bomb on board. So, sit!

From the rear of cabin, passengers used GTE airphones and cell phones to call friends on the ground. They explained that the hijackers wielded knives and wore red bandannas. Two people were sprawled on the forward cabin floor, both evidently dead. Another had been stabbed but was still conscious.

During the phone calls, friends on the ground told passengers about the two airliners that already had crashed into the World Trade Center. The passengers also learned that a third airliner had slammed into The Pentagon. The reality of their plight gradually dawned on them. They could remain passive and die, or they could try to fight back.

Although several people had been killed by the armed hijackers, many passengers stormed forward. Through the cockpit door the CVR recorded their desperate struggle to regain control of the airliner. Armed with their fists and raw courage, they attacked the hijackers in the forward cabin. After a long struggle they subdued or killed them. Then they began bashing down the locked and blockaded door to get into the cockpit.

The portion of the *reconstructed* CVR and ATC transcript, below, begins at 0957 Hours as passengers and flight attendants attack the armed hijackers in the cabin:

Hijack-Pilot-1: . . . . Hijacker-Pilot No. 1, Flight 93
Hijack-Pilot-2: . . . . Hijacker-Pilot No. 2, Flight 93
UnidHijack: . . . . . . Unidentified Hijacker, Flight 93
Pass-1: . . . . Passenger No. 1, Flight 93
Pass-2: . . . . Passenger No. 2, Flight 93
Center: . . . . Cleveland Center (ARTCC)

*[sound of a **violent struggle** and the sound of many shouts and screams beginning at 0957]*

[the hijacker-pilot rolls the aircraft left and right, then pitches it up and down, trying to throw the passengers off balance]

[a hijacker in the cockpit screams to another hijacker for help in blockading the locked cockpit door at 0958:57]

[the attack continues; sound of screams, shouts, loud thumps, loud crashes, and breaking glass at 0959:52]*

Hijack-Pilot-1: Is that it? Shall we finish it off? (1000:08)

Hijack-Pilot-2: No, not yet! When they all come [into the cockpit] we finish it off. (1000:12)

*[sound of **loud crashes and blows** against the cockpit door]*

Pass-1: [Get] in the cockpit! If we don't, we'll die! (1000:26)

Pass-2: Roll it! (1000:42)

Hijack-Pilot-1: Allah is the greatest! Allah is the greatest! Is that it? I mean, shall we put [the airliner] down? (1001:00)

Hijack-Pilot-2: Yes, put it -- put it down!

UnidHijack: Put it down! Put it down! (1002:23)

[the hijacker-pilot turns the control column hard to the right; the aircraft rolls right, then rolls inverted]

UnidHijack: Allah is the greatest! Allah is the greatest!

*[passengers break into the cockpit; sound of shouts, screams, and a **continuing violent struggle**]*

[the airliner impacts the ground at 1003:05]

Center: United ninety-three, do you still hear Cleveland?

Center: United niner-three, do you hear Cleveland?

Center: United ninety-three, do you hear Cleveland Center?

[there is no response]

At 503 knots the aircraft plunged to earth in a rural farm field near Shanksville, Pennsylvania, only 20 minutes flying time from Washington, DC. The impact instantly killed all 44 people on board. The commission would later note:

> The nation owes a debt to the passengers of United [Flight] 93. Their actions saved the lives of countless others.

Intelligence would later confirm that the hijackers had targeted either the White House or the U.S. Capitol building. The unarmed passengers and flight attendants had thwarted that plan.

How the Hijackers Boarded the Planes: Nineteen uneducated and neer-do-well men had, in baseball lingo, *batted a thousand.* They went 19 for 19. Without serious challenge each of them had foiled all airport screening measures that the American commercial aviation industry had in place to prevent hijackings:

> 19 men armed with knives, box-cutters, Mace, and pepper spray penetrated the defenses of the most powerful nation in the world.

Each of the targeted airliners had been loaded with up to 11,400 gallons of flammable jet fuel. The hijackers converted the four airliners into huge guided missiles. They managed to get aboard the four flights in the following manner:

American Airlines Flight 11: In Boston around 0740 Hours, five hijackers approached security checkpoints operated by Globe Security. Each of the men passed through a walk-through metal detector calibrated to detect items with at least the metal content of a .22 caliber pistol. An x-ray machine screened their carry-on bags. Also each man was subjected to a Computer Assisted Passenger Pre-screening System (CAPPS).

None of the men triggered the metal detector and nothing in their carry-on baggage set off an alarm. However, the CAPPS flagged all five men as "suspicious." The only consequence of the CAPPS alert was that their checked baggage would be held until after they boarded. All five hijackers walked down the ramp and into the Boeing 767 without further incident.

United Airlines Flight 175: In another terminal in the same airport at Boston, five hijackers checked-in for United Airlines Flight 175. Two of them had trouble understanding the routine security questions. Yet, after the agent repeated the questions slowly the two men gave *acceptable* responses.

None of the five men were flagged by CAPPS. They passed through the security screening checkpoint operated by Huntleigh USA. Neither they nor their carry-on bags triggered an alarm. With whatever weapons they had in their carry-on baggage or on their persons, they boarded the plane around 0725 Hours.

American Airlines Flight 77: At Dulles International Airport near Washington, DC, five hijackers checked-in for American Airlines Flight 77. CAPPS flagged three of them. The other two were selected for extra scrutiny because one spoke no English and had no photo identification, and both acted in a "suspicious" manner. Thus, the checked baggage of all five men would be held until after they boarded the aircraft.

The five men approached the security checkpoint operated by Argenbright Security. The checkpoint had video cameras that recorded each passenger as he was screened. Three of the men set off the alarm at the first x-ray checkpoint. Two of them set off the alarm when they were x-rayed a *second* time. A security officer used a metal-detecting wand to check their arms, torsos, and legs. They passed this inspection, and the five men then walked aboard the aircraft.

United Airlines Flight 93: The four hijackers checked-in at the ticket counter for United Airlines Flight 93 in Newark. Two of them checked baggage, and CAPPS flagged one of these men for more scrutiny. His bag got screened for explosives, and then handlers loaded it into the aircraft.

The four men walked through the Argenbright Security checkpoint. Without a video recording there is no evidence of what alarms might have been triggered or what security checks might have been performed. The men boarded between 0739 and 0748 Hours. Each of them had reserved seats in the First Class cabin, right behind the cockpit.

The Role of the FAA: The FAA is responsible for the safety of civil aviation in the United States. FAA air traffic controllers work at major airports and at 22 Air Route Traffic Control Centers, commonly called "Centers." Each Center is linked to a central location in Herndon, Virginia, but Centers often get information and make decisions independently of each other. On 11 September the four hijacked airliners were monitored by separate Centers in Boston, New York, Cleveland, and Indianapolis. Thus, each Center had only *part* of the knowledge of overall events:

> No one at the FAA or the airlines that day had ever dealt with multiple hijackings. Such a plot had not been carried out anywhere in the world in more than 30 years.

The FAA had adopted the premise that the best way to deal with a hijacking is to prevent it from happening. Screening and other security measures at airports were designed to stop potential hijackers from boarding airliners. However, if a hijacker foiled the security measures, got aboard, and commandeered an airliner the FAA assumed that the hijacking would be traditional. In the past, hijackers had threatened an act of violence and had told the pilots to fly to a specified airport. En route or at the destination the hijackers made demands, usually political in nature. Negotiations had taken many hours, and often several days. There had been plenty of *time* to formulate a plan to deal with the hijackers and prevent loss of innocent life. Unfortunately the hijackings on 11 September were totally different.

The Role of NORAD: The military binational North American Aerospace Defense (NORAD) command had been set up by Canada and the United States in 1958. NORAD's purpose was to defend the airspace over the continent from any air attack. At the outset the primary threat was the Soviet Union's intercontinental ballistic missiles (ICBMs) and bombers. In recent years the threat expanded to include cruise missiles. In the 1990s NORAD realized that rogue states or terrorists might use airliners to strike North America with chemical, biological, or nuclear weapons:

> NORAD . . . occasionally considered the danger of hijacked aircraft being guided to American targets, but only aircraft that were coming from *overseas [emphasis added]*.

NORAD could identify and track inbound bombers, cruise missiles, or hijacked airliners. It could scramble jet fighters to intercept and shoot down any threat before it reached America's shores. However, little thought had been given to threats that might originate *within* North America.

FAA and NORAD Hijacking Coordination: The FAA and NORAD had worked out a protocol for dealing with a *traditional* domestic hijacking. Pilots on a hijacked airliner would squawk Code 7500 and notify ATC verbally by radio. ATC would inform FAA headquarters in Washington, and a "hijack coordinator" would contact The Pentagon. The FAA would request that a fighter plane shadow the hijacked flight. The request would be approved, and The Pentagon would notify NORAD.

With assistance from ATC, NORAD would locate the hijacked aircraft and scramble fighters. Controllers would vector the fighter pilots to a location several miles behind the airliner. There, out of sight of the hijackers, the military pilots would follow the airliner, verify its identity, and report its direction and progress.

On 11 September the FAA and NORAD found that they faced an unexpected threat from within, a threat that evolved minute by minute. Forced into a totally reactive mode, they had no way to anticipate the intentions or destinations of the hijackers. They had little time in which to act. Defense of North American airspace was improvised by people who had (1) never dealt with a hijacked airliner, (2) never anticipated that such an airliner would cut off communication with ATC, and (3) never dreamed that the airliner itself would be used as a lethal guided missile:

> Existing protocols on 9/11 were unsuited in every respect for an attack in which hijacked planes were used as weapons.

The FAA and NORAD struggled to comprehend the unfolding chaos. On the basis of what they knew, they did the best that they could. Unfortunately, on that Tuesday morning it was not enough.

The President of the United States: In Sarasota, Florida, the President of the United States had been sitting in a classroom at the Emma Booker Elementary School. Earlier an advisor had told the presidential party that a "small twin-engine plane" had struck the World Trade Center. Everyone assumed it was an accident, but at 0905 Hours another advisor whispered to the President:

> A second plane hit the second tower. America is under attack.

Until that time no one in the President's entourage had known that commercial airliners had been hijacked. During a rapid ride to the airport the President learned of the attack on The Pentagon. In a call to the Vice-President he explained: "We're at war, [and] somebody's going to pay!"

To Shoot -- Or Not to Shoot? Shooting down an airliner full of innocent passengers had been almost unthinkable. How would the NORAD pilots identify the proper aircraft from among the hundreds of airliners plying the skies? Who would give the nightmarish and fateful order to fire?

> Prior to 9/11 it was understood that an order to shoot down a commercial aircraft would have to be issued by the National Command Authority, a phrase used [by the Armed Forces] to describe the President and Secretary of Defense.

At 0837 Hours on 11 September, nine minutes before the first aircraft struck the World Trade Center north tower, Boston Center ignored the red tape and called directly to NORAD:

> Boston Center: We have a problem here. We have a hijacked aircraft headed towards New York, and we need . . . someone to scramble some F-16s or something up there. Help us out.
>
> NORAD: Is this real world, or [an] exercise?
>
> Boston Center: No, this is not an exercise, not a test.

That morning, with the Cold War a dim memory, the NORAD eastern air defense sector had only two alert sites, (1) Otis Air National Guard Base in Massachusetts and (2) Langley Air Force Base in Virginia. Each site had two armed jet fighters on alert.

NORAD scrambled the Otis fighters. They took off at 0853 Hours, but by that time the first airliner had already hit the World Trade Center. NORAD did not know that. It also did not know that three more airliners already had been hijacked. It vectored its fighters to military-controlled airspace east of New York. The fighters were told to hold there and await instructions.

After the second airliner hit the World Trade Center at 0903 Hours, NORAD dispatched the fighters to airspace over Manhattan. They arrived at 0925 Hours and set up a CAP. They had *not* been authorized to shoot down an airliner. And, although they did not then know it, there would be no more attacks on New York.

ATC alerted NORAD after learning that the third airliner was streaking toward Washington, and NORAD scrambled the Langley fighters. They took off at 0930 Hours and headed north. Like the Otis fighters, the Langley fighters had not been authorized to fire on a civilian airliner. When the third airliner hit The Pentagon seven minutes later the fighters were 150 miles away.

Earlier, when the third airliner *first* had been detected heading toward Washington, the Vice President was in the White House. The Secret Service, responsible for presidential protection, hustled him down toward the underground bunker. He entered at 0936 Hours, one minute before the third airliner hit The Pentagon:

> The Vice-President . . . called the President to discuss the rules of engagement for the CAP. . . . It did no good to establish the CAP unless the pilots . . . were authorized to shoot if the plane would not divert. The President emphasized . . . that he had authorized the shootdown of [such] hijacked aircraft.

At 1002 Hours the Secret Service agents in the bunker told the Vice-President that an unidentified aircraft was screaming toward the White House at high speed. The Vice-President reaffirmed the shoot-down order. Yet, somehow in the chaos and confusion and the *fog of war* that authorization did not get passed on to NORAD or the CAP pilots over Washington and New York:

> A shootdown authorization was not communicated to the NORAD air defense sector until 28 minutes after United [Flight] 93 had crashed in Pennsylvania. . . . and once the shootdown order was given [to NORAD] it was not communicated to the pilots. . . . The only orders actually conveyed to the pilots were to "ID type and tail."

NORAD was not told that a fourth aircraft (United Flight 93) had been hijacked until *after* it crashed in Pennsylvania. When NORAD first learned of that hijacking the FAA said the aircraft was heading toward Washington. A few moments later NORAD recontacted the FAA to get an update on this latest threat:

> <u>NORAD</u>: [About] United [Flight] ninety-three, have you got

[an updated location] yet?

FAA: Yeah, he's down.

NORAD: He's down? When did he land?

FAA: He did not land.

NORAD: Oh, he's down? Down?

FAA: Yes, somewhere up northeast of Camp David.

As late as 1010 Hours the CAP fighter pilots again had been cautioned: "Negative clearance to shoot." The shoot-down order did not reach NORAD until 28 minutes after the last of the four hijacked airliners had crashed.

Who Are the Terrorists? The terrorists are extremists who have been left out and rejected by the mainstream of society. The commission found that they are motivated by a pseudo-religious ideology based upon hate and fear. Their leaders despise the progressive cultures in the modern Western World, and with respect to the United States their mantra is simple:

It is God's decree that each [terrorist] should try his utmost to kill any American, military or civilian, anywhere in the world.

Terrorist organizers exploit the political turmoil and cultural changes sweeping though parts of the Middle East and the Third World. With a message of violence and death, they prey upon men who have been (1) unable to adapt to modern methods and modern thinking, those who (2) mentally cling to the past. Such a terrorist "candidate" rejects evolving cultural and social mores. He is not able to cope with any type of change. He fears both progress and change, and he hates those who advocate it. He desperately tries to live in the past, and he is unable to *fit in* with modern society. He tries to hide his social failures by berating progressive people, the "enemies" of his way of life.

[Terrorist organizers] appeal to people disoriented by cyclonic change as they confront modernity and globalization.

Left behind culturally and socially, these frustrated men become fodder for terrorist organizers. The terrorist leaders promise these men the opportunity to become martyrs in a holy war against the non-believers and oppressors. Leaders use illusionary religious rhetoric to whip these men into an emotional frenzy. They are soon eager to die in a war against their perceived enemies, for their leaders have assured them of great happiness in an afterlife.

Probable Cause: The bipartisan National Commission on Terrorist Attacks Upon the United States (commonly known as "The 9/11 Commission") issued an exhaustive report on 22 July 2004, almost three years after the hijackings and crashes. With the benefit of hindsight the commission found that the United States had failed to comprehend the scope of the international terrorism threat:

> On that September day we were unprepared. We did not grasp the magnitude of a threat that had been gathering over time.

The homicidal attacks should not have come as a surprise. In the prophetic words of the Director of the Central Intelligence Agency (CIA): "The system was blinking red."

The 11 September 2001 attack on the World Trade Center was not the first. Eight years earlier in 1993, terrorists had detonated a huge truck bomb in a parking garage under one of the towers. That attack was designed to topple the building. It failed to do so, but it killed six people and injured over 1,000 others. The same group of terrorists had planned to blow up the Lincoln and Holland tunnels in New York. Law enforcement officers ferreted out that plot in the nick of time and arrested the would-be bombers.

In 1995, law enforcement agents foiled a terrorist plot to blow up 12 American airliners in flight. Thwarted only for the moment, the terrorists succeeded months later in a less grandiose attack in Saudi Arabia, killing 5 Americans. They had better luck the next year in the same country when their bomb killed 19 Americans and injured several hundreds more. The attacks would continue, and they would become more deadly:

> In August 1998 [the terrorists] carried out near-simultaneous truck bomb attacks on the U.S. embassies in Nairobi, Kenya, and Dar es Salaam, Tanzania. The attacks killed 224 people.

The next year, 1999, law enforcement agents squelched a plot to bomb overseas hotels frequented by Americans. Closer to home,

U.S. Customs officers arrested a terrorist as he tried to smuggle explosives from Canada into the United States for an attack on the Los Angeles International Airport. In a harbor in Yemen in the year 2000 the terrorists took a bold new step. They attacked a United States warship, the *USS Cole*. The bombing killed 17 U.S. Navy sailors and injured dozens more.

When investigating the attacks of 11 September, commissioners were startled to discover that the original plan had been far more grandiose. The original scheme had called for:

> ten aircraft to be hijacked, which would crash into targets on both coasts [including the] CIA and FBI headquarters, nuclear power plants, and the tallest buildings in California . . . .

Terrorists later limited the plan to only four aircraft because of logistic concerns. In regard to the total success of those attacks the commission found a number of *Causes*, including:

To date, diplomatic efforts had failed to thwart terrorism.

The American Armed Forces did not have viable options for preemptive attacks on known terrorist sanctuaries overseas.

America's homeland defense posture faced *outward* and was not designed to counter threats from within.

The Department of Defense had not been postured to effectively counter terrorism.

The military response had not been effective. Fighter aircraft had been scrambled, but the pilots did not know where to go, what to intercept, and were not authorized to shoot if necessary.

The intelligence and law enforcement agencies had not shared information effectively.

Border, immigration, and aviation security agencies had not been integrated into a unified anti-terrorism effort.

The CIA had only a minimal ability to conduct paramilitary operations overseas.

FBI investigations focused primarily on after-the-fact events.

Airport security screening measures were woefully inadequate.

Airliner cockpit doors had not been adequately "hardened."

Collectively, the hijackers who struck on 11 September:

-- Included known men who should have been watchlisted.

-- Used fraudulently manipulated passports.

-- Made false statements on visa applications.

-- Made false statements to border and customs officials.

-- Violated immigration laws once inside the United States.

Postscript: The commission pointed out that terrorism and the threat it poses to the United States will continue as long as (1) political turmoil, (2) resistance to change, (3) hopelessness, and (4) economic malaise exist in under-developed regions of the world. With their now-endless supply of willing recruits, terrorist leaders "seek creative methods to kill Americans in limitless numbers, including the use of chemical, biological, and nuclear weapons." The commission bluntly warned citizens of the United States:

The American people must be prepared for a long and difficult struggle. We face a determined enemy who sees this as a war of attrition, indeed, as an epochal struggle. We expect further attacks. Against such an enemy there can be no complacency.

The commission unanimously concluded that attacks "against ever more ambitious targets" in the United States can be expected. The commissioners pointed out:

An attack of even greater magnitude is now possible -- and even probable. We do not have the luxury of time.

American Airlines Flight 587

Airbus Industrie A-300, registration N14053
12 November 2001, at Belle Harbor, New York
260 aboard, 260 killed (plus 5 killed on the ground)

Overview: Shortly after takeoff an Airbus Industrie A-300 flew into a powerful wingtip vortex. When the pilot applied hard rudder inputs the entire vertical stabilizer broke off of the fuselage. The Airbus crashed into a residential area of Belle Harbor, New York. The near-vertical impact killed all 260 people on board.

The Flight: American Airlines Flight 587 pushed back from the gate at JFK International Airport in New York at 0859 Hours on 12 November 2001. The 251 passengers, 7 flight attendants, and 2 pilots were bound for Santo Domingo in the Dominican Republic. As the airliner taxied toward the runway the pilots ran through their checklists and the flight attendants prepared for takeoff. No one knew that the flight would last only 1 minute and 53 seconds.

The many parts of the airliner had been manufactured at various locations in Europe. Airbus Industrie, a consortium of European aerospace companies, assembled the A-300 at its plant in Toulouse, France, and the airliner received its certification in that country. It was certified in the United States under a bilateral airworthiness agreement between the governments of the United States and France. The new A-300, registration N14053, was delivered to American Airlines in 1988. By the time of this final flight it had accumulated 37,550 flying hours.

The Airbus grossed 349,370 pounds as it neared the runway. The captain, age 42, was a former U.S. Air Force pilot. He had logged 8,050 flight hours, including 1,723 hours as an Airbus pilot-in-command. The young first officer, age 34, had logged 4,403 hours of flying time.

Trouble Ahead: Kennedy Tower cleared the airliner to taxi into takeoff position on Runway 31L and hold there. A big Boeing 747 was on its takeoff roll on the same runway ahead of them. ATC would delay the Airbus takeoff so that the big twin-jet would have the proper separation interval behind the heavier Boeing airliner.

The portion of the CVR and ATC transcript, below, begins as Flight 587 gets takeoff clearance from the tower. The first officer will be flying the aircraft:

<u>Capt</u>: . . . . Captain, Flight 587
<u>FO</u>: . . . . First Officer, Flight 587
<u>Radio-</u>: . . . . (prefix) Radio transmission, Flight 587
<u>Tower</u>: . . . . John F. Kennedy Airport Control Tower
<u>DepControl</u>: . . . . New York Departure Control
<u>Delta 79</u>: . . . . . . Delta Airlines Flight 79
<u>UnidSource</u>: . . . . Transmission from unidentified source

<u>Tower</u>: American five-eighty-seven heavy, wind three-zero-zero at niner, Runway three-one left, cleared for takeoff. (0913:27)

<u>Radio-Capt</u>: Cleared for takeoff, [this is] American five-eight-seven heavy. (0913:31)

<u>FO</u>: Are you happy with that [separation] distance? (0913:35)

<u>Capt</u>: We'll be all right once we get rollin'. He's supposed to be five miles [ahead] by the time we're airborne. (0913:38)

<u>FO</u>: So, you're happy. Lights? (0913:45)

<u>Capt</u>: Yeah, lights are on. (0913:47)

<u>FO</u>: Takeoff checks are complete, I'm on the roll. (0913:47)

[sound of engines spooling up at 0913:54]

<u>FO</u>: You got [the] throttles. (0914:03)

<u>Capt</u>: Eighty knots, thrust blue. (0914:08)

<u>Capt</u>: V-one. (0914:23)

<u>Capt</u>: Rotate, V-two. (0914:24)

<u>Capt</u>: V-two plus ten. (0914:25)

<u>FO</u>: Positive rate [of climb], gear up, please. (0914:30)

<u>Capt</u>: Gear up. (0914:31)

Tower: American five-eight-seven heavy, turn left, fly the Bridge Climb, contact New York Departure [Control]. (0914:42)

Radio-Capt: American five-eighty-seven heavy, so long. (0914:48)

FO: Check speed . . . flaps up, climb power. (0914:52)

Radio-Capt: New York, American five-eighty-seven heavy [is at] thirteen-hundred feet, we're climbing to five-thousand. (0915:00)

DepControl: American five-eight-seven, New York Departure, radar contact, climb [and] maintain one-three-thousand. (0915:04)

FO: . . . slats retract. (0915:14)

Capt: Clean machine. (0915:28)

DepControl: American five-eighty-seven heavy, turn left, proceed direct [to] Wavy [Intersection]. (0915:36)

*[the airliner flies into a **wingtip vortex** at 0915:36]*

Radio-Capt: We'll turn direct [to] Wavy, American five-eighty-seven heavy. (0915:41)

Capt: [We are in a] little wake turbulence, huh? (0915:44)

FO: Yeah -- [airspeed] two-fifty, thank you. (0915:45)

*[the aircraft again flies into a **wingtip vortex** at 0915:51; the First Officer responds with large aileron and rudder inputs and addresses the Captain in a strained voice]*

FO: Max power! (0915:54)

Capt: You all right? (0915:55)

FO: Yeah, I'm fine. (0915:55)

Capt: Hang on to it. Hang on to it. (0915:56)

[sound of a "snap" at 0915:56]

FO: Let's go for power, please. (0915:57)

[sound of a "loud thump" at 0915:57]

*[sound of a "loud bang" at 0915:58; at 251 knots the **vertical stabilizer and rudder tear off of the aircraft**, causing the Airbus*

to sideslip and yaw out of control]

FO: Holy [expletive]! (0916:01)

[sound of stall warning chime at 0916:04]

[the pilots do not know why the airliner is out of control; they assume that the wingtip vortex is causing the problem]

FO: What the hell are we into? We're stuck in it! (0916:07)

Capt: Get out of it! Get out of it! (0916:12)

[end of the CVR tape at 0916:15]

[the aircraft impacts the ground at about 0916:18]

UnidSource: Tower, look to the south, an aircraft's crashing! An aircraft just crashed to the south of the field! (0916:19)

Tower: An aircraft just crashed south of the field? (0916:21)

UnidSource: Affirm, a fireball. (0916:24)

Tower: OK, thank you, sir, . . . we're trying to figure it out now, sir, we're trying to see if we are missing any aircraft. (0916:31)

[53 seconds pass]

Delta 79: . . . it was a heavy jet. (0917:24)

Tower: It was a heavy jet, sir? (0917:27)

Delta 79: Yeah, it looked like it. (0917:28)

The Accident: Gear up, flaps and slats retracted, the Airbus had been climbing through 2,300 feet. For the second time it flew into a wingtip vortex (sometimes called "wake turbulence") from the Boeing 747 that took off ahead of it. The first officer was already in a 23 degree left bank and turning toward Wavy Intersection. The swirling vortex airflow rolled the aircraft farther to the left.

The first officer countered the rolling motion by turning the control column to the right and applying hard right rudder. He made a series of cyclic corrections: right, then left, then right, then left again. Suddenly the entire vertical stabilizer, including the rudder, ripped off of the fuselage.

Without the vertical stabilizer there was no way to control the yaw and sideslip of the airliner. Out of control, it tumbled down into a residential neighborhood in Belle Harbor, New York, four miles from the airport. The engines tore away prior to impact and landed nearby. The vertical stabilizer and rudder fell into Jamaica Bay almost a mile away. The crash of Flight 587 killed the 260 people on board plus five people on the ground.

The Investigation: Investigators from the NTSB probed through the wreckage. They discovered that the 12 fittings that attach the vertical stabilizer to the empennage had broken under overstress conditions, not because of fatigue, and they reported:

> The in-flight separation of the vertical stabilizer from the fuselage of a transport category airplane is an extremely rare, if not unprecedented, occurrence.

Many years before in 1966, British Overseas Airways Flight 911 had swooped low over Mt. Fuji, in Japan, so that passengers could enjoy the spectacular view. The Boeing 707 flew into a violent *mountain wave* that tossed the airliner like a terrier shaking a rat. The vertical stabilizer ripped off and the airliner crashed, killing the 124 people on board. Now, fast-forward 35 years to 2001. Could an invisible wingtip vortex have caused a similar vertical stabilizer failure on the French-built Airbus?

The FDR revealed that the first officer responded aggressively when he encountered the vortex. He twice turned the control column hard to the right, then all the way (78 degrees) to the left. He also used hard rudder in an effort to level the wings:

> The first officer made five subsequent alternating full rudder pedal inputs until the vertical stabilizer separated from the airplane.

The vertical stabilizer on the A-300 is constructed of composite material, carbon fiber reinforced plastics that are cured under heat and pressure. Structural analysis showed that all 12 attachment fittings had failed under aerodynamic loads "two times the loads defined by the limit load design envelope." In other words, the vertical stabilizer had not been designed to withstand the stress that doomed Flight 587. Despite its failure it performed "consistent with its design and certification."

Investigators reviewed the design of the airliner. They found that the A-300 variable stop rudder travel limiter system required the *lightest* rudder pedal pressure of any airliner they evaluated. As the airspeed increases, rudder pedal sensitivity increases. At high airspeeds only very slight rudder pedal movement is required to obtain high degrees of rudder deflection:

> Because of its high sensitivity (that is, light pedal forces and small pedal displacements), the Airbus [A-300] rudder control system is susceptible to potentially **hazardous** *[emphasis added]* rudder pedal inputs at higher airspeeds.

Probable Cause: It took the NTSB almost three years to issue a report dealing with the crash of Flight 587. Finally the board adopted the Aircraft Accident Report, NTSB-AAR-04-04, on 26 October 2004. Amid howls of derision from many in the aviation industry the board opined that the design of the vertical stabilizer and rudder system had not been the root cause of the accident.

On one hand, the board explained that the first officer's control inputs were "too aggressive" and were "unnecessary to control the airplane." On the other hand, the board acknowledged that the American Airlines' training program encouraged pilots to use rudder input to assist in recovery from rolls induced by wingtip vortices. Further, the board found that the American Airlines' excessive bank angle simulator exercise promoted an "unrealistic and exaggerated" view of the effects of wingtip vortices.

The board noted "widespread misunderstanding" among pilots about the degree of structural protection that exists when full or abrupt flight control inputs are made. A crude automobile analogy over-simplifies that reasoning:

> *Car drivers believe that, if they slam on the brakes, their wheels will not fall off. Pilots believe that, if they apply hard rudder, their vertical stabilizer will not fall off.*

Yet, flying a modern airliner is infinitely more complex that driving a car. Further, there are scores of aerodynamic principles applicable to aircraft which do not apply to cars. In aviation, many factors foreign to automobile drivers come into play. The board found the ***Probable Cause*** of this accident to be:

> the in-flight separation of the vertical stabilizer as a result of the loads beyond ultimate design that were created by the first officer's unnecessary and excessive rudder pedal inputs.

The board found two factors that ***contributed*** to the accident:

> [First were the sensitive] characteristics of the Airbus [A-300] rudder system design.

> [Second were unrealistic training] elements of the American Airlines Advanced Aircraft Maneuvering Program.

Postscript: The NTSB makes recommendations for corrective and proactive action following major airline accidents. As explained in "Prologue: Setting The Stage," these recommendations are *another story* and are not included in this book.

A ***limited exception*** will be made for Flight 587. Regardless of a pilot's flight control inputs, regardless of the flight regime, the vertical stabilizer should *never* rip off of an aircraft.

On page 161 of NTSB-AAR-04-04 the board began outlining recommendations dealing with pilot training, inspection procedures, overstress reporting, etc. However, the long-awaited and crucial NTSB edict -- the edict the aviation industry was waiting for -- was sent directly to the French government:

> . . . ***require modifications*** *[emphasis added]* to the [Airbus] to provide increased protection from potentially hazardous rudder pedal inputs at high airspeeds.

6 March 2005: While French engineers were blindly defending their airliner, 270 innocent people aboard Air Transat Flight 961, an Airbus A-310, winged their way toward Quebec City, Canada. At flight level 350 in smooth air the rudder suddenly "broke off" of the vertical stabilizer. One aviation pundit would explain:

> The plane's 28 foot long carbon-fiber rudder disappeared. One moment it was there, and the next [moment] it was gone.

The Transportation Safety Board of Canada began investigating this recent Airbus structural failure. Meanwhile, Airbus engineers began reevaluating the design of the French-built transport.

Air Midwest Flight 5481

Beechcraft 1900, registration N233YV
8 January 2003, at Charlotte, North Carolina
21 aboard, 21 killed

Overview: A Beechcraft 1900 accelerated down the runway at Charlotte, North Carolina. After liftoff the aircraft pitched up, out of control. It stalled, rolled inverted, and dove down into a hangar at the airport. The fiery crash killed all 21 people on board.

The Flight: Early on 8 January 2003 the passengers began filing aboard Air Midwest (d.b.a. US Airways Express) Flight 5481 at Charlotte, North Carolina. The popular commuter airliner had 19 passenger seats, and all of them were filled for the short flight to Greenville-Spartanburg Airport in Greer, South Carolina.

The Beechcraft (Beech) 1900 regional airliners entered service in 1984, and since then they had accumulated over 11 million hours of reliable airline duty. The Beech 1900 scheduled for this flight, registration N233YV, had been delivered new to Air Midwest in 1996 and had accumulated 15,003 hours flying the line. Two Pratt & Whitney turbine engines mated to four-blade Hartzell propellers powered the twin-turboprop commuter.

The young captain, age 25, had been flying with Air Midwest for three years. She held an ATP certificate and had been type rated in the Beech 1900 since March 2001. She began flying while she was a student at Louisiana Tech University, where she became a flight instructor and the flight school supervisor. She had logged a total of 2,790 flying hours, including 1,100 hours as pilot-in-command in the Beech 1900. Her first officer, age 27, held a Commercial Pilot certificate and had logged 1,096 hours.

Trouble Ahead: From the terminal, Flight 5481 taxied out toward Runway 18R. The portion of the CVR transcript, below, begins as the pilots wait for takeoff clearance. The captain will be flying the small airliner during the ill-fated takeoff:

Capt: ...... Captain, Flight 5481
FO: .... First Officer, Flight 5481
PassCabin: ... Unidentified passenger in the cabin, Flight 5481
Radio-: ..... (prefix) Radio transmission, Flight 5481
Tower: ..... Charlotte Airport Control Tower

FO: ... I'm doing to you right now what you were doing to me with the Krispy Kremes yesterday. (0844:49)

[sound of laughter at 0845:01]

Capt: At least I got Ann to eat one. (0845:05)

FO: Did 'ja? Nice. Ann was probably lookin' for any excuse she could find to eat one. (0845:07)

Capt: Sometimes I secretly go get them at the store. (0845:18)

FO: Oh yeah? Yeah, I've been known to do that . . . . (0845:21)

Tower: Air Midwest fifty-four-eighty-one, Runway one-eight right, taxi into position and hold. (0845:25)

Radio-FO: [Taxi into] position and hold, Runway one-eight right, Air Midwest fifty-four-eighty-one. (0845:28)

FO: Before takeoff checklist is complete . . . clear on the right, position and hold. (0845:38)

Capt: Clear on the left . . . . (0845:45)

FO: . . . I just started to say . . . you need to get a box of those and wrap them up in wedding gift wrap paper and take them to Ann's wedding. (0845:55)

[sound of laughter at 0846:05]

Capt: That's a good call, I'm gonna do that. (0846:05)

FO: Like, a huge box . . . you know, like the size box that was in the crew room yesterday. (0846:08)

Capt: That is an awesome idea. (0846:13)

[sound of laughter at 0846:14]

FO: Wouldn't that be great? (0846:16)

Capt: Yeah. (0846:17)

Tower: Air Midwest fifty-four-eighty-one, turn right heading two-three-zero [after takeoff], cleared for takeoff. (0846:18)

Radio-FO: [Heading] two-three-zero [after takeoff], cleared for takeoff, Air Midwest fifty-four-eighty-one. (0846:22)

FO: Two-[hundred]-thirty [degrees], cleared to go. (0846:26)

[sound of engine power increasing at 0846:28]

Capt: Set takeoff power, please. (0846:35)

FO: Power is set. (0846:35)

FO: Eighty knots, cross-checked. (0846:43)

FO: V-one -- V-r. (0846:49)

[the aircraft lifts off and climbs steeply]

FO: V-two. (0846:52)

[the Captain begins trimming nose-down pitch at 0846:53]

FO: Positive rate [of climb]. (0846:55)

Capt: Gear up. (0846:55)

[sound of landing gear retracting at 0846:58]

FO: Wuuuhhh? (0847:02)

[despite full nose-down trim and forward pressure on the control column, the aircraft pitches to 20 degrees nose-up by 0847:02]

Capt: Oh! Help me! (0847:02)

Capt: You got it? (0847:04)

FO: Oh, [expletive]! (0847:05)

[sound of human exertion at 0847:05]

FO: Push down! Oh, [expletive]! (0847:05)

[sound of landing gear warning horn at 0847:08]

[sound of several human exertion "grunts" at 0847:08]

Capt: You, uuuhhh --. (0847:10)

[sound of stall warning horn at 0847:10]

*[sounds of **extreme human exertion** at 0847:11]*

Capt: Push the nose down! (0847:11)

Capt: Aaahhh! Oh, my God! (0847:13)

Radio-Capt: We have an emergency for Air-m'west fifty-four-eighty-one! (0847:16)

*[the aircraft pitches **54 degrees nose-up**, then stalls and rolls inverted at 0847:16]*

PassCabin: Daddy! *[shouted from within the cabin]* (0847:18)

Capt: Pull the power back! (0847:20)

[sound of stall warning horn at 0847:21]

[sound of increase in engine and propeller noise at 0847:24]

Capt: Oh, my God! Aaahhh! (0847:26)

FO: Aaahhh, [expletive]! (0847:26)

[the aircraft impacts a hangar and the ground at 0847:26]

[end of the CVR tape at 0847:26]

The Accident: The FDR showed that the aircraft took off in a normal manner, although the captain had held the elevator at six degrees nose-down. Both pilots quickly realized that something was wrong -- horribly wrong. Although they pushed forward on the control column, the aircraft nose continued to rise.

The aircraft pitched all the way to 54 degrees nose-up, and the airspeed dropped to 31 knots. The airliner stalled, rolled over on its back, and pitched nose-down. Flight 5481 and its mortal human cargo dove earthward. The Beech airliner plunged down into a concrete and steel US Airways hangar. The impact sent flaming wreckage cartwheeling in all directions.

Triggered by the tower controller, the crash alarm wailed at the airport fire department within two seconds. Four fire trucks braked to a stop beside the blazing inferno only 1 minute and 42 seconds later, and EMS showed up within seven minutes. The firefighters quenched the flames, but the 21 souls aboard Flight 5481 were beyond earthly aid. The Mecklenburg County Medical Examiner ruled that the airplane occupants all died instantly upon impact. His autopsy report for each victim reflected the same cause of death: "multiple blunt force injuries due to airplane crash."

The Investigation: NTSB investigators found no evidence of any preexisting structural or systems failures. The FDR made clear the cause of the crash. After takeoff the nose had pitched up too high, and the pilots were unable to regain control.

Investigators checked the Load Manifest and found alarming problems. Excessively heavy pieces of baggage weighing 70 to 80 pounds had not been so labeled, and the "average weight" of 175 pounds per passenger proved to be inaccurate. The aircraft had been overloaded by about 580 pounds. Nonetheless, the crux of the problem lay not in the gross weight, but instead in the *distribution* of the weight. The investigators would report:

> Flight 5481 had an excessively aft center of gravity. *[and also]* Air Midwest's weight and balance program is also unacceptable.

The weight and balance program used by Air Midwest proved to be faulty. The heavy load in the cargo compartment behind the passenger cabin placed the aircraft's center of gravity (CG) far aft of the rearmost CG limit. This put the Beech and its occupants in grave peril. Yet, the NTSB discovered that it got much worse:

> The . . . elevator control system was incorrectly rigged during the Detail Six maintenance check, and the incorrect rigging restricted the airplane's elevator travel to 7 degrees nose-down, or about one-half of the downward travel specified by the airplane manufacturer.

Two days before the accident the airliner went through a "Detail Six" maintenance check by the Air Midwest contract maintenance vendor. One of the many items on the maintenance schedule was a check of the elevator control cable tension. The mechanic who was assigned this task held the required A&P certificate, but he was getting on-the-job training. He properly adjusted the cable tension, but he skipped nine crucial steps in the *rigging* procedure.

A performance study revealed that, standing alone, neither (1) the aft-of-limit CG nor (2) the improper elevator rigging would have caused the uncontrolled pitch-up. Nonetheless, in the words of the analysts, these two conditions together "rendered the airplane uncontrollable in the pitch axis."

Probable Cause: The NTSB adopted the Aircraft Accident Report for Flight 5481, NTSB-AAR-04-01, on 26 February 2004 over a year after the accident. The board found that the vendor's quality assurance inspector did not provide adequate on-the-job training and supervision for the errant mechanic. Also, Air Midwest's deficient weight and balance program resulted in inaccurate weight and balance calculations. The board found that the ***Probable Cause*** of this accident was:

> the airplane's loss of pitch control during takeoff. The loss of pitch control resulted from the incorrect rigging of the elevator control system compounded by the aircraft's aft center of gravity, which was substantially aft of the certified aft limit.

The board found many factors that ***contributed*** to the accident, and among these factors were:

> [First], Air Midwest's lack of oversight of the maintenance work being performed [by its contractor].

> [Second], the quality assurance inspector's failure to detect the incorrect rigging of the elevator control system.

> [Third], the faulty Air Midwest weight and balance program.

> [Fourth], the FAA's [incorrect] average weight assumptions [for passengers] in its weight and balance program guidelines.

> [Fifth was] the FAA's lack of oversight of Air Midwest's maintenance program and its weight and balance program.

NASA Space Shuttle
Columbia

NASA Space Shuttle *Columbia*, mission STS-107
1 February 2003, over the southern United States
7 aboard, 7 killed

This will be the second in-flight loss in the NASA space shuttle program. Although, technically, the shuttle is not an airliner, the accident and investigation hold valuable safety lessons for the commercial aviation industry.

Overview: After 16 days in orbit the NASA winged reusable space shuttle *Columbia* began its return to Earth. Superheated air entered a breach in the left wing and progressively melted the wing support structure during atmospheric reentry. *Columbia* tumbled out of control and ripped apart at about 10,400 knots. The in-flight disintegration killed the seven astronauts aboard.

The Flight: *Columbia* was the first NASA space shuttle, and she first flew in 1981. She was named for the United States' naval vessel that circumnavigated the Earth over 200 years ago. She had completed 27 missions into space. Including her external fuel tank and the two solid rocket boosters, her complex structure included over 2.5 million parts, 230 miles of electrical wire, 1,060 valves, and 1,440 circuit breakers The huge external fuel tank held over 528,000 gallons of liquid oxygen and liquid hydrogen, and the shuttle weighed over 4.5 million pounds at launch. Her coming flight would mark the 113th mission of the shuttle program.

At 15,225 knots (17,500 miles per hour) *Columbia* soared into orbit 175 miles above Earth on 16 January 2003. Over the next 16 days her astronauts conducted microgravity research and science experiments. The onboard payload specialist was a fighter pilot in the Israeli Air Force, Israel's first man in space.

At 0815 Hours on 1 February 2003, tail-first and upside-down over the Indian Ocean, the crew initiated a 158 second engine burn to slow the craft for reentry. Within 29 minutes *Columbia* began to enter the atmosphere as it descended through 400,000 feet.

Trouble Ahead: At 0850 Hours, screaming down through the upper atmosphere at Mach 24 and descending through 243,000 feet, *Columbia* entered an expected 10 minute period of peak thermal stress. Friction from air molecules striking the craft at hypersonic velocity created extreme heat. As the shuttle neared the California coastline the leading edges of her wings reached 2,650 degrees Fahrenheit. Thus far all appeared normal in Mission Control:

> *Columbia* crossed the California coast west of Sacramento at 0853 [Hours] traveling at Mach 23 [at] 231,600 feet.

At 0854:24 Hours the telemetered data readout for four hydraulic sensors in the left wing suddenly fluctuated, then dropped to "off scale low." Within a minute the wing leading edge temperature increased to nearly 3,000 degrees as *Columbia* streaked high over Nevada at Mach 22. A minute later she zipped over the Arizona-New Mexico border, and soon she was streaking across Texas.

Mission Control suddenly lost the telemetered pressure readings on both left landing gear tires. At 0859:32 Hours a radio message from the shuttle commander got cut off in mid-word. Thereafter all voice and data radio signals from the craft were lost.

The portion of the *reconstructed* NASA radio transcript, below, begins five minutes earlier as Mission Control reports the loss of data from the four hydraulic system sensors:

> Columbia: . . . Space Shuttle *Columbia*, Mission STS-107
> Flight: . . . . . . NASA Fight Director
> MMACS: . . . Maintenance, Mechanical, and Crew Systems
> GNC: . . . . . . Guidance, Navigation, and Control
> CapCom: . . . . Capsule Communicator
> INCO: . . . . . . Instrumentation and Communication
> GC: . . . . Ground Control
> FDO: . . . . . . Flight Dynamics Officer

MMACS: I've lost four separate temperature transducers on the left side of [*Columbia*], hydraulic return temperatures. (0854:24)

Flight: Four [hydraulic] return temps?

MMACS: [Yes], to the left outboard and left inboard elevon.

Flight: OK, is there anything common to them? . . . I mean, you're telling me you lost them all at exactly the same time?

MMACS: No, not exactly, they were [lost] within probably four or five seconds of each other.

Flight: Where is that instrumentation located?

MMACS: All four of them are located in the aft part of the left wing, right in front of the elevons, and there is no commonality.

Flight: Tell me again which systems they're for. (0856:02)

MMACS: All three hydraulic systems.

Flight: GNC, Flight, everything look good to you? Control rates and everything [are] nominal, right?

GNC: I don't see anything out of the ordinary.

Flight: [MMACS], all other indications for your hydraulic system indications are good?

MMACS: They're all good, we've got good [hydraulic] quantities all the way across.

Flight: And the other temps are normal?

MMACS: The other temps are normal, yes sir.

Columbia: And, uh, Hou --. *[message interrupted]* (0858:00)

  [75 seconds later MMACS reports another sensor problem]

MMACS: We just lost tire pressure *[meaning, telemetered sensor data]* on the left outboard and left inboard, both tires. (0859:15)

CapCom: And *Columbia*, Houston, we see your tire pressure messages and we did not copy your last call.

Flight: Is it instrumentation, MMACS? [It's] gotta be.

MMACS: Flight, MMACS, those are also off-scale low.

Columbia: Roger, bu --. *[interrupted in mid-word]* (0859:32)

[loss of all telemetered sensor data at 0859:32]

[the shuttle onboard Roll Alarm activates at 0859:46]

["bright flashes" envelop Columbia and she starts to break apart at 180,000 feet at apx. 0900:20; Mission Control does not know this because of the loss of telemetered data]

[30 seconds later, aerodynamic forces breach the crew module at 148,800 feet at apx. 0900:50]

[5 seconds later, aerodynamic and thermal destruction of the crew module begins at apx. 138,680 feet at apx. 0900:55]

*[24 seconds later, **destruction of the crew module** is complete at apx. 105,483 feet at apx. 0901:19]*

[Mission Control still has no indication of a serious problem, exclusive of the data and communications loss]

Flight: There's no commonality between all these tire pressure instrumentations and the hydraulic return instrumentations?

MMACS: No sir, there's not. We also lost the nose gear down [data] and the right main gear down [data].

Flight: INCO . . . uh, you were expecting a little bit of ratty [radio] comm[unication], but not this long? (0902:21)

INCO: That's correct, Flight.

Flight: [There were] no onboard system config[uration] changes right before we lost data?

INCO: That is correct, Flight. All looked good.

GC: Two minutes to MILA. *[meaning, two minutes before the Merritt Island Tracking Station in Florida should be able to detect Columbia on radar]*

CapCom: *Columbia*, Houston, comm[unication] check.

CapCom: *Columbia*, Houston, comm check.

[there is no response]

MMACS: On the tire pressures, we did see them go erratic for a little bit before they went away, so I do believe [the problem] is instrumentation. (0903:45)

CapCom: *Columbia*, Houston, UHF comm check.

CapCom: *Columbia*, Houston, UHF comm check.

[there is no response]

GC: [Kennedy Space Center in Florida] is not reporting any RF *[meaning, voice or data radio transmissions]* at this time.

Flight: FDO, when are you expecting [radar] tracking?

FDO: [I was expecting it] one minute ago, Flight.

CapCom: *Columbia*, Houston, UHF comm check.

[there is no response]

*[minutes pass and **concern soars** in Mission Control; there is no telemetered data, no radar contact, no voice communication]*

GC: MILA is taking one of their antennas off into a search mode [in an effort to find *Columbia*]. (0908:25)

Flight: Did we get -- have we gotten any tracking data?

FDO: We got a blip of tracking data. It was a bad data point, Flight. We do not believe that was [*Columbia*]. We're entering a search pattern with our C-bands at this time. We do not have any valid data at this time.

[another minute passes; by 0909:29 Columbia's speed should have dropped to Mach 2.5 near the Kennedy Space Center]

Flight: OK, [are there] any other trackers that we can go to?

[3 more minutes pass; Columbia should have lined up to land at Kennedy Space Center by 0912:39, but she never arrives]

[Mission Control gets a phone call; public television coverage has shown Columbia breaking apart in flight]

The Accident: As *Columbia* descended into increasingly dense air its sensors began documenting yaw and drag increases on the left wing. The automated flight control system compensated by firing the yaw jets. Finally, despite all four thrusters firing and maximum aileron trim, the yaw to the left could not be stopped. *Columbia* tumbled out of control. Thermal stress and aerodynamic pressure tore the shuttle apart:

> A crackling [sonic] boom that signaled the break-up of the *Columbia* startled residents of East Texas.

Debris ripped through the upper atmosphere at 10,440 knots, then slowed, then fell to the ground. Law Enforcement dispatch centers got flooded with reports of smoking objects falling from the sky. Thousands of small pieces slowly fluttered down. Larger pieces, such as the 800 pound remnant of a main engine, plowed into the ground at about 1,200 knots.

Later that day the President of the United States addressed the nation on television. He reported what most of the world already knew: "The *Columbia* is lost, and there are no survivors."

The Investigation: The accident investigation team sprang into action within two hours of the loss of *Columbia*. The 13 board members, backed up by 120 staff investigators and over 400 NASA engineers, would examine more than 30,000 documents. They would hear testimony from hundreds of experts and examine reams of data. They discovered that:

> *Columbia* reentered the Earth's atmosphere with a pre-existing breach in the leading edge of its left wing.

Photographic evidence pinpointed the initial event that led to the accident. Only 81 seconds into the launch while speeding upward at Mach 2.46, two pieces of insulating foam had broken off from the huge external fuel tank to which *Columbia* and its two booster rockets were attached. The larger piece of foam was over 20 inches long and over 12 inches wide. Whipped downward by the supersonic slipstream, it slammed into the leading edge of the left wing. The impact knocked a small hole in the wing, but no one knew it at the time. Investigation would later determine that:

> the physical cause of the loss of *Columbia* and its crew was a breach in the Thermal Protection System on the leading edge of the left wing.

When the craft began its return to Earth there was no indication of any anomaly until 0848:39 Hours. A sensor on the left wing then began showing increasing strain. This stress on the wing was recorded and stored on board (and recovered after the accident). Hypersonic aerodynamic forces tugged at the damaged wing. At temperatures near 3,000 degrees Fahrenheit, superheated air under extreme pressure began whistling through the hole in the wing. Slowly this "blow-torch" effect began to gnaw at the structure:

The breach widened, destroying the insulation protecting the wing's leading edge support system.

As early as 0853:46 Hours small snippets of debris from the damaged wing began tearing away. Sensor data (stored onboard) revealed that the craft's automated flight control system began reacting to changes in the *shape* of the wing. Less than a minute later the extreme heat inside the wing fused the electrical wiring leading to four hydraulic sensors. Mission Control detected this loss of data, their first indication that something was amiss:

At 0858:20 [Hours], traveling at 209,800 feet and Mach 19.5, Columbia crossed from New Mexico into Texas, and about this time shed a Thermal Protection System tile.

Loss of the protective tile subjected the wing to even more heat damage. Molten debris whipped away in the hypersonic slipstream. The increasing temperature within the wing caused failure of the tire pressure sensors, and the superheated air began melting the wing spar. Gradually the airfoil deformed beyond the capability of the flight control system to compensate, and the craft tumbled out of control at over 10,000 knots:

At 0900:18 [Hours] the postflight video and imagery analysis indicate that a catastrophic event occurred. Bright flashes suddenly enveloped the Orbiter.

The crew module broke away from the rest of *Columbia* at about 180,000 feet at 0900:20 Hours. After break-up the G forces in the crew module were not lethal. Destruction of the crew module would take place later in more dense air.

Over a period of 24 seconds -- starting at about 138,680 feet (at 0900:55 Hours) and ending at 105,483 feet (at 0901:19 Hours) --

thermal and aerodynamic forces shredded the crew module. The Armed Forces Institute of Pathology and the Federal Bureau of Investigation later conducted forensic studies on the remains of the astronauts. Each was killed by "blunt force trauma and hypoxia":

> The break-up occurred in a flight regime in which . . . there was no possibility for the crew to survive.

Probable Cause: The *Columbia* Accident Investigation Board adopted an exhaustive report and presented it to the President of the United States, the U.S. Congress, and NASA on 26 August 2003. The board found that when the first sensor anomaly occurred, the craft had already sustained damage from which there was no chance of recovery. Survival of the crew was not possible. The board found that *The Physical Cause* of the accident was:

> a breach in the Thermal Protection System on the leading edge of the left wing. The breach was initiated by a piece of insulating foam that separated from the . . . External Tank and struck the wing . . . 81.9 seconds after launch. During reentry this breach . . . allowed superheated air to penetrate through the leading edge insulation and progressively melt the aluminum structure of the left wing, resulting in a weakening of the structure until increasing aerodynamic forces caused loss of control, failure of the wing, and breakup of the Orbiter.

The board found that the *design* of the space shuttle system is not inherently unsafe. However, the board concluded:

> NASA's management system is unsafe to manage the shuttle system beyond the short term, and the agency does not have a strong safety culture. *[and also]* We are convinced that management practices overseeing the space shuttle program were as much a cause of the accident as the foam that struck the left wing.

Epilogue: Into the Future

This book begins with the sentence: "The ancients dreamed of soaring with the birds." Some mused wistfully, idly. However, men of vision and science dreamed knowledgeably of the future and labored to convert those dreams into reality.

Europeans began flying crude tethered kites over 2,000 years ago. In the first half of the Second Millennium several visionaries formulated viable designs for manned flying machines, but the state of technology at the time prevented their construction. Yet, in France in 1783, man first ascended from the surface of the Earth in a hot-air balloon. Thereafter the citizens of Western Europe became obsessed with the possibility of powered flight. Grandiose plans for building an ornithopter, a machine designed to fly by mimicking the flapping wings of birds, were soon replaced by plans for more practical fixed-wing craft.

The latter years of the Nineteenth Century were marked by exponential advances in aerodynamic theory and experimentation with gliders. Otto Lilienthal was the first to combine an arched lifting wing with vertical and lateral control surfaces in manned gliders. Within a decade the Wright brothers developed a practical propulsion system. They married the engine-airscrew combination to adequate control and stability features, and a manned powered flying machine finally evolved from fantasy into reality. Within 66 short years after the first "aeroplane" flight in 1903, technological advances and engineering excellence enabled man to journey to the moon and return safely to Earth.

Today an international system of air traffic control facilitates commercial airline transportation worldwide. High speed, high altitude, high power, high technology aircraft increasingly rely upon automated and computerized systems. Some argue that automation has become too complex and may force pilots "out of the loop" in the manner of the berserk "HAL" systems computer in the fictional thriller, *2001: A Space Odyssey*. Nonetheless, most professional analysts point to more traditional aviation perils such as terrorism, lapses in human judgement, and mechanical anomalies.

The airline accident rate continues to decline. This remarkable safety record is the result of professionalism within the airline industry. Combined with after-the-fact accident investigation, this professionalism has made airline transportation the safest mode of travel on the planet. Over the past decade, on average, about 100 travelers per year have been killed in airline accidents in the United States. If (1) terrorism and (2) crashes at sea near the continental United States are excluded, the fatality rate drops to about 40 per year. This pales in comparison to almost 50,000 deaths each year in surface transportation accidents.

Barring a global economic collapse or Divine Intervention, the Twenty-First Century will witness exponential advances in aviation technology and capability. There will be no room for worshipers of the status quo, those who are mired in the past, those who are unwilling to accept change. Even now, engineers are working on blended-wing-body airliners. Boeing and Gulfstream have sonic-boom noise reduction programs in the mill, and supersonic business jets are taking shape on drawing boards. Aided by computational fluid dynamics, physicists are unlocking mysteries of hypersonic aerodynamics, and dual-mode scramjets are evolving from theory into fact. Launched from a B-52 aerial platform, NASA's X-43 experimental air-breathing hypersonic aircraft has already flown at Mach 10 speed.

The aerial road into the future will be charted by progressive dreamers. Listed below are some of our ancestor's visions for our future. They knew that man would be limited only by his will and his imagination. They foretold our destiny in the skies:

****

Man must rise above Earth, to the top of the atmosphere and beyond, for only thus will he fully understand the world in which he lives.
[Socrates (470-399 BC), Athenian philosopher]

An instrument may be made to fly if one sits in the midst of the instrument, and turn[s] an engine by which the wings, being artificially composed, may beat the air in the manner of a bird.
[Roger Bacon (1214-1294), English scholar and philosopher]

I have discovered that a screw-shaped device such as this, if well made from starched linen, will rise in the air if turned quickly.
[Leonardo da Vinci, Italian inventor and artist, writing about his helical air screw, 1480]

Once you have tasted flight you will forever walk the Earth with your eyes turned skyward, for there you have been, and there you will always return.
[Leonardo da Vinci, Italian inventor and artist, circa 1486]

I do seriously and on good grounds affirm it possible to make a flying chariot in which a man may sit and give such a motion unto it as shall convey him through the air.
[John Wilkins, English churchman, *A Discourse Concerning a New World and Another Planet*, 1640]

The art of flying is only just being born. It will be perfected, and some day we will go as far as the moon.
[Bernard Le Bovier de Fontenells (1657-1757), French scholar]

We shall soon travel by air-vessels, make air instead of sea voyages, and at length find our way to the moon in spite of the want of atmosphere.
[Lord Byron (1788-1824), English poet and philosopher]

The time would come when gentlemen, when they were to go on a journey, would call for their wings as regularly as they call for their boots.
[Maria Edgeworth, *Essay on Irish Bulls*, 1802]

I am well convinced that Aerial Navigation will form a most prominent feature in the progress of civilization.
[Sir George Cayley, English glider enthusiast, 1804]

We shall be able to transport ourselves and our families, and their goods and chattels, more securely by air than by water, and with a velocity of from 20 to 100 miles per hour.
[Sir George Cayley, English glider enthusiast, 1809]

Of all the inventions of which it is possible to conceive in the future, there is none which so captivates the imagination as that of a flying machine.
[*Scientific American*, 1860]

In spite of the opinions of certain narrow-minded people who would shut up the human race upon this globe, we shall one day travel to the moon, the planets, and the stars . . . .
[Jules Verne, French novelist and visionary, 1865]

Mankind will migrate into space, and will cross the airless Saharas which separate planet from planet and sun from sun.
[Winwood Reade, *The Martyrdom of Man*, 1872]

The airplane has unveiled for us the true face of the Earth.
[Antoine de Saint-Exupery, *Wind, Sand, and Stars*, 1939]

Aviation is proof that, given the will, we have the capacity to achieve the impossible.
[Edward V. "Eddie" Rickenbacker (1890-1973), World War I flying ace, and later an airline executive]

The moon is the first milestone on the way to the stars.
[Arthur C. Clarke, British author and inventor, circa 1968]

That's one small step for [a] man, one giant leap for mankind.
[Neil Armstrong, first man to set foot upon the moon, 1969]

I'm an optimist. We will reach out to the stars.
[Stephen W. Hawking, physicist, in *The Daily Telegraph*, 2001]

The past is but the beginning of a beginning, and all that is, and has been, is but the twilight of the dawn.

[H.G. Wells, *The Discovery of the Future*, 1901]

About the Author

Marion Sturkey began his flying career in the U.S. Marine Corps. He earned the Naval Aviator designation in 1965 and flew both fixed-wing aircraft and helicopters. His certifications include Instructor Pilot, VIP Pilot, NATOPS Check Pilot, and Maintenance Test Pilot. In March 1968 he established the un-refueled endurance record for the Boeing CH-46 series of military aircraft.

Marion became a Commercial Pilot after he left active duty. For two years he flew helicopters to support off-shore oil exploration and oil production operations in Louisiana and Texas. He then left flying behind and worked in various management capacities for the BellSouth Corporation for 25 years. During the last ten years of that career he served as guest instructor at the Bell Communications Research centers in Illinois and New Jersey.

After retirement from the corporate world, Marion returned to his idyllic rural hometown of Plum Branch, South Carolina. There he began writing and publishing books and articles about military and aviation affairs. He is a frequent guest speaker at military bases and at functions for military veterans. His book reviews and articles appear in professional journals and magazines. *MAYDAY*, his first project dealing exclusively with commercial aviation, is his seventh book.

Glossary

Like most technical pursuits, aviation has developed a unique jargon. Much of it is unfamiliar to laymen. This glossary of common terms, phenomena, and acronyms will assist readers who are not versed in aeronautical terminology:

ADF: Automatic Direction Finder. A low-frequency radio receiver that provides *homing* direction toward ground stations.

AFCS: Automatic Flight Control System.

Ailerons: On the trailing 'edge of wings, moveable surfaces that control the bank and roll of an aircraft.

Airspeed: Expressed in knots, the speed of an aircraft relative to the air mass through which it travels. (see "Knots")

Altitude: Unless otherwise specified, height above mean sea level, measured in feet. When used, the suffix "agl" means height "above ground level." (see "Flight Level")

Angle-of-Attack: Measured in degrees, the angle at which the wings meet the relative flow of air.

Approach Chart: Also called Approach Plate. A small chart that provides IFR electronic navigation instructions and altitude limits for a specified landing approach at a given airport.

Approach Control: (see "ATC")

APU: Auxiliary Power Unit. A small engine that can provide interim electrical and hydraulic power.

ATC: Air Traffic Control. The system for directing and separating aircraft in flight. It is subdivided into several domains; generally speaking: (1) the "Tower" is responsible for aircraft taking off and landing, (2) "Departure Control" and "Approach Control" are responsible for aircraft near the vicinity of the airport, and (3) the "Center," is responsible for the en route phase of flight.

<u>ATIS</u>: Automatic Terminal Information Service. A recorded radio message detailing weather and other concerns at an airport.

<u>Attitude</u>: The roll and pitch of an aircraft relative to the horizon.

<u>Attitude Indicator</u>: A gyroscopically controlled instrument, crucial for IFR flight, that displays the aircraft "attitude" relative to the horizon. For obvious reasons, also called an Artificial Horizon.

<u>Black Box</u>: (see "CVR" and "FDR")

<u>Bug</u>: An adjustable setting on the rim of aircraft instruments to highlight crucial airspeeds and altitudes.

<u>CAB</u>: The former Civil Aeronautics Board.

<u>Center</u>: Air Route Traffic Control Center. (see "ATC")

<u>"Clean" Aircraft</u>: An aircraft in cruise configuration with its high-lift devices and landing gear retracted.

<u>Clearance</u>: An approval by ATC for an aircraft to land or take off at an airport, or to fly specified routes and altitudes. Also called an ATC Clearance.

<u>CVR</u>: Cockpit Voice Recorder. Also called a Black Box, although it is painted bright orange. A crash resistant recording device that preserves cockpit verbiage and sounds.

<u>Departure Control</u>: (see "ATC")

<u>DME</u>: Distance Measuring Equipment. An electronic device that provides a constant cockpit display of the distance, in slant-range nautical miles, from an aircraft to a selected ground station.

<u>EFCS</u>: Electronic Flight Control System.

<u>EFIS</u>: Electronic Flight Information System.

<u>Elevation</u>: Height of terrain, or an obstacle, above mean sea level. (see "Altitude")

<u>Elevator</u>: A movable surface, usually mounted on the horizontal stabilizer, that controls the vertical pitch of the aircraft.

<u>FAA</u>: Federal Aviation Administration.

FDR: Flight Data Recorder or Digital Flight Data Recorder. Also called a Black Box, although it is painted bright orange. A crash resistant recording device that documents operating parameters such as airspeed, altitude, rate of climb or descent, engine performance, acceleration, flight control movements, etc.

First Officer: The copilot, the second-in-command.

Flaps: Adjustable control surfaces on the wings. Flaps can be lowered to several incremental settings, usually up to a maximum of about 50 degrees, depending upon the type of aircraft. Lowering the flaps increases the curvature of the wing and increases aerodynamic lift and drag, allowing the aircraft to land or take off at a lower airspeed. (see "Slats")

Flight Director: A "glass cockpit" computerized display of aircraft attitude plus electronic flight and navigation data.

Flight Engineer: A cockpit crewmember (on some aircraft) who is responsible for operation of aircraft systems.

Flight Level: Height in hundreds of feet, based upon a standard barometric setting (for example, 22,000 feet is *flight level 220*).

G: The force, positive or negative, acting upon an aircraft and its occupants in flight, measured in multiples of the gravitational force of the Earth.

GPWS: Ground Proximity Warning System. An electronic aircraft transceiver that can sense dangerous *ground proximity* conditions. If the GPWS detects such a condition it warns the pilots with an appropriate digitized verbal message such as (1) *"sink rate, sink rate"* or (2) *"whoop whoop, pull up, whoop whoop, pull up."*

GMT: Greenwich Mean Time. Formerly called Zulu Time; more recently called Universal Coordinated Time.

GPS: Global Positioning System. The satellite-based navigation system funded, controlled, and operated by the U.S. Department of Defense. GPS was designed for the U.S. Armed Forces, but it can be used by anyone. With a GPS radio receiver one can determine his position anywhere on, or above, the Earth.

Ground Speed: Expressed in knots, the speed of an aircraft relative to the surface of the Earth. May be less or greater than airspeed, depending upon the wind direction.

Guard: Also called Guard Channel and Guard Frequency. The UHF (243.0 MHz) or VHF (121.5 MHz) aviation emergency radio frequency monitored by military and commercial aircraft.

Hours: Local time on a 24 hour clock (for example, 0915 Hours equates to 9:15 am, and 2215 Hours equates to 10:15 pm). If a colon and two digits follow the time (for example, 0915:51 Hours), the two digits represent *seconds*, not hundredths of a minute.

ICAO: International Civil Aviation Organization.

ICS: Internal Communications System. Also called Intercom.

IFR: Instrument Flight Rules. Rules and procedures for navigating by cockpit instruments alone under poor visibility conditions. Refers to either (1) the procedures, or to (2) the visibility condition that necessitates the procedures. (see "IMC")

ILS: Instrument Landing System. An electronic landing aid that provides (1) glideslope and (2) glidepath displays in the cockpit.

IMC: Instrument Meteorological Conditions. The poor visibility conditions that mandate IFR flight. (see "IFR")

Knot: One *nautical mile* per hour. A nautical mile is 6,076 feet in length (as opposed to 5,280 feet in a statute mile). Thus, 100 knots equals roughly 115 miles per hour.

Mach: Also called Mach Number. The numerical relationship between airspeed and the speed of sound.

Mayday: The international distress message, traditionally repeated three times. Mayday is derived from *m'aidez*, which means "help me" in French. It is the verbal equivalent of the former Morse Code "SOS" distress message.

MDA: Minimum Descent Altitude. During a landing approach on an IFR flight, the altitude below which an aircraft must not descend until the runway environment is in sight.

MEA: Minimum En Route Altitude. On an IFR flight, the en route altitude below which an aircraft must not descend. Flight at or above the MEA will ensure that the aircraft remains clear of high terrain and other obstructions to flight.

NASA: National Aeronautics and Space Administration.

Nautical Mile: (see "Knot")

Navaid: The common term for an electronic *Navigation Aid.*

NDB: Non-Directional Beacon. A low-frequency transmitter of navigational use to aircraft with ADF equipment. (see "ADF")

NOTAM: Notice to Airmen. A cautionary written notice which details irregularities with airways, airports, and navigation aids.

NTSB: National Transportation Safety Board.

Pitot Static System: Interconnected aircraft tubes and sensors that measure airspeed, altitude, and rate of descent or climb.

Radial: A bearing from a VOR ground station. (see "VOR")

Rudder: A moveable surface, mounted on the vertical stabilizer, that controls the lateral yaw of an aircraft.

RVR: Runway Visual Range.

Sink Rate: The vertical descent rate, measured in feet per minute. It is crucial in the final seconds as an aircraft prepares to land.

Slats: Enhanced lift devices on the leading edge of the wings. Slats can be incrementally extended to increase the curvature and the aerodynamic lift and drag of the wings, thereby lowering the landing and takeoff airspeeds of the aircraft. (see "Flaps")

Spatial Disorientation: A condition that exists when a pilot, because of poor visibility, can not detect the horizon and thus becomes disoriented because of vestibular illusions of the inner ear. Usually called "vertigo" by laymen.

Speed Brakes: (see "Spoilers")

Spin: A perilous low airspeed condition which can occur at -- or slightly above -- stalling speed when an aircraft is turning left or right. The wing on the "inside" of a turn has a lower airspeed than the wing on the outside of a turn. Consequently, the *slower* inside wing can *stall* and lose lift, while the faster outside wing has not stalled. In such a condition (1) the *inside stalled wing* will drop, and (2) the fuselage will revolve -- *spin* -- around the stalled inside wing as the aircraft spirals toward the ground. (see "Stall")

Spoilers: Flat panels which lie flush against the surface of the wings in flight. When extended after touchdown they *spoil* the smooth airflow over the wings and decrease unwanted lift. Spoilers also can be used in *cruising flight* to expedite a descent or to slow the aircraft, and in this capacity they are called Speed Brakes.

Spool: The increase or decrease (as in *spool up* or *spool down*) of the revolution speed of a turbine engine.

Stall: A phenomenon that occurs when the airspeed of an aircraft decreases below the minimum at which the wings can create sufficient lift for flight. (see "Spin")

Stick-Shaker: An electro-mechanical device that shakes the control column to warn of an approaching stall.

TOGA: Take-off, Go-around.

Tower: (see "ATC")

Transponder: An aircraft radio transceiver that enables Air Traffic Control radar to identify an aircraft and its altitude.

Trim: Adjusting the control surfaces so that no pressure on the rudder or control column is required for a given flight regime.

UHF: Ultra High Frequency. An aviation radio frequency band used primarily by military aircraft. (see "VHF")

V-1: The calculated "go or no-go" *decision airspeed* on takeoff.

V-2: The calculated takeoff *safety airspeed*; the minimum control airspeed in case of engine failure, plus a safety margin.

V-r: The calculated airspeed at which to *rotate* for takeoff.

VASI: Visual Approach Slope Indicator.

Vertical Stabilizer: At the tail of an aircraft, the vertical airfoil that provides directional stability in flight.

<u>VFR</u>: Visual Flight Rules. The rules under which a pilot may fly and navigate by visual reference to the ground while remaining clear of clouds and other aircraft. (see "VMC")

<u>VHF</u>: Very High Frequency. An aviation radio frequency band used primarily by commercial aircraft. (see "UHF")

<u>VMC</u>: Visual Meteorological Conditions. The conditions under which a pilot may fly under Visual Flight Rules. (see "VFR")

<u>VOR</u>: Very-high-frequency Omni-directional Range. Electronic navigation equipment for use by aircraft. Refers to either the (1) ground transmitting station, or to the (2) aircraft equipment that receives and displays the signal from such a ground station.

Ladies and gentlemen, this is your captain speaking. We have a small problem. All four engines have stopped.

[Public Address System announcement from the cockpit of British Airways Flight 009, a Boeing 747 with 263 people on board, over the Pacific Ocean near Indonesia at night, after the airliner flew into the caustic ash cloud from an erupting volcano on 24 June 1982]

-- Military and Aviation books by Marion Sturkey --

BONNIE-SUE: A Marine Corps Helicopter Squadron in Vietnam (first published in 1996) 509 pages, 21 photographs, 4 maps. A classic, the definitive work on helicopter warfare in Vietnam. Against the backdrop of the turbulent 1960s, *BONNIE-SUE* evolves into a saga of commitment, sacrifice, and brotherhood.

Warrior Culture of the U.S. Marines (first published in 2002) 212 pages, 3 illustrations. Axioms for warriors, Marine quotations, USMC battle history -- and much more -- for the world's warrior elite. Plus, plenty of upbeat and gung-ho satire exclusively for U.S. Marines. "Politically Incorrect" and proud of it!

Murphy's Laws of Combat (first published in 2003) 241 pages. A walk on the humorous side of military life. Military satire for the U.S. Armed Forces. Hundreds of tongue-in-cheek combat laws, axioms, and principles -- hilarious because of the inherent truth they contain. "Politically Impossible," but no profanity.

MAYDAY: Accident Reports and Voice Transcripts from Airline Crash Investigations (this book, first published in 2005) 461 pages, 23 photographs, 6 illustrations. For each accident the author walks the reader through the flight, the crisis, the "black box" transcript, the crash, the investigation, and Probable Cause. Learn from past accidents in order to further aviation safety in the future.

MID-AIR: Accident Reports and Voice Transcripts from Mid-Air Collision Investigations (coming soon) With the format used in *MAYDAY*, the author examines mid-air collisions involving commercial airliners, military planes, and general aviation aircraft.

That's it, I'm dead!

[Final words from the cockpit of Surinam
Airways Flight 764, a Douglas DC-8 with 187
people on board, after the aircraft descended
below the MDA at Paramaribo, Surinam, on 7
June 1989]

Errata: On a project of this complexity it is possible that errors may have crept in. The author will appreciate notification (*with credible documentation*) of any such errors so that they may be corrected in future printings or editions.